NORMAN RICHARDSON was born in the no̲
lived in Northern Ireland since 1972. After
mainly Religious Education and Music in
and Belfast before being appointed in 1
Churches to work in an inter-church pea̲ ───── ₚᵣₒᵧᵣₐₘₘₑ. He
became closely involved in the development of the educational themes of
Education for Mutual Understanding and Cultural Heritage and in the
promotion of wide-ranging and inclusive programmes of Religious
Education. After three years based in the School of Education at Queen's
University, Belfast, where he was engaged in research and in-service teach-
ing on various aspects of diversity education, he was appointed in 1997 as a
Lecturer in Religious Studies at Stranmillis College. He is a Diocesan Lay
Reader in the Church of Ireland and also has Presbyterian connections.
Other involvements include the Corrymeela Community, of which he
has been a member since 1969, and the Northern Ireland Inter-Faith
Forum, of which he is currently Secretary. He is married with two
children.

A
TAPESTRY
of
BELIEFS

CHRISTIAN
TRADITIONS
IN
NORTHERN
IRELAND

edited and with
an introduction by

NORMAN
RICHARDSON

foreword by
LADY JEAN MAYHEW

THE
BLACKSTAFF
PRESS

BELFAST

First published in 1998 by
The Blackstaff Press Limited
3 Galway Park, Dundonald, Belfast BT16 2AN, Northern Ireland
in association with the Community Relations Council

Typeset by Techniset Typesetters, Newton-le-Willows, Merseyside

Printed in Ireland by ColourBooks Limited

A CIP catalogue record for this book
is available from the British Library

ISBN 0-85640-633-3

Contents

Foreword

LADY JEAN MAYHEW

Many of the denominations and movements represented in this fascinating and very valuable book resulted, at least in part, from a desire to follow what was perceived to be the truth. So often when outsiders consider or discuss other denominations it is difficult for them to know the truth about them, in particular to know the current beliefs and practices as distinct from those in the past. Frequently unjust criticism, suspicion and even fear can result from poor information. There is a problem in obtaining contemporary facts, since asking others about their beliefs and practices involves inquiring about very personal matters and, for many, appropriate opportunities are rare. Such questions are specially sensitive in Northern Ireland where I have often heard people, when speaking of friends across the traditional community divide, add 'but we never discuss religion or politics'. This reticence may be understandable but, if even friends from different denominations find it hard, or even impossible, to talk about such matters, it is difficult for knowledge and understanding to develop, let alone to lead on to the possibility of increased mutual understanding or respect in relation to these areas of fundamental importance.

That is why this book is particularly helpful. It supplies answers to a wide range of questions, provided not by outsiders, but by leading members of each denomination or tradition which is being written about. It, moreover, conveys far more than dry facts, however useful. Time and again it is the atmosphere displayed by the way each author has tackled the subject which has most effectively highlighted similarities and differences and which makes the book, at times, difficult to put down.

I greatly welcome this book, which fills an important need, and warmly congratulate the editor, Norman Richardson, the Community Relations Council, the contributors and all those who have played a part in its production. It deserves to be widely read.

JEAN MAYHEW
MARCH 1998

Editor's Preface:
An Explanation

'I didn't know that there were so many different churches in Northern Ireland!'

In conversations between members of different religious or cultural communities it is quite common to hear people expressing surprise at the number of religious denominations and frustration that they do not know what the various traditions – including the well-known ones – either practise or believe. A glance at the Northern Ireland Census Religion Report confirms that there are several dozen such groups, all but a few of which are Christian denominations of one kind or another. In the 1991 census there were seventy-five groups with ten or more adherents, including seven from religions other than Christianity and four categories of a non-religious nature, including atheists, agnostics and so on, leaving a substantial remainder of Christian and Christian-related groups. (Of these, more than one-third were recorded as having under one hundred adherents, and there were a further seventy-four religious groups identified as having fewer than ten adherents in Northern Ireland.)

WHY THIS BOOK CAME ABOUT

Many people are aware that their perceptions of other religious traditions may well be based on myth and misinformation and would like to be better informed, but it has never been easy for the ordinary reader to gain access to clear information on the different churches. Sometimes this leads to the overemphasis of differences and subsequent blanket dismissal of other people's views. On the other hand it can lead to an underplaying of differences and the naive supposition that 'We're all the same really, aren't we?' Neither approach is helpful to the development of a mature society with improved community understanding and co-operation.

Over recent decades various processes have been initiated to attempt to overcome this – in schools and colleges, in church-based education programmes, in other adult education programmes and in the religious peace and reconciliation movements. Interest in inter-church studies at school level has been stimulated by bodies such as the *Churches' Peace Education Programme* and the *Christian Education Movement in Northern Ireland*, the work of John Greer and colleagues at the University of Ulster at Coleraine and that of some of the Education and Library Boards. It is now not uncommon to discover groups of pupils visiting a range of local churches to learn about their similarities and differences. Study programmes such as *Irish Christianity* (J. Greer & E. McElhinney, Gill & Macmillan, 1985), *Looking at Churches and Worship in Ireland* (Churches' Peace Education Programme, 1985 & 1993) and *Opposite Religions?* (Brian Lambkin, Northern Ireland Centre for Learning Resources, 1992) have proved the most frequently used school materials for this purpose. The inclusion of a section in GCSE Religious Studies dealing with comparisons between two Christian denominations has reinforced this interest since the late 1980s, and the 1993 Common Core Religious Education Syllabus, agreed by the four largest denominations in Northern Ireland, has also helped to create a new ethos in which awareness and understanding of a range of Christian traditions is seen as important and desirable.

Resources for teachers and leaders in this work, however, are extremely limited, and little has been available for the non-specialist reader. Until recently few Christian denominations in Northern Ireland were in the habit of producing information about their beliefs, practices and structures. Some of them have now begun to improve their own provision for teaching about themselves, both to their own members and to those who do not belong to their tradition, but many people still complain that there are few obvious sources for their own background reading in a comparative study of Christian traditions. In 1977 Christian Journals (now defunct) published *Who Are We? What Do We Believe?*, edited by Stanley Worrall, which attempted to meet this need. But valuable as it was at the time, the book was limited by its unattractive appearance and its focus on the four largest denominations (Roman Catholic, Presbyterian, Church of Ireland and Methodist) with only a brief chapter covering just some of the rest of the smaller Churches. It also lacked a standard format in relation to each denomination. It went out of print in the mid-1980s, and despite various attempts to get it revised and reprinted, this was never achieved.

Following discussions between Joe Hinds of the Community Relations Council and the present writer in 1993–4, it was agreed that the time was right to pursue such a project again. The proposed book was commissioned by the Council, an editor was appointed and a team of consultants was set up to monitor and support the process. The aim was to produce an attractive and readable resource which would serve as an approachable introduction for a range of readers, with or without church affiliations, including teachers and leaders in educational, cross-community, church and inter-church work. It is hoped that the new publication will offer a survey and comparative study of the Christian traditions active in Northern Ireland which should be regarded as complementary to materials being produced by some of the denominations themselves. It is most important to do this in a way that holds the confidence of the various traditions, and at the same time to attempt to maintain a positive critical distance and a sense of fairness and relative objectivity.

CRITERIA FOR INCLUSION

The principal focus of the first part of this book is on the range of Christian traditions as they are currently to be found in Northern Ireland. Of course, most of the denominations in Ireland pre-date partition and have largely continued to be organised on an all-Ireland basis, but it is in Northern Ireland that the diversity of denominations is at its greatest and the potential for exchange between them is more significant. The aim was to be as comprehensive and inclusive as possible, but such a policy is not without its difficulties and it is not unlikely that there will be some groups who feel excluded.

It was decided, for instance, not to include those groups perceived by many to be on the fringes of Christianity – such as the Jehovah's Witnesses and the Church of Jesus Christ of Latter-Day Saints (the Mormons). These and a number of other groups would be widely regarded as *sects* in that most of them believe themselves to be the only authentic bearers of Christian truth. It is not the purpose of this book to be judgemental of such groups, but one suspects that they themselves would be unhappy with inclusion in a compendium of this kind.

Certain other groups have not been given separate chapters but are dealt with in relation to other similar denominations. Some of the smaller Pentecostal denominations, for instance, have been included in the chapter on the larger (in Northern Ireland terms) Elim Pentecostal Church. Differences between the Pentecostal Churches are not very substantial, and they are normally in good relationship with each other. A very different kind of relationship usually exists between the Christian Brethren and the Exclusive Brethren, and there are some references to the latter in the chapter on the Brethren. Neither group is a denomination as such, and it is extremely difficult to make contact with the Exclusive Brethren (as their name might suggest), who, in any case, might well be regarded as a sect in terms of the definition offered above. Indeed, for a minority of Protestants in Northern Ireland the very inclusion of a chapter on the Roman Catholic Church is likely to create a similar dilemma. These, however, are all difficult decisions which must be faced when planning a work of this kind and it may ultimately prove impossible to avoid offence whether by inclusion or exclusion! It is hoped that the majority of readers will at the very least understand the basis on which these decisions have been made.

SEQUENCE

The sequence in which these denominational chapters appear may be of significance to some. The rationale used is perceived numerical strength in Northern Ireland, starting with the greatest number of members. However, this too may be fraught with difficulties, as only estimated figures are available for some groupings (for instance, the Brethren and the 'New Churches') and different Churches use quite different criteria for calculating their memberships, a point which is discussed more fully in the Introduction. It is hoped that all concerned will understand that this sequence was an attempt to be fair and democratic.

BEYOND THE DENOMINATIONAL BOUNDARIES

Any study of Christian traditions in Northern Ireland, as elsewhere, must, however, take into account that the differences *between* the denominations are only a part of the overall picture. Several denominations, in particular the larger ones, contain *within* them a number of different traditions and perspectives. Some issues and concerns cross the boundaries between the Christian traditions, and for this reason the second part of the book is devoted to broader themes relating to the experience of Christians of various kinds in Northern Ireland. Several of the 'isms' which influence the Churches in quite different ways are explored in these chapters – evangelicalism, fundamentalism and ecumenism, for example. Other chapters in this section deal with concerns which affect the whole Church and which therefore require cross-denominational awareness and experience, such as approaches to spirituality, Christian responses to the political divisions of Northern Ireland, sectarianism and the role of women. These chapters should help to add a sense of context and perspective to the distinct experiences of the various denominational traditions.

CHOOSING THE AUTHORS

Authors were chosen following a process of discussion with the Reference Group and wider consultation, on the principles indicated below. In some cases the persons who were initially approached declined or passed the request on to others.

In Part 1 of this book the authors are, with only one exception (the chapter on the Orthodox Churches), members of the denominational traditions of which they have written. This is most important because it means that the different denominations are being allowed to speak for themselves. It was agreed at an early stage that it would be unwise to ask for official representatives of the various denominations (by request to Assemblies, Synods, Conferences, et cetera) or to seek contributions from church leaders, but rather to find authors who are in good standing with their various traditions and able to interpret their denomination clearly to others. In a few cases, however, especially where the smaller denominations are concerned, chapters *have* in fact been written by senior leaders, past or present, and some, indeed, have been submitted to various denominational bodies and leaders for scrutiny. Nevertheless, none of these chapters should be perceived as having the status of an official denominational statement.

The relationship struck up with the contributing authors has been one of the real pleasures of this whole process, although it is a matter of personal disappointment to the editor that there are very few women in the final line-up. Several women were approached as first choices for various chapters but almost all declined, for a diversity of reasons.

A brief biography of the contributor appears at the end of each chapter.

STRUCTURE OF THE DENOMINATIONAL CHAPTERS

Once a contribution had been provisionally agreed, authors were provided with a printed outline of the project and invited to submit a draft, taking account of certain guidelines. The purpose of this remit was to try to ensure that the denominational chapters had structure and cohesion while permitting flexibility appropriate to the differences between the Churches in question. Some readers, it was assumed, would wish to read about particular denominations as a whole while others might prefer a comparative study, following topics in parallel across a range of traditions. Thus it was recommended that each denominational chapter take account of the following pattern and themes, while recognising that not all themes (or titles of themes) are equally applicable from one tradition to another:

- Origins – especially Irish origins
- Relationships with the world church – e.g. other denominations within the same tradition, alliances, et cetera
- A survey of the denomination at the present time – numbers, distribution, trends, et cetera

- Doctrinal position – including formal statements, distinctive features and variations
- Basis of authority
- Membership, church government and ministry
- Sacraments and ordinances
- Spirituality
- Worship and liturgy
- Buildings and artefacts
- The church in the community
- Attitudes to other denominations and to inter-church/ecumenical activity
- Other special features

THE EDITORIAL PROCESS

Authors were asked to prepare their chapters in a readable style which would be approachable by non-members and non-experts in respect of each denomination. They were encouraged to write positively about their own traditions rather than negatively about those of others, but at the same time they were strongly advised that difficult or controversial issues should be broached openly and honestly. Each contributor was also invited to provide a bibliography of key texts for further reading, although in the case of some smaller denominations this has not proved possible.

Guidelines on the length of contributions were also given, once again on the basis of the perceived numerical strength of each denomination. Thus the four largest denominational traditions were offered a more substantial number of words than the smaller Churches. A flexible approach was maintained on chapter length, however, in recognition of the need for fuller explanations in places.

No attempts were made to seek stylistic unity between the thirty or so contributing authors. This would have been contrived and impossible, but even more importantly it was felt to be quite undesirable. In compiling a series of essays on living religious and cultural traditions the last thing on earth that would be required to stimulate interest is any sense that it had been written by a committee!

Once drafts were received a process of dialogue was entered into in relation to the length, structure and content of the chapters until each contribution was shaped to the mutual satisfaction of author and editor. Members of the Reference Group were also invited to read submitted drafts, and further suggestions from them were considered and, where appropriate, incorporated with the agreement of the authors. Authors were given a final opportunity to read over and correct their submissions at a late stage in order to ensure their confidence in the whole process.

USING APPROPRIATE NAMES

One difficulty with a book about religious traditions in Northern Ireland is that members of some churches have difficulty with the names used by others. In the past this was sometimes an issue in relation to the *Church of Ireland*, which may have been perceived in some quarters as a presumptuous title, especially after Disestablishment in 1871. That no longer appears to be a major concern, but the same kind of discussion often arises over the terms *Catholic* or *Roman Catholic*. At its most pedantic this can be as heated and insoluble as *Derry* or *Londonderry*! Generally speaking, members of the *Catholic Church in Ireland* (its official designation) speak of themselves as *Catholics*; many Protestants add the epithet *Roman* as a way of making the point that *Catholic* is an appropriate description for the whole Church in its orthodoxy and universality. Thus in several of the chapters about the Protestant denominations, the authors have emphasised that they regard themselves as Catholic as well as Protestant.

There is no solution to this which will satisfy everyone. Two editorial principles have therefore been employed. The first is that the right of members of particular traditions to use the name with which they themselves are most comfortable must be respected. This is no less applicable in relation to some of the Protestant denominations (thus 'Christian Brethren' is preferred to 'Plymouth Brethren'; 'New Churches' is used in preference to 'House Churches', et cetera). The second principle is that out of respect for differing points of view other authors have been permitted to use the terms with which they are most at ease. In editorial chapters 'the BBC approach' has been adopted – to use both terms at different points according to the context. Having made this point, it will be evident that the author of the chapter on the Catholic Church in Ireland appears to be equally at ease with the terms Catholic *and* Roman Catholic, which may be indicative of a trend and a readiness among committed (as opposed to nominal) members of the various traditions to be sensitive to each other's ideas and preferences.

One further linguistic issue concerns the use of *Church* or *church*. Generally speaking, the capital C is employed in this book when writing of a denominational title (e.g. the Methodist Church) or a specific local parish or congregation (e.g. Windsor Baptist Church) or of the concept of the Church as the whole People of God. The lower case is employed when using the term of an unspecified building or group (e.g. a Pentecostal church). However, some inconsistencies may be evident on this point.

POINTS OF VIEW

All books have their point of view, even those which set out to offer a

fairly objective survey of a particular phenomenon. This book is no exception. Its fundamental point of view is the belief that religious awareness
and understanding must be based on accurate information, on first-hand
accounts presented from inside the various Christian traditions rather than
on second-hand perceptions or misrepresentations. The presentations of
the various traditions offered in Part 1 can be an important part of such a
process if they are accepted as the first stage in a dialogue. As in any true
dialogue, *listening* is crucial before there can be a serious exchange of ideas.

The second part of the book takes the dialogue a stage further in
encouraging analysis and discussion of cross-denominational themes from
a number of different points of view.

If this book can contribute in small ways to fuller, more frequent and
better-informed religious dialogue, and nudge its readers towards being
able to live with each other's differences in a spirit of fairness and mutual
respect, then it will have achieved an important part of the editor's purpose
in undertaking the task.

THANKS AND ACKNOWLEDGEMENTS

Special thanks in the development of this book are due to a number of
people.

Joe Hinds of the Community Relations Council was responsible for
taking forward a number of aspirational conversations and gaining the
support of the Council for the initiation of this process. Joe's enthusiasm
for the idea was not diminished when he moved on and passed the oversight of the project on to Elaine Rowan, who has continued to combine
patience with encouragement and considerable practical support. Other
members of staff at the CRC, including Micháela McCabe and Ellana
Tomasso, have been most helpful.

The editor is also very grateful to the members of the Reference Group
(named below), some of whom have also been involved as contributors.
Particular thanks are due to Johnston McMaster for much wisdom and
guidance at all stages, and to Robert Brown who, as the editor's Head of
Department at Stranmillis College, has been a wonderful support and
encouragement as well as making many most helpful suggestions on reading some of the chapters. Karen Clarke in the College has also been a tower
of strength in so many practical ways.

At a late stage in the process two people not otherwise involved with
the book were invited to read the almost-complete text and to offer
comments. Special thanks are due to Sr Roisín Hannaway and the Rev.
Doug Baker for undertaking this task and for their helpful observations.

The privilege of being able to shape a book of this kind owes much to the many people from different Christian traditions, in Northern Ireland and further afield, with whom there have been opportunities to share and from whom there have been so many insights over the years. Conversations at Corrymeela or with teachers, students and a wide range of lay people and clergy in different churches, have all enriched the experience from which this book has grown.

It has also been a particular pleasure to work with such a large number and wide range of authors who, while coming from a very broad range of Christian traditions and theological perspectives, have understood the nature of this project and entered enthusiastically and sensitively into the process. The personal meetings, telephone conversations and endless other forms of correspondence with them have been a highlight of the period in which this book has taken shape and, of course, without them and their willing co-operation nothing would have been possible.

Most especially I am grateful to my long-suffering family and several close friends who have listened endlessly, patiently and supportively over the past three years to the accounts of the trials and tribulations of an editor with thirty contributing authors!

NORMAN RICHARDSON

MARCH 1998

Members of the Reference Group

Robert Brown	Stranmillis College, Belfast
Daphne Gilmour	formerly Southern Education and Library Board
Brian Lambkin	formerly Lagan College
Duncan Morrow	University of Ulster at Jordanstown
Johnston McMaster	Irish School of Ecumenics, Belfast
David Porter	Evangelical Contribution on Northern Ireland (ECONI)
Sr Breige Vallely	St Mary's College, Belfast
David Stevens	Irish Council of Churches

Introduction
Mixed Blessings: A View of Christian Practice in Northern Ireland

NORMAN RICHARDSON

Religion in Northern Ireland can be a perplexing semantic wilderness. The religious words that we use are loaded with all kinds of subtleties which can be pitfalls for the unwary, even among those who live in the province. Especially to the outside observer, we don't always seem to say what we mean, or to mean what we actually say – our words about religion are often coded messages about so many other layers of life in our turbulent corner of Ireland. One of the purposes of this book is to attempt to get behind the loaded words and the familiar (as well as the unfamiliar) religious labels and to discover something of the reality of religious life in Northern Ireland.

It is, however, important to emphasise at the outset that part of this reality is expressed in the faith and commitment of ordinary church members – laypeople, clergy and members of special groups such as religious orders – those whose religious convictions form an integral part of their personal and social lives and who live out their faith in the everyday situation in which they find themselves. However much the situation in Northern Ireland may appear to direct people's perception of the Churches towards one of conflict or of failure to live up to the ideals of the Christian faith, it must be recognised that many people gain strength and courage to deal with life from their personal devotions, their study of the Scriptures, from worship in the faith community, from prayer and sacraments and from the support of their fellow believers. Whatever their failings, the Churches have provided much that is positive to the lives of many people, in helping to give them value and to help them to see value in others. Equally it has often been argued, although it is difficult to prove, that the Churches have contributed enormously to social and political stability in Northern Ireland at a time of great social upheaval, at the very least by providing a rationale for restraint. Some of this is seen at its best in the positive and honest statements of denominationally expressed Christian faith provided in many of the chapters in Part 1 of this book. If the primary focus of this introductory chapter is to consider some of the difficulties and contradictions within the experience of the Christian communities of Northern Ireland, then these positive points should be kept in mind as a backdrop and a necessary corrective.

TALKING ABOUT RELIGION IN NORTHERN IRELAND

The clichéd joke about the Jew who was asked if he was a Catholic Jew or a Protestant Jew is not without foundation in reality. Most people are only too well aware that the terms *Catholic* and *Protestant* are more likely to be used to describe where people went to school or where they live rather than where they go on Sundays, but our words and labels about religion do carry much unexpected baggage and many misapprehensions. This is regularly confirmed by a range of experiences. It is not unusual to hear people prefacing any discussion about religion with a hope that they will not offend anyone, indicating a widely held belief that the very mention of a religious topic in Northern Ireland needs to be guarded with extreme sensitivity. Seamus Heaney's oft-quoted lines from the poem 'Whatever You Say Say Nothing' – ' "Religion's never mentioned here", of course'[1] – ring very true in this context. For some people one of the cardinal rules of community relations work remains (despite much encouragement to the contrary) a naive prohibition on the discussion of religion and politics! Lambkin[2] has explored the nature and origins of terms like 'the other religion', 'different religions' and even 'opposite religions' and shown how they reflect a sense which goes well beyond a perception of differing denominations. Such expressions, he proposes, reflect the significance and impact of traditional terminology such as 'the true religion' in various historical church statements.

At a more anecdotal level several experiences from the present author's work with cross-community groups and church members across a range of denominations have highlighted the difficulties of making progress in relation to the ways in which people speak (if at all) about religion. For instance there were the two women, Protestant and Catholic, who, after a week at the cross-community Corrymeela Centre during which they faithfully attended the voluntary daily acts of shared worship, remarked, 'This place is great – there's no religion here!'

This anxious perception of religion as almost synonymous with conflict and mutual hatred is very hard to shift. On another occasion a teacher who had agreed to help with the piloting of primary school materials on different Christian Churches seemed most concerned to state, 'I'm *not* ecumenical! But,' she added, without any apparent irony, 'I do want the children from different denominations to know about and understand each other better.' A denominational youth leader some years ago described the anxiety and, in some cases, distress which was experienced by a group of Northern Irish young adults when they attended an international conference with their peers from the equivalent denomination in other countries and discovered a startlingly wide range of theological and ideological views very different from their own. More disturbingly there was the Protestant clergyman who insisted that if children from the controlled school of which he was a governor were to have any contact with a linked Catholic school then there should be 'no religious discussion'. No less worrying was the Catholic lady who admitted that she never used the word 'Protestant' because she was aware that there were different kinds of Protestants but she had no knowledge of the differences and was thus afraid of offending them by using the generic term 'Protestant'. A small-scale piece of research carried out in Belfast by an educational community relations worker[3] indicated that some teachers were more open to the possibility of visiting the local mosque or Hindu temple than they were to exploring different Christian churches.

Undoubtedly Northern Ireland is a place where religion is taken very seriously. This statement is not intended to be either ironic or cynical. Proportionately more people do attend church than in other parts of the UK, if this can be taken as any kind of indicator. Without doubt the churches perform a very important social function in the province, especially, though by no means exclusively, in rural areas. One is more likely to be handed religious tracts in the street in Northern Ireland, or to be confronted with street preachers, than in other parts of Ireland and Britain. A glance at the letters pages of the province's press is likely to reveal almost on any day a number of letters quoting Scripture passages to support one argument or another. It is well known that the presenter of one of the province's most listened-to live radio programmes, *Talkback* on BBC Radio Ulster, long ago learned that it was necessary to keep a Bible on the studio desk to be able to look up all the biblical references that were being telephoned through.

Does this indicate that Northern Ireland is a 'religious' society, and is that quite the same thing as a Christian society? Perhaps it would be more appropriate to describe it as a society in which the Christian influence appears to be overtly stronger than that in many other European countries.

Its religious diversity sets it apart from its rather more monolithic southern neighbour, the Republic of Ireland, and its religious intensity distinguishes it from its eastern partner, Britain. Some observers have seen more parallels with the religious scene in the United States, where diversity is even greater but where levels of active church membership do appear to be similar.

STATISTICS

Finding out the actual membership numbers of the various denominations is a less straightforward task than it might seem and is complicated by the loose use in Northern Ireland of the 'Protestant/Catholic' terminology. Thus while at the level of community and cultural identity the traditional perception of the province as 'two-thirds Protestant; one-third Catholic' would still appear to be reasonably accurate (although it is narrowing towards a 60/40 relationship), attempts to discover the statistics of genuine religious involvement can lead to confusion.

Sources for such information are approximately threefold: the Northern Ireland Census, conducted every ten years; the *Irish Christian Handbook*,[4] published every three years or so by a London-based organisation, Christian Research; and figures collected and issued by the denominations themselves (though not in every case), sometimes supplemented from other sources (such as the authors of chapters in this book). This information is set out in parallel in Figure 1 (p. 6), but the considerable divergence between the figures requires some attempt at explanation.

Census figures are of interest in that they permit some insight into the identities which people perceive for themselves, but they mostly seem very inflated when set against the Churches' own representations of actual religious allegiance. The reasons why people might claim such a denominational identity can only be for speculation. In many cases people are expressing an unambiguous Christian commitment in their statement of denominational membership. Theirs is an active involvement, born out of conviction and expressed in regular attendance at worship and usually other activities too. In such cases children are encouraged and nurtured in the faith and the church is probably a significant orientation in social life. Others may be expressing no less real and important a conviction, but one which is looser in terms of attendance and involvement, perhaps because of movement away from a home church base, or because of marriage to a partner with whom denominational allegiance or general religious commitment is not shared, or through personal circumstances of loss or disappointment or even falling out with clergy or other local church members. It may still be very important for such people to express their personal sense of allegiance through a statement on a census form, even though the simple expression of a denominational name only gives a superficial account of a much more complex relationship. In the case of others claiming an allegiance which may be influenced by baptism or family background but which does not appear to reflect either current personal commitment or attendance, there may be a genuine reluctance in an ostensibly religious society like Northern Ireland to admit to having 'left' a particular tradition, and even perhaps a lingering sense of social pressure to be seen to conform to outward religious 'assent'.

There are indications, however, that this readiness to acknowledge allegiance in name only is changing. For the first time in 1991 the Northern Ireland Census included an option of stating 'no religion', and 59,234 people (about 4% of the population) chose it – almost exactly as many as described themselves as Methodists (generally perceived to be the fourth largest denomination in Ireland).[5] Other surveys suggest that the number claiming 'no religion' has grown significantly over the years,[6] suggesting a movement towards the increasingly secular society which has been a feature of Britain and Europe for some decades.

The editors of the *Irish Christian Handbook* (*1995/6 Edition*) are cautious about the findings of the Northern Ireland Census and attempt a fuller analysis based on a distinction between the 'Community' figure (indicated by the census) and actual members. In many cases an 'active members' figure is given as a percentage estimate of those claiming membership, based variously on attendance figures issued by the denominations themselves and on findings from other surveys. Thus, for instance, in respect of the Church of Ireland and the Presbyterian Church in Ireland the percentage on which 'active membership' is based is given as 58% of the 'community' figure. In other instances – sometimes surprisingly – different percentages are given to distinguish 'active' members from the community figure (for example 25% in the case of Congregationalists; 50% in the case of the Lutheran Church in Ireland and the Church of the Nazarene; 60% in the case of Free Presbyterians). Roman Catholic membership figures are based on the Church's own mass attendance numbers (generally taken as 85% of the Catholic population in the early 1990s). Several other denominations are given with membership figures which do not make the 'active/community' distinction (for instance the Pentecostal Churches and the Quakers), presumably on the assumption that there is little ambiguity about who is actively involved. This makes the *Irish Christian Handbook* both confusing and fascinating at one and the same time, but the generally useful point is well made – that actual active membership is normally significantly lower than bald census figures might indicate, though with some important exceptions (for example in the case of

Figure 1
Denominational Statistics for Northern Ireland

	1991 NI Census	Denominational sources	Irish Christian Handbook[1]
Catholic Church	605,639	*as Irish Christian Handbook*	518,016[e 2]
Presbyterian (PCI)	336,891	288,000	194,718[e]
Church of Ireland	279,280	not issued	161,500[e]
Methodist	59,517	approx. 30,000[3]	19,357[e]
Baptist Union	19,484	over 8,000[4]	8,890[e]
Christian Brethren	12,446	12,000 approx.[e]	6,300[e 5]
Free Presbyterian	12,363	not available[6]	13,400[e 7]
Congregational	8,176	2,200[8]	1,900[e]
Elim Pentecostal	5,537	approx. 10,000[9]	6,500[e]
Assemblies of God	326	not available	360[e]
Apostolic	254[10]	not available	260[e]
Non-Subscribing Presb.	3,213[11]	4,600[12]	3,600[e]
Reformed Presb.	3,184	approx. 4,000[13]	1,865[e]
Salvation Army	1,918	approx. 1,000	1,110[e]
Church of Nazarene	1,149	not available[14]	630[e]
Free Methodist	1,119	729[15]	296[e]
Independent Methodist	835	not available[16]	260[e]
Quakers	804	*as Irish Christian Handbook*	925[e]
Evangelical Presb.	730	458[17]	494[e]
Moravians	714	600[18]	340[e]
Lutherans	123	not available[19]	55[e]
New Churches	(1,300)[20]	not available	1,800[e]
Chinese Church	—	not available[21]	70[e]
Orthodox	72[22]	as census	183[e 23]

([e] estimate)

Notes
1. Figures from the 1995/6 edition of the *Irish Christian Handbook* – published in 1994.
2. Average weekly mass attendance as given in 1995/6 edition of the *Handbook* (assumed to be 85% of the Roman Catholic population).
3. Comprising 19,000 active adults and 11,000 children.
4. Baptised members only; children and other active adherents to be added.
5. Plus approximately 1,000 members of the 'Exclusive Brethren'.
6. There are approx. 100 Free Presbyterian congregations, mostly in NI but including some in other parts of the world.

7. 1995 estimate of the 'community' figure. The *ICH* adds: 'Active adult members could be taken as approximately 60% of the community figure.'
8. Full communicant members; children and others to be added.
9. Estimate of Sunday attendance figures.
10. The census also showed, as a separate group, 'Apostolic Pentecostal': 156.
11. The census also showed, as a separate group, 'Non-Subscribing Old Presbyterian': 152.
12. Figure includes active adults plus Sunday School attenders.
13. Figure comprises 2,500 communicant members plus 1,500 children and other adherents.
14. There are 13 Church of the Nazarene congregations in Northern Ireland.
15. Average Sunday service attendance in 1991. NB: The author of the chapter on the Free Methodist Church gives the much lower figure of 170 active full members in 1998.
16. There are 16 Independent Methodist congregations in Northern Ireland.
17. The figure is for communicant membership in 1995. Average morning worship attendance in 1995 was 662.
18. A further 200 adherents should be added to this figure.
19. There are approximately 50 Lutheran families in Northern Ireland.
20. The figure of 1,300 is for the Christian Fellowship Church – only one component of the 'New Churches' movement.
21. There is so far only one congregation in Northern Ireland.
22. The census figure is for Greek Orthodox only.

the Pentecostal churches, where the *Handbook* figures suggest steady growth since 1991). There is some wariness in denominational circles about the basis on which the *Irish Christian Handbook* figures are drawn up, and like all such figures they should be read with caution.

One of the main problems with figures issued by the denominations themselves is that they use quite different bases for counting. Of the larger denominations, the Presbyterians and Methodists issue their own statistics, the Catholic Church in Ireland provides mass attendance figures but the Church of Ireland does not engage in any comparable process. In some other denominations, such as the Baptist Union, figures are issued based on baptised members but these do not include the active membership of children and others. This makes comparisons difficult if not impossible.

What most of these sources do show, along with other surveys of religious attitudes (Rose's survey of 1968 and Moxon-Browne's of 1978;[7] periodic Social Attitudes surveys), is that in the case of many denominations both attendance and membership are declining. This appears to be particularly marked in the large denominations (especially the three larger Protestant denominations where the decline has been evident for many decades), in urban areas, and most evidently in the case of young males. However, there has been an increase in the membership (including young people) of the smaller and theologically conservative-evangelical

Protestant Churches, notably the Elim Pentecostal Church and the 'New Churches' movement.

(A very useful summary and synthesis of this statistical information has been prepared by David Stevens of the Irish Council of Churches[8] and is updated from time to time. Some of the non-statistical aspects of Stevens's analysis form part of his contribution to this book: Chapter 23, 'Differences and Commonalities'.)

VARIATIONS

Beyond the numbers and statistics there is a great deal more to be discovered about the Christian communities of Northern Ireland. Perceptions of unified communities of Protestant believers and Roman Catholic believers quickly give way, on even the most straightforward of examinations, to a recognition of considerable diversity particularly at the Protestant end, as indicated by a glance at the contents page of this book. But the tapestry of beliefs and practices does not end there (which is why this book is in two parts rather than just one).

Very few of the diverse denominations are within themselves monochrome and some contain within their membership a significant range of theological approaches, liturgical styles and other variables. This has been very effectively demonstrated by Boal, Keane & Livingstone in their studies of attitudinal variations among Protestant and Catholic churchgoers in Belfast.[9] They propose that it is important to question the 'monolithic stereotypes' implied by the terms Catholic and Protestant and that this can be done by examining 'the variety of religious spaces – both material and metaphysical – which are occupied by significant numbers of people in Northern Ireland'. Such 'religious space', they argue, is significant in terms of ethnic identity which often manifests itself in religious ways, and they cite C.S. Lewis's remark about the 'semi-political churchgoing of Ulster'. They acknowledge that religious space is 'multidimensional space, material and metaphysical, physical and social, in which ideology, iconography, and sociability are explicitly and/or tacitly integrated'.[10]

In their summarised data Boal, Keane & Livingstone offer a picture of churchgoing Catholics and Protestants in the Belfast area. Churchgoing Catholics, they indicate, are 60% female, predominantly middle-aged or elderly (two-thirds over forty-five; one-third over sixty-five; only 7% under twenty-five), representative of the whole spectrum of educational levels, evenly divided between manual and non-manual occupational backgrounds but very under-representative of the unemployed members of the wider Catholic community. At an ideological level churchgoing

Catholics also display a 'range of theological convictions and attitudes on Church affairs and moral and doctrinal teachings', and these variations often seem to relate to age and educational level. 'Indeed, on a very wide range of issues there is little to indicate internal coherence or consensus. However, when it comes to the matter of identity . . . Catholics are united in being non-Ulster, non-British and non-Unionist.'[11]

The parallel picture for Belfast's Protestant churchgoers indicates that they are predominantly female (59%), over forty-five (73%) and middle-class (64%). Comparison with earlier studies suggests that for Protestants 'churchgoing is increasingly an activity practised by the elderly and by women', although there is significant denominational variation. But the study indicates considerable variation *within* churchgoing Protestantism 'on a theological spectrum from conservative to liberal, social class membership, demographic structure, congregational affiliation, stances on public morality, and attitudes towards cross-community relations'.[12] On the issue of the constitutional future of Northern Ireland within the United Kingdom the study shows that churchgoing Protestants 'overwhelmingly speak with one voice', but, the authors suggest, this may well arise 'from a plurality of motivations'.[13] Overall the indications suggest a more marked general conservatism among Protestants as compared with Catholics, and a trend towards even greater *theological* conservatism.

Nevertheless, despite the evident variations within each tradition, the Boal, Keane & Livingstone study indicates that churchgoing Protestants and Catholics each believe the other group to be more monolithic: 'Even if "us" do not exhibit social solidarity there is a strong perception that it exists among "them".'[14]

RELIGION, CONFLICT AND CAUTION

The debate about the extent to which Northern Ireland's conflict is a religious one tends to excite irritation in those who live in the province. An early BBC documentary on the Troubles in 1970, entitled *Christians at War*, provoked many angry letters from those who insisted that 'true Christians' were not fighting each other and that theology and religious observances were not at issue. Yet, substantially true as this is, the close tie-in between religion and identity, religion and culture, religion and politics, means that it is simply not adequate to claim dismissively, as some do, that the conflict has 'nothing to do with religion'. As Duncan Morrow has put it, 'Churches are crucial markers of identity in Northern Ireland.'[15]

Although there is sometimes a reluctance to acknowledge it, the Northern Ireland conflict is at many points reinforced by religiously motivated practices and activities, religious perceptions and religious fears.

There can be little doubt that people from Catholic and Protestant backgrounds are likely to have substantially different understandings and
experiences in relation to those activities, perceptions and fears. Concern
about the perceived religio-political role of the Roman Catholic Church
is still very significant for many people from a Protestant background (still
expressed at gut level in the phrase *Home Rule is Rome Rule*); anxiety about
the activities and influence of institutions such as the Orange Order in relation to the Protestant Churches is very powerful for many of those from
Catholic backgrounds, especially in some parts of the province. The role
and significance attached to church funerals, especially of those who have
been involved in acts of violence, has been another marker of cultural difference and misunderstanding.

If, on the one hand, people make simplistic assumptions about religion
being the primary issue, and therefore that all that has to be done is to hold
a few ecumenical services to set things to right, it will be hard to do justice
to the complexities of the problem. If, on the other hand, the reality of the
religious dimension is denied, the result will be to neglect an area of life
which needs to be dealt with if the communities of Northern Ireland are
to get to grips with the issue of how to live together in mutual peace,
justice and respect.

Yet there is a great reluctance on the part of many people, inside and
outside the Churches, to deal with the religious aspects of the conflict.
They are perceived as too hot to handle, too controversial, too likely to
create problems rather than solving them. This may be understandable,
but it is surely very mistaken.

There are many reasons for this reluctance, but they can only be hinted
at here. Duncan Morrow's research, *The Churches and Inter-Community
Relationships*,[16] a study by Inge Radford for the Community Relations
Council[17] and aspects of the Belfast Churchgoers Survey[18] have been
invaluable in helping to classify and quantify the difficulties, but their conclusions are not particularly surprising. They indicate a society in which
attitudes to religion are cautious, conservative and often defensive, no less
than attitudes to politics. Outside observers often find that the whole theological spectrum in Northern Ireland stands somewhat to the right (if one
may borrow political imagery) relative to the scene in Britain and many
other places.

Church leaders and others have, of course, issued frequent statements
condemning violence, and some have been courageous in their approach
to dealing with paramilitary organisations. In particular some in the
Churches have offered strong cross-community leadership in sensitive
areas and at times of great anxiety. The Churches' pastoral record with
their own communities can hardly be faulted, but overall there is too

strong a sense of standing back, of being unwilling to take a stand, of risk-
ing losing members, of looking over shoulders at the more strident members of our religious communities. There have been prophetic voices from
within various traditions which have often challenged and leavened the
community, but they have not been powerful enough to overcome what
would seem to be the more dominant message from the Churches. This is
well summed up in the writings of the excellent Inter-Church Group on
Faith and Politics:

> The Churches have been chaplains to their communities,
> comforters, reflectors of feelings, understanders, restrainers.
> They have often helped to moderate the crisis, but at the
> same time, have largely been unable to provide the spiritual
> resources, vision and hope which would enable people to
> find new paths and ways forward.[19]

One commentator has suggested, succinctly, that while the Churches are
bigger than the Northern Ireland problem, sadly they have often not been
big enough to cope with it.

(Several of the chapters in Part 2 of this book explore different aspects of
these issues of the relationship between religion, political life and conflict in
Northern Ireland.)

DIVISIVE ISSUES AND INTER-CHURCH CONTACT

As the Belfast Churchgoers Survey would appear to suggest, there seems
little doubt that the greatest and most significant religious division in
Northern Ireland is not, in fact, between Catholic and Protestant approaches to Christianity, but between those in all the Churches who are
open to 'the other community' and those who are closed. This is a rift
which divides all but the already most narrowly defined of denominations, though it is more marked in the larger Protestant traditions. For a
significant minority of Protestants the question of whether or not you
can regard the Roman Catholic Church as a Christian Church at all is a
live issue. It is very difficult to contemplate ecumenical encounter in that
context.

During the period of the Troubles these divisions have been particularly
marked within Irish Presbyterianism, although by no means exclusively
so. In 1980 the Presbyterian Church in Ireland withdrew from its international links with the World Council of Churches, partially on the grounds
that the WCC was supporting terrorism in South Africa, and a decade later
it declined to join the Council of Churches for Britain and Ireland (CCBI),
which drew together into a new relationship most of the members of the

former British Council of Churches (of which the Presbyterian Church had been a member) and the Roman Catholic Church. Observers have suggested that these moves had much more to do with internal church and political conflicts in Ireland than with the ostensibly significant international issues. Many Christians from the various Presbyterian traditions in Britain and elsewhere viewed these developments with sadness and disappointment, as did those within the Presbyterian Church in Ireland who had wanted to retain these links.

Membership of ecumenical organisations within Ireland has been only slightly less contentious for many of the other denominations. The Irish Council of Churches (ICC), formed in 1923,[20] has retained the membership of the larger Protestant denominations and some of the smaller ones but never had the support of the wholeheartedly conservative evangelical denominations. The Congregational Union, which had been among the founder members of the ICC, later withdrew. The Catholic Church in Ireland has never been in membership of the ICC, but has worked closely with it in various projects and, since the 1970s, has been a full partner in the Irish Inter-Church Meeting, which links it to all the ICC member denominations. Nevertheless, for not a few Protestants, including some members of the ICC member Churches, such a relationship is frowned upon even though most lay members of these denominations have little or no contact with any of these bodies. For many Protestant and Catholic Christians in Northern Ireland, clergy and laity alike, the issues of inter-church co-operation appear to be largely irrelevant because they simply do not impinge on their day-to-day involvement in their local church.

The pressure for ecumenical co-operation which in Britain has often risen from local congregations is largely absent in Northern Ireland, where ecumenism has normally been perceived as the preserve of church leaders. Morrow's and Radford's surveys both demonstrate that even where there is local contact it is usually the preserve of clergy, and even then there often seems to be a great wariness of dealing with anything too controversial. In many areas contact between lay members of different churches seems largely limited to very token and very occasional functions such as Christmas carol services and perhaps during the Week of Prayer for Christian Unity (although this latter event is not widely observed). It is sad to note that theological narrowness sometimes seems to be particularly strong among some members of the younger clergy – but this is perhaps unsurprising for a generation which has known almost thirty years of political uncertainties and major civil disruption.

A certain defensiveness is evident in issues such as mixed (or, more accurately, inter-church) marriages and integrated education. Both issues are regarded in some quarters as a potential threat to the identity and survival of a minority group, perhaps especially in rural areas. The movement to promote integrated education, in its origins very much a lay Christian movement, has often been regarded with great suspicion (to the point of hostility) by some in leadership positions in the Churches, perhaps because it is one aspect of education which seems significantly beyond their control. Noting this tendency towards defensiveness, Professor Simon Lee once somewhat cuttingly observed that the Churches in Northern Ireland 'sometimes give the impression of being more worried by women of intelligence, or lay people of independence, than they are by men of violence'.[21]

CHRISTIANS IN A PLURAL SOCIETY?

Our denominational traditions in Northern Ireland are still substantially able to feel self-sufficient, which may be one of the most significant reasons for the reluctance to seek broader visions. Research programmes and census returns do suggest that this may well be a false sense of security, in terms of the decline in numbers for most of the Churches, the greater readiness to state religious affiliation as 'none' and the increase in secular attitudes among many people, but for the most part the leaderships do not yet seem to behave as if they identify this as a significant threat to the status quo. There are still relatively few members of other faith traditions and ethnic minorities present to challenge our homogeneously Christian perceptions (only about two hundred and fifty active members of the Jewish community, about fifteen hundred Muslims, some two hundred and fifty Hindu families and a number of others) although in most cases their numbers are growing and their presence is increasingly being felt.[22] The perception of Northern Ireland as a plural society is undoubtedly growing, albeit latterly in comparison with many other European countries and regions, but this is not an issue which has yet made much impact on the Christian Churches.

This may be exemplified by considering the attitude of the Churches to religious education in schools, an area which they have traditionally regarded as 'their territory'. In 1992 a new Core Syllabus for Religious Education in Northern Ireland schools was drawn up by representatives of the four largest Churches (Catholic, Presbyterian, Church of Ireland and Methodist) and incorporated by the Department of Education into the Common Curriculum for Northern Ireland. Having been written by a panel of teachers and others appointed by the Churches, it is perhaps unsurprising that it proposed an exclusively Christian syllabus. Nevertheless there was a strong case made at the time (by some Christians as well as members of other faiths and none) for a more inclusive programme appropriate to a plural society. (Even the Conservative government of the day seemed uneasy about this apparent exclusivism and the Minister of Education officially requested that there should be some optional guidance material made available for the study of faiths other than Christianity.[23]) It seemed an exciting achievement to have got the Catholic Church and the three largest Protestant Churches together for this task in the first place, but some would believe that it is an achievement limited by the very structure which made it possible. Notwithstanding several positive judgements which can be made about the RE Core Syllabus, it appears in retrospect to represent a flawed process which owes more to church politics than to social, educational or even ecumenical vision.

(An excellent study by Ian Ellis, *Vision and Reality*,[24] includes other uncomfortable examples of the territoriality of the Churches in relation to educational policy during the earlier parts of the twentieth century.)

MUSTARD SEEDS

Much of this may appear to be a very negative and disappointing analysis of the situation in the Churches in Northern Ireland, although it is undoubtedly one shared by others from within the Christian community. It can be the cause of sadness, frustration and sometimes even anger. But it is not, of course, the whole story. There are mustard seeds, and they do grow. In religion, as in many other aspects of life in Northern Ireland, the period since 1969 has had a two-way pull. While many people, including Christians, have undoubtedly been polarised towards narrowness and sectarian bitterness, there are many others who have been pulled towards new relationships which would have been quite unthinkable only a few years ago.

While there are many criticisms which one may make of the Churches – leaders, clergy and laity – in relation to sins of commission and omission, it is no less important to set the record straight. There have been some strikingly prophetic voices which have gained great respect on both sides of the community. Some have made an impact at national level, perhaps by helping to bring calm in potentially inflammatory situations. Others have contributed at a local level, consistently chipping away at fears and ignorance by persisting in establishing good relationships in their area, especially when others wish to threaten and create instability – for instance the clergy, and sometimes laypeople, who have visited bereaved families across the community divide, or who have attended the funerals of victims of violence from 'the other side of the community'. Some will be aware of the west Belfast priest who led a silent vigil to the place where two army corporals were shot by the IRA in 1988; or the Presbyterian minister who spoke movingly at the funeral of a Catholic victim of loyalist sectarian violence; or the local priest and minister who went together to the local RUC station following a bomb attack on it the previous night. Despite the apparent paucity of local inter-church initiatives, there are many such examples – some dramatic, some mundane, some 'official', many unofficial, but all creative and seeking to heal – of positive leadership, working for the whole community, not just for one side of it.

Despite the inevitable, at times almost turgid, slowness of official inter-church initiatives, channels of communication now exist and are even taken for granted. There are the regular meetings between the leaders of the four largest Churches (although in some years the Presbyterian Church has elected a moderator who has refused to take part), and the various inter-church structures described above. (A fuller analysis of the inter-church processes in Ireland is given by Ian Ellis in Chapter 26.) One of the more useful outcomes of this contact has been in the reports which are from time to time commissioned by these bodies, best known among which are the 1976 report on *Violence in Ireland*,[25] and the 1993 report of a working party on *Sectarianism*,[26] although reports alone do not demand a costly response and are no substitute for concerted action.

The work of Christian peace and reconciliation organisations is well known (and is fully considered by John Morrow in Chapter 27). Their strength has often been in their focus at the fringes rather than within official denominational activities and in their significant involvement of lay-people. Such groups have normally seen 'the ministry of reconciliation'[27] as an imperative of the Gospel; or, as the founder of the Corrymeela Community, Ray Davey, once said: 'If we Christians cannot speak the message of reconciliation, then we have nothing to say.' Perhaps the more unexpected developments of this kind have been among some of the Protestant evangelical groups, who have traditionally been perceived as being much more wary of ecumenical contact and peace and reconciliation work. Organisations like the YMCA and ECONI (Evangelical Contribution on Northern Ireland) have worked with great commitment to urge their fellow evangelicals towards the view that biblical Christianity challenges people's relationships, not just in terms of personal salvation, and not just as individuals but in society, and have become most active in promoting cross-community understanding through study and joint action.

Yet mustard seeds must be nourished if there is to be a process of healthy growth. There has been no shortage of advice from within and to the Churches in Ireland as to how such processes might be developed further. While too many in the Churches remain to be convinced that such a process is important at all, there is a growing body of literature and teaching within the Christian communities of Northern Ireland, some of it clearly evident from the chapters of this book, which is encouraging Christians of all traditions to engage more fully with the issues and in new ways of being Christian *together*. There are several important recurrent themes among the approaches proposed to this end.

Foremost among these is a call by many commentators for processes of open, honest dialogue – including a readiness to talk about the things which *divide* – based on trust, between the Churches at *all* levels, most particularly among ordinary members of congregations and not just for clergy and church leaders. This is one of the key proposals of the Irish Inter-Church Meeting's Department of Theological Questions in its publication *Ecumenical Principles*,[28] which offers valuable guidelines for such dialogue. It begs the question, however, as to how ordinary local congregations can become involved in such a process, for inter-congregational co-operation of any kind would appear to run counter to the culture of many Christian communities in this part of the world.

Others have regularly called for more substantial educational programmes, particularly for adults, in order to increase understanding of the various Christian traditions and positions and to counter the shallow misinformation which has so often characterised awareness of Christian diversity in Northern Ireland. Some such programmes have been organised by the denominations themselves, or by voluntary bodies and academic institutions (notably the Northern Ireland studies programme of the Irish School of Ecumenics), and in 1990 Professor Simon Lee called for the Churches to support the work of schools in Education for Mutual Understanding and Cultural Heritage by providing courses for parents.[29] Again the difficulty with the implementation of valuable suggestions like this is that traditionally Churches have not been very good at setting up adult educational programmes of any kind.

Such study should progressively enable those involved to clarify and enunciate together *shared* Christian principles (as opposed to those which are singularly denominational or sectional). In the words of Archbishop Robin Eames such principles should 'transcend loyalties and instincts so often dictated by events'.[30] The challenge to Northern Ireland's Protestant and Roman Catholic Christians is to be able to eschew sectarianism by developing a shared biblical approach to issues of peace, mutual justice and reconciliation, and then to agree ways of acting creatively together on it.

At a different – and probably more sensitive – level there are growing numbers of Christians whose commitment to greater sharing and joint social action has directed them towards promoting integrated education. On present evidence it seems likely that a growing number of such schools will emerge over the coming years. So far most of those involved in developing the planned integrated schools have looked for partnership arrangements with the Churches, locally and nationally, but have often been disappointed with the response and this has sometimes led to estrangement from other members of their denominational tradition, especially in the Roman Catholic community. Greater openness on this issue within and between the Churches will be most important, and if joint Christian action is to go beyond the safe and token then a significant attitude change on the part of church leaderships will be required.

In a book entitled *Churches Working Together*,[31] Johnston McMaster has offered case studies of Christian groups who are attempting to develop a practical dialogue through study programmes, social action, joint prayer and worship and single community projects. McMaster proposes a model which uses the idea of a faith journey (like that of Abraham), and this he likens to discipleship, citing the clergy and elders of a Presbyterian church who had perceived that 'discipleship means that we have to break down barriers'.[32] This, he suggests, is the fundamental model of discipleship for Northern Ireland today.

PILGRIMAGE

This brief, selective analysis of Christian faith in Northern Ireland may have been deeply irritating for some readers. Is it always so necessary to focus on the divisive issues, on the role of the Churches in the conflict, or on the relationships (or lack of them) between the denominations? Surely for most churchgoing people their involvement is about none of these things, but rather about personal commitment and devotion to Christ, about regular worship and Christian service, about ordinary everyday things and a straightforward way of life?

True as this undoubtedly is, it is the conviction of this writer that the Christian Church was never intended to function simply as some kind of comfort zone. The strength which people gain from their everyday faith and worship is not intended to be an end in itself, but it is in the very nature of the Christian faith that it should be an outward-looking, serving community working to bring about the kingdom of God. The old adage remains appropriately challenging: 'It is the job of the Church to comfort the troubled and to trouble the comfortable.'

This is a vision of the Church which has motivated many in Northern Ireland and made them dissatisfied with the approach which does not allow religion to impinge too much on the key issues of society and politics. It is a model which sees the Church not as a static institution but as a living, growing organism, a people on the move.

In his historical survey of inter-church relationships in twentieth-

century Ireland, Dr Ian Ellis has written of the concept of the Christian
Church as a pilgrim people. 'For Irish Christians,' he writes, 'there is an
abiding challenge in the call to be a pilgrim people ... to stand back and
truly to recognise the need to transcend the cultural and societal moulds
and to choose another pilgrimage.'[33] Perhaps this sense of pilgrimage can
help to renew the vision of the Churches in Northern Ireland and lead
them towards creative participation in a new, plural community.

NOTES
1. Seamus Heaney, 'Whatever You Say Say Nothing', from *North* (London:
   Faber & Faber 1975).
2. B. Lambkin, *Opposite Religions Still?* (Aldershot: Avebury 1996), pp. 26ff.
3. C. Curran, unpublished report on teachers' attitudes towards the religious
   dimensions of Education for Mutual Understanding (Belfast: Columbanus
   Community 1995).
4. P. Brierley (ed.), *Irish Christian Handbook: 1995/6 Edition* (London: Christian
   Research 1994).
5. *Northern Ireland Census: Religion Report* (Belfast: HMSO 1993).
6. D. Stevens, 'A Profile of Irish Religion' in the 1995 *Annual Report of the Irish
   Council of Churches* (Belfast: Irish Council of Churches 1995).
7. See R. Rose, *Governing Without Consensus: An Irish Perspective* (London:
   Faber & Faber 1971); E. Moxon-Browne, *Nation, Class and Creed in Northern
   Ireland* (Aldershot: Gower 1983).
8. D. Stevens, 'A Profile of Irish Religion'.
9. F.W. Boal, M. Keane, & D.N. Livingstone, *Them and Us? Attitudinal
   Variation among Churchgoers in Belfast* (Belfast: Queen's University Institute
   of Irish Studies 1997).
10. Ibid. p. 5.
11. Ibid. pp. 66–7.
12. Ibid. p. 141.
13. Ibid. pp. 141–2.
14. Ibid. p. 67.
15. D. Morrow, *The Churches and Inter-Community Relationships* (Coleraine:
    University of Ulster Centre for the Study of Conflict 1991), p. 121.
16. Morrow, ibid.
17. Inge Radford, *Breaking Down Divisions: The Possibilities of a Local Church
    Contribution to Improving Community Relations* (Belfast: NI Community
    Relations Council 1993).
18. Boal, Keane & Livingstone, *Them and Us?*
19. An Inter-Church Group on Faith and Politics, *Breaking Down the Enmity:
    Faith and Politics in the Northern Ireland Conflict* (Belfast: 1993), p. 125.
20. J. Barkley, *The Irish Council of Churches* (Belfast: Irish Council of Churches
    1983).

21. S. Lee (ed.), *Freedom From Fear: Churches Together in Northern Ireland* (Belfast: Queen's University Institute of Irish Studies 1990).

22. M. Ryan, *Another Ireland* (Belfast: Stranmillis College 1986).

23. DENI, *Core Syllabus for Religious Education* (Belfast: HMSO 1993).

24. I. Ellis, *Vision and Reality: A Survey of Twentieth-Century Irish Inter-Church Relations* (Belfast: Queen's University Institute of Irish Studies 1992).

25. *Violence in Ireland: A Report to the Churches* (Belfast/Dublin: Christian Journals Ltd/Veritas Publications 1976).

26. *Sectarianism: A Discussion Document* (Belfast: Department of Social Issues of the Irish Inter-Church Meeting 1993).

27. 2 Corinthians 5:18.

28. *Ecumenical Principles* (Dublin: Veritas Publications/Irish Inter-Church Meeting 1993).

29. Lee (ed.), *Freedom From Fear*, p. 78.

30. R.H.A. Eames, 'The Future: The Contribution of the Christian Churches' in E. Hanna (ed.), *Reconciliation in Northern Ireland* (Dublin: Social Study Conference 1986), p. 61.

31. J. McMaster, *Churches Working Together: A Practical Guide for Northern Ireland* (Belfast: Community Relations Council 1994).

32. Ibid. p. 14.

33. Ellis, *Vision and Reality*, p. 162.

PART I

———

The Denominational Traditions

1

The
Catholic Church in Ireland

OLIVER CRILLY

INTRODUCTION

The Christian Church exists in paradox. The Church is a mystery in which the presence of the Risen Christ and the life of the Holy Trinity may be experienced. But the Church also has a human face, often disfigured by weakness and sinfulness, by contradictions and divisions. It lives and grows according to the divine principle within it, but also in the context of the historical time and the geographical place in which it is found.

It is probably impossible to find the perfect vantage point from which to view the Roman Catholic Church in Northern Ireland at the end of the twentieth century, but the Second Vatican Council (1962–5 – referred to as Vatican II) certainly offers a significant perspective. The years 1958–65 are years of privileged insight into the reality of the Church. These were the years of Pope John XXIII and Vatican II, the years which, for a Catholic, might well be described as the gathering of the authentic tradition of the Church and the articulation of it for our generation.

The Church in the modern world

Cardinal Leon Joseph Suenens, who died in 1996, a few months before his ninety-second birthday, proposed to Pope John a structure for presenting the large volume of material to be dealt with by the Council. At the centre of the picture was the Church, looked at both inwardly in terms of its own identity, and outwardly in terms of its relationships with the world around it. As the two great doctrinal Constitutions (*The Church*, and *The Church in the Modern World*) developed, reflection on the internal identity of the

Church focused on its unity as the Body of Christ – drawing its reality and perfection from Jesus Christ as its head, and on its ongoing struggle with its human imperfections as the Pilgrim People of God whose journey has not yet been completed: *'ecclesia semper reformanda'* – the Church always in need of reform.

When a change of perspective takes place in a large institution, it takes a very long time for that change to become effective or normative both within the institution and in public perception outside it. It is probably not surprising, then, that the image of the Catholic Church from before Vatican II is the image which prevails in the popular imagination – an image of a monolithic, authoritarian structure with mysterious pious practices rooted in the Latin language and Mediterranean sentiment.

Seeing what is essential

The remarkable thing is the strength and clarity of the vision of the Church which was articulated at the Second Vatican Council, which cut through the accretions of centuries to highlight what is essential and lasting. Richard P. McBrien, in the HarperCollins *Encyclopedia of Catholicism* (1995, p. 1306), summarises some major changes of perspective in the documents of Vatican II:

> Among the distinctive teachings of Vatican II, by contrast with some common beliefs of the pre-Vatican II era, are the following:
>
> 1. The Church is, first and foremost, a mystery, or sacrament, and not primarily an organisation or institution.
>
> 2. The Church is the whole people of God, not just the hierarchy, clergy and religious.
>
> 3. The Church's mission includes action on behalf of justice and peace and is not limited to the preaching of the word and the celebration of the sacraments.
>
> 4. The Church includes all Christians and is not limited exclusively to the Catholic Church.
>
> 5. The Church is a communion, or college, of local churches, which are not simply administrative subdivisions of the Church universal.
>
> 6. The Church is an eschatological community; it is not yet the kingdom of God.
>
> 7. The lay apostolate is a direct participation in the mission of the Church and not simply a sharing in the mission of the hierarchy.

8. There is a hierarchy of truths; not all official teachings of the Church are equally binding or essential to the integrity of Catholic faith.

9. God uses other Christian churches and non-Christian religions in offering salvation to all humankind; the Catholic Church is not the only means of salvation.

10. The dignity of the human person and the freedom of the act of faith are the foundation of religious liberty for all, over against the view that 'error has no rights'.

ORIGINS

Catholic teaching today, renewed and articulated for our time by the Second Vatican Council, is the visible tip of two thousand years of faith and reflection. At its origins we find the person of Jesus Christ, the words of the Scriptures, the lived experience of Christian communities, the writings of saints and scholars, of evangelisers and pastors, of people of prayer and vision. We find the great Councils of the Church, and the great Creeds which were anguished over and chiselled with fine precision. We find the great monastic traditions and movements and schools of spirituality: Columban, Franciscan, Dominican, Ignatian, Carmelite, and the lived experience of the religious life and of individual Christians and Christian families. We find the great medieval theologians like Thomas Aquinas. It is acknowledged now more than before, also, that Catholic theology and Scripture scholarship are indebted to the insights of the Churches and theologians of the Reformed tradition, a result of creative exchanges at the ecumenical level.

The Irish tradition

Within the Irish context, the Catholic Church finds its roots in a Christianity whose love of the Scriptures is expressed in the great illuminated manuscripts; whose sense of the Church as family goes back to the writings of St Patrick, and is etched in stone in the great High Crosses and stone lintels like that of St Lurach's Church in Maghera, Co. Derry, inspired by the Gospel of John, and portraying the glorified Christ on the cross and the birth of the Church from the side of Christ, whose lengthened arms gather the disciples, and even the two soldiers, into unity with himself. Sometimes also it is not just the sophisticated theological insights which touch us across the centuries, but the human warmth and immediacy of the lyrics scribbled on the margins of manuscripts by monastic scribes whose hands have grown weary with writing, or who are distracted by

the dappled shadows of moving branches from outside the window of
the scriptorium or the clear note of a blackbird on a yellow-heaped
branch.

ORGANISATION AND STRUCTURES

The external structures of the Roman Catholic Church are so clearly
defined as to lend themselves to simplification – perhaps even to caricature. There is a strict hierarchical order where the chain of command runs
from a monarchical Pope to a similarly monarchical bishop in each diocese
to a similarly monarchical parish priest/pastor in each parish.

The caricature, of course, needs to be corrected. The Second Vatican
Council sought to balance the chain of command by an awareness of
'collegiality' – a process of discernment, co-responsibility and joint decision making where all in the Church, clergy and laity, participate and
reflect the movement of the Holy Spirit: a process based on 'the very
nature of the Church, which calls for communion and for the co-operation of all' (Suenens, *Memories and Hopes*, p. 192). This is a continuing
struggle in the daily life of the Church. It has parallels in the experience of
other Christian denominations, for example in the balancing of the roles of
the teaching elder and the ruling elders in a local Presbyterian community.

The diocese

The Catholic Church in Ireland, like its main sister Churches, is organised
on an all-Ireland basis, unaffected by political structures. The key unit is the
diocese. Each diocese has a geographical boundary, but is defined in the
Code of Canon Law as 'a portion of the people of God, which is entrusted
to a Bishop to be nurtured by him ... in such a way that, remaining close
to its pastor and gathered by him through the Gospel and the Eucharist in
the Holy Spirit, it constitutes a particular Church'.

The Bishops' Conference

There are twenty-six dioceses in Ireland, grouped in four ecclesiastical provinces around the Archdioceses of Armagh, Dublin, Cashel and Tuam.
Because of the quirks of history, the Archbishop of Armagh, Patrick's
See, is given the title 'Primate of all Ireland', and the Archbishop of Dublin
is given the title 'Primate of Ireland'. Clearly, it is not only in politics that
language has to be allowed a certain leeway for personal interpretation. All
the bishops together used to be referred to as 'the Hierarchy'. While this
term is still used, the more frequent term nowadays is the Irish Catholic
Bishops' Conference. The Conference is usually, though not necessarily,
chaired by the Archbishop of Armagh. The title of *Cardinal* (a member of

the College of Cardinals, who advise the Pope and serve as papal electors) is not part of the local structure as such, though the Archbishop of Armagh has frequently been made Cardinal by the Pope.

Since 1969, the Catholic Bishops' Conference, following on recommendations in the aftermath of Vatican II, has established a series of Commissions and other bodies, to advise and help it in fields like Communication, Justice and Peace, Third World Development (*Trócaire*), Social Welfare, Liturgy, Ecumenism, et cetera. Before these were established, the annual budget of the Bishops' Conference for central administration was practically nil, which indicates how self-contained each diocese was. From this time, also, structures were put in place in collaboration with the Church of Ireland, Presbyterian Church, Methodist Church, and with the Irish Council of Churches, to deal with ecumenical relations and matters of common interest. The structures began as the *Ballymascanlon Talks*, so called because they took place at the Ballymascanlon Hotel, near Dundalk. Later they took on a more permanent form as the *Irish Inter-Church Meeting*. The Roman Catholic Church is not a member of the Irish Council of Churches, but is a full member of the Inter-Church Meeting. These links have been vital during the period of the Northern Ireland Troubles. One sad feature is that the full extent of co-operation has been publicised more abroad than at home, for fear of some people's objections.

The parish

Internally, each diocese is divided into parishes, again usually with a geographical boundary, but defined in Canon Law as 'a certain community of Christ's faithful stably established within a particular Church, whose pastoral care, under the authority of the diocesan Bishop, is entrusted to a parish priest as its proper pastor'. In larger parishes the parish priest is assisted by a curate or curates. The standard abbreviation for parish priest is PP, and for curates is CC. Just as the Bishops' Conference has established various commissions since Vatican II, many parishes have established pastoral councils. These are not meant to be executive committees on the model of secular business administration, but a core group in the faith community of the parish whose role is to work with the priests and religious in discerning the direction in which the Spirit is leading the community and in helping to facilitate the growth and activity of the local church.

As well as the involvement of lay people in pastoral councils, and in the many traditional supporting roles in parish life (often centred on fund-raising and maintenance), an increasing number of people in parishes now exercise a role in ministry, for example in the Liturgy as Ministers of the Word, reading the Scriptures at Mass or on other occasions, as Ministers of the Eucharist, distributing Communion within Mass and bringing Communion to the sick and elderly on a regular basis in music ministry (choir, folk group, instrumental) and in various other ministries.

The religious orders

As well as the diocesan and parish structures, a certain flexibility for the expression of different spiritual insights and different apostolates within the broader church structure is provided in the Catholic tradition by the existence of religious orders of women and men. Some of these are closely linked to the local diocesan structure and some are established on a more international basis, reporting directly to the Church's central administration in Rome. The Franciscans draw on the commitment to poverty of their founder, St Francis of Assisi (1181–1226), and his sense of being called to work for the renewal of the Church. The Dominicans, following St Dominic (1170–1221), are known as 'the Friars Preachers', and with members like the famous St Thomas Aquinas (1225–74) are naturally known for their intellectual contribution in the tradition of Scholasticism, right down to the present day, and also for their contemplative spirit and their work in education. St Ignatius Loyola (1491–1556), an ex-soldier, founded the Jesuits as a kind of spiritual 'flying column', ready to go anywhere in the world as the Pope might request. In recent times, however, the Jesuits have gained great respect for their contributions to academic theology and their great commitment to working with the poor and underprivileged around the world. Some orders are monastic, like the Cistercians, the Benedictines, the Carmelites, for example, and some respond to a practical pastoral need. The Sisters of Mercy were founded in Ireland to work for the poor in areas like education, and another well-known Irish order, the Medical Missionaries of Mary, were founded to address by personal presence, prayer and professional medical training, the health needs of what we now call the developing countries, especially in the great missionary territories of Africa.

MEMBERSHIP AND STATISTICS

The faithful (*Christifideles* in recent official documents) of the Roman Catholic tradition constitute the largest of the individual Christian denominations in Northern Ireland. Recent census figures show over 605,600 Catholics, spread throughout the dioceses of Armagh, Derry, Down and Connor, Dromore, Clogher and a tiny piece of Kilmore, Archbishop Seán Brady's home diocese. The statistics hide the fact that most of the 'northern dioceses' run across the border into the Irish

Republic. Derry, the ancient diocese of the Cineál Eoghain, runs from Tyrone to Inishowen (part of the present Co. Donegal), taking in most of Co. Derry on the way. Armagh runs all the way from Magherafelt in the north to Drogheda, just thirty miles north of Dublin. Some significant demographic changes have been taking place over the past fifty years, and are still going on. The overall Catholic population is increasing, to the extent that in the younger age groups the Catholic population tends to equal the sum of the Protestant denominations, while simultaneously the commitment to religious practice has fallen off substantially against a background of political and social change. Another factor, directly related to the Troubles and associated sectarian tension, is the movement of population away from religiously mixed areas to areas more or less confined to one side of the community.

THE CATHOLIC DOCTRINAL TRADITION

Several currents of renewal in the Catholic Church during the twentieth century, liturgical, scriptural, ecumenical, were assimilated into the mainstream of church life at the Second Vatican Council. Since the Council, many aspects of renewal have been spelled out in documents like the revised Code of Canon Law and the new Catechism of the Catholic Church. In that sense, there probably has never been a time when Catholic teaching and practice has been so open to view. New technology plays its part also, so for example it is possible to have the whole Bible in various languages and translations, the documents of Vatican II, the new Code of Canon Law and the Catechism of the Catholic Church, plus a variety of reference works and encyclopedias, all on CD-ROM, not to mention the Internet.

Continuity

However, the various forms of renewal, and all the modern technology which provides immediate access to such a variety of information, has to be placed in the context of a continuing tradition – a thread of continuity which links today's Church poised on the edge of the Third Millennium with those early disciples who went in and went out with Jesus and witnessed his death and resurrection.

In Catholic theology, the authoritative transmission of that faith experience, rooted in the transforming relationship with Jesus Christ who died on the cross and was raised in glory, takes place through Sacred Scripture and Tradition. It is a 'both-and' dynamic. We are *the people of the Book* in that the Christian community cannot be conceived of without the life-giving Word of God in the Spirit-filled book of the Scriptures, received in personal reading or in public proclamation. Conversely, the Scriptures are *the Book of our people*, in that we receive the gift of the Scriptures through the continuity of a faithful Spirit-filled community.

The faithful community of God's people in the Old and New Testaments, found in the Bible, touch us, the faithful community of God's people now in the Church. The people gathered round the Book meet the people within the Book, who draw them close to God, and challenge them to hear God's Word and live by it. The Word of God speaks to us in the continuing community of faith. As the First Letter of John puts it: 'we declare to you what we have seen and heard so that you also may have fellowship with us; and truly our fellowship is with the Father and with his Son Jesus Christ. We are writing these things so that our joy may be complete' (1 John 1:3–4).

The recent Catechism of the Catholic Church presents the various elements of the Catholic Church tradition following a simple structure:

- faith (the great Creeds: the Apostles' Creed; the Nicene Creed; the Athanasian Creed)
- the sacramental life
- the spiritual and moral life (including the life of grace and the Ten Commandments)
- Christian prayer as an expression of the Christian life

I believe

There is great reassurance in going back to the words of the great Creeds, the core statements of faith which all Christians share. There is great wonder and power also at the Baptism of a newly born child, the most recent Christian arrival in the local church community, when the ancient faith is proclaimed in the dialogue around the font:

Do you believe in God, the Father almighty,
creator of heaven and earth?
I do.

Do you believe in Jesus Christ, his only Son, our Lord,
who was born of the Virgin Mary,
was crucified, died and was buried,
rose from the dead,
and is now seated at the right hand of the Father?
I do.

Do you believe in the Holy Spirit,
the Holy Catholic Church, the Communion of Saints,

the forgiveness of sins, the resurrection of the body,
and life everlasting?
I do.

The sacraments

While the Creeds highlight our common heritage, the theology of the
sacraments is an area of diversity between Christian denominations. We
can oversimplify by taking a purely mathematical approach to difference
and saying that the Catholic Church counts seven sacraments as opposed to
two in most Protestant traditions. It is more important to look at the
Catholic approach to sacraments and sacramentality. The Second Vatican
Council roots the understanding of the sacraments in the reality of the
Church as the basic sacrament of the presence and saving action of Christ
among us. Jesus Christ himself is the primordial sacrament of our encounter with God.

The sacraments of initiation – Baptism, Confirmation and Eucharist –
bind us to that reality as members of the Body of Christ, filled with the
power of the Spirit, nourished into unity. There are two sacraments of
healing: the sacrament of Reconciliation (formerly known as Confession
but, since Vatican II, given fuller meaning) is a privileged way of restoring
our unity in Christ when it has been damaged by sin (only, of course,
when our repentance is genuine); the sacrament of Anointing of the Sick
is an expression of the healing presence of Christ in the community of his
Church, at times both of illness and of danger of death (from which the
sacrament was called *Extreme Unction* – anointing of a person *in extremis*).
In the Irish language there is the appropriate usage: *ola an bhisigh* – the oil of
healing or recovery. The sacraments 'at the service of communion', as the
new Catechism says, are Matrimony and Holy Orders. They sanctify the
married couples and clergy whose duty it is to build the unity of the family
(the domestic church) and the local church community (in the case of
priests the parish, in the case of bishops the diocese, and in the case of the
Pope the universal Church).

The usual experience of Baptism locally in the Catholic Church is the
Baptism of infants. The rite is expressive and full of symbolism. The celebration takes the shape of a little journey, beginning with the welcome at
the church door, moving into the church for Scripture readings, then to
the font for the Baptism itself, and finally to the altar, at the heart of the
church, for the 'Our Father' and the final blessing.

Adult Baptism happens occasionally in Ireland in exceptional circumstances – not, of course, in the case of an already baptised Christian joining
the Catholic Church, as all Christian Baptism is acknowledged as valid.

The Baptism of adults is a more frequent experience in mission territories, and in recent years in countries like Britain and the USA following the Second Vatican Council.

Of all the documents that followed the Council which addressed the practical application of the norms of the major Constitutions and Decrees of the Council itself, none was more striking or more radical in its implications than the Rite of Christian Initiation of Adults, usually referred to simply as the RCIA. Not only does it apply to the Initiation of adults, but it is clearly stated that the approach which it defines is to be normative in all rites of initiation into the life of the Church. Put very simply, it marks a clear change of emphasis from a preparation by information − 'Father Doherty instructs James' − to a process of involvement and commitment. It restores the gradual preparation and the stages of initiation associated with the ancient catechumenate (those who were being prepared for Baptism) and it reaches its climax in the final preparation during Lent and the celebration of Baptism at the Easter Vigil, in the presence of the worshipping community. There are liturgies to mark the various stages, and some of the prayers are very beautiful and very demanding:

> That in preparation for the Easter Feast we may seek a change of heart, give ourselves to prayer, and persevere in our good works. That throughout the whole world whatever is weak may be strengthened, whatever is broken restored, whatever is lost found, and what is found redeemed.

It is very moving to see a group of adults make their final commitment and move to the front to be baptised in the newly blessed Easter water on Holy Saturday night. It is not just a joy for them, it is a great renewal of faith for the whole community who are present, which is part of the significance of the restored adult rite.

Apart from the specific list of seven sacraments, which are carefully defined, there is a 'sacramental' aspect to life in the Catholic Church which simply means that external signs − things that can be seen or heard or felt − are frequently used as stepping stones to prayer, or reminders of the nearness of God or of specific moments in Christ's saving work. Examples are the Angelus bell, the use of holy water (which has its origins in water blessed for the celebration of Baptism), rosary beads, and the custom of physically making the sign of the Cross on the forehead or over forehead, shoulders and breast at the beginning and end of prayer, or as a prayer for protection from harm.

Prayer

The Catholic Church's rich tradition of prayer and spirituality is indicated by the large final section of the new Catechism. It is obviously an area where Christians can learn from one another, and draw from the huge quarry of each other's traditions without feeling insecure or defensive. Sharing in services of public prayer on occasions like the Week of Prayer for Christian Unity may be a valuable encouragement. An increasing number of Christians have spent at least some time in a deeper sharing within a mixed faith community, whether with a specifically ecumenical objective, or bringing Christian commitment and prayer to bear on the need for peace and reconciliation in society.

ISSUES OF DISTINCTIVENESS

In spite of the overwhelming volume of truth which we share, we Christians have always been inclined to define each other by those comparatively few things on which we differ, or on which we place a different emphasis. Many devotional practices of Catholics, for example, can be seen by others as at best distractions and at worst idolatrous. Regarding the external expressions of the Catholic experience, particularly the visual and tactile aspects of lighted candles, pictures and statues, rosary beads and the like, many of these are about emotional support for faith, rather than about theological definition of faith. The artist Patrick Pye once wrote: 'Religious art does not tell us what to believe; it tells us what it feels like to believe.'

Supports to devotion

From a Catholic perspective, rather than taking over from the reality, these aids to concentration provide a concrete support to personal devotion, bringing a warmth and immediacy to realities which are otherwise expressed in terms of a more abstract thought and theology. Being reminders and audio-visual aids, of course they are even more subject to distortion than the words which we generally use to express mysterious reality, and therefore, in keeping with our limited human vocabulary, require continual correction and critical examination. There are many examples of sentimental art forms which distract rather than enlighten.

There is no need to pretend, however, that the devotional externals of Catholic life are unreal or irrelevant. Underlying them is a real Catholic 'sensibility'. However, that sensibility cannot be artificially created or analysed, as if it were an aromatherapy created by warming up a mixture of candlelight and incense: it can only be experienced where we find people

living out the deeper commitment of the Christian life as expressed specifically in the Roman Catholic tradition, not for effect, but as a genuine
searching for God, following the one Way and Truth and Life – the Lord
Jesus Christ. An American author, Fr Chuck Gallagher SJ, expressed this
fact – that we find Christian faith and expression where we find Christian
people – in the phrase: 'We cannot have the faith without the faithful.'

There are a number of areas in Church life and practice, and in the
expression of a particular faith perspective in prayer, for example, where
the Catholic approach would be recognised as having a particular emphasis; some of these which come to mind are: the funeral liturgy and praying
for the dead; devotion to Mary, Mother of God; and the sense of belonging to the Church even while being 'a bad Catholic'.

Prayer for the dead

The Catholic sense of praying for the dead is well expressed in a little
prayer from the graveside part of the funeral liturgy:

> We pray for all who are buried in this cemetery:
> may their suffering be lessened,
> may their joy be increased,
> may the light of glory shine on them
> and may they rest in peace.

The Irish language tradition has some lovely phrases about the departed
faithful: 'They have fulfilled their Baptism', for example, and 'They are on
the way of truth' – *ar shlí na fírinne*.

Devotion to Mary, Mother of God

In an introduction to religious life for new members of the Blessed Sacrament Fathers, published as 'Rule for a new Brother', there is a little section
which captures something of the warmth and simplicity of the Catholic
approach to Our Lady:

> Mary will have her own place in your life.
> You cannot separate her from the Lord
> who chose her as his mother and his bride.
>
> She is the selfless space
> where God became man;
> she is the silence in which God's Word
> can be heard.
> She is the free woman, subject to none,
> not even to the powers of evil.

She is the image of the Church.
Her self-effacing service will guide you to the Lord.
Her faith and fidelity
are a model for your life.

Being 'a bad Catholic'

In a famous filmed interview, Brendan Behan rejoiced in being a bad Catholic. He wasn't rejoicing in being bad, though he loved to shock his audience. He rejoiced that, being bad, as he saw it, he could still hold on to the belonging which had made him part of the Church since his Baptism. Where an evangelical Protestant might say he was saved, or born again, a 'bad Catholic' might confirm his conversion from his wayward lifestyle by 'making a good Confession', like making up a family quarrel – though without ever having left the family home.

Many Catholics might well say: 'If Brendan Behan was all we had to worry about in the context of being a bad Catholic, wouldn't we be well off!' The story of the Popes over the centuries provides plenty of examples of immorality and every kind of corruption. There were times in the history of the papacy when it seemed to be just a plaything in the power politics of families like the Borgias. When Pope John XXIII took his name, he was in a way rehabilitating the name John, which had been so dishonoured by some of his predecessors of that name. While recent Popes have been hard-working and dedicated, the Church has never been without its scandals, and in Ireland in recent years the faith of ordinary churchgoers has been sorely tested by incidents of clerical sexual impropriety and even child abuse.

As on many occasions in the past, it has not so much been charismatic leadership as the persevering prayer and faith of 'ordinary' people in the Church which have brought us through these crises. The comment has frequently been made that 'if God weren't with his Church, and it depended on the likes of you and me, it never would have survived for two thousand years'. Throughout our lives we have continual need to turn to God and seek his faithful love and his faithful forgiveness. It is no wonder every Mass begins with a penetential rite: 'Lord, have mercy.'

Jesus in the Eucharist

The Catholic Church has a strong tradition of devotion to the real presence of Jesus in the Eucharist, not just during Mass, but in the reserved Sacrament (that is, bread and wine remaining after communion), expressed in the tabernacle in church, in Eucharistic devotions like Benediction and periods of Exposition (when the Blessed Sacrament is presented in the monstrance on the altar), and in the practice of bringing Communion to the sick in their homes.

Charles de Foucauld, trying to write a rule for a religious order which later became the Little Brothers of Jesus, wrote various forms of a rule of enclosure. Eventually he scored it all out and wrote simply: 'The Eucharist is my enclosure.' When someone asked Mother Teresa of Calcutta why her sisters spent so much time in prayer before the Blessed Sacrament, she said: 'There is only one Jesus; if we do not touch him in the poor we cannot touch him in the Eucharist, and if we do not touch him in the Eucharist we cannot touch him in the poor.'

Though there is a very Catholic thing about all of that, there is evidence that we are learning once again from each other how to understand the presence of Jesus in the Eucharist. The Catholic Church in Wales uses the Eucharistic hymns of nonconformist Ann Griffiths, and there has been an extraordinary degree of convergence on the understanding of the presence of Jesus in the Eucharist between the Anglican and Roman Catholic theologians in the ARCIC documents (Anglican and Roman Catholic International Commission) and between theologians of virtually all the major Christian Church traditions in the World Council of Churches Lima document, 'Baptism, Eucharist and Ministry' (Faith and Order Paper 111, 1982). What we are learning as we address these questions of faith together is that we are closer than we had realised, and, in relation to the Eucharist, that our faith in the reality of the presence of Jesus in the Eucharist is more important than the technical terminology we use to explain the 'how' of that presence.

Liturgy and architecture

It was interesting that, although the major documents of Vatican II centred on the Church, the first Constitution to be completed was the document on the Liturgy. In fact it became in a sense normative and prophetic for a great deal that was to follow, and for the spirit of the Council. The Liturgy was seen as 'the summit towards which the activity of the Church is directed' and also 'the source from which all its power flows'. The centre of the Liturgy is the paschal (Easter) mystery of the suffering, death and resurrection of Jesus Christ. In order to make the central truth and action of the Liturgy more clearly visible in the life of the Church, the Second Vatican Council set about renewing the Liturgy, cutting away anything which over the centuries had obscured the essentials, and restoring what was central and significant.

The liturgical renewal affected the shape and layout of the buildings in which the Liturgy was to be celebrated. Many older churches were reorganised, not always sensitively, as altars were removed or relocated so that the celebrant could face the congregation during Mass, and so that more participation of the laity could take place, including the exercise of ministries like reading the Word of God and distributing Holy Communion.

Many excellent new churches were designed, in Ireland as elsewhere. In the best of the new churches, the main focal points of the Liturgy are clearly established, and the highest-quality workmanship can be seen in the altar, the lectern (ambo), the celebrant's chair, the tabernacle (where the reserved Sacrament is kept), the baptismal font, and in furnishings like the crucifix and the stand for the paschal candle. Though not central to the main liturgical celebration, traditional devotional works of art like the Stations of the Cross are often of high quality also in recent church buildings, though people sometimes miss the more representational and perhaps more sentimental art with which they had grown up. Many of the developments in church architecture in the Catholic Church, such as the visible gathering of the community around the altar and the clearer highlighting of the place of the Word, have been understood and appreciated by other Christian denominations.

THE CATHOLIC CHURCH IN RELATIONSHIP

In recent years movements like Charismatic Renewal have brought the churches closer in the vocabulary and practice of the spiritual life, and of course there is a huge overlap of shared values and norms in the moral life, focused in all denominations by the Ten Commandments. Perhaps it is in the area of sexuality, marriage and family that we most see divergence, as the Catholic Church maintains a stricter regime in matters like contraception and divorce – although some Churches of the Reformed tradition, certainly in Ireland, like the Catholic Church, have a very firm line on abortion.

On the question of ecumenism in general, Catholics can take steps to build ecumenical relationships locally, secure in the knowledge that they have the backing of the Church at a public policy level both in the documents of the Second Vatican Council and in the teaching of every Pope since then. Pope John Paul II put down a marker in his first encyclical letter, *Redemptor Hominis*, in which he wrote:

> The unforgettable Pope John XXIII set out the problem of Christian unity with evangelical clarity as a simple consequence of the will of Jesus Christ himself, our Master, the will that Jesus stated on several occasions but to which he gave expression in a special way in his prayer in the Upper

Room the night before he died: 'I pray, Father, that they may all be one.' The Second Vatican Council responded concisely to this requirement with its decree on ecumenism. Pope Paul VI, availing himself of the activities of the Secretariat for Promoting Christian Unity, began the first difficult steps on the road to attaining that unity.

The Christian denominations in Ireland have done a lot of work on inter-church understanding and dialogue in recent years. One of the better-known examples of this is the Report of the Working Party on Sectarianism, drafted for the Irish Inter-Church Meeting under the co-chairmanship of John Lampen and Mary McAleese, who was then Pro-Vice Chancellor of Queen's University. There have been several joint projects between the Roman Catholic Church's Irish Commission for Justice and Peace and the Irish Council of Churches.

Education and intermarriage

Nevertheless, it has been difficult for communities separated by geography as well as by fears and prejudices to address effectively, together, areas like education and intermarriage, which over the years have been seen as the focus for inter-church tension and disagreement. There has been some lessening of pain on the marriage front because of more open public attitudes and efforts at dialogue and accommodation, particularly on the question of the Catholic upbringing of children: the Catholic Church's concern is to support the faith commitment of the Catholic partner. There is much misunderstanding on the issue of education, and views range from those who cannot see any deviation from totally denominational education to those who present integrated education as a way of engineering the healing of community relations.

There is now a range of experience in education which, if addressed realistically, would provide many useful insights. However, up to the moment there has never been the widespread confidence for the Churches and the other partners in education to sit down together and acknowledge the ideals and needs of the various sectors as well as their fears and insecurities, including the financial implications of radical educational development, and to look calmly and creatively at each group's vision and at the extent to which that can be integrated with shared objectives and the future well-being of the whole community. Paradoxically, some contentious moral issues, which might be expected to divide, and do divide people, such as the issue of abortion, have tended to unite Christians in Northern Ireland, including church leaders, and indeed politicians from otherwise very different backgrounds.

Church and state

The relationship between Church and state is never easy. In a divided society like Northern Ireland it is particularly fraught with difficulty. Dr John Dunlop used the title *A Precarious Belonging* for his book on the Presbyterian experience; it could well apply to all the Churches, and perhaps with particular aptness to the experience of the Roman Catholic Church in the context of British jurisdiction in Northern Ireland. For a Catholic to accept a title in the New Year's honours list is read by some fellow Catholics as a kind of apostasy, in line with John Dunlop's observation that we define ourselves by what we are not: unionists being not-Catholic, and Catholics being not-British.

The leaders of the Catholic Church have had to confront the difficulty of being in dialogue with the civil authority without seeming to acquiesce in injustice; being outspoken about injustice without appearing insensitive to the fears of unionists; standing for the transformation of Northern Ireland society while condemning absolutely the efforts of paramilitary organisations to bring about that transformation by violence, death and destruction. During the worst of the Troubles, many Protestants have found it difficult to understand, for example, the Catholic Church's celebration of funerals for IRA members, while some republican supporters have given up Catholic practice because of the limitations placed by the Church on those same funeral services.

Christians working together

Yet through the shared experience of many of these paradoxes and apparent contradictions, church leaders have learned that often, perhaps always, the best way to deal with situations of conflict and apparently insurmountable contradiction is to deal with them together. Republican prisoners in the Maze, meeting an inter-church group, not only found it easier to trust the Protestant members because of the religious mix, but strangely, and in some ways more importantly, found that the same mix helped them to have greater trust in the Catholic members also. It is encouraging that over the years many from all the Churches have had the courage and the mutual respect and simply the Christian conviction rooted in the Gospel of Jesus Christ to work together and to be seen to work together, to forgive and then to forgive again.

THE WORLDWIDE DIMENSION

The Irish Church over the centuries has never feared to look outward. The strength of the faith community, so clearly evidenced in the visual expressions of Christian art which have come down to us, overflowed in a missionary outreach, to Europe in the dark ages and further afield to North and South America, to Africa and to the Far East in recent centuries. The outreach, significantly, was not confined to priests and religious, or to more 'professional' missionary personnel. The faith was carried abroad by the faithful people who emigrated because of oppression or famine or unemployment, and who established and developed the Church in many countries simply by living their Christian faith in their adopted territories. The pain of the years of suffering was expressed in the little 'penal crosses' which witnessed to Mark's image of Jesus isolated and forsaken on Calvary. Once again, through faith lived in anguish and perseverance, the cross became the source of new life.

Extending relationships

The Second Vatican Council pointed to a new universal outreach for the Catholic Church, not just geographical, but in extending concentric relationships of reconciliation and inclusiveness – to fellow Christians, to the Jewish people, to the great world religions and to all people of good will. The election and pontificate of Pope John Paul II has drawn considerable attention to the countries of Eastern Europe, including his native Poland, at a time of extraordinary political change with the fall of Communism, and of horrific conflict, most notably in the countries of the former Yugoslavia.

Catholics in Ireland in recent years have begun to use the term 'Roman Catholic' more frequently, out of courtesy to their fellow Christians of the Catholic though not of the Roman variety. However, that is not in any way to narrow the emphasis on the Church to a Roman or even to a European perspective. Irish Catholics are very much aware of the worldwide dimension of their Church, and of the vast range of perspectives which that brings to bear on history and doctrine and discipline. It is remarkable that the same Church is mother to European colonial powers and to millions in the developing countries who resist exploitation, whether political or economic, by those same powers, finding in the Christian Scriptures a 'theology of liberation' to sustain them in their search for freedom and self-esteem.

Transformation

The experiences of struggle and the effort at transformation in societies in such different parts of the world has not only been a challenge to the Catholic Church, but is a resource for Christian reflection on a much broader front. It is paralleled by the work and reflection of people like

Jim Wallis, from an evangelical Protestant background, in addressing the need for real social transformation within supposedly affluent and egalitarian societies in Europe and North America, including the poor and under-privileged areas of Washington DC. Another factor in the conscientisation of Irish Catholics about developing countries, along with the missionary tradition, has been the work of Trócaire (Gaelic for 'compassion' or 'mercy'), the Catholic Church's aid agency, which along with the Irish Commission for Justice and Peace has put a great deal of effort into development education.

CONCLUSION

In the second half of the twentieth century we have found the Church experiencing itself and reflecting on that experience. When we reflect on our experience, we are not always pleased with what we discover about ourselves. We face an ongoing struggle. There is a threefold dimension to the effort at growth, renewal and development in the Catholic Church. There is the building of new relationships, no longer dependent but inter-dependent, within the Catholic Church. There is the inter-church dimension: learning new relationships with fellow Christians. And there is what the Second Vatican Council called 'the Church in the modern world' – the life and witness of the Church in the wider society. We have begun to learn that Churches witness better together. Chiara Lubich, foundress of the Focolare movement in Italy during the Second World War, had a phrase about working in unity; she said: 'Jesus among us makes Jesus within us grow.'

The sense of church is at the core of the experience of Catholic Christianity. That is why the Catholic Church has always been so adamant about the duty of each member to attend Mass every week, on Saturday night or Sunday morning. It is in the midst of his disciples that the Lord Jesus is to be found. Religion is not just a private affair, but is rooted in the experience of a faith community. Like Ruth in the tradition of the Jewish faith experience, the individual Catholic does not seek God alone, but by drawing close to God's people:

> Where you go, I will go;
> where you lodge, I will lodge;
> your people shall be my people,
> and your God my God.
> Where you die, I will die –
> there will I be buried.
>
> (Ruth 1:16–17)

It's a bit like the old Donegal proposal of marriage: 'Would you like to be buried with my people?'

We began with Cardinal Suenens, with his friendship with Pope John XXIII and his contribution to the shape of the Second Vatican Council. Before his death, Cardinal Suenens wrote a lovely prayer, full of his vibrant faith, his great sense of the Holy Spirit, and his openness to all his fellow Christians and to all people of the world – reminiscent, in fact, of the thrust of the documents of Vatican II. It is an expression of Christian optimism, an optimism based not only on any organisational structure, not on any great efforts of ours, but on the centrality of the Risen Christ in our lives, and on the power of the Holy Spirit, released among us as at the first Pentecost:

PRAYER FOR THE YEAR 2000

Looking at the world:
Lord, we are afraid to face the world of tomorrow;
we have lost faith in ourselves;
we no longer believe in that boundless progress
which was supposed to ensure our future happiness;
nor do we believe any longer in science as the salvation of
    mankind;
nor do we believe that man is the supreme end of man
nor that death is the last word of life.

And we know, too, that if tomorrow there were to be
another nuclear disaster such as Chernobyl,
whether by accident or design,
there could be an apocalyptic explosion
from which none of us would survive,
no one even to number and bury the dead.

Looking at the Church:
Lord, if I turn my eyes to the Church,
who received from your Son the promise of eternal life,
I feel how poor and weak we, your disciples, are today;
so poor and so poorly Christian;
but I hear on every side
the pressing call of our pastors
for a new and second evangelisation
to make us true and faithful Christians,
conscious of the imperatives of our Baptism.

Help us to discover the fervour of the early Christians
and the power of the first evangelisation,
that morning of Pentecost, as it started
in the Cenacle of Jerusalem
where your disciples, with Mary, gathered in prayer,
awaited, Father, the fulfilment of your promise.

Give us the grace to be renewed
'in the Spirit and in fire'.
Teach us to speak to the world in tongues of fire;
let us bring to an end this time of uncertainty
where Christians are timid and mute,
discussing anxiously problems of today,
as in the past on the road from Jerusalem to Emmaus,
without realising that the Master is risen and alive.

Prayer for the future:
Lord, open our hearts to welcome your Holy Spirit;
teach us to await his coming, as Mary did,
at the time of the Annunciation
and again at Pentecost – the nativity of the Church –
when she became also our mother.
Teach the coming generations that your Son, Jesus Christ,
    remains
for ever and ever, the Saviour of the world.

Help us to proclaim, loudly and boldly,
that he is
'the Way,
the Truth
and the Life':
the Way, which leads us towards our final destiny;
the Truth, which lights our way through the night;
the Life, which gives us a profound peace, serenity and joy
which nothing created can destroy.

May your disciples, on the eve of the third millennium,
hasten their steps to obey the order given by the Master,
to be 'one' in the unity of
the Father,
the Son,
the Holy Spirit.

And may they approach the Lord together,
radiant with his light,
with no shadow on their face,
so that the whole world will recognise Jesus Christ
alive in his disciples,
now and for ever.

Amen.

BIBLIOGRAPHY

Scripture quotations: from the *New Revised Standard Version*
Catechism of the Catholic Church, Veritas Publications 1994
The Code of Canon Law, Collins 1983
McBrien, Richard P. (ed.), *Encyclopedia of Catholicism*, HarperCollins 1995
Flannery, Austin (ed.), *Vatican Council II – The Basic Sixteen Documents*,
     Dominican Publications 1996
Glazier, Michael, *The New Dictionary of Catholic Spirituality*, Liturgical Press
     1993
Rahner, Karl, *Foundations of Christian Faith*, Darton, Longman & Todd
     1978
Stacpoole, Edward, *Vatican II by Those who were There*, Geoffrey Chapman
     1986
Suenens, Leon, *Memories and Hopes*, Veritas Publications 1992

BIOGRAPHICAL NOTE

After ordination in 1965, FR OLIVER CRILLY, a native of Co. Derry, taught
in St Patrick's High School, Maghera, and then spent thirteen years in
Dublin, first as Director of Veritas Publications, and then as Director of
the Catholic Communications Institute of Ireland. In 1982 he returned to
the Derry diocese as a curate in the parish of Strabane. Since August of
1989 he has been Parish Priest of Melmount, Strabane.

He has been a member of the Irish Commission for Justice and Peace,
the Western Education and Library Board, the interdenominational
Religious Press Association of Ireland, the Irish Book Publishers' Associa-
tion (CLÉ) and the National Conference of Priests. He worked on *Northern
Ireland's Prisons – A Report to the Churches* (1990) and on *The Independent
Review of Parades and Marches* (the North Report, 1997).

He has broadcast frequently in Irish and English, and presented the first
Irish language documentary on BBC Television in Northern Ireland. Other
interests include leisure cycling, amateur drama and drawing cartoons.

2

The
Presbyterian Church in Ireland

JOHN ERSKINE

ORIGINS

Presbyterianism is Catholic, Protestant, Reformed and evangelical. Its roots reach not simply to the Reformation of the sixteenth century but to the pre-Reformation Church, to the Church of the Early Fathers, and to the Church of the Apostles in Jerusalem. In common with the other traditions of Western Christendom, Presbyterianism acknowledges the Trinity and shares the creeds of the Early Church. In this way Presbyterianism forms part of the wider Catholic tradition.

Presbyterianism is also Protestant. That is, it is a product of the widespread religious movement of Reformation that emerged in Europe under the influence of Martin Luther. But Presbyterian Churches are also Reformed because they derive their particular structures, practices and doctrines not simply from Luther's Reformation in Germany but, in particular, from the branch of the Reformation which developed in Geneva under the leadership of John Calvin. Presbyterian Churches are part of the Reformed family within Protestant Christendom. And Presbyterianism is evangelical in the broadest sense of the term. In other words, Presbyterians maintain that the message of the Gospel is for everyone and includes everyone.

Reformation teaching was formally adopted by the Scottish parliament in 1560. At that time Scotland was an independent nation and so the origins and development of the Scottish Reformation differed markedly from those of the Reformation in England. Scotland's Reformation drew on her historic links with Europe and in particular with those places in which the Reformation had been influenced by the Genevan Reformers.

The Reformation in Scotland was further shaped by individuals like John Knox (who had himself been a refugee in Calvin's Geneva) and Andrew Melville (who developed its distinctly Presbyterian traditions).

Shaped in Scotland, Presbyterianism came to Ireland, and largely to Ulster, with the Scottish settlers of the seventeenth century. Migration from Scotland to Ulster was no new phenomenon for there had been links and movement between the two countries for centuries. However, the significance of this seventeenth-century movement of population lay both in its scale and in the fact that it post-dated the Reformation.

Initially, Scottish Presbyterian ministers and people in Ireland formed part, although an uneasy part, of the reformed Protestant Church in Ireland. This Church, although episcopal in its structure, was broadly Calvinist in its theology and therefore provided a theological home, at least at first, for the Presbyterian settlers. The arrangement, however, was fraught with fundamental tensions between episcopal and presbyterian parties and a break had to come. The arrival of a Scottish army in Ulster in 1642, in the wake of the 1641 rebellion, provided the opportunity for the formal establishment of Presbyterianism in Ireland. When the chaplains and elders of the Scottish army formed the first presbytery at Carrickfergus in June 1642 they were quickly joined by local congregations. Irish Presbyterianism traces its formal beginnings to this date.

By the eighteenth century there were in Ulster (as in Scotland) several different Presbyterian groupings. They had much in common but differed in outlook and, to some degree, in doctrine. In 1840 the two largest groupings merged to form the Presbyterian Church in Ireland, the major Presbyterian denomination in Ireland today. Of those groupings which remained outside the new Church, two later united to form the Non-Subscribing Presbyterian Church, and another became the Reformed Presbyterian Church. The Evangelical Presbyterian Church and the Free Presbyterian Church are independent formations of the twentieth century.

Presbyterianism in Ireland therefore regards itself as part of the Catholic Church, re-formed in the sixteenth century but with its roots firmly in the Church of the New Testament. While its Scottish origins mean that Presbyterianism did not arise from a reformation of the Irish Church, Presbyterians none the less find much with which to identify in the writings of St Patrick and much to admire in the scholarship and mission of the Celtic Church, on which Scottish Presbyterianism itself also draws. Presbyterianism, therefore, introduces and represents an important Ulster-Scottish and also a European dimension in the story of Christianity in Northern Ireland.

WORLDWIDE PRESBYTERIANISM

Strictly speaking, the word 'Presbyterian' (from a Greek word meaning 'elder') describes a system of church government – a way of organising a church – and not a system of doctrine or belief. However, in the English-speaking world, the term 'Presbyterian' is commonly used to describe those Churches which adopt a particular theological point of view, one usually termed 'Calvinist' or 'Reformed'. On the Continent, such Churches usually describe themselves as 'Reformed' rather than 'Presbyterian'.

The Presbyterian Church in Ireland – 'presbyterian' in its church structure and 'reformed' in its theology and doctrine – is therefore part of the family of European Reformed Churches. Presbyterianism was introduced into North America and the old British Commonwealth by emigrants, many of them from Scotland and Ulster. The development of Presbyterianism and Presbyterian Churches in Africa, Asia and South America is largely the consequence of missionary activity – not least by Irish Presbyterians – in the nineteenth and twentieth centuries.

An awareness of their common ecclesiastical heritage and of their European and world connections led Presbyterians in Ireland at the end of the nineteenth century to join other Churches in establishing a world-wide organisation of Reformed Churches. The 'Alliance of the Reformed Churches throughout the World holding the Presbyterian System', formed in 1875, owes much of its origins to the work of Irish Presbyterians. The organisation has evolved since then and continues today, with its headquarters in Geneva, as the World Alliance of Reformed Churches.

The World Alliance, while important as a central voice for world Presbyterianism, in no way constitutes a higher authority over its member Churches. It is an organisation of equal partners and has no power to interfere in the internal workings of any one Church. However, its one sanction is to suspend Churches from membership and it did so in the case of the South African Dutch Reformed Church during the years of apartheid. It is estimated that there are some seventy million Presbyterian and Reformed Christians worldwide.

SURVEY OF THE DENOMINATION TODAY

In its geographical distribution, the Presbyterian Church in Ireland in many ways still reflects its seventeenth-century origins. It is strongest in those areas of predominantly Scottish settlement: in Cos. Down, Antrim, Londonderry and east Donegal (the Laggan). It is also well represented in Armagh and Tyrone, and in Cavan and Monaghan; but it is much more thinly represented in the rest of Ireland, where it is confined largely to urban centres.

While it is possible to trace and date the spread of individual congregations during the seventeenth and eighteenth centuries, it is much harder to
make an estimate of actual Presbyterian numbers at this period. The Presbyterian community appears to have grown steadily since the foundation
of the first presbytery, although considerable numbers of people, and at
times whole congregations, emigrated to North America in the eighteenth
century. It is not until the nineteenth century that it becomes possible to
establish Presbyterian numbers with acceptable accuracy. Figures in the
1861 census put Presbyterian numbers in what is now Northern Ireland
at 457,000 (and in what is now the Republic of Ireland at 66,000). By
1926 the figures for Northern Ireland were 393,000 and in the 1991 census
some 337,000 people claimed Presbyterian allegiance. (Some of this is
nominal since congregational returns would claim lesser numbers.) The
decline in numbers is shared by other Churches and has been a cause for
considerable concern. Many reasons have been put forward to account
for the decline: among these are the growth of secularism, the movement
of young people to education and employment in other parts of the UK,
'leakage' to smaller and newer Christian groups, and, to a lesser degree,
intermarriage.

There are currently 562 congregations throughout Ireland, all but 100
of them in Northern Ireland.

DOCTRINAL POSITION

No single characteristic distinguishes Reformed theology. Indeed, many
tenets of Reformed theology are shared with other Protestant Churches
– the Sovereignty of God, the Kingship of Christ, the authority of the
Bible, salvation by Grace, and the priesthood of all believers – but
Reformed theology also has its own emphases and its own insights.

Within the Reformed tradition, theology is never merely speculative. It
has a purpose. That purpose is to discover truth and in particular the
supreme truth about God and His purpose for men and women in the
world. Theology exists, therefore, not simply to understand God but also
to ensure that life and society conform to the will of God. Doctrine and
practice must be continually tested against truth, so that God's will may be
known and obeyed. Through this objective pursuit of truth, Reformed
teaching emphasises the importance of loving God with the mind as well
as with the spirit. Reformed theology is not satisfied with faith simply as
piety. Nor is theology simply an intellectual exercise.

Reformed doctrine begins and ends with the Sovereignty of God.
Calvin and Luther agreed in many things, but they brought different

perspectives to the theology of the Reformation. While Luther's theology may have begun from a sense of his own sin, Calvin's began with a conviction of the Sovereignty of God and an overwhelming belief in God's Grace. Sovereignty and Grace are the foundations of Reformed theology. And since Sovereignty and Grace are revealed through the insights of Scripture, so the Word of God – the Bible – has a central and unchallengeable position in the Reformed tradition. Reformed theology is more biblical than philosophical.

Sovereignty means that God is Creator of all, is lord of all, and that everything within this world is somehow contained within His good purposes. Reformed theology has also always maintained a firm distinction between the Creator and the creature (a created person), so that what is divine is never confused with what is human. Yet God is not a remote Creator for He is always dynamically at work within His creation. He has established a covenant with men and women, a covenant with and for people which arises from His Grace. Grace describes God's free and saving activity and is fully expressed in Jesus Christ. Men and women do not and cannot earn Grace by their actions: instead, it is freely given to them by God.

However, Reformed theology has also placed great emphasis on the direct relationship between Creator and creature, between God and individual. Men and women are called to respond to God's Grace and to respond directly and individually, unimpeded by any intermediary. (They do not have to respond – for they do have free will – but their true fulfilment is found in response.) Furthermore, men and women exist not simply as individuals but also as members of society, called to different tasks and functions within society. Those tasks, whatever they may be, are invested with value. For Calvin it was society, and not the cloister, which was to be the arena for the exercise of spirituality. Men and women, individually and collectively, were called to create a society that would reflect God's glory. They were and are called to witness to God *in* the world and to participate in God's transformation *of* the world.

Reformed doctrine can be misunderstood (not least by Presbyterians themselves) and easily caricatured. It can be depicted as portraying a harsh, unforgiving and judgemental God who capriciously predestines an abject, miserable and irretrievably worthless humanity to salvation or perdition. Yet this is to misunderstand the nature and purpose of Reformed theology. 'What is the chief end of man?' asks the first question of the *Shorter Catechism*. 'Man's chief end,' it states, 'is to glorify God and enjoy Him for ever.' This is a much more accurate reflection of the nature and understanding of Reformed theology.

One 'difficulty' encountered in Reformed theology is the doctrine of predestination and the elect (those chosen). (It should be remembered that 'chosen' in Reformed terms means chosen for service and not for privilege.) Predestination was not invented by Calvin: it was something he had found in Scripture and was a doctrine with which both St Augustine and Thomas Aquinas had wrestled. Predestination rules out human merit but not human freedom. Predestination is contained within the Sovereignty of God and is intended to emphasise the Grace of God. Men and women cannot earn salvation by their merit; nor are they condemned to perdition by their failings. Salvation is wholly a matter of Grace. Calvin himself was aware of the dangers of too narrow an interpretation of predestination and urged caution, a warning unheeded by many of his less able followers. Ultimately, predestination seeks to assure men and women that their destinies are in the hands of a loving God and not of a capricious fate. They can cease worrying about themselves and can direct their attention to the concerns and needs of others.

Another potential area of misunderstanding in Reformed theology is the 'total depravity' of humanity. This does not mean that there is no goodness in people – clearly there is and God makes use of it for His purposes – but it does mean that there is no aspect of the life and being of people, however good they may be, that is not corrupted to some degree. 'Depravity' is not intended to denigrate or dismiss men and women as irretrievably lost but rather to contrast their imperfection with the complete perfection of their Creator.

BASIS OF AUTHORITY

At their ordination, ministers and elders of the Church are required to subscribe to (or affirm) the 'standards' of the Church. These standards are of two sorts: the supreme standards and the subordinate standards. The supreme standards of the Church are the Scriptures of the Old and New Testaments: these form the undisputed heart of the Church's faith and belief and the standard by which all controversies are to be determined. (These Scriptures do not include the Apocrypha, later Hebrew writings recognised by some denominations.)

However, experience showed that the Scriptures could be variously and often 'erroneously' interpreted. Therefore, in the sixteenth and seventeenth centuries, many European Churches sought to codify their understanding of the Scriptures in 'confessions' which they adopted as subordinate standards. For Presbyterians in Britain and Ireland, the most important of these codifications are contained in the documents drafted by the Assembly of Divines convened at Westminster in the middle of the seventeenth century. The major Westminster documents are the

Confession of Faith (usually known as the *Westminster Confession*) and its two accompanying catechisms, the *Larger Catechism* and the *Shorter Catechism*. The mid-seventeenth century was a time of political and ecclesiastical upheaval and the Westminster documents, like all such documents, bear the hallmark of their age. Not all Reformed Churches adopt the Westminster documents as their subordinate standards: there are many other Reformed confessions, some of them written this century, all of which represent attempts to express the faith in contemporary terms.

The Westminster documents, since they are man-made and therefore fallible, are by definition *subordinate* standards. Consequently, no one is asked to subscribe every jot and tittle of the subordinate standards: subscription is made to the *substance* of the faith and to a *system* of related fundamental doctrines. Liberty of conscience is allowed, indeed expected, in the interpretation of those matters which do not enter into the substance of the faith. Subscription is made under the terms of the Rule of Faith, which states that it is the 'privilege, right and duty' of each individual to search the Scriptures and to decide thereby what God's purpose may be. However, in exercising 'the inalienable right of private judgement' the individual must not set himself above Scripture and must not 'refuse light from any quarter'. In other words, decisions must be made in an informed way, using the insights of Scripture often supported by scholarship and experience. In this way the struggle between order and ardour is held in creative tension.

Furthermore, in subscribing the documents, ministers and elders agree that the Presbyterian form of church government 'is founded on and agreeable to the Word of God'. This is not understood to mean that it is the only form possible.

MEMBERSHIP, CHURCH GOVERNMENT AND MINISTRY

Membership

Membership of the Church may be viewed in two ways. The membership of a congregation includes all those, adults and children, who are formally attached to a particular congregation. Full communicant membership is constituted by those who have been received as communicants and have thereby been admitted to the Lord's Table. Communicant members who contribute financially to the church have voting rights and are thereby fully involved in the running of the congregation through, for example, election to kirk session and to committee.

Church government

Fundamental to Presbyterian belief and practice is an egalitarian ideal of the people of God whereby no one individual is given status or authority over another. However, as in all societies, direction and order are necessary. In Presbyterianism this is achieved, not through a hierarchy of clergy and bishops, but through a system of democratically elected and representative committees known as 'courts'. These courts exist at various geographical levels: at congregational level the court is the 'kirk session'; at district level, the 'presbytery'; and at national level, the 'General Assembly'. Each court has a chairman or 'moderator' and a secretary or 'clerk'. These names – 'moderator' and 'clerk' – reflect the Reformed tradition's French-speaking origins; and the system of government by committees owes its genesis to Presbyterianism's European roots and – ironic though it may seem – in particular to the 'conciliar' (government by councils) system adopted by the alternative papacy at Avignon in the fourteenth century.

Within each **congregation** it is the responsibility of the kirk session – a body made up of the elders elected by the congregation and of the minister (who acts ex officio as moderator) – to provide leadership and to exercise spiritual oversight. (The temporal affairs of the congregation – its finances and buildings, for example – are the responsibility of another elected body, the congregational committee, which is not a court. Within each congregation, office-bearers are responsible to the congregation as a whole and are required to present their reports and accounts to the annual general meeting of the congregation for scrutiny and approval.)

Each congregation is represented at **presbytery** by its minister and one of its elders. Ministers and elders together in presbytery have oversight of the congregations within the presbytery's district. The work of a presbytery, however, consists not only of oversight but of ordination, discussion, debate, training and various other responsibilities.

All the presbyteries, made up of their congregational representatives, ministerial and lay, meet together, for one week in June, to form the **General Assembly** of the Church. By virtue of the fact that *all* the presbyteries meet together in the General Assembly, it is deemed to be the 'supreme' court.

At first sight such a structure might indeed seem to be hierarchical since each larger court exercises jurisdiction over the smaller courts within its bounds. On closer examination, however, the structure is shaped not so much as a pyramid but more as a wheel, with congregations on the rim and the General Assembly at the hub. However, it is also important to note that, within this structure, power is devolved from the periphery to the centre, and not from the centre to the periphery. This reflects and derives from a deep-seated Presbyterian distrust of centralised authority. Furthermore, an unwillingness to vest power in one individual is reflected in the position of the moderator of any church court. A moderator may represent his (or her) court only if he or she reflects the decisions and views of that court; he has no right or responsibility to create or direct policy; and he has no vote other than the casting vote of a chairman. Such a system is not particularly 'media-friendly': it is hard to assemble a committee for a quick sound bite. The role of the moderator-as-chairman is summed up in the motto on the back of the chair used by the Moderator of the General Assembly: *Primus inter pares* – First among equals. Moderators of presbytery and General Assembly (but not of kirk session) are elected by their peers and hold office for one year only.

Since the General Assembly meets for only one week in each year it cannot respond to situations that arise from day to day or take time adequately to formulate policy in detail. Consequently reports and policy proposals from the General Assembly are submitted to presbyteries for further and more detailed consideration before being adopted or passed into church law. Certain other continuing aspects of the Assembly's work are delegated to Boards and Committees which report annually to the General Assembly. Boards and Committees are made up of members of Assembly and others with expertise to offer. The Church also has a permanent staff – for example its Clerk and General Secretary – based at its headquarters in Church House in Belfast.

Ministry

Presbyterianism recognises four orders of ministry: ministers, elders, doctors and deacons. All orders are open equally to men and women.

Ministers (sometimes called 'teaching elders') undergo a period of education and training at a recognised theological college before being ordained to the ministry of word and sacrament. Ministers are 'called' to serve a congregation by the congregation itself. No Church authority appoints a minister to a congregation.

Unique to the Reformed tradition is the office of **elder**. Understood to have biblical warrant in the Old and New Testaments, elders are elected by the congregation by and from its communicant members, both men and women, and are ordained for life to the office by the local presbytery. Together in the congregational court, the kirk session, it is their responsibility to provide leadership and to exercise spiritual oversight of the congregation.

The office of **doctor** is now exercised through the professors of the Church's college, Union Theological College. These professors are

ordained ministers of the Presbyterian Church in Ireland or of another
Reformed Church in communion with the Presbyterian Church in
Ireland.

The order of **deacon** no longer exists within Irish Presbyterianism, the
duties of the office now being largely exercised through the congregational committee. There is, however, an office of deaconess within the
Presbyterian Church. This office, at present solely for women, is not an
order as such (for deaconesses are not ordained). It was designed to afford
women the opportunity for full-time pastoral service (for example, in
congregations or hospitals) at a time before they became eligible for the
ordained ministry.

SACRAMENTS AND ORDINANCES

In common with other Protestant traditions, Presbyterianism recognises
two sacraments: Communion, or the Lord's Supper; and Baptism. The
sacraments are believed to be those ordinances which were instituted or
given sanction by Christ in the New Testament and are defined as 'means
of Grace'. Certain other ordinances – such as the reception of communicants and marriage – are of course observed but are not sacraments.

Communion

Most Presbyterian congregations celebrate the Lord's Supper regularly but
infrequently – up to three or four times each year – although some celebrate it monthly. (Calvin himself actually preferred weekly celebration.)
However, the rarity of its celebration makes it a solemn – some might
say sombre – but a very dignified occasion for each congregation.

In Presbyterianism only an ordained minister may officiate at communion. This is, however, a 'functional' provision: in other words, it is
intended to ensure that the sacrament is celebrated decently and properly,
and is not designed to elevate the minister above other participants.
Furthermore, communion may not be celebrated without the exposition
of the Word, otherwise the sacrament is deemed to be mere ritual. The
elements – bread and wine – are distributed to the people for sharing with
each other: they are not handed to each individual communicant by the
minister. The intended symbolism is that the people of God gather
together round the table to share the sacrament with each other in the
way that the disciples did in the upper room. Within Presbyterianism the
table is open to communicants of all Christian denominations: Presbyterians insist that it is the Lord's Table and not simply a Presbyterian table.

The elements themselves are not considered to have any special quality:
they remain simply bread and wine. Christ is present but not inherently in

the elements. The real symbolism of the sacrament is in the breaking of the bread, just as Christ's body was broken, and in the pouring of the wine, just as Christ's blood was poured out for all. What takes place is a spiritual nourishing, an action by which Christ's sacrifice is remembered and by which communicants are helped to grow in Grace.

Until the beginning of this century the elements (or 'symbols' as they are also known) consisted of alcoholic wine and a specially baked shortbread-style biscuit. Today, however, non-alcoholic wine and bread are generally used. The introduction of non-alcoholic wine was a consequence of the temperance movement of the nineteenth century and the replacement of the common cup by individual glasses was largely a matter of hygiene.

The style of celebrating communion has changed much over the past centuries. Until the beginning of the present century, tables were erected in the aisles and the people gathered round them. The elements were consecrated by the minister (as they are today) and then passed by hand from communicant to communicant around the tables. Often the congregation was too large to gather round the tables at the one time so the sacrament was celebrated by the congregation in two or three successive 'tables'.

Today, however, most Presbyterian churches have a small communion table at the front of the church on which the elements are placed. The minister and one or two laypeople sit at the table to represent the whole community gathering around the Lord's Table. (The minister never sits alone at the table as this would accord him a status not recognised by the Church.) The elements are then carried into the body of the congregation, usually by the elders, and passed along the pews to each communicant. While more 'efficient' than the practice of former days, much of the egalitarian symbolism of the people gathering together round the table can be lost and an inappropriate separation of people from minister and elders introduced.

The 'communion token' is a feature unique to Presbyterianism. Initially tokens were precisely that – metal tokens – which were distributed to those members of the congregation considered fit to be admitted to the sacrament. The withholding of a token was a severe sanction which the kirk session could (indeed, still can) administer. Today, tokens are made of card and, with the communicant's name written on them, have become, in effect, records of attendance.

Baptism

Baptism is administered by an ordained minister to the children of believing parents and (much more rarely) to adults. Parents present their child for baptism and promise to bring it up in the Christian faith. There are no godparents in the Presbyterian tradition; instead, the congregation as a whole pledges itself to assist in the spiritual upbringing of the child. The minister places water – to which no particular quality is attributed – on the forehead of the child and baptises it in the name of the Trinity. Baptism is not considered essential for the salvation of the individual but it is in many ways essential to the life of the Church. Through Baptism it is acknowledged that children are Christian children and are within the Church.

Other ordinances

The funeral service within the Presbyterian tradition consists of two parts: memorial and committal. These two parts may be physically separate: for example, the service of memorial (and consolation and encouragement) may be held in a church or home to be followed later by a short service of committal at the graveside or crematorium. Prayers are offered at the funeral for the family and friends in their time of grief but no prayers are said for the deceased, who is considered to be already in God's hands and thereby beyond human intercession.

The service of marriage, which is generally solemnised in church, places its primary emphasis on the companionship of the couple rather than on the procreation of children.

SPIRITUALITY

Within the Reformed faith people have to deal directly with God. This direct relationship requires a life of personal piety and obedience so that everything, from the most menial of tasks to one's relationships with others, is influenced by God and is undertaken for the glory of God. Yet this is not a self-conscious or oppressive undertaking: it is one which arises naturally, and joyfully, from a faith which also requires men and women, individually and as a community, to identify and to fulfil God's purpose for the world. Given this background, Presbyterian spirituality is often characterised by earnestness. But it also tends to be private and personal; it is undemonstrative; and it distrusts outward show.

Central to Presbyterian thinking, to the worship of each congregation and to the private devotion of each individual, is the Bible. Bible study, therefore, undertaken privately or in groups, is an essential part of worship for both the individual and the Christian community. (A wide variety of schemes exists to aid structured reading.) With Bible study comes prayer, which is fundamental to the spiritual life of both individual and community. However, Presbyterians have no ready-made treasury of liturgical prayers or actions on which to draw for personal devotion. On the other hand, a prominent feature of Presbyterian worship, until recently at least, was the use of the psalms; and in many ways the words of the psalms, known to most Presbyterians from their childhood, became the liturgy of Presbyterianism. From the psalms could be drawn images and phrases adaptable to everyday life and to private devotion. And at the heart of the psalms is the relationship between the individual and God, the relationship that is also at the heart of Calvinism.

The absence of a fixed liturgy in Presbyterianism and the rejection of a range of religious artefacts (both in themselves a conscious part of the tradition) perhaps make a particular spirituality less easy to define. Furthermore, certain active practices of a couple of generations ago, such as formal family worship, are no longer as widespread as once they were – for various reasons – and have been, or have yet to be, replaced by new forms of nurture. And certain other traditional attitudes, such as Sabbatarianism, are also changing. The obligation to observe the Sabbath is no longer as rigidly interpreted by Presbyterians as once it was. Yet, while many now enjoy family recreation on a Sunday, most still feel uncomfortable with the radical, secular transformation of Sunday into a day for sport or shopping. Some other traditional attitudes, like temperance and opposition to gambling, which arise from a sense of community responsibility, also remain deep-seated but are not necessarily embraced by all Presbyterians.

WORSHIP AND LITURGY

Presbyterians are said to worship God with their mind as much as with their heart. Such an attitude helps to explain the form and nature of Presbyterian worship. While a Presbyterian church service has an overall framework, it is marked by the absence of a fixed liturgy. (Calvin, however, was not completely opposed to regular liturgical elements.) No general service book for the use of the worshipper will be found in a Presbyterian church pew and, with the exception of the Lord's Prayer, the congregation is unlikely to join in the saying of any prayer. This may seem curious in a denomination which is theologically founded on the equality of believers and which prides itself on its democratic structures.

A church service begins by highlighting the centrality and undisputed importance of the Word of God. A Bible is often carried into the church and the minister opens the service by reading a sentence or two from Scripture. The service follows with readings, prayers, singing and preaching.

Although Presbyterianism lacks a fixed liturgy, the normal church service falls clearly into three parts: the approach to the Word; the proclamation of the Word; and the response to the Word.

Approach: Prayers of adoration and confession.
Proclamation: Readings of the Bible (normally two: one Old
                 Testament, one New Testament); preaching.
Response: Prayers of intercession (for ourselves and others);
                 offering.

Most services today will also include a children's address after which
children often leave for children's church or Sunday School. The service
ends with the benediction.

The rejection of a fixed liturgy is derived from a Presbyterian concern
that, in the unthinking repetition of set items, form may replace substance, that worship may be replaced by ritual. Such is this concern that
congregations used to place great emphasis on the use of free prayer, that
is, of a minister using extempore prayer. 'It was written,' was a once
common dismissal of a minister's best endeavours in prayer or sermon.
Most ministers today, however, will enter the pulpit with some or all of
their prayers either written out or adapted from different sources. For
special services, such as funerals and weddings, many ministers will use
the forms of service suggested in the Church's *Book of Public Worship* or
its Scottish equivalent, the *Book of Common Order*. None the less, the
Presbyterian service is still marked by a variety and liberty of content
within a familiar structure.

Sermons today last generally from fifteen to thirty minutes, a reduction
on past practice when they could last up to a couple of hours. An ability to
preach was, and often still is, considered to be a minister's greatest recommendation and asset.

Throughout the service the congregation joins in the singing of hymns.
There was, until the late nineteenth century, a general reluctance among
Presbyterians to sing anything other than the metrical version of the
psalms. This reluctance stemmed from the belief that the use of anything
that was not scriptural was unacceptable for worship. Similar objections
were raised to the introduction of organs, which are a late – and once
highly controversial – addition to Presbyterian churches. Previously, the
singing had been unaccompanied and led by a precentor, a man appointed
to 'raise the tune' from the front of the church.

The introduction of hymns and of organs, the greater informality of
worship, and the wide variety of hymns and songs in use in today's congregations all mark a considerable departure from the practice of the past.
Indeed, such change was encouraged by the General Assembly in 1992
when it was urged that worship should use 'language, form and music
appropriate both to Scripture and to our time and culture'.

BUILDINGS AND ARTEFACTS

In their attempts to recover the simplicity of the New Testament Church, the Reformers abandoned much of what they saw as the distracting accretions of the past. While many of these had been introduced in order to aid worship, the Reformers came to believe that such introductions in fact obstructed rather than facilitated worship. Their desire for simplicity and the removal of distraction applies equally to buildings and artefacts.

Church design should reflect worship. The classic Presbyterian church is a rectangle with the pulpit placed centrally in the long wall. The centrality of the pulpit exalts not the minister but the Word and its proclamation. The pulpit's place in the long wall enabled the people symbolically to gather round the Word: all were to be as close to the Word as possible. Balconies also aided the gathering of the people round the Word, particularly in a small building. Rectangular churches were often later extended by a return to create a T-shape. The most familiar pattern for a Presbyterian church – or 'meeting house' as it used to be called (the church being the people and not the building) – is the 'barn' church, often later enhanced by the addition of a 'classical' façade. In the nineteenth century, church building became more ambitious as the Presbyterian community became wealthier and more confident, especially towards the time of the Disestablishment of the Church of Ireland. These later churches are often too big for today's needs and can be a drain on resources – a problem experienced by other denominations. They have also lost much of their symbolism by having the pulpit in the short wall, away from the people. Communion tables and organs, as late introductions into Presbyterian churches, can often sit awkwardly in a small church. Some churches today have a central communion table and off-centre pulpit, representing a sacramental centrality which is not typical of Presbyterianism. Much new church building better reflects the purpose and nature of worship.

The determination to avoid distraction also accounts for traditional ministerial dress – a black cassock and a black gown (often called the 'Geneva gown') – which is intended to concentrate the mind of the congregation on what is said and not allow it to be distracted by the colour and finery of vestments.

The desire for simplicity also means that there is little ornament in Presbyterian churches, where often the only decoration is the pulpit fall. The fall is embellished with a symbol, very often a burning bush – the symbol of Presbyterian Churches in many lands – which represents Moses' encounter with God on Mount Horeb and once again emphasises the individual's direct encounter with God. The origins of this symbol are unclear, but are probably French. Sometimes also to be found on the pulpit fall is a

cross, either plain or Celtic (reflecting both the Irish and Scottish background to Irish Presbyterianism), a Chi-Rho (the Greek letters for CH, as
in 'Christ') or an Alpha-Omega (the first and last letters of the Greek
alphabet, representing the eternal nature of God) symbol. None the less,
it is noticeable that churches are now beginning to hang decorative ban-
ners, often based on or illustrating biblical texts, as aids to devotion. The
cross used by Presbyterians, in common with most Protestant Churches, is
the empty cross, reflecting the risen rather than the suffering Christ.

Memorials in Presbyterian churches are always dedicated first to the
glory of God and then in memory of the donor or person commemorated.

CHURCH AND COMMUNITY

Fundamental to the Reformed tradition is the belief that faith demands a
response, that faith should inform our every action. Belief dictates practice.
So it was that the Reformed revolution in Geneva saw not simply a radical
change in religious belief and practice but also a sweeping programme of
social reform. A godly society was to be manifest physically as well as
spiritually. How such an ideal is to be realised at the end of the twentieth
century poses many questions for today's Church.

Until the middle of the nineteenth century, Presbyterianism formed a
self-contained and self-regulating community in which the personal conduct of church members was subject to scrutiny by the kirk session. However, the kirk session also had wider, social responsibilities which included
the alleviation of need, both inside and outside their congregations. Today
the Church exercises its social responsibility through its Boards, Committees, agencies and officers (and not least its full-time Adviser on Social
Services first appointed in 1986) as well as through congregational initiatives and joint social action with other churches. The Church also publishes a wide range of reports on issues of social and moral concern, many
of which generally deserve wider attention than they receive.

The formation of the Presbyterian Church in Ireland in 1840 saw the
new Church emerging into a broader society and identifying issues and
concerns for social action in the changing conditions of the middle of the
nineteenth century. The Church's attitude to drink, for example, changed
dramatically and its drive for temperance – often in fact total abstinence –
was particularly manifest in the latter part of the century. In the twentieth
century, and not least since the introduction of the Welfare State after the
Second World War, the Church has sought to develop new areas of social
outreach in addition to its existing concerns. The provision of sheltered
housing for the elderly, well in advance of the growth industry seen today,
and the creation of facilities for the rehabilitation of young offenders, are
two examples.

The merger of 1840 also saw the Church looking beyond the horizons of the British Isles. Missionaries were commissioned by the General Assembly and a long tradition of missionary activity, chiefly in China, Africa and India, was begun. That tradition continues today although 'mission' is now viewed as a partnership with sister Churches overseas. It also includes work with Asian communities in Britain.

Experience of the Third World and concern for the alleviation of its poverty and deprivation led the Church to make a commitment to fund projects for world development through an annual appeal to congregations. The Church decided against the establishment of its own agency and instead channels funds through existing organisations like Christian Aid and the TEAR Fund.

Education has been a central concern of the Church since the time of the Reformation. The Reformers taught that each individual should be able to read the Bible for himself; and John Knox was insistent that there should be a school as well as a church in every parish. Such attitudes in the past led to a comparatively high rate of literacy within the Presbyterian community, but in an era of universal schooling this particularly Presbyterian emphasis on education has perhaps been lost. In the late 1920s the Church handed its schools over to the Northern Ireland government and received in return transferor representation on boards of school governors. However, this by no means marked the end of the Church's concern for education, which is still an important topic for debates in the sessions of the General Assembly. Indeed, the Church has often differed with government in regard to curriculum and other matters. The Sunday School, originally a means of widespread social improvement, remains today simply as an important aspect of the nurturing of the congregation's children.

The Church has also sought, particularly in the last thirty years, to comment, through the Assembly and its various committees, on the political situation in Northern Ireland. Tensions exist in the Church's role in this matter as it seeks both to lead its people in prophetic terms and to speak on behalf of its people to government. Many contacts have been made, many discussions undertaken, and many thoughtful and useful papers have been produced. Among these is the Church's 'Peace Vocation' statement, adopted by the General Assembly in 1994. This statement asserts that the Christian's 'vocation to peace ... is both the gift and mission placed on us by God' and affirms that the Christian's calling is 'to seek peace, and the things that make for peace in our day'.

How well the Church identifies and responds to the needs of the community and how adequately it addresses the broader issues of social justice are matters for constant questioning.

ATTITUDES TO OTHER DENOMINATIONS AND
INTER–CHURCH/ECUMENICAL ACTIVITY

Fundamental to the Church's attitude to inter-church activity are two principles of the Reformation which are often in tension. The first is a conviction that the True Church, the invisible Church, is not encompassed within any one earthly denomination; and the second, that the pursuit of truth should never be compromised. For some Presbyterians these principles seem complementary and lead naturally to inter-church activity, while for others they present barriers to such activity.

Just as Irish Presbyterianism was involved in the formation of the Alliance of Reformed Churches in the nineteenth century, so, in the twentieth century, Irish Presbyterianism became involved in the formation of the World Council of Churches, the British Council of Churches, the Irish Council of Churches and the Corrymeela Community.

However, unease at membership of some of these interdenominational bodies has always been experienced by certain sections of the Church; and, in the increasingly conservative climate of the last quarter of the twentieth century, this unease began to spread more widely. The Church's membership of the World Council of Churches in particular became subject to sustained opposition from a group within the Church calling itself the Campaign for Complete Withdrawal. A decision by the WCC to introduce a 'programme to combat racism' was perceived by many to condone if not to promote terrorism and, in the political climate of Northern Ireland in the 1970s, was viewed with deep concern. It was further argued that contacts between the WCC and the Roman Catholic Church inevitably compromised the Presbyterian Church's evangelical position. Eventually, a majority of the General Assembly voted to withdraw from the WCC. Similarly, when the British Council of Churches was restructured in 1990 to form the Council of Churches for Britain and Ireland, in order to allow for the inclusion of the Roman Catholic Church, the Presbyterian Church in Ireland, unlike Presbyterian Churches in Great Britain, voted not to join.

The withdrawal of the Church from these ecumenical bodies is perceived by a majority of the Assembly to defend its evangelical and Reformed position. Other Presbyterians believe that it has, on the contrary, contributed to an inward-looking disposition and has failed to evince the revival of evangelical endeavour which withdrawal was said to herald. Furthermore, withdrawal has led to a situation whereby some of the major ecumenical organisations are no longer made fully aware of the insights which the Reformed tradition has to offer. The standing of the Church could be said to be impaired thereby.

This is not to say, however, that there is no ecumenical activity within Irish Presbyterianism. The Church remains a member of the Irish Council of Churches and also of the Conference of European Churches and continues, apparently without compromise, its membership of the Irish Inter-Church Meeting (originally known as the Ballymascanlon Talks). Practical, local inter-church activity has been realised in some joint building enterprises and joint charges with, for example, the Methodist Church. In addition, many congregations are involved in local inter-church activity through membership of local councils of churches, clergy fellowships and other, individual initiatives.

REFLECTION AND SUMMARY

Being a Presbyterian is simply one way of attempting to be the people of God. Presbyterian traditions of simplicity and rigour, the inalienable right of private judgement and the emphasis on the importance of the individual's response to God have often generated within Presbyterians an independent and sometimes cantankerous disposition. The emphasis on the individual and the nature of Presbyterian theology have also meant that Presbyterianism can be prone to schism, hence the creation of so many different Presbyterian bodies over the past centuries.

Resistance to central authority in Church and state has sometimes almost become a point of principle in itself. Presbyterians in the past, with their notions of democracy, were notorious for their lack of deference. William Drennan, the United Irishman, attributed his political outlook to the democratic and independent principles of his Presbyterian upbringing. Exclusion from full participation in the state until the nineteenth century meant that the Presbyterian community was in many ways a state within a state: apart, separate and self-sufficient. This heightened its sense of independence. Presbyterian political traditions in the last century were largely Liberal, encouraged by the egalitarianism inherent in Reformed theology. Yet Presbyterianism, though radical in its origins and many of its structures – and once perceived to be a social and political threat, with its dangerous ideas of democracy, accountability and egalitarianism – is often considered today to be both socially and politically conservative. Indeed, it may well be that the experience of the twentieth century in Northern Ireland has developed attitudes which are defensive and in marked contrast to those of previous centuries. Furthermore, attitudes informed by Old and New Testament teachings of separation can often come into conflict with the Church's call to the transformation of society.

Yet Presbyterianism has not by any means been wholly resistant to social change. For example, women, who have always played an important role within the congregation and in the mission field – especially when other opportunities for service were denied them – were admitted to the office of elder in the 1920s and to the ministry in the 1970s. However, these changes were, and still are, not without their opponents.

Presbyterianism experiences tensions between liberal and fundamentalist or 'conservative-evangelical' points of view (although the Church is by definition evangelical); and from generation to generation the balance in the Church moves between them. The more conservative view tends to emphasise the individual, a concern for the salvation of the individual, biblical literalism, and a wider, less denominationally differentiated, evangelicalism. The more liberal view tends to emphasise community, the role of the Church, a more interpretative view of the Bible, ecumenism, and the broader dynamic of Reformed thinking. The tension between the two can be, but is not always, creative.

Presbyterians are people of the Word. The Word and words generally are important to them. They prefer words to mean what they say. They distrust 'clever' use of words and they distrust wordiness. As a result they can often appear inflexible and blunt. 'Their manners,' remarked the Ordnance Survey Memoirs of the 1830s, 'even when intending civility are far from being courteous ... they are more than a little stubborn.' Such attitudes derive from a literal use of language and an attachment to hard-won principle. Presbyterian conviction, while seemingly at odds with its tradition of questioning, often seems simply unimaginative. Yet Presbyterians are creative although, as in their theology, they have a preference for the practical over the theoretical, for the applied over the abstract: Presbyterians, it has been said, are more likely to be engineers than poets.

Given their religious background and the attitudes which develop from it, how well do Presbyterians manage to be the people of God? One Church publication makes the following statement:

> The best test of our Church and its members lies in what their faith compels them to do for others, not just what has been done for them as individuals. The King and Head of the Church loved us and gave Himself for us so that we should no longer live for ourselves. We are called to service.

In seeking to fulfil its role in the world, the Presbyterian Church also has before it one of the tenets of the Reformation: *ecclesia reformata semper reformanda* – a church re-formed but always in need of reformation.

BIBLIOGRAPHY

Barkley, John, *Presbyterianism*, Belfast: the author 1951

Dunlop, John, *A Precarious Belonging: Presbyterians and the Conflict in Ireland*, Belfast: Blackstaff Press 1995

Holmes, Finlay, *Our Irish Presbyterian Heritage*, 2nd edn, Belfast: Presbyterian Church in Ireland 1992

Irish Presbyterians (GCSE pupils' book), Belfast: Presbyterian Church in Ireland 1988 (with accompanying video cassette)

Leith, John H., *An Introduction to the Reformed Tradition: A Way of Being the Christian Community*, Atlanta: John Knox Press 1977

McKim, Donald K. (ed.), *Encyclopedia of the Reformed Faith*, Edinburgh: St Andrew Press 1992

Patterson, Carlisle, *Over the Hill: Ecumenism in the Presbyterian Church in Ireland*, Belfast: T.C. Patterson 1997

Presbyterian Church in Ireland, *Brief Statement Concerning Faith and Order*, Belfast: Presbyterian Church in Ireland 1974

Presbyterian Church in Ireland, *Agreements and Disagreements of Irish Presbyterianism and Roman Catholicism*, Belfast, Presbyterian Church in Ireland 1990

BIOGRAPHICAL NOTE

JOHN ERSKINE is a member of his local congregation in Belfast, an elder of the Presbyterian Church in Ireland, a member of the Council of the Presbyterian Historical Society of Ireland, and editor of the Society's Bulletin. His enthusiasm for Presbyterian history is tempered somewhat by his wife's Anglican indifference to the whole subject and by the low boredom threshold inexplicably displayed by his two children on this topic alone. John is a Librarian by profession and works at Stranmillis College, Belfast.

The
Church of Ireland

edited by

ELIZABETH GIBSON HARRIES AND EDGAR TURNER

INTRODUCTION

The Church of Ireland (as a Protestant Episcopal Church) is that part of the Irish Church which accepted the sixteenth-century Reformation. From the time of the Reformation for 320 years it was the established state Church, headed by the crown, and had considerable legal and political privileges. Since 1 January 1871, it has been disestablished, and is now an entirely voluntary Church where neither crown nor parliament has any role in its government in either part of Ireland.

The Church of Ireland, as that title implies, is conscious of three things: its claim to relate directly with Christianity from its very beginnings in this island; its awareness of its presence throughout the island; and its adherence to the Christian Faith in its fullness.

In response to a request to set down a number of characteristics which make the Church of Ireland and its members distinctive, a standing committee conference in 1993 produced a document of ten short paragraphs with the following headings:

1. We are Christians.

2. We are Irish.

3. We are Catholic, holding all the Christian faith in fullness.

4. We are a Reformed Church.

5. We are committed to unity within Christ's sadly divided Body.

6. We are Anglicans.

7. We respect freedom.

8. We regard Worship, public and private, as a priority for every Christian.

9. We are a Church affirming the place of the ancient threefold ministry of bishops, priests and deacons within our common life.

10. We believe in the equality within the Body of Christ of all the baptised.

The Church of Ireland, for historical as well as practical reasons, finds itself in a traditional Anglican position in Ireland. Theologically, pastorally and geographically it stands between the ethos and outlook of Roman Catholicism on the one hand and Presbyterianism on the other. Catholic and Reformed in doctrine, composed of members in both north and south of the island, reflecting an entire spectrum of political, economic and cultural outlooks while maintaining practical allegiance to 'unity in diversity', the Church of Ireland has found itself, despite great pressure, reflecting a middle ground. The Church's organisation and ministry transcends the political border. The General Synod, its supreme legislative assembly, is composed of elected clergy and laity from all parts of Ireland and this is reflected in all membership of boards or committees. While its numerical majority live and worship in Northern Ireland, its members in the Republic are fully represented in its administration, and its administrative office and theological college are in Dublin.

Despite political developments which over the years have divided Ireland and her people, the Church of Ireland has managed to maintain a degree of unity which has allowed its voice to be heard clearly in both jurisdictions. It is widely accepted that the Church of Ireland has played a role in Irish life far in excess of its numerical strength. Among the other Churches of the Anglican Communion, the Church of Ireland has provided expertise, advice and leadership in many important aspects of the life of that Communion.

The cause of reconciliation has been a priority for the Church of Ireland north and south. A significant number of its members have been killed in the violence in Northern Ireland. Its bishops and members have played key roles in the peace process and in the building of bridges between divided communities.

Although it has many large city parishes its real strength lies in rural communities. The farming community provides a large proportion of its membership. The movement of population in urban Ireland has necessitated the building of new churches and the creation of new parochial units. The essential priority of its ministry remains pastoral, and consequently a relatively small number of its clergy are in specialist, non-parish-based, positions.

Given its acceptance in both parts of Ireland, the Church of Ireland has influenced political debate, political developments and community thinking in many ways. Through its Role of the Church Committee it has supported the individual initiatives of bishops by an ongoing dialogue with party politicians. In all such instances the Church of Ireland has emphasised reconciliation, justice and fairness. In its liturgy and pastoral ministry the Church of Ireland reflects the historical Celtic tradition, while emphasis on the concerns of youth has given it fresh impetus in meeting the needs of a new generation. It sees sectarianism in Northern Ireland as a corrosive and destructive element in society, and has taken a lead in combating this evil element to Northern life.

ORIGINS

The very title 'Church of Ireland' conveys to its members its sense of Irish identity. At Disestablishment in 1871 this title was legally confirmed although from the seventeenth century church writers had referred to the titles Church of England or Church of Ireland as alternative descriptions of the same body. Yet the Church of Ireland has always emphasised its separate identity, despite sharing the same doctrine and discipline as its English counterpart.

The Irish origins of the Church of Ireland are as varied as the many traditions which make up the Irish identity. The scholarly Archbishop James Ussher (1581–1656) was convinced that the faith which St Patrick professed was at one with his own, and this strong sense of continuity with the past, in particular with Celtic times, has remained influential. This was keenly expressed in a hymn written at the time of Disestablishment by the Rector of Banbridge, Canon James E. Archer:

> Lift thy Banner, Church of Erin,
> To thine ancient faith we cling.
> Ages pass yet with St Patrick
> Firm we hold the faith of God.

In 1863 in his life of Patrick, Dr J.H. Todd asserted the claim of his Church as 'the original Irish Church', an attitude accepted by other writers. (The building of the memorial church to St Patrick at Saul, Co. Down, in 1932 was a visible testimony to this conviction.) As history this attitude has been discarded by modern scholarship, but as a mythology it is a vital part of the Church of Ireland's understanding of itself.

In the wider understanding of Irish origins the Church has seen its heritage as enriched by the integration of Ireland into European Christendom in Norman times. This was the tradition which its members saw reformed by the Protestants so there was nothing against their sense of being Irish in accepting influences from a wider world. In the eighteenth century the Church of Ireland saw itself as in the forefront of the struggle for Ireland's freedom to govern itself. When, years later, Church members fought for unionist beliefs it was for all Ireland, not just Ulster, that they contended. They accepted partition as second-best, but as a Church continued to view themselves within the framework of Ireland. Although much battered by the Northern Ireland Troubles, this concept is still part of the 'ethos' of the Church of Ireland.

NUMBERS, DISTRIBUTION, TRENDS

At Disestablishment in 1871 the Church of Ireland had about 700,000 members throughout the island, that is about 10.7%. Its present population is believed to be 279,280 in Northern Ireland and 89,187 in the Republic of Ireland, totalling 368,467 throughout Ireland, that is about 5% of the total population. These figures show that about one-quarter of the members of the Church of Ireland live in the Republic – that is many times greater than any other 'protestant' denomination – and account for the relative ease with which bishops, clergy and people of the Church of Ireland cross the political border and find themselves at home in either jurisdiction.

There is a steady decline in the Republic of about 0.65% per year and of about 0.2% per year in Northern Ireland. There are about 475 churches in Northern Ireland and about 640 in the Republic. There are 310 clergy serving in Northern Ireland and 230 in the Republic. This shows that while many parishes in Northern Ireland may have just one church building and perhaps two clergy, most parishes in the Republic have quite a number of churches served by one cleric.

The Church of Ireland now has twelve bishops, two of whom have dioceses which are completely contained within Northern Ireland (Connor; Down and Dromore), four of whom have dioceses with parishes on each side of the border (Armagh; Clogher; Derry and Raphoe; Kilmore) and six of whom have dioceses which are entirely contained in the Republic (Dublin; Meath and Kildare; Cashel and Ossory; Limerick and Killaloe; Cork; and Tuam). While some Northern dioceses like Connor have over a hundred thousand members in a county the size of Antrim, some of the Southern dioceses like Limerick may have a mere six thousand members spread over as many as seven counties.

Within Northern Ireland it is possible to identify certain trends and movements of church members. The movement into cities like Belfast, so marked a generation ago, seems to have ceased. Instead there appears to be a drift away from Belfast, from both the Co. Antrim side (Connor Diocese) and the Co. Down side (Down Diocese). Newtownards, Banbridge, Carrickfergus, Larne and Limavady all show an increase of over 10%.

There is no indication of any drastic change in the numbers of Church of Ireland children. In fact the number of those aged between zero and four is slightly higher than those between five and nine, and only a little lower than those between ten and fourteen.

The last census showed that slightly fewer Church of Ireland people were divorced than in the other major denominations, the figure being 7.78%.

DOCTRINE

The Church of Ireland's doctrinal position is well summed up in the dictum of Lancelot Andrewes (1555–1626): 'one canon ... two testaments, three creeds, four general Councils, five centuries and the series of the Fathers in that period ... determine the boundary of our faith'. ('One canon' refers to the Bible.)

The Church of Ireland sees itself as an Apostolic Church. (The Greek word for apostolic has the root meaning of 'sent'.) We believe that we are members of a Church sent by God, in the apostolic tradition of St Patrick, who himself received the apostolic teaching in France (Gaul). The Church of Ireland is one in faith and order with the New Testament Church described in the Acts of the Apostles. 'Those who ... were baptised ... devoted themselves to the apostles' teaching and to the fellowship, to the breaking of bread and to prayer' (Acts 2:41–2, New International Version).

The Church of Ireland sees itself as a part of the Catholic Church in that it has come to us from the earliest days of Christianity in Ireland. It has experienced great changes at the time of the Anglo-Norman invasion, at the Reformation, at the Cromwellian intrusion, at Disestablishment and during the past hundred years; but there has been no break in all that is essential in its continuity. It has always remained the same Holy, Catholic and Apostolic Church with the same Scriptures, the same Sacraments – Baptism and Eucharist, instituted by Christ himself – and the same apostolic ministry – the three Orders of Bishops, Priests (or Presbyters) and Deacons. Furthermore it maintains the age-old obligation to worship Almighty God, to preach the Gospel declaring the mighty works of God and to practise social penetration – to comfort the disturbed and to disturb the comfortable.

The Church of Ireland is a scriptural Church. It has always valued the open Bible, requiring its clergy to study it daily and encouraging its laity to read it. In the teaching of the Faith it appeals to the Scriptures as containing all doctrine necessary to salvation 'so that whatsoever is not read therein nor may be proved thereby is not to be required of any man, that it should be believed as an article of the Faith or be thought necessary to salvation' (*Articles of Religion*, vi). Much of its liturgy is built around the Bible; the Psalms and readings from the Old and New Testaments occupy a large part of the daily services. Most of the versicles and responses, so much a feature in its worship, are quotations from the Bible while the prayers and thanksgivings bear the impression of scriptural language. 'The Church to teach and the Bible to prove' sums up the position of the Church of Ireland.

The Church of Ireland is Reformed and Protestant. In the *Preamble and Declaration* (1870) prefixed to the Constitution of the Church of Ireland it is stated that the Church of Ireland as Reformed and Protestant reaffirms 'its constant witness against all those innovations in doctrine and worship, whereby the Primitive Faith hath been from time to time defaced or overlaid and which at the Reformation this Church did disown and reject' (1.3). This is the only place in the Irish Book of Common Prayer (1926) where the word 'Protestant' is found. When used nowadays of the Church of Ireland, it conveys the idea of the Latin *pro testor* – witnessing for and not just against. To reform is not to set up a new church with a New Faith. Archbishop Bramhall of Armagh (1594–1663) suggested the analogy of a garden: a garden full of weeds and the same plot after it has been weeded are not two gardens; it is one and the same garden. So the Church before the Reformation and the Church Reformed, freed from all accretions to the Faith, is the same Church. John Cosin put it this way: 'Protestant and Reformed, according to the Ancient Catholic Church'.

The Church of Ireland is a disciplined Church. It is not an 'à la carte' Church. It has set forms of prayer and there are good biblical and traditional precedents for this. The Lectionary follows the Church's Year with its thematic approach Sunday by Sunday. This discipline is dictated by the Bible, the Book of Common Prayer, the Catechism, the Thirty-Nine Articles, et cetera. The Church of Ireland combines authority with freedom. It speaks plainly and uncompromisingly on the central doctrines of the Christian Faith, yet it values spiritual freedom. It keeps its rules to a minimum, preferring to say 'you ought' rather than 'you must'. It makes its special appeal to the Bible and tradition, reason and conscience, encouraging its members to discuss and criticise in their search after a deeper understanding of the Truth.

BASIS OF AUTHORITY

The sixteenth-century Reformation, in which the Church of Ireland was actively engaged, raised profound issues of authority. The question of how the Church was to be reformed, and how far that reform should be carried, was virtually indistinguishable from the question of who had authority to do it.

That instrument was the king working through parliament. While the desire of the crown to maintain the unity of the national Church by a policy of avoiding sharp theological definition had something to do with reasons of state, it laid the foundation of that distinctive Anglican distaste for, and distrust of, theological authoritarianism. Reinforced by the theological traditions of the great sixteenth-century Anglican apologists and the Caroline divines in the succeeding century, this openness to debate predisposed the Church in the long term to conciliar forms of government.

The Church of Ireland is governed by a constitution that ensures consultation with the elected representatives of both clergy and laity at parochial, diocesan and national levels. It is consultative rather than democratic. This is perhaps best illustrated in the case of the incumbent of a parish. He or she is elected by representatives of both the parish and the diocese, and must consult the representatives of the parish (the Select Vestry) in those matters that concern finance, fixtures and fabric as set down by the Constitution. But the pastoral care of the parish, and the authority to conduct worship, are received from the bishop alone. This is ultimately because, as the *Preamble* to the same Constitution carefully points out, the Church of Ireland derives its authority 'from Christ, who is the head of all things over the Church'.

MEMBERSHIP, CHURCH GOVERNMENT AND MINISTRY

The Church of Ireland is a self-governing member of the Anglican Communion, which means that it is in communion with the See of Canterbury (the seat of the senior archbishop in the Church of England). The Archbishop of Canterbury has no authority in the Church of Ireland: he is not an Anglican pope. Neither does the Anglican Communion have any authority over it: there is no Anglican curia. The bishops of the Church of Ireland attend the ten-yearly Lambeth Conference convened by the Archbishop of Canterbury and attended by all the bishops in the Anglican Communion. While that Conference frequently issues major statements for the guidance of the Churches of the communion, these must be accepted by the governing bodies of the individual member Churches before they become effective.

The Church of Ireland is subject only to its own Constitution. The *Preamble and Declaration* to that Constitution require the Church to:

- accept and unfeignedly believe all the Canonical Scriptures of the Old and New Testament as containing all things necessary to salvation
- profess the faith of Christ as professed by the Primitive Church
- maintain inviolate the three orders of bishops, priests or presbyters and deacons in the sacred ministry.

The Church of Ireland follows the pattern of the Early Church where there was an 'episcopos', a bishop or overseer, in most cities. Each of the twelve diocesan bishops has a number of parishes which meet under the authority of the bishop in an annual diocesan synod which consists of all the clergy of the diocese together with two laity for each cleric. The diocesan synod has an executive body, the diocesan council, which exercises control over the finances, property and affairs of the parishes in the diocese.

In each diocese there is a cathedral – that is, the church where the bishop has his 'cathedra' or seat. The incumbent in charge of the cathedral is known as a dean, and has a number of canons to assist him – although in practice the canons continue to serve in their own parishes and their canonry is regarded as a honour for notable work or long service.

As a member of the parish each parishioner can sign the roll of registered vestrymen, as either 'resident' or 'accustomed', and so be able to take part in the affairs of the parish. At Eastertide each year every parish has a General Vestry which chooses the churchwardens, glebewardens (i.e. two people to oversee the care of the rectory or other church property) and a Select Vestry of twelve other persons to guide the finances and business of the parish for the ensuing year. Every third year the Annual General Vestry chooses its two lay members for the diocesan synod. That synod chooses the clergy and laity to act for it on the diocesan council. It also elects its representatives – clerical and lay – who are to be part of the 215 clergy and 432 laity on General Synod.

The *Preamble and Declaration* to the Constitution adopted by the General Convention of the Church of Ireland in 1870 affirms the legislative power of the General Synod and gives it 'such administrative power as may be necessary for the Church and consistent with its episcopal constitution'. Thus, while bishops and clergy have their prerogatives, the laity also have theirs, and participate fully in decision making, not only at parish level, but in dioceses and at General Synod. They also have a constitutional role in the appointment of parochial clergy and of bishops.

Candidates for the ministry are examined by an Advisory Committee on

Ministry, and if accepted are sent for training to the Church of Ireland Theological College in Dublin (or to a similar college elsewhere). After satisfying the college authorities a candidate must receive a 'title' – that is, a position as assistant (usually 'curate') to a rector – and is ordained deacon by the diocesan bishop. Usually about one year later the deacon is ordained priest and could thereafter be nominated for a vacant parish as 'incumbent'.

Two major changes in the nature of ministry have taken place in recent years. In 1974 an auxiliary ministry was introduced – that is, clergy who have been ordained but receive no stipend, and can act only as assistants to an incumbent. (At the time of writing there are forty-eight auxiliaries.) Since 1990 all three orders of the ordained ministry have been open to women as well as men. While most of the thirty-two women priests are auxiliary ministers or assistants, a few have already become incumbents of parishes. One has been appointed as a canon, but none, however, has so far been appointed as an archdeacon, or dean, or bishop.

Some lay people are involved in ministry as commissioned Diocesan Lay Readers. They may lead Morning and Evening Prayer, preach, and assist a priest in the administration of Holy Communion. Some lay readers also help with parish visitation and in a range of other ways.

SACRAMENTS

The sacraments of Christ, in Church of Ireland understanding, are Baptism and Holy Communion. Other rites are sometimes called sacraments, or sacramental ministries, provided it is understood that they are not in the same category as the two instituted by our Lord, which are necessary for fullness of life in Christ for all Christians.

Baptism is a sign and means of grace. It is a sign of God's gift and a divinely appointed means he uses to impart it. *'The inward and spiritual gift in Baptism is union with Christ in his death and resurrection, the forgiveness of sins, and a new birth into God's family, the Church'* (the Revised Catechism, p. 17).

Baptism has several aspects:

- *Participation in Christ's death and resurrection.* Christ died to sin and rose that we might be raised to new life with him.
- *Forgiveness of sins.* Forgiveness is applied individually in baptism.
- *Regeneration*, new birth, or birth from above.
- *Incorporation into the Church.* In the New Testament entrance into the Church is always by baptism.
- *The Gift of the Spirit.* Those baptised into the Church receive the Spirit for the common good.
- *Faith and repentance* always accompany baptism in the New Testament.

Infant baptism is practised by the Church of Ireland and justified because of the corporate nature of faith. The baptised infant becomes a member of the believing community. His baptism and the faith of the community help to elicit his own personal faith. A person's baptism, whether in infancy or later, marks God's decisive, objective act in making him a Christian, though he may need a lifetime to lay hold on what God has made him in baptism.

As people who live in community our individual personal faith affects, and is affected by, the faith of others. The Church of Ireland encourages the public celebration of baptism at a main Sunday Service to make clear its corporate aspect.

The Church of Ireland regards **Holy Communion** as the highest act of Christian worship, by which the Church is constantly renewed by the Body and Blood of Christ. How this mystery takes place it is reluctant to define precisely. 'Shall I wish that men would give themselves to meditate with silence what we have by the sacrament and less to dispute of the manner how?' (Richard Hooker, c. 1554–1600).

Holy Communion can be described as

- *Thanksgiving (Eucharist)*. Thanksgiving occurs throughout the Eucharistic celebration, but especially in the great thanksgiving over the bread and wine.
- *Memorial*. 'Do this in remembrance of me.'
- *Sacrifice*. Christ's once-for-all sacrifice is effective now.
- *Communion in Christ's body and blood*. Christ gives himself through the consecrated bread and wine received with faith.

Communion with Christ always involves communion with other Christians (1 Corinthians 10:17).

The Church of Ireland values and uses the five other 'commonly called' sacramental rites, i.e. confirmation, absolution, marriage, ordination and anointing of the sick. *Confirmation* – when the person can say the Creed, the Lord's Prayer and understand the Church Catechism – involves the laying on of hands by the bishop and is normally the prelude to communicant membership. *Ordination* in the Church of Ireland invariably includes the laying on of hands on the person being ordained by a bishop in the context of the prayers of the whole congregation. The Church of Ireland values the threefold ministry of bishops, priests and deacons as an essential strand in the unity and continuity of the Church throughout the world and throughout the centuries.

SPIRITUALITY

The Church's authorised prayer books: the *Book of Common Prayer* (as revised in 1926), the *Alternative Prayer Book* (1984) and the *Alternative Occasional Services* (1993) contain the materials for regular worship and show, better than anything else, how the Church of Ireland understands the Christian faith.

The *Book of Common Prayer* has provided for all the members of the Church of Ireland a kind of 'handbook' to their spiritual life. Not only does it deal with the words and actions of the Church's services, but it spells out its doctrine or teaching about marriage, sickness, death, ordination, sacraments, theological issues, the use of 'protestant' and 'catholic', et cetera – and even gives the text of the Constitution or rules of procedure. For about three hundred years that Book has continued in use – with only minor changes. Its Elizabethan cadences, fitting the language of the Authorised Version of the Bible, have governed the Church's worship, expressed its theology and ensured the continuity of a rich literary style.

The spirituality of the Church of Ireland is fed mostly by participation, week by week, in the corporate liturgy of the Church. By its concentration for seven months in each year on the biblical events of the Christian Faith – Advent, Christmas, Epiphany, Lent, Passion, Easter, Ascension, Pentecost – and for the remaining five months on particular aspects of Christian practice, it has created a broad basis for its spirituality. Additional activities, such as commemoration of saints on weekdays, can rest easily on this basis. These can be biblical people like the Blessed Virgin Mary, or Celtic saints like Patrick, Columba and Brigid who have found their way into the Prayer Book, or Columbanus, Kevin, Finbarr and Brendan who have only local commemoration.

In addition to their public worship and private prayers the members of the Church of Ireland have many opportunities and options for finding and expressing their spirituality. Extra activities such as midweek prayer meetings, Holy Week services, occasional Mission services, and for some people a retreat or a pilgrimage, can be an adjunct to their normal weekly worship. In a parish there may be a communicants' guild or prayer groups, or branches of the Mothers' Union or Men's Fellowship. Shared outlook or interests enable many to join those of other parishes or other local churches for Bible study, ecumenical or practical concerns – as is indicated by the increasing popularity of shared Holy Week or Christian Unity Week services. Parish groups may form 'links' with far-off parishes with quite different concerns, or take part in a diocesan 'twinning' in another country. Individuals can join with 'kindred spirits' of other parishes or dioceses to discuss religious issues, or share a common spiritual need, or take part in an evangelistic enterprise, or go off on a pilgrimage to enrich their knowledge and understanding, or go for a time of quiet and spiritual enrichment in conference or retreat.

The custom – practised until recently – of learning by heart the collect of the Sunday, the whole of the catechism, and many of the psalms, gave a basis and a reference point for establishing the nature of the private prayers and theological opinion of most Church of Ireland members. The Collects (short, often theme-based prayers) form a handbook of doctrine as well as a manual of devotion. They constantly remind us that God is 'the fountain of all goodness', 'the author and giver of all good things', the person 'from whom all holy desires, all good counsels, and all just works do proceed', that he 'hates nothing that he hath made', and of 'his power most chiefly in shewing mercy and pity'. The constant use of such phrases, and meditation on them, not only teach about God's true nature, but help us to 'worship in spirit and in truth'.

The *Irish Church Hymnal*, used by almost every congregation, contains hymns from ancient Latin and Greek sources and traditional Victorian hymnology, side by side with hymns from the Celtic past such as St Patrick's Breastplate, 'Be Thou my Vision', 'It Were my Soul's Desire', and hymns by St Columba or from the Bangor Antiphonary – all helping to create a sense of continuity with the worship of the Church in this island for centuries.

The roots of the tradition which had shaped the spirituality of so many members of the Church of Ireland, such as Bishop Jeremy Taylor, Mrs Cecil Frances Alexander and C.S. Lewis, can easily be seen from their writings to lie in the fertile soil of the liturgy of the Church of Ireland. What they, and those thousands who live by it week by week, have valued most are the close link between word and sacrament; the reading of the Scriptures combined with participation in the Holy Communion after preparation the day before; the observance of Sunday as a day of worship which marks a renewal of life for Monday's work; an ordered pattern which gathers private devotion and corporate public prayer into a recreating experience. These are the common roots from which the spirituality of its members still grows.

As the introduction to the *Alternative Prayer Book* puts it, 'Liturgy becomes worship when the people of God make the prayers their own prayers, and turn in faith to God, Father, Son and Holy Spirit.'

WORSHIP AND LITURGY

The worship of the Church of Ireland consists mainly of two services, the Holy Communion or Eucharist and the Offices of Morning or Evening

Prayer. The Eucharist originated as the commemoration of the Last Supper as instituted by Christ, while the Daily Offices were the short series of daily monastic services following the Jewish pattern of daily prayers. These services, adapted and reformed from their use in the Celtic and pre-Reformation Church, were made available to both clergy and laity in their own language in the *Book of Common Prayer*, with a liberal use of directions or 'rubrics' on how to conduct the services.

Since 1972 there have been *Alternative Service Books* which, while still containing the same services, express them with clearer structure and in more modern language. The rubrics are now much more 'user-friendly'. In addition, the canons (laws) of the Church now allow more alternatives and opportunities for clergy to add to and vary many of the forms – but always in obedience to the rule to 'use the form in the said book prescribed and none other, except so far as may be allowed by the lawful authority of the Church'.

When the pre-Reformation Mass with mostly non-communicating attendance was superseded by the Order for the Administration of the Lord's Supper or Holy Communion there was a tendency for the laity, feeling uneasy about the strong exhortation about 'unworthy receiving' of the sacrament, to prefer the less demanding services of Morning or Evening Prayer. It is only in recent years, due largely to the influence of the Parish Communion movement, that the primacy of the Holy Communion as the major service has been re-established. It is found now as the principal service in each church on at least one Sunday in the month and in very many churches as the regular weekly form of worship – 'the Lord's own service on the Lord's own day' as it is sometimes described.

The structure of the Eucharistic service is clear, and follows a pattern which other Christian communities can readily follow: introductory prayer for 'purity'; theme collect of the season; set readings from psalms, Old Testament, Epistle and Gospel usually related to the theme; sermon; Nicene Creed; prayers of intercession and of penitence; presentation of and Thanksgiving over the elements of bread and wine (i.e. consecration); communion; post-communion prayers and dismissal.

The structure of Morning and Evening Prayer is equally full of biblical material. After an optional penitential beginning there is a plea to God that he would 'open our lips' and an immediate response that 'our mouth will proclaim your praise'; then follows a psalm (usually sung to an Anglican chant); an Old Testament Lesson; a canticle (i.e. a biblical or early Christian hymn); a New Testament lesson; Apostles' Creed; prayers (including the collect of the Sunday from the Eucharistic service). By tradition there follows a hymn; prayers for people and concerns both general, topical and local; a sermon; and a concluding hymn.

There is a considerable amount of congregational response – and laity can not only read the lessons but often lead the prayers, and even (if authorised) preach. The music varies according to local competence and ability: it may be full cathedral-type choral service, or there may be a choir which can provide an anthem on occasions, or a group who give a congregational lead to the music. Sometimes services are simply said, thus giving even more scope for congregational participation.

The use of an ordered liturgy such as this ensures that most of the Bible is read 'in course', that all its main themes are dealt with so that neither clergy nor congregation are tempted to concentrate narrowly on favourite subjects. While adequate provision is made for 'biddings' and 'free forms', the use of corporate prayers of penitence or response ensures that worship will be conducted 'decently and in order'.

The introduction of the *Alternative Prayer Book*, the commemoration of saints' days, the use of ancient Irish forms of litany, the introduction of a new hymn book – *Irish Church Praise*, with hymns in Irish like 'Ag Críost an Síol', the wide sanction allowing special forms of service for special occasions, permission to use musical 'groups' with rhythmic beat and charismatic participation – all these are ways by which experiments in widening the scope and nature of worship can be used, under the restraint of the 'ordinary' (i.e. the bishop), without destroying the main character of worship.

BUILDINGS AND ARTEFACTS

The Church of Ireland has inherited the ancient parochial structure of the country, as described by Bishop Reeves in his *Ecclesiastical Antiquities of Down, Connor and Dromore* (Dublin, 1847). As a consequence, the reformed church was the legal possessor of the ancient ivy-clad ruins which can still be seen in many parts of Ireland. St Patrick's and Christ Church Cathedrals in Dublin along with St Nicholas's Church in Carrickfergus and Down Cathedral in Downpatrick lay claim to be the oldest buildings still in use, each dating from the twelfth or early thirteenth centuries.

In the century following the Reformation many churches were built, although few survive. Perhaps the best known is St Patrick's, Newry, erected by Sir Nicholas Bagnal in 1578. The destruction wrought during the 1641 rebellion destroyed most of these churches; many of the ruins which we see today date from this time. After the Restoration in 1660 there was a significant increase in building new and larger churches. As Dublin was the centre of government, so it became the headquarters of the Established Church; many of the fine Dublin city churches were built during the late seventeenth and eighteenth centuries. Other areas were not neglected; there was a significant Anglican population in Cork and also in the upper Lagan and upper Bann valleys in Ulster, as well as Co. Armagh stretching through the Clogher valley to Co. Fermanagh. The eighteenth century marked the zenith of church building, because of the wealth and social standing of the Establishment.

The Board of First Fruits was established in 1712 and was empowered to grant loans or gifts towards the building of churches and glebe houses (rectories) within specific guidelines. This facility led to the almost universal provision of churches in every parish. The standard design was a simple structure, divided into chancel and nave, the chancel being for the clergy and the nave for the people. Some had a small belfry at the west end and many went so far as to have a square pinnacled tower as well. These 'First Fruit' churches are still to be seen in almost every town in Ireland. Many churches were built by private patronage, where the local landowner felt the necessity to provide for the spiritual welfare of his tenants. Such churches tended to be somewhat more freely designed as in the exquisite example at Hillsborough, built by Wills Hill.

The Board of First Fruits was succeeded in 1833 by the Ecclesiastical Commissioners, who carried on the extensive programme of church building and replacement. Indeed the mid-nineteenth-century religious revival necessitated in some cases the total replacement of the earlier church, and in others the enlargement of the church, with the addition of transepts, extra aisles, chancels and galleries. Most of the old box pews were swept away in favour of the Victorian style of open pew. Very few churches escaped the 'improving' architect. The religious revival was bound up with the population move into urban centres – hence the provision of large Gothic piles in Belfast and elsewhere. It is these outsize churches, then attracting full congregations, which are now creating a problem as to how best to use or dispose of them.

With Disestablishment in 1871 the provision of government funding came to an end. In subsequent years, the Church of Ireland was responsible for finding its own resources. The pace of building slowed dramatically; in fact, work carried out during the next fifty years was largely extension work to existing buildings. The period between the wars brought a modest boost to new building, particularly in Ulster as the city of Belfast pushed its suburbs farther into the countryside and along the northern and southern shores of Belfast Lough. Buildings of this period retained the recognisable look of a church, i.e. they were still traditional in architectural terms. However, the post-war relocation of population, particularly during the 1960s and 1970s, brought a need for new church buildings in new areas. Architects did not feel obliged to keep to traditional design and found new freedom in architectural form. The Church of Ireland has always stood in the forefront of church development and employed the best of modern architects to design new churches. Examples can be found in many Belfast suburbs, Bangor, Carrickfergus, Craigavon and indeed wherever a 'new' housing estate has made them necessary. Many of these churches represent the new spirit in our worship and liturgy, involving greater congregational involvement and a greater feeling of belonging. (Even in its church buildings the Church of Ireland can be seen to be Reformed and Catholic, in the widest sense.)

Many Church of Ireland churches are repositories for a wide variety of furnishings and artefacts which in themselves are of fascination to the interested student. Bow-fronted box pews, early organs, old silver and a variety of baptismal fonts, some possibly of medieval date, grace our churches.

INTER-CHURCH/ECUMENICAL ACTIVITY

While always anxious to be co-operative with other Christians, particularly at the social level, the Church of Ireland has in recent years become much more conscious of improved relationships with other denominations. Membership of the Irish Council of Churches and the Irish Inter-Church Meeting, the extension of invitation to all other Christian bodies in Ireland to send observers to the General Synod, the participation of bishops and senior clergy at ecumenical conferences and the like, have encouraged much more co-operation at local and parish level. Almost all parishes now participate regularly in shared services, Christian Unity Week observances, 'fraternals', et cetera. At a broader level the Church is a member of the Council of Churches for Britain and Ireland and the World Council of Churches.

Clergy and laity are encouraged to associate with joint activities such as the Columbanus Community for Reconciliation, Corrymeela, PACE, Cornerstone, Education for Mutual Understanding in schools, ecumenical lectures in St Anne's Cathedral or Benburb, and so on. At parish level the old concept of 'fencing the altar' against members of other denominations has long gone. Following a Lambeth Resolution, the Church of Ireland now happily invites all who are communicant members of their own church, and whose conscience allows it, to participate in the Holy Communion – though confirmation is still the normal Anglican way towards full membership.

Many Church of Ireland clergy are accustomed to sharing with priests or ministers of other denominations in weddings, funerals, et cetera. Some even go on joint pilgrimages or retreats. In a few cases there are shared church buildings as in Monkstown, near Belfast, or Shannon Airport – and inevitably in such cases congregations are invited either to create joint worship or to attend the services of the other denomination. Joint Bible study between churches at local level is now commonplace and is encouraged. Some parishes have studied international inter-church documents (from the World Council of Churches or Anglican–Roman Catholic discussions, for instance) although most local groups would be primarily concerned with local issues.

The ending of the *Ne Temere* decree, by which both partners at a mixed marriage had to promise that all children of the marriage would be brought up as Roman Catholics, and the growing understanding since Vatican II of the concentration on the importance of the family and of intelligible worship has – in most places – created a much warmer climate between the Church of Ireland and Roman Catholics.

There is still little contact and co-operation with the smaller religious bodies, but the animosity and fear of proselytising which characterised former relationships has largely disappeared.

In a few places – but only in a few – charismatic services have brought together people who are more concerned about sharing in the Spirit than they are about denominational allegiance.

CHURCH AND COMMUNITY

At Disestablishment the Church of Ireland inherited social welfare bodies with names like the 'Association for Discountenancing Vice', the 'Ladies' Committee of the Ragged School', the 'Ulster Magdalene Asylum for the Reception of Penitent Women', et cetera. These bodies indicated that the Church had two objects in view: a desire to inculcate a high moral tone, and a concern for the needy and destitute.

Over the years these concerns found expression in the reports to General Synod of the Temperance and Total Abstinence Society, although these reports were not considered sufficiently important to be preserved or recorded. Later still the Moral Welfare Association, inspired and founded by a bishop returned from China, became the focus of the Church's welfare work. This was accompanied by the work of the Protestant (i.e. Church of Ireland) Orphan Society, which in each diocese assisted those children unfortunate enough to lose their wage-earning parent.

Today those Victorian societies have been subsumed into the Northern Ireland Board of Social Responsibility, which has links with the local boards and committees of the dioceses. It is a board set up by the General Synod of the Church, and is made up of clergy and laity from across Northern Ireland who also represent different interests within the Church, e.g. Mothers' Union, Church Army. The Board of Social Responsibility still provides an adoption service and a counselling service for women with an unplanned pregnancy, putting before them all the options and offering them support rather than directive advice.

A major part of its work involves dealing with problems caused by past secrecy, because in today's more open society adult adoptees are seeking their original birth records and trying to trace their birth parents. The Board also counsels birth mothers who gave up their children when adoption was the only option open to them.

It has a contract with the Royal Victoria Hospital to provide a counselling service for childless couples undergoing medical treatment for infertility. In addition, couples attending other hospitals can approach the Board directly – some research suggests that one in six couples require medical intervention in order to conceive children.

In the past the Board has commented on proposed government legislation for Northern Ireland – e.g. licensing laws, health issues, national lottery or social issues such as the Brooke Clinic.

At present the Board is co-ordinating and subsidising the training of clergy in marriage preparation in each of the dioceses in Northern Ireland. A similar course in bereavement counselling has just commenced. A small amount of money is still available to help needy people, especially children. Referrals are made via the parish clergy to the relevant orphan society.

Most social welfare in the Church of Ireland takes place quietly within the parishes themselves. Some of these may be small ventures such as visiting elderly parishioners – a community service which involves Christian stewardship. Other ventures may involve a whole parish, such as the Shankill Parish (Lurgan) Caring Association. Other groups, such as Clogher Care, Rathcoole Self-Help Group, Ballyclare Community Concern and the Churches Trust in Londonderry, have an interdenominational base. Shankill parish has a cross-community scheme for primary school children.

One indication of a way that the Church of Ireland has altered its attitude in response to changes in society can be seen in the removal from the porches of the Church of Ireland of a notice which was there during the days of *Ne Temere* warning against marriage with Roman Catholics. Instead the greatly increased frequency with which Church of Ireland clergy now assist at mixed marriages in Roman Catholic churches, and Roman Catholic clergy at services in the Church of Ireland, has become apparent. One of the demographic studies issued after the 1991 census in Northern Ireland showed that if a Roman Catholic was involved in a mixed marriage it was much more likely to be with a member of the Church of Ireland than with someone of any other denomination or none.

In recent times the understanding by the Church of Ireland of its own 'identity' has undergone great change. The culture shock of Disestablishment might well have destroyed it, but by a tremendous effort of self-assessment it came to realise that it could maintain itself and hold a recognised and well-respected position as a 'bridge' church in Ireland. Again, at the division of Ireland between two states in 1920–1, the Church was fearful that it would be irrevocably split into two inharmonious groups. It survived both of these shocks, partly by continuing to emphasise its continuity with the faith of former centuries, and proudly claiming its Celtic heritage. Today in the Church of Ireland there is gradually emerging a sense of identity shed of its political trappings, a realisation that what matters is our theological identity, and that this has been for too long submerged under an accretion of social and political characteristics.

The effect of this shedding is also traumatic, particularly as there does not seem to have been enough trouble taken to explain what was happening other than in terms of what was being lost – whether in prestige, in historical claims or in mere numbers.

In view of the changes in Irish life in recent years the Church of Ireland in the Republic needs to demonstrate not that Irish society is being 'protestantised', but that things are happening there which are consonant with its theological views, with its view of authority and with its theological method. In Northern Ireland the Church of Ireland needs to demonstrate that it is not tied to any particular political view, and must constantly be seen as advocating in public and political life the principles of justice, fairness, dialogue, human dignity, reconciliation and friendship.

BIBLIOGRAPHY

Acheson, A., *A History of the Church of Ireland: 1691–1996*, Columba Press/APCK 1997

Akenson, D.H., *The Church of Ireland – Ecclesiastical Reform and Revolution, 1880–1885*, Yale University Press 1971

Alternative Prayer Book of the Church of Ireland, New Haven 1971

Book of Common Prayer

Deane, J.L.B., *Church of Ireland Handbook: A Guide to the Organisation of the Church*, APCK 1982

Ford, A., J. McGuire & K. Milne, *As by Law Established – The Church of Ireland since the Reformation*

Johnston, T.J., J. L. Robinson & R.W. Jackson, *History of the Church of Ireland*, APCK 1953

Journal of the General Synod, annually since 1870. (This gives the text of

Statutes (passed in a form similar to parliamentary bills), resolutions, annual reports of Boards to General Synod and a summary of business done each year.)

MacCarthy, Dr R.B., *Ancient and Modern: A Short History of the Church of Ireland*, Four Courts Press 1995

Milne, Dr Kenneth, *The Church of Ireland – A History*, APCK, n.d.

Neely, Dr W.G., *Be thou my Vision: the Church of Ireland, Past and Present*, APCK 1994

Phillips, W.A., *History of the Church of Ireland*, 3 vols, Oxford University Press 1933–4

White, Stephen Ross, *Authority and Anglicanism*, SCM Press 1996

BIOGRAPHICAL NOTE

This chapter was edited by the REV. CANON R.E. TURNER and MRS E. GIBSON HARRIES, with contributions from the following: Dr W.G. Neely; Dr K. Milne; Rt Rev. S. Poyntz; Dr W. Marshall; Mr R.F. Rankin; Mr I. Slaine; Dr I.M. Ellis.

4

The
Methodist Church in Ireland

GEORGE E. ORR

ORIGINS

The Methodist Church originated in England in the eighteenth century. As the Methodist Catechism puts it, 'The Methodist Church was founded in the eighteenth century, mainly through the instrumentality of John Wesley, who, at a time of gross irreligion in England, having received the assurance of the forgiveness of his sins for Christ's sake, gave himself at the call of God to the spread of scriptural holiness throughout the land.'

John Wesley was born in 1703 in Epworth in Lincolnshire where his father, Samuel, was rector of the local parish church. One of a very large family, he was strongly influenced by his mother, Susannah, a keen disciplinarian, who believed that a child's will had to be broken before right understanding and true spiritual development could ensue. From her example, he developed an ordered and disciplined mode of conduct which persisted throughout his life.

Wesley was ordained as a deacon in the Church of England in 1725 and as a priest in 1728, and lived mainly in Oxford, as student and tutor, until 1735. His time there was characterised by a persistent, methodical search for personal spiritual fulfilment and assurance. As part of this quest, Wesley and some friends established what became known as 'The Holy Club'; another of its many nicknames was the term 'Methodists'.

In 1735, John and Charles Wesley emigrated to the newly settled area of Georgia. In his *Journal*, John Wesley states that their purpose in doing so was 'singly this – to save our souls, to live wholly to the glory of God'. His stay in Georgia was not a happy one, either personally or politically, and in early 1738 he returned to England, dismayed to discover 'that I, who went to America to convert others, was never myself converted to God'.

There followed a few months of intense self-analysis and soul-searching, as he struggled to be assured of his faith. This period reached a climax in his experience of 24 May 1738. As he puts it in his *Journal*:

> In the evening I went very unwillingly to a society in Aldersgate Street, where one was reading Luther's preface to the Epistle to the Romans. About a quarter before nine, while he was describing the change which God works in the heart through faith in Christ, I felt my heart strangely warmed. I felt I did trust in Christ, Christ alone for salvation; and an assurance was given me that he had taken away my sins, even mine, and saved me from the law of sin and death.

Following this experience, Wesley commenced a round of preaching engagements, and by 1741 he had formed several religious societies, visited and supported by him and his brother, Charles, and by a growing band of lay preachers. By 1744 the societies had become so numerous that a formal structure was necessary if some common form of discipline and practice were to emerge; consequently John Wesley convened the first conference, where a small number of invited clergymen and laymen discussed doctrine, discipline and the organisation of the Methodist societies. Despite the formation of these societies, however, Wesley was determined to maintain his connection with the Church of England.

From such tentative and piecemeal beginnings emerged an organisation which was to have a profound influence on England during the remainder of the eighteenth century and beyond.

Before long this influence extended across the Irish Sea. One of Wesley's helpers, John Cennick, preached in Dublin in 1746 and Wesley himself made the first of his twenty-one visits to Ireland in August 1747. During these visits he travelled the length and breadth of the land, preaching in every county, apart from Kerry. He established a number of religious societies, frequently returning to them on subsequent visits to offer encouragement and guidance. He presided over the first Irish Methodist Conference in Limerick in 1752, though it was not until 1782 that an annual Irish Conference was formally instituted. At first, most of the preachers in Ireland were, like Wesley, from England, but gradually, especially towards the end of Wesley's life, Irish preachers became more prominent, some of them, such as Dr Adam Clarke, serving in England. It was an Irish preacher, William Thompson, who presided at the first British Conference, following Wesley's death in 1791.

Both John and Charles Wesley were ordained priests of the Church of

England. Neither wished for any separation from the Church of England but circumstances made a separation inevitable. Initially John Wesley felt that he and his helpers had a merely preaching role, seeking to promulgate the gospel of salvation through faith. He had no wish to usurp the authority of the Church of England in, for example, the administration of the sacraments. For many years members of the Methodist societies in Ireland continued to receive the sacraments in the Church of Ireland, the Established Church. But Wesley offended the Anglican community, in England and Ireland, not only through his enthusiasm but through his condoning of practices such as the use of extempore prayers and sermons, his use of lay preachers and open-air preaching, and, towards the end of his life, his ordination of ministers to carry on his work.

After his death there was a division among his followers in Ireland, then numbering about fourteen thousand. Some wished the Methodist connexion to become an autonomous Church, separate from the Established Church of Ireland. Others wished to retain strong links, even dual membership, with the Established Church. A split finally occurred in 1818: the former became Wesleyan Methodists and the latter Primitive Methodists. The two connexions existed in parallel until after the Disestablishment of the Church of Ireland in 1871. By then the rift had been healed, a disestablished church was less attractive to the Primitive Methodists and the two branches, Wesleyans and Primitives, were united to form the Methodist Connexion in 1878. There was a similar history of division in England but it was not until 1932 that three different Methodist connexions merged to form the present Methodist Church in Great Britain.

The Methodist Church in Ireland includes Methodists from all parts of the island, both the Republic of Ireland and Northern Ireland. It does not have any official political viewpoint and includes within its membership those with a wide divergence of political views and aspirations.

METHODISM IN THE WORLD CHURCH

The Methodist Church in Ireland continues to have close links with Methodism in Great Britain. The British President, as the successor of John Wesley, presides at the Annual Conference of the Irish Church and representatives of the British Conference, both ministerial and lay, also attend; in return, six Irish representatives sit as members of the British Conference and there are strong links between Irish Methodism and departments of the British Church. The Methodist Church in Ireland is a constituent member of the European Methodist Council and of the World Methodist Council, which represents some sixty million Methodists in ninety countries, including within its membership a diversity of Churches with

Wesleyan roots and traditions. Some of these Churches have forms of organisation which differ greatly from Irish Methodism. Those which owe their origin to the American Methodist Church are *episcopal* in form, in that bishops provide spiritual oversight.

The Irish Methodist Church is a member of the Irish Council of Churches, the Council of Churches of Britain and Ireland, the Conference of European Churches and the World Council of Churches.

The Methodist Women's Association, including the Young Women's Association, with a current membership of about four thousand, exists to promote the spiritual growth of its members. The Association is a constituent member of the World Federation of Methodist and Uniting Church Women, a recent ex-President of which is an Irish Methodist.

SURVEY OF THE DENOMINATION TODAY

At the time of Wesley's death in 1791 there were about fourteen thousand members in the various Irish societies or congregations. The membership reached its peak in 1844 when there were forty-four thousand members altogether in the Wesleyan and Primitive Methodist connexions. By 1855, mainly as a consequence of the Irish Famine, it had dropped dramatically to about twenty-seven thousand. The membership remained fairly constant for about one hundred years, reaching a peak of about thirty-two thousand around 1960. In the last thirty-five years there has been a gradual decline in active adult membership to the current figure of just under nineteen thousand. In addition to those who are full members of the Church, there are over eleven thousand junior members and about thirty thousand names on the congregational registers. Figures from the 1991 Northern Ireland census indicate that just under sixty thousand people in the province claim to be Methodists.

Methodism is not, and never has been, evenly distributed throughout the land. It has been strongest in those areas which had a strong Anglican church and weakest in areas where there was a strong Presbyterian influence or few Protestants generally. Traditionally in the Republic of Ireland it has been strong in Dublin, the Midlands, Cork, Limerick (where it flourished among German immigrants) and Sligo. It has not been strong in Connemara, Kerry or the south-east of Ireland. In Northern Ireland the incidence of Methodism has been highest in Belfast and in the area extending west from Belfast to Co. Fermanagh. The northern and eastern counties of Ulster never had a strong Methodist tradition.

There has been a very significant decrease in the Methodist membership in the Republic of Ireland, where many Methodist churches have been closed: currently the total Methodist community in the Republic is about forty-three hundred, of whom about thirty-one hundred are full members.

Since the Second World War there has been a sharp decline in the numbers of Methodists in Belfast. Many inner-city churches have closed or have suffered significant reductions in membership; there are now only a few Methodist churches in north and west Belfast. These decreases are largely due to demographic changes as people have moved to the developing areas of Greater Belfast and to places such as Carrickfergus, Newtown-abbey, Bangor, Comber and Lisburn. As the inner-city churches closed there has been a corresponding development of new churches established within these areas.

Throughout the island of Ireland there are ninety-six chapels or other preaching places where worship is conducted twice on Sunday, one hundred and thirty where there is one service on Sunday and twenty-six where worship is conducted less frequently. There are approximately two hundred ordained ministers, of whom about seventy are retired. Widespread use is made of lay (or local) preachers, particularly in rural areas where there are more preaching places than ministers. There are, in total, about three hundred fully accredited local preachers.

DOCTRINAL POSITION

A formal Statement of Belief is found in the Constitution of the Methodist Church in Ireland as recorded in the Manual of Laws. Part of this statement reads as follows:

> The Methodist Church claims and cherishes its place in the Holy Catholic Church, which is the Body of Christ. It rejoices in the inheritance of the Apostolic faith, and loyally accepts the fundamental principles of the historic creeds and of the Protestant Reformation. It ever remembers that, in the Providence of God, Methodism was raised up to spread scriptural holiness through the land.

> The doctrines of the evangelical faith, which Methodism has held from the beginning, and still holds, are based upon the divine revelation recorded in the Holy Scriptures. The Methodist Church acknowledges this revelation as the supreme rule of faith and practice . . .

> The Conference is the final authority within the Church with regard to all questions concerning the interpretation of its doctrines.

The main thrust of Wesley's preaching can be summed up in four statements:

All need to be saved.
All can be saved.
All can know that they are saved.
All can be saved to the uttermost.

MEMBERSHIP, CHURCH GOVERNMENT AND MINISTRY

In the Constitution of the Methodist Church as recorded in the Manual of Laws, membership of the Church is defined as follows:

> The members of the Methodist Church in Ireland are those who, desiring to be saved from their sins through faith in our Lord Jesus Christ, and to associate themselves with the people of God in Christian fellowship, have been received into full membership in accordance with the rules and regulations of the Conference. The baptised children of such persons also are junior members of the Church, and it is their duty and privilege when they reach the age of discretion to enter into full membership.

When young people reach the age of discretion, around the age of fourteen or fifteen, they are enrolled in a Preparation Class, where they are instructed in the duties and privileges of church membership. Those who confess Jesus Christ as Saviour and Lord, promise to follow in the way of His commandments and submit themselves to the discipline of the Methodist Church are received into full membership, usually at a service of worship; they publicly declare their allegiance to Christ and receive an assurance of welcome and support from the members of their local church.

In addition to those who are full members, there are those who wish to maintain links with the Church, but who are unprepared to accept the conditions of membership. Each society maintains a congregational register containing the names of all those in this category. They are offered pastoral care by the ministers and by lay congregational visitors; many of them are regular worshippers, and actively participate in aspects of the Church's work.

The members of the Church are enrolled in classes, each class being under the pastoral care of a leader. The classes in a locality are grouped into a Society, based on a particular church, the administration of which is the responsibility of the Leaders' Meeting, which consists of the Minister or Ministers and such Society Officers, Class Leaders, Local Preachers and other members as may be appointed under the rules and regulations of the Conference. These local officers include two society stewards, who have responsibility for finance and property, the Sunday School superintendent, secretaries of organisations such as World Development, Home Missions, Overseas Missions and the Methodist Women's Association, together with some others. The term 'society' has been retained from the time of Wesley when groups of people who met for spiritual debate and education were referred to as religious societies.

One or more societies in a larger area constitute a circuit, a term originating from the practice of Wesley and his helpers of undertaking a tour, or circuit, of a number of societies. The administrative body of the circuit is the Quarterly Meeting. Most rural circuits consist of several societies, each with its own church building; a few, mainly urban, circuits consist of a single society. Each circuit has a superintendent minister and in larger circuits there are additional ministers. The membership of the Quarterly Meeting consists of the ministers of the circuit, and various officials appointed under the rules and regulations of the Conference. Each circuit appoints two circuit stewards, a senior and junior, who may not serve in the same office for more than three successive years. They have responsibility for co-ordinating the financial affairs of the circuit, for the maintenance and upkeep of manses and for representing the circuit at the representative session of the District Synod.

Circuits are grouped into Districts; the business is administered by a District Synod which meets twice a year and which is presided over by the Chairman of the District, a minister elected by the members. The District Synod consists of all the ministers, active and retired, from the circuits within the districts, together with the circuit stewards and two lay representatives from every circuit. The District Synod is a committee of the Conference; its function is to give effect to the regulations of Conference within its area and to make recommendations and suggestions for consideration at the ensuing Conference.

The Governing Body of the Methodist Church in Ireland is the Conference. It has two sessions, a ministerial session and a representative session, and meets for about a week in mid-June. In recent years it has met in Dublin, Belfast, Cork, Londonderry, Portadown, Bangor and Enniskillen. The ministerial session consists of 128 ministers; the representative session of the Conference consists of these 128 ministers, together with 128 lay members, elected or appointed according to the Rules and Regulations of the Conference. Each of the seventy-six circuits in Irish Methodism is represented by its superintendent minister and at least one layperson. Traditionally the Irish Conference is presided over by the President of the Methodist Church in Britain. A vice-president is elected from among the Irish ministers and this person becomes the President of the Methodist Church in Ireland for a one-year term.

The ministerial session of the Conference has responsibility for all matters related to the admission, probation, discipline, appointment, expulsion and retirement of ministers; appeals on matters of discipline relating to members of the Church; and all ministerial and pastoral concerns. The representative session of the Conference deals with all matters pertaining to the government and management of the Church, except such as are reserved for the decision of the ministerial session. It receives ministers into full connection on the recommendation of the ministerial session.

The Conference appoints a number of committees which have responsibility for aspects of the Church's work, such as, for example, home missions, overseas missions, world development, property, church extension, education, ministerial training, faith and order, youth and social responsibility. These committees produce reports for discussion and adoption at its representative session.

The office of a minister, according to the Manual of Laws, 'is to win and watch over souls as he that must give account. In order thereto he must feed and guide the flock by regular and faithful preaching, teaching and pastoral visitation.' A candidate for the ministry must be a fully accredited local preacher, whose candidature is supported by his or her superintendent and circuit quarterly meeting; the educational requirement is the minimum academic qualifications for entry to the Diploma in Theology course at Queen's University, Belfast. Following nomination by the superintendent minister, a candidate is required to undertake a range of tests before candidature is approved: these include oral and written examinations, aptitude and personality tests, interviews, and the conducting of a trial service. Approval is recommended by the District Synod and by the Church's Board of Examiners and the final decision is made by Conference.

The normal period of probation is, for a university graduate, five years and, for others, six years. The period spent in Edgehill Theological College, Belfast, a foundation of the Church for the training of its ministers, is normally three years, the remaining period prior to ordination being spent on circuit work. Ordination takes place during the annual Conference. Edgehill College also provides training for laypersons in a range of theological, pastoral and related disciplines.

All appointments of ministers to particular circuits or to other duties are made by Conference. The basis of appointment is the itinerant system, which goes back to Wesley's travelling preachers. The current arrangement is that a minister serves in any post for a maximum of eight years when he/she automatically is allocated to a different circuit. There are a few exceptions to this general rule: tutors in the theological college and superintendents of city missions, for example, usually serve in those posts for longer periods, at the discretion of Conference.

There have been two major recent developments in recruitment for the ministry. Increasingly, since about 1960, there has been a tendency to recruit mature candidates, those in their thirties and, sometimes, forties. The first woman entered the ministry in 1977 and at the time of writing there are six women in the active work.

SACRAMENTS AND ORDINANCES

The Methodist Service Book, for use throughout Great Britain and Ireland, was most recently revised in 1975. A further revision is in progress at the time of writing. It contains guidance for the conduct of worship but as the Preface indicates, 'These forms are not intended, any more than those in early books, to curb creative freedom, but rather to provide norms for its guidance.' The Service Book includes an order of service for the Sacrament of Baptism, both infant and adult, and general directions for the conduct of the Sunday Service, both with and without the Sacrament of Holy Communion.

The children of members, and of others prepared to undertake the requisite promises, are normally baptised in infancy. Their parents promise to provide a Christian home for their children, to help them renounce all evil and put their trust in Jesus Christ as Saviour, and to encourage them to enter into the full membership of the Church and to serve Christ in the world. The congregation promises, on its part, so to maintain the common life of worship and service that the children may grow in grace and in the knowledge and love of God and of His Son, Jesus Christ the Lord. In recent years a minority of parents have chosen not to have their children baptised; they bring them to a service of thanksgiving, but leave the decision about baptism to the person when he or she reaches the age of discretion.

Methodists believe that the risen Christ is present in the Sacrament of Holy Communion. The bread and wine are symbols of his presence. As we participate we obey His command, 'This do in remembrance of me.' The service should be an occasion of joy and celebration as well as for self-examination and repentance.

It is customary for the Lord's Supper to be observed, usually at the morning service, on the first Sunday of the month. Sometimes it is an integral part of the service but most commonly it follows the normal service of worship. Those who wish to participate in the sacrament remain for the service of Holy Communion; others leave before it occurs. Usually the set order of service from the Methodist Service Book, which is closely akin to the services in the various Anglican prayer books, is used, but occasionally the service is less formal. There has been an increasing tendency for the officiating minister to use laypersons, both male and female, in the distribution of the elements of bread and wine.

In addition the Methodist Service Book contains orders of service for the Public Reception into Full Membership, or Confirmation, of those baptised, the Covenant Service (more fully described later), the Marriage Service, the Service for the Burial or Cremation of the Dead and the Service of Ordination of Ministers, together with a lectionary of collects, lessons and psalms for all the services in the church calendar.

In practice, little use is made of the formal liturgy for the Sunday Service, most churches making use of a free form of worship, including extempore prayers. Very limited use is made of the church lectionary.

WORSHIP AND SPIRITUALITY

All that nourishes the moral and religious life, whether free or liturgical prayer, and all that contributes towards a careful analysis of one's walk with God relates to piety or spirituality. In the early Methodist Church, where many of Wesley's followers came from an Anglican background, there was a regard for traditional liturgical patterns which were practised alongside freer, more spontaneous forms of worship. There was, too, a strong emphasis on the cell structure of the class meeting where small groups of believers met regularly, usually weekly, for prayer, study, self-examination, confessional testimony and mutual admonition and encouragement.

The influence of such a background is seen in the practices of today. The Church's formal Order for the Sunday Service is seldom used, free worship and extempore prayers being normal practice. The set liturgical forms are, however, used in the Sacraments of Holy Communion and Baptism and in the Service for the Burial of the Dead. The Methodist Hymnbook, most recently revised in 1983, is a rich source of spiritual challenge and nurture. Alongside the hymns of Charles and John Wesley, many of which are seminal statements of biblical theology, are found those written by contemporary authors. In most churches the worship is enriched by a blend of the ancient and modern. Most members and ministers appreciate the freedom and flexibility which is available within Methodist worship.

The Class Meeting, as originally envisaged, has fallen into disuse, though some vestiges of its practice remain. Most societies have midweek services for prayer and Bible Study and many have other prayer and devotional meetings but, generally, they are not well attended. The members of most societies continue to be organised in classes, under the spiritual oversight of a lay class leader, but the classes no longer meet and the class leader tends merely to carry out the duties of a congregational visitor.

The Covenant Service, a distinctively Methodist ordinance, was instituted by John Wesley. The first formal Covenant Service, in which members renew their Covenant with God, was held in London in 1755. It is now widely used throughout the Methodist Church and has been adopted for use in other Christian communions. The general custom is that the Covenant Service is held once a year, usually on the first Sunday in January. The central moment of the service is when the people make a solemn covenant with God, using the words:

> I am no longer my own, but yours. Put me to what you will, rank me with whom you will; put me to doing, put me to suffering; let me be employed for you or laid aside for you, exalted for you or brought low for you; let me be full, let me be empty; let me have all things, let me have nothing; I freely and wholeheartedly yield all things to your pleasure and disposal. And now, glorious and blessed God, Father, Son, and Holy Spirit, you are mine and I am yours. So be it. And the covenant now made on earth, let it be ratified in heaven. Amen.

There is a strong emphasis on the nurturing, teaching and training of the young. The Sunday School plays a key role in every society and most societies cater for the children of members and for children in the wider community through uniformed organisations such as the Boys' Brigade, Girls' Brigade and Scout Movement or through less formal structures such as the Shell Club for children of primary school age, and Youth Club for those who are older. The Department of Youth and Children's Work co-ordinates the work of youth clubs through IMAYC (the Irish Methodist Association of Youth Clubs), promoting interaction and competition between clubs throughout the island and with their British counterparts. The Department of Youth and Children's Work also sponsors a team of about five young people, who give a year's voluntary service in working with young people in different churches throughout Ireland.

A feature of the church is the degree of lay participation in all aspects of church life. There is a firm belief, which is worked out in practice, in the priesthood of all believers, the doctrine that all believers have a role in ministry. There is a heavy dependence on local preachers, laypersons who conduct worship and preach within the churches of a local area; they make a particular contribution in rural circuits where there are several societies. Laypersons participate fully in the committees of the Conference and make a major contribution to the running of youth organisations, to the organisation of women's work which offers strong support to missions, both at home and overseas, and to the church's work in the wider community.

BUILDINGS AND ARTEFACTS

Although Wesley preferred and endeavoured to erect octagonal buildings the traditional Irish Methodist chapel or preaching place was a rectangular building, seating from one to two hundred people, with a slightly elevated area behind the Communion Rail. Most churches did not even have a vestry; when a vestry did exist it was usually a very small room abutting on to the church. Churches of this type are still found in many rural areas.

As larger churches became necessary, particularly in urban areas, the planners became more ambitious and the buildings more impressive. Some of these church buildings, which seat up to five hundred people, particularly those fronted by classical pillars, appear strong, well proportioned and graceful; such churches usually have a gallery which considerably increases their capacity. To facilitate the participation of all the congregation the pulpit is usually elevated. Hymn singing is normally accompanied by organ music, most large churches having pipe organs. Several of the larger churches have been designated as preserved listed buildings.

The most notable characteristic of Methodist churches generally, particularly those in rural settings, is that they are plain, unadorned and functional. A single, simple church building served the needs of a society which met only for worship and prayer. As churches expanded their activities to include work with youth organisations and recreational pursuits, there was a need for additional accommodation. Most churches, even small rural societies, have a hall to cater for such activities: some have quite elaborate suites of buildings purpose-built to meet their needs; others make use of renovated schoolrooms which became vacant when the responsibility for education was transferred to the state. Some recently built churches are dual-purpose, the building serving both as a worship centre and as a community amenity.

The interior of most Methodist churches is simple and plain, the bareness of the walls being relieved only by the occasional memorial plaque, although many churches have stained-glass windows. At the front of each church, enclosed by the Communion Rail, is the pulpit, behind a simple Communion Table. Usually the pulpit is centrally placed, immediately behind the Communion Table. This arrangement symbolises the centrality in Methodist worship of the Preaching of the Word and of the Sacraments. In some churches a simple cross sits on the Communion Table or hangs on the wall behind the pulpit; a few are beautified by the use of wall hangings but it is customary to find that the only splash of colour is provided by the weekly arrangement of fresh flowers.

CHURCH AND COMMUNITY

Since its inception Methodism has been concerned not only with people's spiritual conditions but with their social welfare. Wesley's message of salvation through grace won a ready response from working men and women – miners, and those engaged in activities engendered by the Industrial Revolution. The conditions in which they lived were a concern to him.

This historical concern for social conditions continues in the current work of the Methodist Church in Ireland. The Council on Social Responsibility examines different aspects of social life, prepares statements and submits them to Conference for debate, approval and adoption. During the past decade declarations have been made on a diverse range of social issues including housing and homelessness, the sexual abuse of children, the terminally ill, the environment, alcohol abuse, community relations in Northern Ireland, abortion and the status of the unborn, business ethics and the role of Methodism in the local community. The Church has produced documents, available upon request from the Secretary of Conference, on subjects such as divorce, family planning, the Methodist position on the use of alcohol, morals and religion, the use of Sunday, euthanasia, the Christian use of leisure, homosexuality and punishment.

The work in some of the city missions goes back for over a century. In these missions (Dublin Central, Belfast Central, East Belfast, Newtownabbey and Londonderry) there is a particular emphasis on making a contribution to solving the social problems facing inner-city areas, problems such as unemployment, broken homes, homelessness, poverty, inadequate housing, violence and crime. Efforts are made to provide opportunities for people to meet to discuss their problems, to provide leisure facilities, to combat the worst effects of poverty and deprivation and to offer support and advice to groups and individuals with particular needs.

As part of this programme, and in other places, the Church has provided children's homes, day and night shelters for the needy, holiday accommodation and sheltered housing, with the approval, and sometimes with the financial support, of the state. In addition to such special projects, many societies offer provision for the community such as youth clubs, drop-in centres, mother and toddler groups, luncheon clubs and leisure facilities. These are open to, and frequently used by, members of other denominations and those who have no church allegiance.

For many years, until education became the responsibility of the state, there were Methodist schools for children of school age. The Methodist contribution to education is recognised by the appointment of Methodist 'transferor's representatives' to the Boards of Governors of controlled primary schools in Northern Ireland. Two grammar schools, Methodist College, Belfast, and Wesley College, Dublin, are under Methodist management, reporting annually to Conference. Methodism was also responsible for the founding over fifty years ago of Gurteen Agricultural College in Co. Tipperary, the aim of which is to prepare young people, Methodists and others, for careers on the land.

The church provides the services of ministers as Chaplains to hospitals, prisons and other institutions throughout the island.

ATTITUDES TO OTHER DENOMINATIONS
AND TO INTER-CHURCH ECUMENICAL ACTIVITY

The following statement on Inter-Church Activity was adopted by the Conference in 1987:

> It is important to understand what Inter-Church activity implies and what it does not. It does not imply that each participating Church accepts all that the others believe. It does not imply that they are actively attempting to 'sink differences' and reach a 'common denominator'. It does imply that each accepts the sincerity and contribution of the others, that all believe that God has a purpose and will for His Church, that each is trying sincerely to discover and do that will, and that each denomination is part of the Body of Christ. In the context of a search for God's will for His Church, joint prayer, study and action to this end and for a better understanding of each other is to be positively encouraged.
>
> In many parts of the country joint worship, prayer and study has become an established fact in relationships with Roman Catholics. This has been a learning and enriching experience for those involved, not least in helping Methodists to a deeper awareness of their own riches and tradition. The basis of sharing is the spirit and mind of Christ.
>
> It is important to recognise that when Roman Catholics extend invitations to participate in joint activities, they most assuredly do not consider that we see everything as they do, nor do they suggest that they approve of all we believe. The issuing and acceptance of such invitations should be regarded

as a declaration of a common recognition of the Christian tradition, in its several forms, as part of our Irish heritage. It should underline a common prayer that the people of this island should come to recognise the Salvation and Lordship of Christ and to know the mind and will of God.

Provided always that these facts are recognised, individuals should be free to exercise their Christian commitment with due regard to all the circumstances . . .

In obedience to Christ and to our Methodist tradition, to act together is a sign of the wholeness of Christ in a broken society. The ultimate loyalty for all Christians is loyalty to Christ and to the standards and values of His Kingdom. When expressed together there is a more effective witness to Christ's healing and reconciling love.

Methodists claim to be 'the friends of all and the enemies of none'. The relationship between the Methodist Church and other Churches is harmonious and friendly. The Church is a member of the Inter-Church Meeting, the forum in which member Churches of the Irish Council of Churches and the Roman Catholic Church meet to discuss issues. The President of the Methodist Church has regular meetings with the leaders of the other mainstream Churches and they co-operate in issuing joint statements on political, social and moral issues. The Methodist Church is deeply concerned with the question of peace and reconciliation in Ireland. Many of its members, both ministerial and lay, have taken leading roles in movements to establish peace during the period of the Northern Ireland Troubles.

In some areas of declining membership, particularly in the Republic of Ireland, and in areas of population growth such as the developing areas around Belfast, the Methodist Church has established formal links with the Church of Ireland and the Presbyterian Church. In Limerick and Galway there is a joint alternating ministry between the Methodist and Presbyterian Churches; in Gorey, Wexford and Enniscorthy there is a similar arrangement. In the west of Ireland, around Sligo, a federation scheme exists with the Presbyterian Church, while at Shannon there is a tripartite arrangement with the Presbyterian Church and the Church of Ireland. In Carnalea, Movilla (Newtownards) and Glencairn the Methodist Church and Church of Ireland co-operated in establishing a building which both churches use. Although morning worship is held at different times there is co-operation in evening services and in some week-night activities. There is co-operation with the Presbyterian Church in places such as Braniel, Knockbreda, Taughmonagh and Lisburn. A joint theological working party with representatives of the Church of Ireland and the Methodist Church has been meeting regularly during the last few years.

Relationships with the Roman Catholic Church vary in different parts of the country. In some areas there are friendly links, which include joint meetings for prayer and worship, either regular or occasional; the closest links are found in parts of the Republic of Ireland and in the Greater Belfast area. A Methodist minister has conducted the Methodist Covenant Service in a Roman Catholic Church and Methodist women share with their counterparts in other Churches, including the Roman Catholic Church, in the Annual Women's World Day of Prayer. Often, however, although good relations exist between the ministers, these have not been developed into formal co-operation between the congregations. Some laypeople, in particular areas, are guarded about promoting joint activities with the Roman Catholic Church.

OTHER SPECIAL FEATURES

The Methodist Church in Ireland is a connexion, not a collection of disparate congregations. Executive decisions are made by Conference, which also determines the allocation of ministers to circuits through the itinerant system. The strong circuits support the weak through a system of financial support. Funds are provided centrally for the work of certain church bodies, such as the Department of Youth and Children's Work, Edgehill Theological College, Church Extension, the Ministers' Retirement Fund and the Candidates' Grants Fund. This money is levied from the circuits through a system of assessment, which is based on the size of membership and the ability to pay. The connexional element provides a strong family ethos in the life of the Church.

There is a marked emphasis on the participation of laypersons, who take a very active role in the various committees of Conference and in Conference itself, where they have equal voting rights with the ministers. Widespread use is made of local preachers, a practice which has been maintained since the time of Wesley. As yet, however, a layperson does not hold office in Conference, unlike Britain where the Vice-President of the Conference is always a layperson.

The Methodist Church in Ireland has had a long history of involvement in Overseas Missions. In the 1760s it was Irish Methodists who founded Methodism in the United States of America. Since then the Church has sent missionaries to all parts of the world, most notably to the Indian subcontinent, China, Africa and the West Indies. Many of these missionaries, both lay and clerical, have served with great distinction, making particular contributions in the fields of medicine and education. Some have received recognition from the governments of the country in which they served and from the British government. At the time of writing four ordained ministers are serving abroad as Mission Partners.

The hymns of John and Charles Wesley are widely used not only in the Methodist Church but in many other Christian communions. As the Preface to the Methodist Hymnbook, published in 1933, states:

> Methodism was born in song. Charles Wesley wrote the first hymns of the Evangelical Revival during the great Whit-suntide of 1738 when his brother and he were 'filled with the Spirit' and from that time onwards Methodists have never ceased to sing. Their characteristic poet is still Charles Wesley.

The hymns of the Wesleys provide a very clear distillation of Methodist theology. Their contribution to Christian hymnody is unique.

BIBLIOGRAPHY

Cole, R. Lee, *History of Methodism in Ireland: 1860–1960*, Belfast: Epworth House 1960

Crookshank, C. Henry, *History of Irish Methodism*, 3 vols, Belfast and London: R.S. Allenson & Allen/T. Woolmen 1885–8

Harper, Steve, *John Wesley's Message for Today*, Zondervan Publishing House 1983

Hurley, Michael, sj (ed.), *John Wesley's Letter to a Roman Catholic*, Belfast: Epworth House 1968

Jeffrey, Fred, *Irish Methodism: An Historical Account of its Tradition, Theology and Influences*, Belfast: Epworth House 1964

A Methodist Catechism, Irish Methodist Department of Youth and Children's Work, Aldersgate House, University Road, Belfast

The Methodist Church in Ireland, *Methodist Belief*, 1992

The Minutes of Conference of the Methodist Church in Ireland (published annually), available from the Book Room, Aldersgate House, University Road, Belfast

Rack, Henry D., *Reasonable Enthusiast, John Wesley and the Rise of Methodism*, London: Epworth Press 1989

Wesley, John, *Journals* (ed. N. Curnock, 1909–16, 8 vols), London: Epworth Press 1909

Wesley, John, *Letters* (ed. John Telford), London: Epworth Press 1931

BIOGRAPHICAL NOTE

Born in Co. Fermanagh in 1934, GEORGE ORR was educated at Portora Royal School and Stranmillis College. He taught in Carr's Glen Primary School, Belfast Royal Academy and Friends' School, Lisburn, before becoming an Inspector with the Department of Education for Northern Ireland. His family has had long-standing links with Methodism. He is a local preacher and leader on the Lisburn and Dromore Circuit where he previously served as Sunday School Superintendent and Circuit Steward. Married, with two children, he has three grandchildren who help occupy his retirement.

5

The
Baptist Union of Ireland

DAVID McMILLAN

DAVID McMILLAN

ORIGINS

The Baptists of today trace their origins to Reformation times. A 'Second Front' (Verduin, p. 11) of reformation was opened up by those who became known as the *Anabaptists* (a term of derision which meant the 're-baptisers'). The term Anabaptist was applied to a broad range of groups who were out of step with the Reformers and included some which indulged in excesses of immorality and sedition. Consequently the label Anabaptist carried a high degree of opprobrium. Heinrich Bullinger, successor to Zwingli at Zurich, was considered an expert on the Anabaptists. He had no hesitation in describing them as 'Satanic'. However, within the various fringe groups at the time of the Reformation were those who paved the way for what are today known as the Baptist Churches.

Many Anabaptists felt there was a need for a return to the kind of simple church order outlined in the New Testament and a more radical break from the inherited structures of the medieval church. European Anabaptists influenced English Separatists of the sixteenth century when John Smyth and Thomas Helwys, who had migrated to Holland to escape persecution, adopted the practice of believers' baptism. Helwys returned to England to establish the first Baptist Church in the British Isles at Spitalfields near London at the beginning of the seventeenth century.

Today there are more than 191 Baptist Unions and Conventions in over two hundred countries of the world. They have a combined membership of more than forty-two million baptised believers.

While we know that by the middle of the seventeenth century Baptist Churches existed in Dublin, Waterford and Cork, the exact circumstances of their foundation are not clear. It was not until the establishment of the Baptist Irish Society in 1814 (an English Baptist Missionary organisation) that Baptist Churches in Ireland began to proliferate.

In the nineteenth century Baptist Churches in Ireland co-operated through the 'Irish Baptist Association', which was affiliated to the 'Baptist Union of Great Britain and Ireland'. In 1895 the Baptist Union of Ireland was established as a separate and independent union of churches and has remained as such to the present day.

ORGANISATION

By the end of the nineteenth century there were some three thousand members in Baptist Churches. Today there are some 109 churches throughout Ireland, 16 in the South and 93 in the North, with a baptised membership in excess of eight thousand people. These churches, which are autonomous and self-governing, continue to co-operate through membership of the Baptist Union of Ireland. The Union is governed by a 'Churches' Council' which meets twice yearly and comprises representatives appointed from each member church of the Union. The Churches' Council appoints an Executive Committee to supervise the work of the Union's departments and officers. The Union's departments include: Youth, Missions, Welfare, Education, Women and Men. There are also two Corporations whose directors administer the legal and financial affairs of the Union. In addition the churches in the North are able to join the Northern Association of Irish Baptist Churches and those in the South are eligible to join the Southern Association of Irish Baptist Churches. The main purposes of these organisations are to foster fellowship between the churches in the two distinct jurisdictions and to engage in evangelism.

As each Baptist church is autonomous and self-governing, the role of the Baptist Union is to serve the churches. It carries no authority other than that delegated to it by the representatives of the churches for the purposes of managing the joint initiatives of the churches as structured in the various departments.

Churches determine and implement their own programmes of activity. Most conduct services on Sundays, midweek prayer and Bible study meetings, Sunday Schools, youth meetings, and meetings or organisations for other specific groups associated with the church. Evangelism is an important aspect of church life and increasingly churches seek to provide services in the community such as parent and toddler groups.

MEMBERSHIP AND LEADERSHIP

Within each local church decision making is exercised by the membership as they seek to discern the mind of the Spirit under the authority of the Scriptures. Men and women are equal members in the church. Having been baptised by immersion as believers and been accepted into membership of the church by vote of the members, they then share in the decision-making process of the church. Each local church would normally elect Deacons to conduct the ongoing business of the church and Elders to provide spiritual leadership and pastoral oversight. Leadership in Irish Baptist Churches tends to be male (some churches have female Deacons) and its appointment is the sole responsibility of the local church.

Pastors are often appointed (by the members of the local church) to serve the church in a pastoral and teaching role. Pastors may be employed on a full-time or part-time basis and may or may not have undertaken formal theological training.

DOCTRINAL POSITION

In 1993 the Baptist Union of Ireland adopted a revised Basis of Doctrine. The first Basis of Doctrine had been agreed in 1895 and was designed to maintain the orthodoxy of the Union and ensure a defence against modernist and liberal theology.

The present 1993 Basis of Doctrine (which is appended) sets out a conservative evangelical and Baptist theological position which churches and those recognised as serving the churches and departments of the Union must affirm. It begins with the Scriptures and affirms their inspiration and inerrancy and 'final authority in all matters of faith and practice'. This view is central to a Baptist understanding of theology. The statement then outlines a summary of belief in regard to God, Jesus Christ, the Holy Spirit, the Devil, Man, Justification, the Future State and Christian Behaviour. There is also a section on the church which sets out a distinctive Baptist understanding of the nature of the Church:

> The local church as a company of baptised believers gathered under the headship of Christ for worship, fellowship, instruction and evangelism; the ordinances of baptism and the Lord's supper;

the significance of baptism:

> baptism being the immersion of believers on profession of their faith in the Lord Jesus Christ and a symbol of their identification with Him in His death, burial and resurrection;

our understanding of Communion:

> the Lord's supper being a remembrance of Christ until He

comes and a renewal of commitment to Him;

and the nature and order of office in the church:

the offices of elder and deacon; the gifts of evangelist and pastor-teacher; the priesthood of all believers and their unity in the Body of Christ; the separation of church and state.

ORDINANCES

Baptists prefer to use the term Ordinances rather than Sacraments when referring to Baptism and the Lord's Supper, reflecting the emphasis on obedience to the express command of the Lord Jesus in their observance.

The Baptist position on baptism

Before he returned to heaven Our Lord gave a command to his disciples: 'Go and make disciples of all nations, baptising them in the name of the Father and of the Son and of the Holy Spirit, and teaching them to obey everything I have commanded you' (Matthew 28:19, 20). This was a divine order (so we call 'baptism' an 'ordinance') and as we read through the Acts of the Apostles we can see how carefully this order was obeyed by the Early Church (cf. Acts 2:38, 41).

Discipleship comes first, then baptism – and that order is always the same in the New Testament. A person becomes a believer first and is then baptised. That is why we talk about **'believers' baptism'**. The Baptist position is sometimes referred to as 'adult baptism', but this term is misleading and inaccurate. It is the profession of faith in Christ and not the age of the candidate which is the determining factor in baptism. In the New Testament a person was not brought to baptism as an infant. A person came to baptism as an expression of his or her commitment to Christ.

Baptism is seen as 'the outward and visible sign of an inward and spiritual grace'. That is a formal, concise way of saying that when believers are baptised they are declaring to everybody, in a visible way, that they know their sins have been forgiven through faith in Jesus and that they are now living a new life. Everybody can see where we stand because we identify ourselves with the Lord Jesus Christ.

The word 'baptism' comes from a Greek word 'baptizō', which means to dip in or under water, to immerse or submerge. So the origin of the word gives a clue as to how a person should be baptised. The significance of baptism further indicates how it ought to be administered. In being baptised believers are identified with the Lord Jesus Christ in what he did to bring about our salvation. The Apostle Paul tells us 'that Christ *died* for our sins according to the scriptures, that he was *buried*, that he was *raised* on the third day according to the scriptures' (1 Corinthians 15:3, 4). These great facts are clearly demonstrated in the ceremony of baptism. Going down into the water symbolises *death*. Going under the water shows that we have been '*buried* with him through baptism into death'. Coming up out of the water is a picture of *resurrection*, 'in order that, just *as Christ was raised from the dead* through the glory of the Father, we too may live *a new life*' (Romans 6:4).

Christians have used rivers, lakes, the sea – anywhere, so long as there is enough water. For convenience (and because of our Irish weather), most Baptist churches have a purpose-built baptistry in the church building. The place should always be public and the ceremony carried out before a congregation who can join in the rejoicing and witness the candidate's confession.

Baptism is a witness to salvation, not a means of bringing it about. In another sense, however, baptism is essential – for two reasons. First, it is essential to be obedient to Our Lord's command in Matthew 28:19, 20. Secondly, baptism is essential to proper discipleship. Our confession in baptism is that we are 'counting ourselves to be dead to sin'. It is our public resolve to live as those who are 'alive to God in Christ Jesus' (Romans 6:11). Baptism is an act of obedience to Christ and a commitment to live for God.

A Baptist view of the Lord's Supper

The Lord's Supper was instituted by Our Lord on the night before his crucifixion. 'He took bread, gave thanks and broke it and gave it to them, saying, "This is my body given for you; do this in remembrance of me." In the same way . . . he took the cup, saying, "This cup is the new covenant in my blood, which is poured out for you." ' (Luke 22:19, 20). In this way Our Lord commanded his followers to remember him and his death for them. The Apostle Paul makes it clear in 1 Corinthians 11:26 that the Lord's Supper is to be observed as a perpetual remembrance of him 'until he comes'.

Various titles are used to describe this ceremony: 'the Lord's Supper' comes from 1 Corinthians 11:20; the term 'communion' from 1 Corinthians 10:16 (Authorised Version); 'the Lord's Table' from 1 Corinthians 10:21; 'the Breaking of Bread' from Acts 2:42.

The service of the Lord's Supper is very simple. After a hymn and a reading from Scripture, there is usually a brief explanation of the scripture by the person leading the service, who is normally the pastor or an elder. He then asks for a prayer of 'thanksgiving' for the bread. Anyone present may be invited to offer that prayer. The bread is then taken to the congregation and each person breaks off a small piece.

The same procedure is carried out for the wine: a prayer of thanksgiving is offered by a member of the congregation and then each person takes a small glass. Different Baptist Churches may vary slightly from this pattern but mostly this is the way it is done.

The Lord's Supper is a simple ceremony in which the bread and the wine are symbols of the body and blood of Our Lord. We do not believe that the bread and wine change into the body and blood of the Lord.

The Lord's Supper is one of the central acts in Christian worship. It is a way of remembering what Christ has done for us and of being strengthened for everyday Christian living; it is for those who see the true worth of the Lord's death for them and have claimed his forgiveness.

Paul's warning in 1 Corinthians 11:27 about eating the bread and drinking the cup of the Lord 'in an unworthy manner' has caused problems for some people who have felt that they must be 'worthy' to come to the Lord's Supper. If they feel themselves to be sinners or weighed down because of failure in the Christian life, they consider themselves 'unworthy' to attend. But the exact opposite is the case. The Lord's Supper is for sinners. To take the bread and the wine in an unworthy manner is to take it without regard to its true worth, to come without a care about your sin or your shame.

What the Apostle Paul makes clear, in 1 Corinthians 11:28, is that 'A man ought to *examine* himself before he eats of the bread and drinks of the cup.' If any sin needs to be forgiven, then things must be put right with the Lord and with other people (1 John 1:9) before coming to the Lord's Table. The Lord's Supper is for sinners who know Christ as Saviour and are seeking to walk in fellowship with him.

Acts 2:46 hints that the early Christians celebrated the Lord's Supper very frequently: 'Every day they continued to meet together in the temple courts. They broke bread in their homes...' Acts 20:7 says: 'On the first day of the week we came together to break bread' – in other words on Sunday. And that is what we do – meeting every Sunday, usually at the end of the morning service.

BUILDINGS

Baptist church buildings tend to be simple and functional. There is little of an ornate nature about the internal decoration and nothing by way of paintings, statues or relics. A particular emphasis will be discernible in that the pulpit will usually be in the centre as will the communion table. This indicates the priority of place given to the Scriptures and the exposition of them in preaching. It also indicates the commitment to meeting around the Lord's Table as part of the regular life of the local church. Some churches may have an open baptistry but most will, for reasons of space, have the baptistry under the pulpit area and uncover it as necessary. Many churches will see their meeting areas as 'multifunctional' and use the same rooms for a variety of activities. Many will have purpose-built facilities for youth work and Sunday Schools.

WORSHIP AND LITURGY

Generally speaking, Baptist Churches do not use a written liturgy. While the format of services may be broadly similar from week to week, prayers are usually offered extemporarily. As a rule, the Church calendar is not followed except at Christmas and Easter. Congregational singing forms an important part of any Baptist meeting and prayer meetings are occasions when people are free to contribute as they feel they should. There is a sense of everyone having an opportunity to contribute to the spiritual life of the church even though leadership and preaching roles are quite clearly defined.

INTER-CHURCH/ECUMENICAL ACTIVITY

'We stand on our Basis of Doctrine free and independent of all outside bodies.' This declaration was made by the Union Council in September 1951 (Thompson, p. 147) and it represents the continued position of the Baptist Union of Ireland. Concerned to maintain its conservative theological ethos, the Union is not a member of, or affiliated to, any other religious body – Baptist or otherwise. In 1991 an amendment to the Constitution and Rules of the Union was agreed which states: 'The objects of the Union are: ... The fostering of spiritual unity (in distinction from every form of false ecumenism) with all who love our Lord Jesus Christ in sincerity and who are faithful to his Gospel.' This amendment was to ensure that there would be no misunderstanding as to the non-ecumenical nature of the Baptist Union. The Union is not a member of any ecumenical council or organisation.

Given the fact that the Baptist Union is an association of independent Baptist Churches throughout Ireland which have distinct and sometimes diverse emphases and attitudes, the Officers of the Union are not in a position to speak on behalf of the churches unless specifically mandated to do so by the Churches' Council. Consequently it is uncommon to hear statements in the media issued by the offices of the Baptist Union of Ireland. It is not possible for the Secretary of the Baptist Union to commit Baptists to a particular opinion or course of action on any social, political or contentious matter. This is not to say that many Baptists will not be involved in political life, the voluntary sector or forms of social action.

CONCLUSION

With a background experience of rejection and persecution Baptists worldwide have recognised the importance of the promotion of the principles of religious liberty and liberty of conscience. They have also maintained a commitment to the principle of the separation of Church and state – being convinced that while both are ordained by God it is not the duty of either to rule the other.

Concluding his *Short History* of the Baptist Union of Ireland Joshua Thompson says:

> Irish Baptists are not ashamed of their stress on the indispensable Gospel, of their reverence for the Holy Scriptures, of their pietism, of their stand for scriptural separation. In some respects they may have pressed some aspects of these features to extremes, and may still have to find more felicitous ways of expressing their convictions. Nevertheless, they have maintained their principles over the past century often in circumstances of extreme difficulty. They themselves are the first to acknowledge that their failures are due to human weakness, and that their successes flow from the grace of God . . . the goals of the churches forming the BUI are still evangelisation, fellowship, co-operation, training and spiritual unity among and through those churches. They are still valid as the churches enter the twenty-first century still awaiting the second advent of our Lord Jesus Christ (pp. 155–6).

APPENDIX

Baptist Union Basis of Doctrine

Each member of the Union shall affirm the following doctrines which are commonly believed among us:

THE SCRIPTURES
The verbal inspiration and total inerrancy of the Holy Scriptures of the Old and New Testaments as originally given by God; their sole sufficiency and final authority on all matters of faith and practice.

GOD

One God in three persons, the Holy Trinity, co–eternal, sovereign and active in creation, providence and redemption.

THE LORD JESUS CHRIST

The essential deity and perfect humanity of our Lord Jesus Christ, the only mediator between God and men; His virgin birth, sinless life and sacrificial death on the cross as the only substitute for sinners; His burial, bodily resurrection and ascension to heaven; His high priestly ministry and personal return.

THE HOLY SPIRIT

The work of the Holy Spirit in regenerating the sinner and indwelling, sanctifying and empowering the believer.

THE DEVIL

The personality of the devil; his evil activity and final doom.

MAN

The creation of man in the image of God; the entrance of sin through Adam's disobedience; the fallen and totally depraved state of all men; their subjection to God's wrath and condemnation; their responsibility to repent and believe the Gospel.

JUSTIFICATION

The justification of the sinner by God's grace through faith alone in the Lord Jesus Christ; the eternal security of the believer.

THE CHURCH

The local church as a company of baptised believers gathered under the headship of Christ for worship, fellowship, instruction and evangelism; the ordinances of baptism and the Lord's supper:

> baptism being the immersion of believers on profession of their faith in the Lord Jesus Christ and a symbol of their identification with Him in His death, burial and resurrection; the Lord's supper being a remembrance of Christ until He comes and a renewal of commitment to Him; the offices of elder and deacon; the gifts of evangelist and pastor–teacher; the priesthood of all believers and their unity in the Body of Christ; the separation of church and state.

THE FUTURE STATE

The unconditional immortality of the soul; the resurrection of the body; the eternal joy in heaven for the believer; the conscious eternal punishment in hell of those who die impenitent.

CHRISTIAN BEHAVIOUR

The responsibility of all believers to obey and serve the Lord and to live self-controlled, upright and godly lives; the duty of each church to exercise godly discipline in a loving and caring fashion.

BIBLIOGRAPHY

Baptists: Who are they? (educational pack), Baptist Union of Ireland, 117 Lisburn Road, Belfast, BT9 7AF
Hulse, E., *An Introduction to the Baptists*, Carey Publications Ltd 1973
Thompson, J., *Century of Grace: The Baptist Union of Ireland: A Short History 1895–1995*, Baptist Union of Ireland 1995
Verduin, L., *The Reformers and their Stepchildren*, Baker Book House 1964

BIOGRAPHICAL NOTE

DAVID McMILLAN is Pastor of Windsor Baptist Church in Belfast, a member church of the Baptist Union of Ireland. For ten years he served as the Pastor of Newry Baptist Church after training at the Irish Baptist College. David comes originally from east Belfast, is married and has two teenage daughters. He often addresses school groups and RE teachers exploring Baptist beliefs. He has written this chapter in a personal capacity and not on behalf of the Baptist Union of Ireland.

6

The
Christian Brethren

DAVID CURRIE

ORIGINS

Around 1825 there was a medical student in Dublin called Edward Cronin who enjoyed fellowship in various local churches during his student days at Trinity College. After he graduated he was put under severe pressure by these same churches to become a member of one of them. Cronin could not reconcile their narrow attitudes to the freedom which he believed was the heritage of all those who as Christians owed their primary allegiance to Jesus Christ. There were others who were also concerned at the sectarian attitudes prevalent at that time, attitudes which ensured that attendance at and participation in Communion was a matter of satisfying the particular requirements of each church. Those who did not satisfy such requirements were effectively banned from Communion with their fellow believers. Very soon Cronin and a few friends began to meet in a simple way to remember the Lord in 'the Breaking of Bread', i.e. in a communion service. They had no thoughts at that time of forming a new church or yet another denomination. Their sole purpose was to have fellowship with other Christians, most of whom retained their membership of their particular denomination and who included clergymen who met with Cronin and others before proceeding to conduct the service in their own church.

At the same time as these happenings in Dublin there is evidence of a great desire to return to New Testament simplicity of worship in other parts of the world, including the British Isles. Foremost in these parallel developments were British Guiana in South America, Bristol and Plymouth (hence the name Plymouth Brethren – almost universally disliked and rejected by Christian Brethren today). There is no evidence that these diverse developments were initially aware of each other. They soon became aware, and finding striking similarities in their beliefs relating to worship and church order concluded that this movement was indeed the work of the Holy Spirit calling the Christian Church back to a pattern of living more akin to that of the first-century Church as portrayed in the New Testament.

There was another important development running in parallel with this spontaneous emergence of groups of Christians who were expressing their desire for unfettered fellowship with one another. This was the Oxford Movement, where at the highest level of Anglican thinking, questions were being asked relative to the church/state dichotomy. Best-known of these men was J.H. Newman, who asked the most fundamental question of all – 'What are our beliefs based on?' His search for an answer to this question led him to reject all confessions and eventually to embrace Roman Catholic teaching in 1845. Two other prominent Anglicans following the same line of questioning came to a very different conclusion. Anthony Norris Groves and Benjamin Wills Newton came to believe that it was not only possible but desirable to reach back beyond all established churches and creeds and to recapture the simplicity and spontaneity of the Early Church, including its order and practice. Taking the New Testament books as being the most authoritative documents of all, they studied these to find church order and practice. Both men became powerful influences in the development of a distinctly Brethren form of worship, Groves in the Middle East and India, Newton in England.

It was almost inevitable that new churches would emerge – the Brethren still vehemently deny that they are a denomination. The next twenty years was to see a spectacular growth of churches with a distinctly Brethren ethos. Many individuals seceded from established congregations, entire congregations came over, often led by their pastor or clergyman. New churches were established often as the outcome of itinerant evangelism by the Brethren.

The Movement had become a potent force in church life, particularly in the English-speaking world and in France and Switzerland. However, in 1847 it divided. The issue which tore it apart was, ironically, that of openness of fellowship.

One group, led by an ex-Church of Ireland clergyman originally from Co. Wicklow, insisted that it was legitimate to establish doctrinal criteria by which to test the orthodoxy or otherwise of members and indeed of individual churches. Failure to pass this test meant excommunication from one's fellow believers and from participation in a service of Communion. This group was led by John Nelson Darby. They eventually became known as either Darbyites or, more often, *Exclusive Brethren*. Their subsequent history is regarded by the mainstream Brethren as a tragic travesty of everything that Cronin and other founders of the Movement stood for. If early Brethren history could be described as a flight from sectarianism then the Exclusive Brethren represent a complete reversal of this and are today one of the most closed and rigid sects in the Christian Church.

All that follows in this chapter describes the other branch of the Brethren Movement. They are known variously as Christian Brethren, Open Brethren or quite simply Brethren. Many prefer to be called Christians or Believers, seeking thereby to emphasise the unity of fellowship for which they stand. (For clarity they will now be referred to as Brethren.)

NUMBERS AND DISTRIBUTION

It is notoriously difficult to obtain accurate numbers for the Brethren. Because of the preference of many to be known as Christians or Believers, even in filling in a government census form they will eschew the use of the name Brethren. There are about one hundred and sixty Brethren churches in Northern Ireland and twenty in the Republic of Ireland. Some are quite small with perhaps thirty members while the largest would have six hundred members. Altogether there are probably around twelve thousand Brethren in Ireland.

BASIS OF AUTHORITY

By 1848 the Brethren had already firmed up much of the thinking which was to make them a distinctive movement within mainstream Christianity. They sought by careful Bible study to base all of their practices on the Bible alone. They were, and are, firmly in the historical line of the Reformation churches, especially in regarding the Bible as the sole rule of faith and practice.

Perhaps the main difference at this stage between the Brethren and the longer-established Churches and indeed between the Brethren and those who eventually formed the Exclusive Brethren was the issue of who could be a member of a Brethren church (often called by preference an Assembly). This position is perhaps best expressed by George Müller, associated with the Brethren at Bristol: 'That we ought to receive all whom Christ has received, irrespective of the measure of grace or knowledge they have attained unto.'

This statement is based on Romans 15:7: 'Accept one another then, just as Christ accepted you, in order to bring praise to God.' With this as a basic undergirding principle it is easy to see why the Brethren did not and could not accept the Darby position but insisted in preserving the openness in which they passionately believed.

KEY PRACTICES AND BELIEFS

The Brethren have a number of practices which are their distinguishing marks to the present. They would contend that all of these are clearly taught in the Bible and indeed that these things are the hallmarks of any church seeking to operate on first-century biblical principles. Brethren practices are therefore derived from what they perceive to be the biblical methods of operation for a church.

Organisation and leadership

- Each local church is responsible and accountable to God alone. No church or group of churches can have any jurisdiction over any other church. There is no central organisation to which all Brethren churches subscribe or owe allegiance – each church is completely autonomous.
- There is no ordained Ministry. The Brethren believe that the Holy Spirit gives the gifts of Teaching, Evangelism, Administration, et cetera to individuals within each church and they are free to develop their particular gift for the benefit of all the members.
- Each church is governed by a group of Elders, all male, who see Eldership as a voluntary service which they give to the local church. They derive their position from a recognition by the membership that they have the necessary spiritual qualities to fulfil this role.

Membership

- Membership is open to all those who have a personal faith in Jesus Christ as Saviour and Lord. Members would be encouraged to be involved in personal Bible study and prayer.

Communion

- There is a very strong emphasis on the importance of the Communion service, more often called the Breaking of Bread. This normally takes place weekly and the worship is not pre-arranged but spontaneous in that various members would contribute a hymn, a prayer, a Scripture reading or a short homily.

Baptism

- The mode of Baptism practised is adult Baptism by full immersion.

In the light of comments made above about the Exclusive Brethren, it might seem that the Christian Brethren are therefore a homogeneous group. To some extent they are but the emphasis on autonomy leads to a number of interesting variations in practices and beliefs. Two of these are fairly widespread, identifiable and significant:

1. *Baptism.* As mentioned above, the mode of Baptism is by immersion. This is only administered to those who are prepared to state publicly their personal faith in Jesus Christ as Saviour and Lord. Within Brethren there are two quite different attitudes to Baptism. Many insist that Baptism is a prerequisite to full membership of the church and will exclude from Communion those who have not been baptised in the appropriate manner. This would be the majority view among Brethren in Northern Ireland. The others, while equally committed to the same form of Baptism, do not make it an absolute requirement for either fellowship or Communion.

2. *Inter-church fellowship.* The same two groups would also differ in their attitudes to inviting teachers and pastors from other denominations to participate in Ministry to a Brethren congregation. Those with the stricter view on Baptism would also take a more 'in-house' attitude to visiting speakers and invite only those from other Brethren churches. The second group would invite itinerant teachers from a wide variety of denominations and would foster links with other churches who hold similar views on important issues such as Evangelism.

STATEMENT OF BELIEFS

The strong emphasis on autonomy means that there is no written statement of what Brethren believe. If asked, they will state that they are seeking to live their personal and church life according to the pattern laid down in the New Testament.

Appended is a statement of *What We Believe* as issued by one Brethren church in Belfast, namely Crescent Church in University Road. This church too believes in autonomy and therefore its statement does not in any way purport to be a statement of what all Brethren believe. It would nevertheless be a fair reflection of the main doctrines held by Brethren.

INTER-CHURCH INVOLVEMENTS

The same emphasis on autonomy means that virtually no Brethren would be involved in the ecumenical movement. Many would, however, be actively involved in such enterprises as the Billy Graham campaigns, the Gideon movement, TEAR Fund, Leprosy Mission and similar groups.

BUILDINGS

The strong emphasis placed on simplicity of worship by those most involved in the founding of the movement has had a lasting effect on the types of buildings used by the Brethren. Most buildings are fairly basic, perhaps best described as functional. Many are quite small, holding about two hundred. Seating is usually movable thus enabling multiple use of the space for different services and activities. On Sunday morning the seats would be arranged in an open square around a table on which would be placed the bread and wine. This arrangement has significance as it portrays the centrality of place accorded to the risen Christ, who is believed to be present on the basis of Matthew 18:20: 'For where two or three come together in my name, there am I with them.' This service is at the very heart of Brethren worship. Their attitude to buildings is such that they have no problems with the idea of rearranging the furniture after the Breaking of Bread service to accommodate a Sunday School in the afternoon. The building is not held to be Sacred or Consecrated in any way.

The most common name for a Brethren church is Gospel Hall, usually prefixed by the name of the street or road on which it is situated. In recent years there has been a marked change in this pattern. Many Brethren now recognise that if they wish to attract unchurched people to their services then a more attractive form of building may be desirable. Consequently any extensions or new buildings tend to be more elaborate and comfortable. There is also a tendency to rename the Gospel Hall as an Evangelical Church.

OUTREACH AND MISSION

It will have been evident that the Brethren are overtly Evangelical. The pattern for this was set right from the start of the movement by the members of the various churches using every means at their disposal to spread the Gospel in their immediate areas. As converts were made and new churches formed they in turn became centres of evangelical outreach. Traditional meetings were used as were cottage and open-air meetings. In many ways the early years of the Brethren Movement are reminiscent of the early years of the Methodists.

Perhaps the outstanding feature of the Movement has been their commitment to overseas mission. Brethren missionaries and Brethren churches are to be found worldwide. The funding of these missions again reflects a typically Brethren attitude, in that just as there is no central organisation for the Brethren churches, neither is there a central Missionary society. Each missionary depends for finance on their home church, supplemented by unsolicited financial support from individuals. This is known as 'living by faith' and stems from a deeply held belief that God can and does move in the hearts of his people to share in the support of those who have gone to other countries with the Gospel. The number of Brethren missionaries is much higher than would be expected from what is in effect a relatively small group.

APPENDIX

What We Believe

A Statement issued by the Crescent Church, Belfast, in *Worshipping and Serving*:

1. The Holy Scriptures (the Bible), as originally given, are inspired by God. Through them God speaks to us and every word is infallible. They are our only authority for what we believe and practise.

2. There is only one God, revealed in the Bible as three persons: the Father, the Son and the Holy Spirit. These three are one God co-eternal and co-equal.

3. The Lord Jesus Christ, the Son of God, became man, being conceived by the Holy Spirit and born of the virgin Mary. He is perfect eternal God, and perfect sinless man.

4. Man, created by God in His image and likeness, sinned. Universal sinfulness and guilt renders everyone subject to God's righteous wrath and condemnation.

5. The death of the Lord Jesus Christ upon the cross was on behalf of sinners and satisfied the claims of God against sin. Through the sacrificial death of the Lord Jesus Christ there is redemption from the guilt, penalty and power of sin. He is the only Mediator between God and man.

6. On the third day after His crucifixion the Lord Jesus Christ was raised in His physical body from the dead. He was seen alive by His disciples during the forty days after His resurrection and in His risen, glorified body He ascended into heaven to the right hand of God the Father.

7. The Lord Jesus Christ will personally return to raise the dead in Christ and they together with living believers will be caught up to meet Him in the air.

8. Salvation is not by works but through repentance for sins and faith in Jesus Christ the Son of God alone. By an act of God's undeserved

mercy the believing sinner is forgiven all his sins, is justified before God and accepted as righteous in His sight.

9. There will be a final judgment when those who have not been saved and whose names are not found in the book of life will suffer eternal punishment.

10. The Holy Spirit convinces individuals of their sin and leads to faith in Christ. He indwells every believer, producing in them increasing likeness to Christ in character and behaviour, empowering them for witness in the world.

11. There is one universal Church, the body of Christ. Into this body, of which the Lord Jesus Christ is Head, all believers have been baptised in the Holy Spirit.

12. In the New Testament, a local church consisted of all believers in a given locality; but now there is practically no complete expression of this principle. Nevertheless, in accordance with the teaching of the New Testament, believers may meet together and function as an independent, self-governing church, recognising the authority of God's Word, the Lordship of Christ and the sovereignty of the Holy Spirit. It will give expression to the teachings of the New Testament in its worship, doctrine and service.

BIBLIOGRAPHY

Beattie, David J., *Brethren – The Story of a Great Recovery*, Kilmarnock: John Ritchie Ltd 1944

Broadbent, E.H., *The Pilgrim Church*, London: Pickering & Inglis 1931

Rowden, Harold H., *The Origins of the Brethren: 1825–1850*, London: Pickering & Inglis 1967

Tatford, Frederick A., *That the World May Know*, 10 vols., Bath: Echoes of Service 1982. (Each of the ten volumes has a useful appendix entitled 'Who are the Brethren?' The articles are contributed by ten different modern writers and give a broad spectrum of views. 'Echoes of Service' is an organisation founded, funded and supported by Brethren churches worldwide to support the various needs of missionaries.)

Veitch, Thomas S., *The Story of the Brethren Movement*, London: Pickering & Inglis *c.* 1935

Walker, William, 'The New Testament Church: Past, Present & Future' in *Steward Ministries in India* (ed. J. Samuel), Madras: Steward Publications 1978

BIOGRAPHICAL NOTE

DAVID CURRIE (BA, DASE) grew up in east Belfast in traditional Brethren circles, gradually moving to a more open viewpoint, best stated as 'Accept one another, then, just as Christ accepted you . . .' (Romans 15:7). He and his wife, Iris, both retired early from education and are actively involved along with their family in Crescent Church, University Road, Belfast. He is currently chairman of Elders there and is a former Brethren Chaplain at Queen's University and Stranmillis College.

7

The
Free Presbyterian Church of Ulster

IAN R.K. PAISLEY

ORIGINS

On St Patrick's Day, 1951, a new biblical witness for Christ was born in the village of Crossgar, Co. Down, Northern Ireland. As a result of the high-handed actions of the Presbytery of Down, the elders of the local Presbyterian church were prohibited from using their church hall for a gospel mission. When the elders refused to acquiesce in the decision, they were immediately suspended. All this took place less than twenty-four hours before the mission was due to commence. Those elders had no doubt as to their duty. They could not go back to their church without denying or compromising the gospel. That was something they refused to do. So they decided to leave a denomination that had no difficulty permitting dances and parties of various kinds in its church halls but which, in this case, banned the gospel of Jesus Christ.

They proceeded with the help of Rev. Ian R.K. Paisley, their guest evangelist, and Rev. George Stears, a Presbyterian minister who had laboured for the Lord for some years in Brazil, to form the Presbytery of the Free Presbyterian Church of Ulster. The Crossgar congregation was soon joined by the Ravenhill congregation of which Dr Paisley was the minister. This congregation had some years before seceded from the Ravenhill congregation of the Irish Presbyterian Church. So, like the Relief Presbyterian Church in Scotland, the Free Presbyterian Church of Ulster had two sources. In the months that followed, two more congregations sprang up as the result of Dr Paisley's evangelism and secessions from the Irish Presbyterian Church. The growth of the new church continued through the years until its witness spread to all the counties of Northern Ireland.

Presbyterian

The new church was Presbyterian in doctrine and government, though it departed from the usual Presbyterian policy by recognising that baptism is variously understood by good men equally committed to Scripture. This being so, the Free Presbyterian Church believed that Christians should not be kept apart by baptismal views, as long as no one held to baptismal regeneration. It was called *Free Presbyterian* to indicate its liberty from any affiliation with a liberal church hierarchy or organisation.

Protestant

The church was unashamedly Protestant. It gladly identified with the great Protestant Reformers. Throughout its history it has stood opposed to the ecumenical movement's efforts to promote union with the Church of Rome, because that church still holds to every dogma that caused the Reformation in the first place. In theology the church is Reformed. It stands foursquare in the great Geneva tradition of Calvin, Knox, the English and American Puritans, and some of the most used revival preachers in history.

Evangelistic

The church has always tied its Calvinism to evangelism. It is a praying church with a burden for the salvation of sinners. Its growth has been through unremitting evangelistic outreach, preaching the gospel 'in season, out of season'.

Emphasis on prayer

Great prayer meetings have been the secret of the church's life. We do not merely pay lip service to prayer. We recognise that we have a long way to go in the experience of power in prayer, but we are seeking to follow on to know the Lord in prayer that will be gloriously effective.

AN INTERNATIONAL FELLOWSHIP

Today there are about one hundred Free Presbyterian churches and extensions in various parts of the world: in all of the United Kingdom (Northern Ireland, England, Scotland and Wales), the Irish Republic, Australia, Canada, USA, Germany, Jamaica and Spain. The spirit of family fellowship among all these far-flung churches is deep and sweet. The church has also missionary work in Kenya. Its associated radio ministry, *Let the Bible Speak*, is heard around the world. It is in fraternal relations with the Orthodox Presbyterian Church of the Cameroon and a group of

Reformed Churches in Spain. In the United Kingdom and the Irish Republic the church is in membership with the *British Council of Protestant Christian Churches*. In America our churches are in membership of the *American Council of Christian Churches*. Its official organ is the *Revivalist*, published eleven times a year, and its youth magazine, *Truth for Youth*, is bimonthly. Its ministerial training college is the Whitefield College of the Bible, situated in Banbridge, Northern Ireland, with extensions in Greenville, South Carolina and Toronto, Canada.

In Northern Ireland the Free Presbyterian Church soon became the largest of the smaller Presbyterian Churches, having, in the last government census, a greater number of members than the other three smaller Presbyterian Churches put together, the Reformed Presbyterian, the Non-Subscribing Presbyterian and the Evangelical Presbyterian.

ARTICLES OF FAITH

1. The Absolute Authority and Divine Verbal Inspiration of the Old and New Testaments as the Word of God.

2. There is but one living and true God, and in the Godhead there are three Persons, equal in power and glory, God the Father, God the Son, and God the Holy Ghost.

3. The Eternal Sonship, Virgin Birth, and Deity of our Lord and Saviour Jesus Christ.

4. The personality of God the Holy Spirit, and the absolute necessity of His work in Regeneration and Sanctification, and His Infilling of the Indwelt Believer for power to live and witness for Christ.

5. The Substitutionary Death of the Lord Jesus Christ and His Resurrection as the only way of Salvation through Faith.

6. God has appointed, besides the Word and Prayer, the Sacraments of Baptism and the Lord's Supper.

(a) *Baptism* – The Free Presbyterian Church of Ulster, under Christ the Great King and Head of the Church, realising that bitter controversy raging around the mode and proper subjects of the ordinance of Christian Baptism has divided the Body of Christ when that Body should have been united in Christian love and Holy Ghost power to stem the onslaughts and hell-inspired assaults of modernism, hereby affirms that each member of the Free Presbyterian Church shall have liberty to decide for himself which course to adopt on these controverted issues, each member giving due honour in love to the views held by differing brethren, but none espousing the error of baptismal regeneration.

(b) *The Lord's Supper* — The Lord's Supper has been appointed by our Lord
for Remembrance of Him in His work as Saviour. Its purpose to the
child of God is for strengthening, and putting of a visible difference
between the redeemed and the unregenerate. This Sacrament will be
observed once each month in every Free Presbyterian Congregation,
or more frequently as each local congregation shall decide.

7.   The visible and personal return of our Lord Jesus Christ.

8.   These Articles, together with the *Larger Catechism*, the *Shorter
Catechism*, and the *Westminster Confession of Faith*, form the
Subordinate Standards of the Free Presbyterian Church.

Presbyterian beliefs

Presbyterian refers basically to a form of theology and of church govern-
ment. The form of theology is that exposition of Scripture which is called
'Reformed'. It sees the Bible as a basic unity, with both the Old and the
New Testaments declaring the one triune God, one Saviour from sin, one
way of salvation, and one covenant of grace. Presbyterians see all of
Scripture falling under two covenants, the covenant of works and the
gospel covenant of mercy. The covenant of works was made by God with
Adam prior to the fall (Genesis 2:16–17; Hosea 6:7, margin). After the fall
God never set before men the possibility of eternal salvation by works. We
reject the notion that God placed fallen man under a series of probations.
Man's probation ended with the fall. After that he could be saved only by
grace without any merit arising from his own works. Thus, throughout
Scripture the Lord presents us with a covenant of mercy that sets forth His
sovereign terms for saving sinners. He has administered that covenant in
various ways, progressively leading up to the full revelation of His grace in
the incarnation and atonement of His Son. Galatians 3 and Romans 4
show that Old and New Testament believers are seen by God in the same
covenant. Romans 11 makes the same point under the figure of the olive
tree. We are grafted into the tree of the Old Testament church. In both
Testaments God's people are saved on the ground of the righteousness of
Christ received by faith (Romans 4:1–13; 5:1). It is a mistake to think that
in the Old Testament God's people were saved by their personal obedience. The law always exposes sin and condemned even the most religious
Jews (Romans 7:7–11), but it was attended by a ceremonial code of sacrifice that prefigured the coming once-for-all sacrifice of Christ. Even
during the period from Moses to Christ, God saved men only by free grace
through faith. Hebrews 11 shows just how real and powerful the faith of

the Old Testament saints was.

We believe it is vital for us today to maintain this basic unity of Scripture. It opens up the Old Testament in a wonderful way and enables us to see Christ as its central message – and, after all, He saw Himself in the same way (Luke 24:27; John 5:39).

Thus, true Presbyterianism maintains the centrality and all-sufficiency of Christ in all its preaching. It sees in Him the perfect revelation of God to men (John 1:18; Matthew 11:27). It refuses to deal with such subjects as God's predestination, or Christ's particular redemption of His people by His blood, or man's moral responsibility, in mere philosophical terms. These are parts of God's revelation of grace in Christ, and it is in the context of His person and work that we must handle these truths. Hence our theology is as biblically warm as it is biblically orthodox. Historic Presbyterianism is biblically Fundamentalist believing that no foundation can any man lay but Jesus Christ (1 Corinthians 1:11).

CHURCH GOVERNMENT AND MINISTRY

Presbyterian also has special reference to a form of church government that seeks to follow Scripture as closely as possible. It differs from Independency in that it works on the biblical principle of the *inter*dependency of local congregations. It differs from Episcopacy in that it has no clerical hierarchy.

In the government of a local Presbyterian church, the spiritual oversight is committed to elders, or *presbyters* (which is merely the Greek word for 'elders' in an Anglicised form). We believe that in the New Testament the apostles committed the administration of church ordinances and the regulation of church affairs to office-bearers, not to a clerical hierarchy or to the congregation at large (1 Peter 5:1–4). Elders had the responsibility for the spiritual affairs, while deacons had special responsibility for the church's temporal affairs (Acts 6).

In Presbyterianism, as in Scripture (1 Timothy 5:17), some elders are ruling elders, and some are ruling and teaching elders. In other words, a minister or preacher is joined by men appointed and ordained (Titus 1:5) to form the spiritual oversight of a local church. These and all other office-bearers are elected by the vote of the communicant members of the church (Acts 1 and 6).

There is clear evidence in Acts 15 that the final court of appeal in church issues does not lie in the local congregation but in a body of elders representing various associated congregations. As Presbyterians we recognise the role of the united eldership of a number of associated congregations as a court of appeal for matters originating in a local church. This presbytery, as it is called, expresses the unity of churches with a common doctrine banded together for mutual support and prayer, for the protection of their common testimony, and for joint effort to spread the gospel and establish new churches.

As Presbyterians we do not deny the legitimacy of churches that disagree with us on church government, but we do believe that the polity we practise is 'founded on and agreeable to the Word of God', to use the language of the Scottish ordination formula.

THE PLACE OF WOMEN IN THE CHURCH

A burning question for many today is whether or not women may be ordained to the ministry of the church. It is often stated that any denial of such a right is demeaning to women and denies their equality with men in Christ. Requiring an all-male ministry and eldership is portrayed as sexism at its worst. More and more churches are sweeping away all restrictions on a woman exercising any part of the ministry of the church, whether in a preaching or a pastoral (including governmental) role. The Free Presbyterian Church takes the biblical position of historic Christianity on this issue and is therefore at variance with the modern trend.

The New Testament shows that women participated in the public prayer meetings of the church (Acts 1:14). As well as praying they prophesied. We are expressly told that Philip's four daughters did so (Acts 21:9). Paul tells the Corinthians that any woman praying or prophesying with her head uncovered dishonours her head (1 Corinthians 11:5) yet in the very same epistle he goes on to make this emphatic statement: 'Let your women keep silence in the churches: for it is not permitted unto them to speak; but they are commanded to be under obedience, as also saith the law...It is a shame for women to speak in the church' (1 Corinthians 14:34, 35).

There are those who do not scruple to say that Paul here contradicts himself. Such people deny the basis of Christianity. If we cannot trust an inspired apostle of Christ at this point, how can we trust him in any other statement of doctrine or practice? Paul made no mistake on this issue. Clearly, from all he says, there are times and places in which a woman may speak and others in which she may not. In 1 Timothy 2:12 he makes it clear what should govern the decision as to when and where it is proper or improper for a woman to speak: 'I suffer not a woman to teach, nor to usurp authority over the man, but to be in silence.' Here is the key. A woman is not permitted a pastoral or governmental position over men in a New Testament church. No ministry that places her in such a position is open to her. There is no question but that a woman may be every bit as spiritual and spiritually gifted as any man. That is not the point. The place of public ministry and pastoral government is not open to her, 'not turned over to' her by the Lord, as the literal force of 1 Corinthians 14:34 has it. The Lord will give her fitting opportunities to exercise her gifts. She has a special role in the teaching of other women and the young (Titus 2:4, 11; 2 Timothy 1:5; 3:15). She may be a Priscilla and use her home as a pulpit to teach needy people the gospel (Acts 18:26). She may be so beneficial to the work of the church as to earn the title Phoebe, 'the servant [or, deaconess] of the church' (Romans 16:1). Here there is no hint that the word *deaconess* has reference to any elected office, but rather to Phoebe's selfless service to the church.

Thus the Free Presbyterian Church, gladly affirming the rich ministry of godly women in the church throughout history, none the less maintains that no woman may scripturally be elected or ordained to any preaching, pastoral or governmental office in the church.

MARRIAGE AND DIVORCE

Marriage is a divine institution (Matthew 19:4, 5), not merely a social convenience. God's original appointment was the uniting of one man and one woman as one flesh. Monogamy and marital fidelity, therefore, constitute the biblical standard (1 Timothy 3:2; Exodus 20:14). Therefore, the Free Presbyterian Church opposes all the philosophies and pressures of this age that tend to weaken or destroy the sanctity and permanence of marriage. Jesus said, 'Wherefore they are no more twain, but one flesh. What therefore God hath joined together, let not man put asunder' (Matthew 19:6).

The permanence of marriage

Marriages between all legitimate partners are legally binding before God. This is true of the marriages of believers and of unbelievers alike. If a person becomes a Christian after his marriage, he ought not to regard his unsaved spouse as anything less than his true and legitimate marriage partner.

Mixed marriages

Christians wishing to enter into marriage are admonished that it must be 'in the Lord'. This is the only stipulation the Bible lays down. The Free Presbyterian Church will conduct marriage services for couples where both parties are saved, or where both parties are unsaved, using the opportunity to seek to point them to Christ. What it will not do is wittingly to join a believer and an unbeliever in marriage.

Grounds for divorce

Under the Mosaic law the penalty for breaking the marriage bond by adultery, sodomy, bestiality or other gross uncleanness was death (Leviticus 20:10, 13, 15). The Mosaic standard was that divorce could be obtained only because of 'uncleanness' in a spouse (Deuteronomy 24:1), that is, gross sexual impurity. The Lord Jesus Christ reiterated this, teaching that divorce on any other ground than 'fornication' is invalid (Matthew 5:32; 19:9). He bluntly terms any remarriage under such circumstances 'adultery'.

Paul addresses the issue of marriage breakdowns from a somewhat different perspective to deal with the problem encountered by Christians whose heathen spouses deserted them (1 Corinthians 7:12–16). He recognises that where a wife is unjustly deserted, she is free (v. 15). He therefore appears to include desertion in such cases within Christ's definition of fornication, making it a just ground for divorce and remarriage. Where there is no such ground, he emphatically states that couples should not divorce or separate, and if they do they must not remarry (1 Corinthians 7:10–11).

Remarriage

While reconciliation is better than divorce, the remarriage of justly divorced people is recognised in both the Old Testament and the New (Deuteronomy 24; Matthew 5:32; 19:9; 1 Corinthians 7:15). It would appear, however, that though divorced people were admitted into the New Testament church, they could not hold the office of elder or deacon. This may be deduced from 1 Timothy 3:2–5, 12.

Divorced people in church

The elders of each Free Presbyterian church may receive divorced people into membership if they are convinced that their present lifestyle is not condemned by Scripture. When received into membership, these brethren and sisters are welcome to participate fully in the life and fellowship of the church and to use their gifts and abilities to advance its ministry. However, no divorced person or one married to a divorced person may be elected to the office of deacon or elder. In addition, no Free Presbyterian church may be used for a marriage service involving a divorced person, nor may any Free Presbyterian minister officiate at such a marriage. This is not to question the legitimacy or propriety of the remarriage of justly divorced people. It is simply a confession that often elders have only partial or very confused evidence relating to the cause of a divorce. If we make a mistake in recognising a remarriage and allow the parties into membership, we can rectify it. If we have actually solemnised the marriage, we cannot. We know that good men and churches differ from us on this matter, but we believe that, on balance, it is more expedient not to conduct marriage services involving divorced people.

As stated, however, we do sincerely seek to minister in love to divorced people. Under the Christ-centred preaching in Free Presbyterian churches, and amid the warmth of Christian fellowship, many a divorced person has come to know the power of the gospel to bring peace and freedom from the feelings of rejection, guilt, shame and remorse that all too often haunt those who have suffered a divorce.

WORSHIP

Worship has been defined as 'reverent devotion and allegiance pledged to God'. Its main elements are prayer and praise (Psalm 105:1–14; Ephesians 5:19; Acts 2:42), the reading of the Word of God (Luke 4:16–17), the preaching of the Word (Luke 4:18–20; Acts 13:5; 2 Timothy 4:1–2), and the administration of the sacraments (Matthew 28:19; 1 Corinthians 11:23–4). This worship is to be spiritual and sincere (John 4:24). It is not to degenerate into a mere mechanical, ritualistic or liturgical form (Matthew 15:8).

The central act of worship: preaching

This we seek to maintain. In line with historical Protestantism, and more importantly, in line with the emphasis of the New Testament, we hold that the faithful preaching of Christ is the central part of Christian worship. Paul said, 'Christ sent me not to baptise but to preach the gospel' (1 Corinthians 1:17). This is not to undervalue baptism, but it is to establish the primacy of preaching in Christian worship. That is why in our services the preaching is central.

The Bible we use in our services

In carrying on this preaching ministry the Free Presbyterian Church has, throughout its history, used the Authorised (often called the 'King James') Version of the Scriptures. We wish to avoid the confusion that arises from the use of many different translations and paraphrases in church services. Modern English translations dilute the great cardinalities of the faith. We believe the Authorised Version is unrivalled as an English translation of the Scriptures and that it reflects the authentic, historical Hebrew and Greek texts that God 'immediately inspired, and by His singular care and providence kept pure in all ages' (Westminster Confession of Faith, I. 8).

The Lord's Table

Fellowship with the Lord is especially sweet at the Lord's Table. In Presbyterian church history, the communion season has often been the time God has chosen to visit His people with revival.

In the Free Presbyterian Church, each session (i.e. board of elders) has the right to determine the frequency of observing the Lord's Supper. We adhere strictly to what is the historic Protestant view of the ordinance. We repudiate the Romish notion of transubstantiation and Luther's idea of consubstantiation. There is no change in the physical elements. There is no bodily presence of Christ. Neither is the Supper a sacrifice for sin. It is a blessed memorial in which Christ's 'death is showed forth; and the worthy receivers are, not after a corporal and carnal manner, but by faith, made partakers of His body and blood, with all His benefits, to their spiritual nourishment and growth in grace' (*Shorter Catechism*, 96). Thus for us a Communion Service is no mere 'add-on' or afterthought to another service. It is a solemn privilege to remember Christ, and as we do so we earnestly crave the manifestation of His glory to the reviving of our souls.

CHRISTIAN BAPTISM

The importance of Christian baptism is clear for all to see in the New Testament (Matthew 28:19; Mark 16:16; Acts 2:38, et cetera). Every branch of the Christian Church has agreed that baptism is a divine ordinance whose observance is part of what constitutes a church. In this the Free Presbyterian Church is at one with all the rest.

Differences over baptism

The Free Presbyterian Church recognises that good men have differed and continue to differ on this emotive subject. Should God's people separate from one another over baptism? Can they not hold their view strongly while allowing conscientious brethren to hold a differing view? We believe they can and should. (See Article 6a of our *Articles of Faith*.)

We do not undervalue baptism, neither do we want needless division. We would not wish to be so exclusively Presbyterian that we could find no place for a C.H. Spurgeon just because he strongly adhered to believers' baptism. Nor would we wish to be so Baptistic that we would exclude a Robert Murray McCheyne just because he strongly held to the baptism for the children of believers.

In the World Council of Churches, Baptists and paedo-Baptists are seeking to work out an acceptable position that will do justice to all their traditions. They are doing this in a spiritual compromise on every major doctrine of the gospel. That is a betrayal. But is it not sad that Baptists and paedo-Baptists who agree in upholding every fundamental of the faith cannot usually find the love, the humility or whatever it takes to stand together in the unity of the gospel? That is the problem the Free Presbyterian Church addressed at its inception. Ever since, it has enjoyed a spirit of unity that has not been marred by the diversity of views on baptism it encompasses.

FREE PRESBYTERIANS: 'SEPARATED UNTO THE GOSPEL'
(Romans 1:1)

The *Free* in our name refers to our total dissociation from the major Presbyterian denominations of the world, which have largely repudiated the historic Christian faith. We have no affiliation with the World Council of Churches or any of its international, national or local organisations, thus *Free* speaks of our liberty to stand without compromise for Christ in a day of apostasy. Many evangelicals have stayed in apostate churches. Others have separated but have not made any strong protest against the betrayal of the gospel by apostates and the compromise of those evangelicals who have put denominational loyalty before obedience to the biblical command to separate. We view our freedom as liberty to stand resolutely for Christ, to defend the gospel, to oppose apostasy and compromise, and to urge God's people to cease all fellowship with the unfruitful works of darkness. For us freedom is freedom to be holy, observing both personal and ecclesiastical separation unto the Lord.

The duty of separation

'Can two walk together, except they be agreed?' (Amos 3:3). We are instructed to 'have no fellowship with the unfruitful works of darkness, but rather reprove them' (Ephesians 5:11). To a Christian, Liberalism, Modernism, Romanism and World Council of Churches Ecumenism are undoubtedly 'works of darkness'. The duty of separation is plain. Paul teaches this duty again in 2 Corinthians 6:14–18. John speaks of it in 2 John 10–11.

Christ the focus of separation

Separation is no mere negative reaction. It is thoroughly positive, because it is basically separation unto Christ. 'Let us go forth therefore unto him without the camp, bearing his reproach' (Hebrews 13:13). Fellowship in any organisation that denies Christ, repudiates His Word, or departs from His finished work of atonement and the gospel of justification through faith without works, is a fellowship that leads away from Christ. Our fellowship with Him demands our separation from apostasy and fundamental error.

We seek to express the fundamental oneness of God's people in any way we can, without compromising the fundamentals of the faith. We are biblical separatists, not isolationists.

PREACHING CHRIST

When Paul said he preached Christ, he meant it. And so do we. Jesus Christ is the great subject of our preaching. We lay great emphasis on the objective work of Christ. He has made an all-sufficient atonement for all His people. In a day of man-centred preaching we constantly proclaim that it is not the strength or merit of our faith that saves, but the strength and merit of Him in whom it rests. Christ is all our merit, and we need no more (1 Corinthians 1:30). By the imputation of His righteousness we are freely justified (Romans 3:20–8). This free justification provides the motive power for our service (Galatians 5:1; 2 Corinthians 5:14). We do not believe in guilt theology – making believers feel bad enough for doing or not doing something, that they will do what we command just to ease their consciences. It never works! We believe in grace theology. We will preach against sin in the lives of Christians, but always to point them to Christ (Hebrews 12:1–3). It is only as 'we see Jesus' (Hebrews 2:9) and understand our full acceptance by God on His merit without our added works (Ephesians 1:6) that we will have the power to do good works and strive after holiness. Thus we preach Christ as the message both sinners and saints need to hear.

This is the heart of the ministry of the Free Presbyterian Church. This is the undergirding reason for every stand we adopt. We expose and oppose the apostasy that is all too clear in many churches. We do not do so because of a desire to be contentious. No, our contending is for 'the faith which was once delivered to the saints' (Jude 3). It is our commitment 'not to know any thing among you, save Jesus Christ and him crucified' (1 Corinthians 2:2). That compels us to be 'set for the defence of the gospel' (Philippians 1:16).

BIOGRAPHICAL NOTE

The REV. DR IAN R.K. PAISLEY, MP, MEP, is Moderator of the Free Presbyterian Church of Ulster. The son of an Independent Baptist pastor, he was born in Armagh in 1926 and brought up in Ballymena. At the age of twenty he was appointed minister of the Ravenhill Evangelical Mission

Church in Belfast, and in 1951 was involved in the formation of the Free Presbyterian Church. As founder and leader of the Democratic Unionist Party (DUP), Dr Paisley has many political involvements. In 1970 he was elected first as a Stormont MP and then to Westminster, and in 1979 he became one of Northern Ireland's first Members of the European Parliament. Alongside these many responsibilities, he travels frequently to conduct missions and revival meetings in many parts of the world.

8

The Congregational Union of Ireland

MALCOLM COLES

ORIGINS

Most denominations in Ireland claim Patrick as their Founder. Congregationalists believe the Patron Saint of Ireland was a Congregationalist in spirit if not in name. The Celtic Church he established had a bishop or pastor in each church and the local congregations enjoyed a considerable degree of autonomy, reflecting the Congregational ethos.

Congregationalism was introduced to Ireland in the seventeenth century in the time of Oliver Cromwell. Many of his soldiers and their chaplains were Congregationalists and the church at Youghal, founded in 1650, was known as the place where 'Cromwell and his soldiers worshipped'. During the Commonwealth and Protectorate, Congregationalists came to Ireland in considerable numbers. Some of these were scholars from Oxford and Cambridge, including John Owen, Stephen Charnock and Samuel Winter (who was Provost of Trinity College). During this period a Congregational church worshipped in Christ Church Cathedral, Dublin.

In the eighteenth century Ireland was favoured with the visits of the great evangelists John and Charles Wesley and George Whitefield, the last of whom was under the patronage of the Countess of Huntingdon. Converts of Whitefield were gathered at first into Societies, from which Congregational churches emerged.

Evangelistic concern for Ireland in the nineteenth century was generated from Scotland and England. The Haldane brothers from Scotland itinerated in Cos. Antrim, Armagh and Down, with churches being formed as a result of their efforts. The Irish Evangelical Society, founded in London in 1814, established an Academy in Dublin training men for the ministry, and by 1832 the Society had fifty-two agents at work in the field, with one hundred stations.

SURVEY OF THE DENOMINATION TODAY

The Congregational Union of Ireland was formed in 1829. In those days the centre of activity was in Dublin and the majority of the churches were in the South. Today only two churches in Co. Donegal and one in Dublin remain in the South. The twenty-four churches in the North are concentrated in the Greater Belfast area and Cos. Antrim and Down. Fermanagh, Londonderry and Tyrone have one church each. The newest churches in the Union, brought into being through local initiative, are Bangor and Erne West (both 1987) and Raphoe (this being a relocation in 1986 from St Johnston). The churches are currently served by twenty-seven ministers. The number of full communicant members is twenty-two hundred and the total community is at least twice this, plus children.

CONGREGATIONALISM IN THE WORLD CHURCH

Congregationalists believe that the simple church order and structure goes back to Apostolic times. It was the desire for liberty and simplicity of worship that led to the Pilgrim Fathers setting sail for New England, taking their Congregationalism with them. It is generally agreed that they were the founders of the United States.

Congregationalism was introduced to many of the countries of the British Commonwealth. The evangelistic and missionary zeal of Congregationalists is legendary, and the great missionary statesmen include Robert Moffat, David Livingstone, Robert Morris and John Williams.

The Union is a member of the World Evangelical Congregational Fellowship, which brings together Congregationalists from the United Kingdom, America, Canada, Brazil, Australia, New Zealand, South Africa, Fiji, Micronesia, Portugal, Macedonia and Bulgaria. Spiritual unity transcends all national and cultural boundaries.

DOCTRINAL POSITION

The churches of the Union all subscribe to a short evangelical basis of faith which allows for a measure of liberty. Calvinists and Arminians, Paedo-baptists and Baptists, Amillennialists, Postmillennialists and Pre-millennialists all find a welcome. On the essentials of the Christian Faith there is agreement.

The doctrinal basis is as follows:

1.   The divine and special inspiration of the Holy Scriptures of Old and
     New Testaments and their sole authority and entire sufficiency as the
     rule of faith and practice.

2.   The Unity of God eternally existing in Three Persons with the proper
     Deity of the Father, of the Son and of the Holy Spirit.

3.   The depravity of man and the absolute necessity of the Holy Spirit's
     agency in man's regeneration and sanctification.

4.   The Incarnation of the Son of God in the Person of the Lord Jesus
     Christ, the Universal Sufficiency of the Atonement by His death and
     Free Justification of sinners by faith alone in Him.

5.   Salvation by grace and the duty of all men to repent and believe in
     Christ.

6.   The Personal Return of the Lord Jesus Christ in Power and Glory.
     The resurrection of the dead and final judgement when the wicked
     'shall go away into everlasting punishment but the righteous unto life
     eternal'.

7.   The one holy, universal Church which is the Body of Christ to which
     all true believers belong.

Each church is governed by a Trust Deed which usually includes a doctrinal schedule, which the Minister and members are required to uphold.
The historic confessions of Faith are the Savoy Declaration of Faith and
Order (1658) and the Declaration of Faith and Order of the Congregational Union of England and Wales (1833).

BASIS OF AUTHORITY

The authority for Congregationalists in all matters of faith and practice is
the Divine Scriptures of the Old and New Testaments. All creeds and
confessions are regarded as subordinate.

MEMBERSHIP, MINISTRY AND CHURCH GOVERNMENT

Membership is on a voluntary basis. Those who make a credible profession
of faith in Christ as Saviour and Lord (that is, a profession which is more
than mere belief but is accompanied with a change of life) are received by
the Church into membership.

The local church (or congregation) is autonomous. It does not concede
authority to any, be it another church, the Congregational Union,
Ecclesiastical Assemblies or a church dignitary. Congregationalists believe
that Christ is the sole Head and King of the Church and that each local

church is accountable only to Him. They believe that His will is made known in the Church Meeting, when the members are gathered under His lordship, with His promised presence (Matthew 18:20), the leading and guiding of the Holy Spirit and the open Bible. Ministers are called forth, set apart and ordained by the churches to the Christian Ministry. Men set apart may be from the home church, from another church of the same Faith and Order or from a background outside the denomination. Men are expected to be able to give clear testimony to their conversion to Christ and the call to the work of the ministry. They will usually have already given proof of their ministry and will have given themselves to theological, spiritual and practical training. Men who have undergone theological training at a recognised college or a course of prescribed study are admitted to a Roll of Ministers of the Union

SACRAMENTS/ORDINANCES

The two Ordinances of Baptism and the Lord's Supper are observed by Congregationalists. They believe that these were instituted by Christ and are to be perpetually observed by the Church.

Traditionally, Baptism has been administered to converts to Christianity and their children. Today some churches practise the baptism of believers on confession of faith only, and this is administered either by immersion or by the pouring of water on the candidate. Where the Baptism of infants does not take place, a simple service of prayer and thanksgiving is held on the birth of a child.

The Lord's Supper is usually held monthly, at the conclusion of Public Worship when all true Christians are welcome to communicate. The service is generally presided over by the minister but this is not necessary to give validity to the observance.

WORSHIP

The emphasis in worship in Congregational churches is both spiritual and simple. There is no liturgy or Prayer Book. Generally, the Minister conducts worship but sometimes this is delegated to spiritually qualified men, such as officers of the church.

The services will usually consist of lively praise (in some instances choirs and soloists participate), the reading of Scripture, solemn and earnest prayer (on occasions open prayer is encouraged), and the climax is the Sermon, in which the Bible is expounded and applied.

BUILDINGS

Church buildings are generally simple and functional with little by way of ornament. The style of building often reflects the period in which it was built. The Pulpit invariably dominates the sanctuary, emphasising the priority of preaching. Good facilities are usually provided in ancillary rooms, where work for children and young people takes place during the week.

CHURCH AND COMMUNITY

Congregationalists believe in the separation of Church and state but this does not mean they have no concern for the community. The very fact that they believe in the local gathered nature of the Church means that they are concerned for the spiritual and social welfare of the community in which they are placed. They seek to be as salt and light, as Jesus Himself taught, and work amongst folk of all ages and backgrounds seeking to win them to the allegiance of Christ.

INTER-CHURCH ACTIVITY

Congregational churches, whilst holding tenaciously to the principle of Independency, are certainly not isolationist. They work happily with like-minded Christians and Churches, who hold to the same Gospel and Faith once delivered to the saints. Minor differences and differing forms of church government are not allowed to become barriers. The Union has links with the Baptist Union of Ireland, the Evangelical Presbyterian Church and the Reformed Presbyterian Church. Local churches have contact with other small denominations and groups of Christians.

However, the Union believes that the form of ecumenicity advocated by the World, British and Irish Councils of Churches is inimical to the Gospel and the Bible. It therefore stands apart but seeks to foster true evangelical ecumenicity and is a member of the *British Evangelical Council*, which brings together almost one thousand congregations from various evangelical denominations in the British Isles, including: the Apostolic Church; an Evangelical Fellowship of Congregational Churches in England and Wales; the Evangelical Movement of Wales; the Evangelical Presbyterian Churches of England, Wales and Ireland; the Fellowship of Independent Evangelical Churches; the Free Church of Scotland; Grace Baptist Churches; and the Union of Evangelical Churches. The Council issues theological journals, arranges study conferences, employs a parliamentary agent to represent its constituency on matters of concern and seeks to promote the interests of Evangelical Christianity throughout the British Isles. (It also has a programme of theological teaching in Romania.)

SPECIAL FEATURES

Congregationalists have always had a great zeal for mission. The Irish churches have well over one hundred personnel in the field, and in 1996 contributed over £180,000 for mission at home and overseas.

BIBLIOGRAPHY

Coles, Malcolm, *I Will Build my Church*, Congregational Union of Ireland 1979

Dale, R.W., *History of English Congregationalism*, Hodder & Stoughton 1907

Dale, R.W., *Manual of Congregational Principles*, 1884 (reprinted by Quinta Press 1996)

Evangelical & Congregational (with the Savoy Declaration of Faith and Order, 1658), Evangelical Fellowship of Congregational Churches 1981

Jones, R. Tudor, *Congregationalism in England 1662–1962*, Independent Press, n.d.

Owen, John, *The True Nature of a Gospel Church* (*Works*, vol. 16), Banner of Truth 1968

BIOGRAPHICAL NOTE

The REV. MALCOLM COLES comes from West Sussex and served in the Royal Army Medical Corps as a National Serviceman in England and the Far East. He studied for four years at London Bible College, where he met his wife. They married in 1967 and have three daughters. Ordained in 1966, he has served pastorates in Essex (1966–73), Albert Bridge, Belfast (1973–6) and Connsbrook Avenue, Belfast (1976 to the present). In 1984 he was appointed Honorary Secretary of the Congregational Union.

9

The
Elim Pentecostal Church
and Other Pentecostal Churches

PETER SMITH

ORIGINS

'Did your church start in America?' is a question we have been asked many times. Imagine the surprise when our reply is, 'No, it began in Monaghan in 1915.' It seems strange to some that the Elim Pentecostal Church, which today has an influence worldwide, should have had such humble beginnings.

At the invitation of a few young men, the Welsh evangelist George Jeffreys conducted a crusade in a tent on the green in Monaghan town. Such were the results that it became necessary to organise after-care for the converts and this resulted in the inception of, initially, the Elim Evangelistic Band. Subsequently, a move was made to Belfast, to a disused laundry in Hunter Street, not far from where Townsend Street is now. After renovation and refurbishment, meetings began there and the Elim Pentecostal Alliance was begun. Headquarters were set up in Belfast with subsequent moves to Essex and then to London, at which time the full name of the Church was changed to the Elim Foursquare Gospel Alliance.

The name 'Elim' was chosen because of its scriptural background in Exodus 15:27, which describes an oasis in the Sinai desert some forty miles from Suez. The seventy palm trees and twelve wells of water must have provided a very welcome refreshment to the weary travellers of the children of Israel as they fled from captivity in Egypt to Canaan. The idea of an oasis in a wilderness is still in the forefront of the thinking of members of Elim churches.

The 'Foursquare' idea was developed from George Jeffreys's emphasis on the centrality of the Person of Jesus Christ in his preaching. He proclaimed that Jesus was Saviour, Healer, Baptiser in the Holy Spirit and Coming King. To be foursquare was a symbol of stability and represented what was felt to be a balanced approach to new things that God was doing in His Church. The Movement depended strongly on the belief that the Bible is the Word of God. Amazingly, tremendous opposition was stirred up both within the established Churches and in the secular world, but the more opposition there was, the greater the response to the Revival and Divine Healing Crusades.

OTHER PENTECOSTAL CHURCHES

In 1916 another stream of Pentecostal Churches emerged with some doctrinal differences relating to the prophetic ministry of the Church, as well as some views on church order and government which were unacceptable to the other two main Pentecostal Churches, Elim and Assemblies of God, which at this stage existed as a loose grouping of independent churches. Today, the **Apostolic Church**, which has its headquarters in Wales, is the smallest of the three main Pentecostal Churches.

Nationally, it was a time of growth for the infant Pentecostal Churches. George Jeffreys had founded Elim on the basis of his great crusades, which filled the largest halls in the country. Meanwhile, his brother, Stephen, was also being mightily used by God and signs and wonders were following the preaching of the Word of God. A number of independent missions and churches were also experiencing growth and an outpouring of the Holy Spirit which showed itself in various manifestations, predominantly speaking with other tongues and dramatic healings. On 1 February 1924 many of these independent assemblies agreed to set up an umbrella organisation in which there would be fellowship, but no overall organisational control. This became the basis of the **Assemblies of God**, which is still a fellowship of independent pentecostal assemblies. What differences exist between Elim and the Assemblies of God are governmental rather than doctrinal.

ELIM MINISTRY TODAY

The Elim Church has continued, throughout the years, to maintain a strong emphasis on evangelism and this is evidenced, in some ways, by the fact that an overseas evangelistic thrust developed so that thirty-two countries are now involved in Elim International Missions work. Schools, hospitals and churches, together with feeding programmes for refugees, form the basis for much of our work and we are now seeing church planting taking place in Europe, the Middle East and the USA based on missionary work in Ghana. At home, evangelism takes place at all levels, especially on a relational basis, although city-wide crusades are still conducted occasionally.

There are today some fifty churches in Northern Ireland, most supporting a full-time minister and on any given Sunday the total attendance in the province is likely to be around ten thousand. This would include churches belonging to the wider ECI (Elim Church Incorporated) fellowship, including churches like the Metropolitan Church at Whitewell in Belfast. Almost all have their own buildings as opposed to using rented halls and several are in the process of extending and improving their premises.

At Elim's inception, a number of ladies were involved in significant ministries. For many years, the ministry within Elim was, as it still is, predominantly male, largely because of the laws of supply and demand. There is a trend, however, for young ladies to seek opportunities for ministry and this is being addressed seriously and jointly by the Elim Church and the Assemblies of God Conferences.

DOCTRINE

The doctrine of the Elim churches is based primarily on the Bible as the inerrant Word of God and we would subscribe to the interpretation of it as set forth by the Westminster Confession of Faith. The distinctiveness of the Church would rest in our attitude to pentecostal phenomena (like speaking in tongues, interpretation, prophecy and divine healing, and the spiritual gifts of 1 Corinthians), since we believe that these activities of the Holy Spirit are present in the Church today just as much as they were in the early Christian Church. We reject the cessationist views on the basis that the giver of these gifts is Jesus Christ, who, the Bible says, is 'the same, yesterday and today and forever' (Hebrews 13:8). We recognise that, throughout church history, the gifts of the Holy Spirit have fallen into disuse, but that has been the fault of the Church, and not because God has withdrawn His giftings.

A few years ago, the Elim churches addressed the problem of divorce and remarriage in a specially convened theological Conference. This took the form of a series of small group discussions and plenary sessions based on position papers presented by ministers of the Movement. The result was the setting of clear scriptural guidelines for dealing with what was regarded as an ever-increasing challenge to the Church in this age. The effect was to allow, in certain clearly defined and limited circumstances, the possibility of remarriage of divorced persons.

The Elim Church has always taken its stand against smoking and, more recently, reaffirmed its long-held view that, as a matter of example, the taking of alcohol was not acceptable for those in leadership positions within the churches locally and the Movement nationally.

The Conference, some years ago, decided that membership of the Masonic Lodge was inappropriate for those claiming a personal relationship with the Lord Jesus Christ and determined that such individuals should not be admitted to membership within an Elim church.

FUNDAMENTAL BELIEFS

The beliefs of the Elim Pentecostal Church are as set out below.

1. *The Bible:* We believe the Bible, as originally given, to be without error, the fully inspired and infallible Word of God and the supreme and final authority in all matters of faith and conduct.

2. *The Trinity:* We believe that the Godhead exists co-equally and co-eternally in three persons, Father, Son and Holy Spirit, and that these three are one God, sovereign in creation, providence and redemption.

3. *The Saviour:* We believe in the true and proper deity of our Lord Jesus Christ, in His virgin birth, in His real and complete humanity, in His sinless life, in His authoritative teaching, in His substitutionary and atoning sacrifice through His shed blood, in His bodily resurrection, in His ascension to the right hand of the Father, in His heavenly intercession and in His second advent to receive His Church.

4. *The Holy Spirit:* We believe in the deity of the Holy Spirit who proceeds from the Father and the Son and the necessity of His work in conviction of sin, repentance, regeneration and sanctification, and that the believer is also promised an enduement of power as the gift of Christ through the Baptism in the Holy Spirit with signs following. Through this enduement the believer is empowered for fuller participation in the ministry of the Church, its worship, evangelism and service.

5. *Mankind:* We believe in the universal sinfulness of all men since the Fall, rendering man subject to God's wrath and condemnation.

6. *Salvation:* We believe in the necessity for salvation of repentance towards God and faith in the Lord Jesus Christ by which the sinner is pardoned and accepted as righteous in God's sight. This justification is imputed by the grace of God because of the atoning work of Christ, is received by faith alone and is evidenced by the Fruit of the Spirit and a holy life.

7. *The Church:* We believe in the spiritual unity and priesthood of all believers in Christ and that these comprise the universal Church, the Body of Christ.

8. *The ministry:* We believe in the ministries that Christ has set in His Church, namely, apostles, prophets, evangelists, pastors and teachers, and in the present operation of the manifold Gifts of the Holy Spirit according to the New Testament.

9. *The ordinances:* We believe in the baptism of believers by immersion in water in obedience to the command of Christ and in the commemoration of Christ's death by the observance of the Lord's Supper until His return.

10. *The commission:* We believe that the gospel embraces the needs of the whole man and that the Church is therefore commissioned to preach the gospel to the world and to fulfil a ministry of healing and deliverance to the spiritual and physical needs of mankind.

11. *The coming King:* We believe in the personal, physical and visible return of the Lord Jesus Christ to reign in power and glory.

12. *The future state:* We believe in the resurrection of the dead and in the final judgement of the world, the eternal conscious bliss of the righteous and the eternal conscious punishment of the wicked.

ORGANISATION, GOVERNMENT AND MEMBERSHIP

The Elim Church works on two levels. There are churches which are recognised as full 'Alliance' churches. They have buildings registered with the Elim Trust Corporation, use ministers who have been ordained by the Alliance and contribute 10% of their income to central funds for the upkeep, administration and development of the work.

There is a broader 'umbrella' grouping known as the ECI (Elim Church Incorporated), which, in addition to all the Alliance churches, provides for independent fellowships to relate to Elim. They maintain their independence, use their own chosen leadership and are not required to make any financial contribution to central funds. In some cases, they can request the services of an Alliance minister and may make voluntary financial contributions. They are encouraged to support the work of overseas missions irrespective of their status. The only demand made upon them is that they subscribe to the Fundamental Truths of the Elim Church.

The Elim Church has a presbyterian form of government. The governing body is the general Conference, which consists of all ministers and one lay representative from each church. The country is divided into

Presbyteries and Regions, and full-time Regional Superintendents have responsibility for pastoral care in their area.

Part of the Elim Church's service is preparing people for ministry – whether as pastors, as missionaries, for work with para-church organisations or for returning to work in the local church. The main centre for this is the Elim Bible College (now known as Regent's Theological College) in Nantwich, Cheshire, which works in conjunction with Manchester University. Here, it is possible to study for any period from one to four years and awards range from the College's own certificate, through Diplomas to Higher Degrees. Because of the college's excellent facilities for the training of young people for ministry, the Elim churches have not had a shortage of candidates for many years. It should be noted that the training provided by the interdenominational Belfast Bible College as well as the Irish Baptist College is considered acceptable for entry to the Elim ministry. In London, a full course of study is provided by IBIOL – the International Bible Institute of London, which has its base in the Kensington Temple Elim Church. The Church Training Programme (CTP) exists to meet a need for people who wish to study locally and at reasonable cost. This leads to a locally presented certificate.

Northern Ireland, as the foundation area, was first to be organised and, for this reason, has always held special status within the Movement. Ireland has its own Executive Council, consisting of a Superintendent Minister, three minister members and three lay members who must be church elders, elected for four-year terms by the Irish Conference. The Irish work raises its own finance, the tithes of the churches being received here rather than being sent to Headquarters in England. Financially, the Irish work has responsibility for the support of several churches in Éire and additionally, approximately 20% of Elim's total overseas missionary budget from the whole of the UK is raised in Northern Ireland by only 10% of the UK's Elim membership. The stationing of ministers in churches here is always the prerogative of the Irish Executive.

Membership of an Elim church is dependent on an individual's clear relationship with Jesus Christ as Saviour. Water Baptism is not demanded as a condition, but is recommended as a token of obedience in the Christian life. It is expected that those entering into membership with a local Elim church should be ready to affirm their acceptance of the Church's doctrinal statement and, in many cases, churches conduct membership preparation classes before admitting new members.

In today's climate in society, there is a great demand for counselling of various types and the Elim churches have made the necessary preparations to have on hand counselling for families, people expecting to be married, bereavement, et cetera. Referrals are made to professional bodies where the need presents itself so that those who are counselled receive the best help possible. Elim churches have been in the forefront in training their workers in all aspects of the new child protection legislation. Seminars have been conducted for all youth and children's workers, and all workers have completed authorised registration forms, thus providing a sense of security to all parents whose children are involved in church activities.

The Church's worship is as diverse as the individual churches themselves, but all would tend to a freedom in music and opportunity given – especially in the Sunday morning meeting, which is always a communion service – for individuals to take part publicly in what is termed 'open worship'. Many churches have broadened their musical base from a piano and/or organ to include other instruments, such as guitars, violins, drums, keyboard and wind instruments. Sunday services would include a service for believers in the morning and a gospel service at night, while midweek, meetings are conducted for prayer and Bible study.

IMPACT ON THE COMMUNITY

Initially, the Elim churches spent their time mainly preaching the Gospel and many believed that to do otherwise was beyond their remit as Christians. Work amongst children took the form of Sunday Schools and 'Sunshine Corner' – usually a midweek meeting for children of all ages using bright choruses, stories, quizzes and Bible games; it was less formal than Sunday School and tended to be a fun time with evangelistic overtones. Many also made use of the good offices of the Child Evangelism Fellowship. There was little to occupy older children and teenagers. Most churches had activities for ladies but nothing for men. Happily, however, they have moved with the times and have recognised that it is impossible to make an impact on a community whilst remaining isolated from it. Accordingly, across the country, in addition to the regular activities mentioned above, there have been added the Boys' Brigade or the Campaigners, which cater for all ages up to eighteen-year-olds. Elim churches are running nurseries, play schools and mother and toddler groups. Men's fellowships are developing and senior citizens' luncheon clubs are providing a needed service. One church in England has bought two disused hospitals and converted them into a senior citizens' rest home, community centre, addicts' centre, single parents' centre and a church. The Elim Church in Ireland has two homes for senior citizens (in Armagh and Hillsborough) as well as a youth community centre in the Shankill area of Belfast working closely with the local Probation Service and other agencies to help young people break out of the negative influences of their environment. Many churches run Saturday night youth clubs to help to keep young people off the streets.

It will be seen that social awareness has a high profile and many churches are seeking ways and means of developing these aspects of their ministry to the communities in which they are placed.

RELATIONSHIPS

It is interesting to note that the early opposition and ridicule which attended the gatherings of the Pentecostal Churches has largely diminished as many denominational Churches have become open to the truths which the pentecostal people proclaimed for years. It is no longer 'strange' for members of other denominations to speak in tongues or to lay hands on the sick for healing. Indeed, for many years, the Church of England, for example, has had its own Commission on Healing.

The Elim Church, nationwide, has always stood back from associations with the 'Charismatic Movement' on the basis that much that was involved was contrary to our perceptions of the standards required for a scripturally based activity. Help and advice were offered in many cases, but generally speaking, these were rejected, the implication being that the classical Pentecostal Churches had run their course and had nothing to contribute to the current debate. The involvement of the Roman Catholic Church also presented a major problem, although most Elim churches have within them a number of Roman Catholic people.

Today, the Elim Church is a member of the Evangelical Alliance and maintains good relations with other denominations. Its associations with the other mainline Pentecostal Churches are cordial and united activities are arranged periodically. On a much broader canvas, the Elim Church is a participating member of the World Pentecostal Conference, a gathering held every four years which brings together pentecostal people from around the world for a week of fellowship and ministry. This has no legislative authority but exists as a forum for the interchange of ideas and the expression of an organic spiritual unity rather than any type of organisational unity.

Elim churches and Elim ministers serve on the boards of various parachurch organisations, for example Lyndon Bowring (an Elim minister) in his work with CARE (which is not an Elim organisation, but is well known for its research and lobbying activities on matters relating to the health of society, such as abortion, Sunday trading, homosexuality, et cetera). Many Elim ministers are involved in chaplaincies of hospitals, prisons and universities. Throughout the country, there is a great interest being shown also in radio work in hospitals and commercial and BBC stations.

The concern for the community which is a mark of Christian

commitment is seen in the setting up of the Elim Church Ethics and Social Affairs Committee consisting of concerned members of the Church whose intention is to bring pressure to bear on the media and government regarding aspects of the life of society which are considered to be unacceptable from a biblical perspective. Current concerns being studied include the abortion and euthanasia debates and the present interest in the National Lottery, together with the wider issues of gambling in general.

BIBLIOGRAPHY

Boulton, E.C.W., *A Ministry of the Miraculous*, London: Elim Publishing Co. 1928

Brumbach, C., *What Meaneth This?*, London: Elim Publishing Co. 1946

Darragh, R.E., *In Defence of His Word*, London: Elim Publishing Co. 1932

Edsor, A.W., *George Jeffreys, Man of God*, London: Ludgate Press 1964

Gee, Donald, *The Pentecostal Movement*, London: Elim Publishing Co. 1941

Jeffreys, G., *The Miraculous Foursquare Gospel*, London: Elim Publishing Co. 1933

BIOGRAPHICAL NOTE

PETER SMITH has been a minister in the Elim Church since 1957, serving in churches throughout the UK and in Northern Ireland since 1979. He has occupied the post of Missions Director for Northern Ireland for some time and has served as Elim's Director of Communications, a member of the International Missions Board and of the Elim Bible College Council. For several years, he has been a member of the Irish Executive of the Elim Churches and Superintendent of various Presbyteries in England.

10

The Non-Subscribing Presbyterian Church of Ireland

TOM BANHAM

ORIGINS

From 1725 successive splinter groups from mainstream Presbyterianism found common ground in their dissatisfaction with the Calvinist Westminster Confession of Faith. This dated from 1643 but was not significant in Ireland before the 1720s. However, there was little agreement over what should stand in its place. The standard accepted at the time with varying degrees of rigour was 'the Bible and the Bible only'; but by the 1800s this was becoming debatable. It was a time of growing biblical scholarship. The eventual result was an appreciation that dogmatism is the enemy of spiritual religion and that many of the things for which men of the past had persecuted one another were indifferent when measured against eternity. This more liberal understanding can be seen from 1835 in the founding for sharing resources of the *Association of Irish Non-Subscribing Presbyterians* in spite of theological differences. The Non-Subscribing Presbyterian Church of Ireland itself was formed only in 1910 when the members of the Association – the Remonstrant Synod of Ulster (1830), Presbytery of Antrim (1725) and some independent congregations, joined later by the Synod of Munster (*c.* 1650) – came together as one denomination.

RELATIONSHIPS WITH OTHER CHURCHES

In spite of fewness of numbers the Church or its predecessors endeavoured to take a responsible part in inter-church and inter-faith work. It was a founder member of the *International Association for Religious Freedom*, which has an office at United Nations Headquarters. Within the British Isles it was an early member of the *General Assembly of Unitarian and Free Christian Churches* (1925) and of the *British Council of Churches*. Owing to its shortage of resources it has asked for Observer status only in the BCC's successor, the *Council of Churches for Britain and Ireland*.

In Ireland itself it was an early member of the *Irish Council of Churches* and the *Irish Inter-Church Meeting*. Recently, with denominational approval, members have supported the *Inter-Faith Forum for Northern Ireland*, which was founded in 1993. This continues the denomination's witness to comprehensiveness in faith and Christian life. As far back as the eighteenth century, for example, Catholic children were accepted into their local schools and several of them went on to become bishops. Also, in 1829 most Non-Subscribers were strong supporters of Catholic Emancipation, and men like Dr Henry Montgomery of Dunmurry worked and spoke publicly in support. Later endeavours have included helping to found groups such as Protestant and Catholic Encounter (PACE) and joint services with Catholic, Church of Ireland, Methodist and some Presbyterian congregations.

STATISTICS

Adult membership listed by name has remained steady over the past ten years at around four thousand adult members. Non-listed adherents and occasional attenders could well be around three times this number. Sunday School numbers total around six hundred. Almost all Non-Subscribing Presbyterian churches are in the counties of Antrim and Down. Only two churches remain of the Synod of Munster, which in the mid-1800s contained over forty congregations in what is now the Republic.

DOCTRINE AND AUTHORITY

By foundation and definition there is no one doctrine binding upon the Non-Subscribers. The ultimate Basis of Authority is the Bible understood in the light of knowledge and reason since knowledge and reason are gifts of God helping us to identify the Holy Spirit and the teaching of Jesus Christ speaking in Scripture. Based on this understanding is the *Constitution and Code of the Non-Subscribing Presbyterian Church of Ireland* (which was revised in 1996). In the eighteenth century Non-Subscribers were often referred to as 'New Light Presbyterians' since Arminian views were widely held and, from the early 1800s, some ministers avowed themselves to be Arian or Unitarian in their beliefs. One or other doctrinal title was sometimes applied to the whole movement. However, this is incorrect and always has been. The Church is Presbyterian in organisation and discipline, and non-dogmatic in its theology. Exercising the right of private judgement an individual may call himself or herself a Unitarian or even a Universalist but this does not commit a congregation or anyone else to holding the same dogmatic views. The NSPC of I is rather a 'free' church inspired by the Spirit of God in which doctrines and dogmas are secondary, and they may grow and change with new knowledge.

MEMBERSHIP

This is shown by inclusion in a congregational list of members which is normally printed with each congregation's Annual Report. Someone wishing to join would approach the church Secretary and the application would be considered and approved by the Committee or Session at its next meeting.

CHURCH GOVERNMENT

Church government in the NSPC of I is through Kirk Sessions, Presbyteries, Regional Synods and the General Synod. Moderators of these church courts are elected annually. In each congregation the Kirk Session of Elders is responsible for the spiritual affairs of the congregation and for representing it in higher courts. A congregation's day-to-day business is dealt with by its Church Committee, whose members are elected for one year, or in some cases three years. The Constitution is perhaps unique in ruling that an ordained minister of another denomination being present at a church court may be invited to 'sit and deliberate'.

MINISTRY

A minister is ordained for life by his or her presbytery. Ministers are required by the Constitution to be educated to graduate level before undertaking theological studies to degree or diploma status. Wherever possible, studies are carried out in colleges outside Ireland in order to give a broader religious perspective. Presbyteries may also recognise personal and religious qualities, and years of lay service, and through these the validity of the Call, of those individuals for whom study outside Ireland would be inappropriate or unnecessary. Ordained ministers of the NSPC of I are eligible to candidate for vacant pulpits in the mainland General Assembly of Unitarian and Free Christian Churches, the associated churches in Commonwealth countries and in the United States.

Each congregation elects a number of Ruling Elders who are ordained to the Eldership and the care of their congregation's spiritual affairs by the appropriate presbytery.

Preaching by lay people is encouraged and voluntary training for Lay

Preachers is provided by the denominational Academic Training Board.

COMMUNION

Communion is celebrated twice a year although in recent years some congregations have introduced a third celebration at Easter. In the revision of the *Directory of Worship* Communion is defined in a simple and biblical way as follows:

(1) its institution by Christ was the designation of a memorial act to be celebrated in the Church to the end of time;

(2) its significance rests in its being a memorial of Christ's once and for all time self-giving life, teaching and death;

(3) its purpose is that of forming a bond of mystical communion uniting those who worship with the eternal Spirit of Christ as signifying the divine imminence, and being in itself a pledge with one another to follow the examples of the apostles and men and women who have shown forth a Christlike spirit of unselfish service and personal dedication.

BAPTISM

Baptism is accepted as the formal and sacramental mark of membership of the Christian Faith. Non-Subscribers hold that there is no such thing as *Protestant baptism* or *Catholic baptism*; these terms apply only to the ritual used. However, the Non-Subscribers follow generally the teaching of Calvin, who held that the outward ceremony is the 'seal' of a sacramental moment which has taken place through grace in the hearts of those most intimately concerned – that is, in his or her own heart in the case of an adult candidate, and in the hearts of a child's parents when they resolve that their child shall have all the privileges of Christian life. There is therefore no necessity for the practice of baptism in an emergency by a layperson; and formally baptism may be administered only by an ordained minister. (However, it is also accepted that the Intensive Care Unit of a Maternity Hospital is not a suitable place for discussions on doctrine.) The baptismal formula in general use is that in Matthew 28:19: *'in the name of the Father and of the Son and of the Holy Spirit'*. The NSPC of I also regards as valid the practice of the Early Church (Acts 2:38, 8:16, 10:48, 19:5, et cetera): *'in the name of the Lord Jesus'*; and some ministers prefer this as better authenticated. The *Common Certificate of Christian Baptism*, which is recognised by many denominations in Britain and Ireland, can be issued only where the Matthew 28:19 formula has been used.

MARRIAGE

This is seen as a solemn and personal contract between one man and one woman, instituted of God since time immemorial, and sanctioned and regulated under civil law. In common with general Presbyterian teaching, marriage is not regarded as a sacrament but as a contract. Since the seventeenth century it has been held in these or similar words that *'adultery, or such wilful desertion as can in no way be remedied by the Church or civil magistrate, is cause sufficient of dissolving the marriage bond'*. Thus, when a new start is wanted in penitence, hope and love, NSPC of I ministers, when the law allowed, have held themselves to be justified legally and morally in conducting the marriages of individuals whose marriages have been dissolved by the courts or declared in law as null and void.

SPIRITUALITY AND ETHOS

The Non-Subscribers see faith as essentially a personal relationship between the individual and God. All else is secondary, supplementary and having a value relative only to how it helps or hinders personal faith. It is this 'sitting loose' to sharp definitions and an awareness of the danger of earthly things of religion becoming idols of worship in themselves which have enabled the Non-Subscribers to hold together. Tolerance and an ability to sense which things are 'indifferent' are both essential in a denomination in which views range from those of senior members of the Orange Order to very loyal members of Protestant and Catholic Encounter (PACE).

WORSHIP

Services of worship follow normal Presbyterian practice with hymns, readings, prayers and sermon. Liturgical prayers with responses are very rarely used. 'Praise Services' may be held from time to time with extra music and no sermon. Regular 'Family Services' are held in some churches. Communion Services are usually held twice a year (and, in a few congregations, also at Easter).

BUILDINGS AND ARCHITECTURE

The main non-subscribing controversies arose early in the history of Presbyterianism in Ireland. As a result the NSPC of I has an undue proportion of historic classified buildings. Early-eighteenth-century meeting houses are usually T-shaped and later in the century square or barn-shaped. Churches rebuilt in the early nineteenth century often have pillared classic façades and later rebuilds are mostly Victorian Gothic. Some churches are open to the public during the week at set times and most have display cabinets for communion sets or other historic exhibits. The most valuable, such as seventeenth-century silver communion cups, are kept more safely. The majority of old baptism, marriage and funeral records still extant are now deposited in the Public Record Office, Belfast.

CHURCH AND COMMUNITY

Most Non-Subscribing Presbyterian congregations are situated in villages or small towns, where they play a full part in communal life. Church halls are used for bringing people together in bowling clubs, whist drives, youth activities, drama groups, et cetera, and members of other denominations are made welcome. In Belfast Non-Subscribers were directly involved in founding both of the oldest grammar schools as well as the university and various hospitals and charitable institutions. Owing to population movements, the number of members living in Belfast has fallen steadily over the century and it is more difficult for Belfast churches to keep up their traditional social role in city life.

BIBLIOGRAPHY

General works on the history of Presbyterianism in Ireland
Haire, J.L.M. (ed.), *Challenge and Conflict*, Greystone Press 1981
Moore, T., *The First Presbyterian Church, Belfast, 1644–1983*, First
    Presbyterian Church, Rosemary Street, Belfast 1983
Numerous local histories – advice is available from the Presbyterian
    Historical Society or from the local church itself.
Video and documentation pack on the Non-Subscribing Presbyterian
    Church of Ireland (twenty minutes). This is intended for schools' use
    under the NI Core Syllabus for RE, but would also be suitable for small
    groups or even individual viewing. Copies are available on loan from
    Resource Centres of the NI Education and Library Boards and the Irish
    Council of Churches, or from the Clerk of Synod, 102 Carrickfergus
    Road, Larne, Co. Antrim, BT40 3JT (tel: 01574 272600).

BIOGRAPHICAL NOTE

The REV. D.G. (TOM) BANHAM was born in Devon in 1929 and went to sea in 1945 as an apprentice, qualifying later as a Royal Navy Electrical Engineer Officer. During foreign service he worked professionally with people of many other religions and cultures. In 1968 he resigned from the navy to enter Unitarian College, Manchester, from which he graduated with an external London BD. Preferring the liberal Christian understanding of faith, he accepted a Call in 1971 to the Old Presbyterian Congregation of Ballycarry, Co. Antrim. In 1975 he was called to First Presbyterian Church, Belfast. He was involved early in Irish Council of Churches committees and the Ballymascanlon Talks. Various representative, secretarial and chairmanship posts in inter-church work were held in the following years until bouts of ill health made a reduction in commitments necessary. He was Moderator of the NSPC of I from 1989 to 1991.

11

The
Reformed Presbyterian Church of Ireland

EDWARD DONNELLY

ORIGINS

The origins of the Reformed Presbyterian Church in Ireland are bound up with the coming of Scottish settlers to Ulster in the early seventeenth century. Most were Presbyterians and they soon made a major impact on the religious life of the province. They were naturally sympathetic towards their co-religionists in Scotland, who drew up a National Covenant in 1638 in protest against the autocratic policies of Charles I and who, in 1643, entered into the Solemn League and Covenant with the English Parliament. One aim of this covenant was 'to work for the reformation of religion in the three kingdoms' and it was warmly approved and signed by many of the Ulster Scots.

The Revolution Settlement of 1690 was welcomed by most Ulster Presbyterians as a vindication of their struggle for religious freedom. A minority, however, objected to the disregarding of the Covenants and the absence of any specific recognition of the kingship of Jesus Christ. These 'Covenanters', ancestors of modern Reformed Presbyterians, stood apart from the Presbyterian Church and began to hold separate meetings for fellowship. They were dependent on visits from Scottish ministers from 1696 until 1757. In 1763 a 'Reformed Presbytery' was formed and rapid growth led to the formation of a Synod in 1811.

THE DENOMINATION TODAY

There are at present thirty-seven congregations, five in Cos. Monaghan and Donegal and the remainder in Northern Ireland. These total approximately twenty-five hundred communicant members, with up to fifteen hundred covenant children and adherents in addition. This is a stronger community than bare numbers might suggest, as most of those belonging to the Church show a high level of commitment. In contrast to some larger bodies, there are few nominal members.

The distribution of Reformed Presbyterians (still often called Covenanters) has generally followed the pattern of the original Scots settlement, with most congregations in Cos. Antrim, Londonderry and Down. For much of her history, therefore, the Church has been rural in membership and orientation. This has been changing in recent years, with significant numerical growth in the Greater Belfast area resulting in the formation of several new congregations. A recovery of confidence in the relevance of the Church's message is leading to a more active and fruitful church expansion programme.

Church buildings are typically simple in design, with a central pulpit, under which is a communion table, symbolising the supreme importance of the Word of God. A widespread building programme has done a great deal to improve the range of classroom, hall and kitchen facilities.

DOCTRINAL POSITION

The supreme standard for belief and practice is the Bible, received as the inspired and inerrant Word of God. In common with all historic Presbyterian Churches, the Westminster Confession of Faith and the *Larger* and *Shorter Catechisms* are held to be a systematic and accurate summary of the teaching of Scripture. Further expansion of the Church's teaching is found in her 'Testimony', which applies these doctrines to various specific topics. These documents are the subordinate standards of the denomination.

Reformed Presbyterian theology is apostolic, Protestant, Reformed (or Calvinistic) and evangelical. There is a desire to maintain in its depth and purity the Christian faith handed down from the beginning. The basic principles of the denomination are not different from those held by many other Churches. Such distinctives as there are lie in the application and implementation of these truths.

In particular, Reformed Presbyterians give prominence to the kingship of Christ. This has implications for human life in all its spheres. Areas which have received special attention (and where Reformed Presbyterian practice is, in this century, somewhat unusual) are worship and politics. The worship of the King must be governed in every detail by what he has required in his Word. The nation is under obligation, once admitted but now repudiated, to recognise Christ as her king and to govern all her affairs in accordance with his will. Words from Colossians 1:18 express the core of Covenanting theology: 'that in everything he [Christ] might have the supremacy'.

MEMBERSHIP, CHURCH GOVERNMENT AND MINISTRY

The terms of membership require acceptance of the Scriptures as the Word of God and the only infallible rule of faith and practice, a profession of personal faith in Jesus Christ as Saviour and Lord and promises of a teachable attitude towards the doctrines of the Church and a sincere endeavour to live a consistent Christian life. Communicant (or full) members are baptised persons who satisfy the Session as to their commitment to these vows. The children of such members, though not yet admitted to full privileges, are also members of the congregation.

The name 'Presbyterian' comes from the Greek word for 'elder', so each congregation is governed by the Session, a group of ruling elders. These are men, chosen by the people and with no distinction of rank. Each Session sends delegates to the regular meetings of Presbytery, a higher court of the Church. Presbyteries, in turn, meet together in a general gathering, or Synod.

The minister of the congregation is one of the elders, of equal rank with his colleagues, though serving as chairman, or Moderator, of Session. In addition to ruling, he has the responsibility of preaching the Word. Ministers are trained, usually after graduation from university, at the Reformed Theological College, located in Belfast since its establishment in 1854. Those who successfully complete the three-year course are awarded a Diploma in Theology.

SACRAMENTS

The only two sacraments instituted by Christ are baptism and the Lord's supper. Baptism is given to unbaptised adults who profess faith in Christ. It is also administered to the children of believers, who are recognised as included in God's covenant of grace, of which baptism is a sign and seal. The sacrament is performed with water, which may properly be administered by immersion, pouring or, preferably, sprinkling.

The frequency of observance of the Lord's supper is decided by each Session, present practice ranging from two to four times a year. In addition to members of the Church, believers from other denominations are welcomed to the table, provided that their Christian testimony and practice are known to the elders.

SPIRITUALITY

Since Christ is Lord over all of life, the daily work of every believer is a vital part of Christian service, to be carried out to the Saviour's glory. The covenant family is regarded as a church in miniature and parents promise to hold regular family worship in the home and to pay conscientious attention to the spiritual training of their children. The Lord's Day is a special blessing, given for rest and worship, apart from duties of necessity and mercy. For over three hundred years Covenanters have met during the week in 'societies', home groups for prayer and Bible study where spiritual experience is shared and the members can minister to one another in love.

WORSHIP

Like most historic Reformed Churches, worship centres on the reading and preaching of the Bible, with the response of the people to God in praises, prayer and giving. Two areas of distinctiveness in the matter of praise are that the only words used in singing are from the Book of Psalms and that no instrumental accompaniment is used. This is the original practice of presbyterian churches, which the Reformed Presbyterian Church, alone in Ireland, maintains to this day. Her rationale, however, is deeper than loyalty to a historic tradition. Since God has revealed in Scripture how he is to be worshipped, nothing is to be introduced which he has not specifically commanded. Nowhere has he instructed his people to praise him with songs other than those provided in the Book of Psalms. Instrumental music was an integral part of Old Testament sacrificial worship, which was fulfilled in Christ, and there is no example of such accompaniment in the Church of the New Testament.

The Book of Psalms provides songs which are inspired, Christ-centred, timeless, non-sectarian and continually relevant, the property of the universal Church. Reformed Presbyterians experience profound spiritual fulfilment in singing, usually in four-part harmony, these glorious praises. The basic version used is the Scottish Metrical Psalter, with supplementary alternative versions. The Church is at present engaged in a major process of Psalter revision.

CHURCH AND COMMUNITY

The primary responsibility of the church to the community is that of evangelism and each local congregation is a centre from which the gospel is communicated to the surrounding neighbourhood. Missionary work outside the bounds of established congregations is being carried on in the

Republic of Ireland and in France. Cameron House, a Christian bookshop at 98 Lisburn Road, Belfast, is also denominational headquarters and home of the Reformed Theological College. Residential accommodation is provided for the elderly in Ballymoney and for students and young people in Belfast. A monthly denominational magazine, the *Covenanter Witness*, is published for the benefit of the churches in Ireland and Scotland.

A distinctive witness to the nation is borne through an emphasis on the duty of recognising Christ as king, as was once done in the seventeenth-century covenants. The Church considers the repudiation of those covenants to be a sin, to be repented of and corrected, and Reformed Presbyterians will only support candidates for political office who promise to work for such a national recognition of the authority of Christ. They seek to be good citizens and to support policies and participate in initiatives aimed at the true well-being of the community.

RELATIONS WITH OTHER CHURCHES

There are several categories of professing Christians with which the Reformed Presbyterian Church can have no official fellowship. Liberal theology, with its attack upon the authority of Scripture and its denial of the gospel, has placed itself outside the faith and under the condemnation of God. Roman Catholicism's failure to accept such cardinal doctrines as the sole authority of Scripture and justification by faith alone, together with innovations such as its teaching on Mary and the development of the papacy, render it impossible for Reformed Presbyterians to accept it as a Christian Church. It is recognised, however, that there may be individual Roman Catholics who are true believers and all harshness and ill feeling between Protestants and Roman Catholics is to be deplored.

Closest relations in the family of Christ are Reformed Presbyterian Churches in Scotland, North America, Australia, Japan and Cyprus. The denomination is a constituent member of the International Conference of Reformed Churches, which brings together Churches from as far apart as North and South America, South Africa, Asia, Australia and Europe. Ministers serve on the boards of such bodies as Scripture Gift Mission, Christian Witness to Israel and the Evangelical Fellowship of Ireland. Links are continually being strengthened with Christians in many other denominations and increasing co-operation with biblical Churches is actively pursued.

BIBLIOGRAPHY

The Code: The Book of Government and Order of the Reformed Presbyterian Church of Ireland, 1989
Loughridge, Adam, *The Covenanters in Ireland,* Cameron Press 1984
Smellie, Alexander, *Men of the Covenant,* Banner of Truth 1975
Testimony of the Reformed Presbyterian Church of Ireland, 1990

BIOGRAPHICAL NOTE

The REV. EDWARD DONNELLY has been minister of Trinity, Newtownabbey, from 1975 to 1987 and from 1990 until the present. Ordained to the ministry of the Reformed Presbyterian Church in 1968, he has also pastored congregations in Dervock and Portrush, and served as a missionary in Cyprus from 1972 to 1974. He was appointed Professor of New Testament Language and Literature in the Reformed Theological College, Belfast, in 1979, a position which he still holds. He and his wife, Lorna, have three children.

12

The
Salvation Army

LESLIE SMYTH

ORIGINS

In a crowded tent on a disused Quaker burial ground at Whitechapel in London's East End the people were sitting on wooden benches. Most could neither read nor write but the preacher held their attention because he seemed to understand them and their needs. The tall, dark, 36-year-old speaker was William Booth (1829–1912), a minister of the Methodist New Connexion.

During this tent mission, in 1865, William Booth had walked through the east London streets and seen the great range of human need around him. One night he reached home just before midnight to tell his wife, 'Darling, I have found my destiny!' This Christian Mission to the East End grew to become the Salvation Army, so named from 1878. Booth initially had no thought of forming a new Church. His aim was simply to get people saved, meet the social needs of the poor and send them to their churches, but the churches didn't seem to want them.

Some years later, on Monday, 3 May 1880, the Salvation Army Headquarters in London was the setting for a very special meeting in which five specially selected Officers were commissioned for the work of the Army in Ireland. Booth had received numerous requests for the Army to extend its work to Ireland and property was already purchased for its use in Belfast and Londonderry. This act of appointing five female Officers showed clearly the mind of William Booth, who believed that all were equal in the sight of God irrespective of class, colour, creed or gender. So began the Salvation Army in Ireland.

It was in the district known as Sandy Row in Belfast that the first Irish

Corps (church), Blackstaff, was established. Early reports from 29 May reveal great interest in the Message of the Gospel as preached by these Salvationist lassies. One account tells of a lady who visited amongst the poor and was anxious for the salvation of their souls. She told the Army members of a street where the vilest people in Belfast lived but said it had been given up by all the Lord's people; no one cared for it. The answer from the Salvationists was: 'Man may have given it up but Jesus has not', and so the pattern was set for the Salvation Army, who believed that 'all have need of God's Salvation'. From this first centre the work spread steadily despite biting sarcasm and in some instances fierce intolerance. By February 1910 there were eleven Corps and two Social Institutions in Belfast. Further north the work was established at Ligoniel, Ballymena, Coleraine and Londonderry. At Ballymena during 1909 no fewer than 220 persons professed conversion in the Army Hall within six months.

STATISTICS

At the time of writing there are twenty-one Corps in Ireland as a whole, most of them in Northern Ireland. There are sixty-six officers and approximately one thousand members.

In the Republic of Ireland the Salvation Army formerly had Corps at Waterford, Cork, Dublin and Kingstown (Dún Laoghaire). In Dublin there were four Corps but in some places in the Republic there was considerable coldness from the Protestant community. (In one town it was said to the Salvationists, 'We know that you are not Catholics, and the Protestants won't look at ye; so, what are ye?') Sadly the work in the South is now limited to Dublin.

In Northern Ireland there has also been a decrease in the number of Corps but this has to be seen against what could be termed a 'Church Culture'.

BELIEFS AND AUTHORITY

The Salvation Army is part of the Christian Church and has throughout its history been seen as part of the Evangelical Tradition with its preaching of:

- the need of salvation and to be 'born again'
- salvation through confession and faith
- the resurrection of Jesus from the dead
- faith that nothing but Jesus' blood can save us
- confession of sin to God
- one God and one Mediator – the man Christ Jesus.

The Salvation Army uses only the Holy Bible for the foundation of its beliefs and preaches that, all having sinned in the sight of God, all need God's Salvation, which can be found only by believing in God and seeking His forgiveness. The Army also preaches 'Holiness', believing that it is truly possible to lead a 'holy life'.

SOCIAL COMMITMENT

Telling others of Christ, the Bread of Life, posed the Salvation Army a great challenge when it realised that for all too many bread and food was in such short supply for people's daily need. This was a challenge that had to be met and so began the social side of the Army's work.

Down throughout the years in over one hundred countries members of the Army are well known for their work amongst the deprived of society. Indeed the quote often used is 'Where there's need there's the Salvation Army.' This part of the Ministry has had something of a rebound effect because a great number of people see it as a Social Mission or, in today's language, 'a group of do-gooders', not realising that it is an expression of their Spirituality that makes them reach out to lift up the fallen and to show to others something of the 'love of Christ'. In the words of John Greenleaf Whittier:

> Follow with reverent steps the great example
> Of Him whose holy work was 'doing good'.

WORSHIP AND SACRAMENTS

What sets the Salvation Army apart from most other Churches is its lack of Sacraments and Ordinances. It is difficult to give the reason for this in a few words, but simply to say that whilst they understand how others interpret Scripture and see the need for such things in their worship, the Army still holds to the basic belief that these are not a requirement for the forgiveness of God and for continuing to lead a Christian life.

The worship of the Salvation Army in all its meetings for public worship is centred on the knowledge that Jesus lived, died and rose again. The songs are often of a rousing style and sometimes members express their praise by hand-clapping to the rhythm of the music. It could be said that in the Salvation Army there is more freedom of expression than in the more orthodox forms of worship.

MEMBERSHIP AND MINISTRY

All members of the Salvation Army must declare that they have sought God's repentance and that they are 'saved'.

The Salvation Army has a Leader and, being a Christian *Army*, the

Leader is called a *General*. Each country in which the Army operates has its own Commander and down to local level each Corps has, in most places, an *Officer* (Minister) in charge with the assistance of local Officers who are members of a *Census* (Advisory) Board.

There are many opportunities of service and many outlets at local level but for full-time Ministry it is necessary to leave home and enter the Army's Training College for Officers in London. In most cases this is for a period of two years with an ongoing period of further instruction. In the Army men and women have equal opportunity in all positions of leadership, even to Officership and the command of a Corps.

RELATIONSHIPS WITH OTHER CHURCHES

The Salvation Army has a good working relationship with all Christian denominations and is held in high esteem by other church members and people in general here in Ireland. The Army is in full membership of the Irish Council of Churches.

In the situation in our province, especially regarding what is called 'ecumenism', any such co-operation is usually limited to a request to supply music for some community event, such as a carol service. The Salvation Army could not take part in any form of worship where, in its considered opinion, there was a departure from Scriptural Teaching.

The Army as a Church never makes any political statement because as a body of people each with his own political outlook it would not be possible to speak as a united voice. However, where it is necessary to speak on what might be deemed 'a matter of conscience' it does express its view.

WORK IN THE COMMUNITY

The Salvation Army as a Church believes that it should be identified with the local community and today there is a greater awareness of this need. Many of its Corps operate a charity shop, a care for the elderly programme, dinner clubs, youth clubs and parent and toddler groups. There is also the province-wide Christmas family appeal. Recently appointed here in Ireland is a Director of the Social Programme.

SPECIAL FEATURES

Understandably the Army has moved with the times and this can be seen in the distinctive uniform that is worn by many of its members. The traditional bonnet has been to some extent replaced by a hat, and tunics which had a military-style stand-up collar are now of the open lapel style. It is not, however, essential for members to wear uniform, which becomes necessary only when one joins the Band or Songsters. Others can wear the uniform if they so desire, and many do not wear it at all.

The Salvation Army makes considerable use of music through its bands and Songster Brigades (Choirs). It publishes its own music but before it can be used in public all music must be passed as acceptable by the Army's Music Board.

Britain's most popular religious weekly, the *War Cry*, is published by the Salvation Army. It is sold mainly in public houses and city centre shopping areas, and sales in Northern Ireland total some thirty-five hundred per week.

A worldwide international body, the Salvation Army after well over one hundred years in Ireland is still faithfully maintaining its Christian Witness and that witness is in many places bearing fruit to the Glory of God and the extension of His Kingdom. The Army is still prepared to do and dare for Jesus and, in the words of one of its songs:

> Weep o'er the erring one
> Lift up the fallen
> Tell them of Jesus
> The mighty to save.

BIBLIOGRAPHY

Barnes, Cyril, *God's Army: An Illustrated History of the Salvation Army*, Lion Publishing 1978
Collier, Richard, *The General Next to God*, Fontana 1965
'The Expedition to Ireland', *War Cry*, 8 May 1880
'The Expedition to Belfast', *War Cry*, 29 May 1880

BIOGRAPHICAL NOTE

LESLIE SMYTH is a lifelong Salvationist, born of Salvationist parents. He has served in several positions in the Londonderry Corps and was Corps Sergeant Major for eleven years. Most of his early working life was spent in the family painting and decorating firm until he joined the civil service. On retirement he took responsibility for the Salvation Army Community Complex in Londonderry City and is also responsible for the Army's Family Tracing Service in the area.

13

The Church of the Nazarene

DAVID TARRANT

ORIGINS

The roots of the Church of the Nazarene lie in Methodism. Dr Phineas Bresee (1838–1915), a presiding elder in the Methodist Episcopal Church in Los Angeles, had the vision of providing full church membership privileges for the disadvantaged masses of that city, who up to that point had been given only mission hall facilities. He asked the Methodist Conference for permission to pioneer a new church project in the downtown area, but was refused. He then felt his call in this direction so strongly that he tendered his resignation from the denomination and set out to pioneer an independent church which would minister to the poor of the city at every level, and at the same time give a revived emphasis to one of the cardinal doctrines of Methodism, which John Wesley had set out in his book, *A Plain Account of Christian Perfection*. The first services were held on 6 October 1895.

Because of the new church's emphasis on ministry to the poor, the despised and the neglected, the name 'Church of the Nazarene' seemed to identify it most directly with the One who was 'despised and rejected' by the establishment of His day, yet gladly welcomed by the common people. It took His words as its watchword: 'The Spirit of the Lord is upon me, because He has anointed me to preach good news to the poor' (Luke 4:18).

During the final decade of the nineteenth century, and the first decade of the present century, the work grew and spread to other cities. A coming together of several small new holiness groups throughout the USA resulted in the establishment of a denominational structure in 1908; and by 1915 the accession of a ten-year-old holiness church in Glasgow provided a bridge-head for the Church of the Nazarene in the British Isles, which now has almost a hundred churches.

The first move into Ireland came in 1935, when Rev. Frank Clark, a Scotsman, began the work in Lurgan, which was officially organised as a Nazarene church in 1937. This was quickly followed by the first church in Belfast, at Skegoneill Avenue, in 1939. Subsequent years have seen success-ful church plantings in Ulster, where there are now thirteen churches; there is also one church in the Republic of Ireland, originally located in Dublin but now operating in Greystones.

THE CHURCH TODAY

In the meantime, the Church of the Nazarene has extended its ministry into more than a hundred world areas, and now has a constituency of around two million members and adherents – half of whom live in de-veloping countries. Haiti, Mozambique and India are countries where the Church is particularly strong; and in the Cape Verde Islands to be a Protes-tant is to be a Nazarene. The Church operates hospitals in India, Swaziland and Papua New Guinea, and hundreds of schools and colleges. Nazarene Theological College in Manchester, affiliated to the University of Manchester, is one of the foremost evangelical colleges in the United Kingdom.

In a day when evangelicalism is becoming increasingly dominated by charismatic influences, the Church of the Nazarene has maintained a strongly conservative stance. While modes of worship and musical styles have reflected modern trends, speaking in tongues is frowned on and so-called deliverance ministries are suspect, though traditional practices in the area of divine healing – anointing with oil, together with the prayer of faith – are encouraged. There is openness concerning modes of baptism, though the dominant practice is believers' baptism. The Lord's Supper, usually celebrated monthly, is open to all believers. Non-alcoholic wine is prescribed for use in the sacrament.

DISTINCTIVE BELIEFS

The experience and lifestyle which Wesley called 'Christian Perfection' is seldom called by that name today, since it would carry negative connota-tions in the minds of the uninitiated, as it did in Wesley's own day. But its basic truth is still firmly held to by today's Nazarenes. It springs from the Bible teaching that the nature of sin is twofold. There are acts of sin, will-ing infringements of the divine law, which attract guilt, but are capable of being forgiven on the ground of Christ's atoning work. There is also inbred sin, the inherited corruption of our nature, which creates within us, even after spiritual regeneration, a bias towards self-centredness and dis-obedience. All Christians believe that this can be controlled, with the aid of the Holy Spirit. Nazarenes believe it can be cleansed away so that man's moral heart may become pure and undivided. Paul's prayer for the Thessalonians, that they might be 'sanctified through and through' (1 Thessalonians 5:23), can be fulfilled as born-again believers, hungering for inner holiness, make a full commitment of themselves to God's will, as defined in Romans 12:1–2, and receive by faith the purifying infilling of the Holy Spirit (see Acts 15:8–9). This 'entire sanctification' needs to be maintained by careful attendance on the means of grace, and is the door-way to spiritual growth. Nazarenes believe that constant watchfulness against Satan's devices is essential. As Jude reminds us, we must 'keep our-selves in the love of God', while remembering that He alone is able to 'keep us from falling' (Jude 21, 24).

AUTHORITY AND MEMBERSHIP

The basis for authority for Nazarenes is solely the Holy Scriptures, fully inspired, an unfailing guide to Christlike living. The Church has formu-lated its own guidelines for those who seek membership in it, but these are dependent on the scriptural injunctions to which, in the Church's official Manual, they are linked. They are reviewed quadrennially by the denomi-nation's General Assembly, and some modifications have been made from time to time in the light of today's society; for example, rules have been relaxed relative to the admission to membership and ministry of persons who have suffered the trauma of divorce. But Church members are still expected to abstain from alcohol and tobacco, and practising homosexual-ity is still regarded as sinful. The place of women in the ministry of the Church has never been questioned; in fact, in the earliest days, one minister in five was a woman. This proportion has steadily declined over the years.

CHURCH GOVERNMENT AND MINISTRY

Church government is a fusion of the congregational with the episcopal. While the Church does not have bishops, it has six General Superinten-dents, who share worldwide supervision of the Church; and a District Superintendent for each assembly district, of which there are two in the United Kingdom. A pastor is called by a local church by a congregational vote, and is amenable to that church, as well as to the District Superinten-dent. He is required to report annually to the District Assembly. In matters of local administration, he is assisted by a church board, which comprises trustees, stewards and leaders of the subsidiary organisations. Matters of substance, such as the purchase of property, must be decided in a church members' meeting and endorsed by the District Superintendent and his Advisory Board.

BUILDINGS

Church architecture, in the Reformed style, centres on the pulpit, for the preaching of the Word is more important than any sacrament. A distinctive item of furniture is the altar of prayer, at the front of the auditorium, formerly called the mourners' bench or the penitent form, at which seekers are invited to come and pray. These days it has a wider use, in that during a family worship time, members often come forward to pray for the needs of others as well as their own. Buildings are simple and functional, without obtrusive artistic embellishments. The importance of Sunday School indicates the need for adequate classroom space.

COMMUNITY CONCERNS

The denomination's original emphasis on ministry to the community has found a new impetus during the past twenty years or so. With the rise of the great interdenominational relief agencies, such as TEAR Fund, Nazarenes have been stirred to concern themselves more urgently with the devastation caused by war and famine in our own mission areas. Hot lunches for schoolchildren in Haiti, relief programmes in Mozambique and Rwanda, hospital supplies for Romania and Russia as well as welfare projects in our own cities have captured the concern of our people. In Belfast the Church has sponsored the LINC project, which has been providing skills training for released prisoners, as well as participating actively in negotiations to help forward the peace process.

ATTITUDE TO OTHER CHRISTIANS

The Church's core doctrine, which is also known as Perfect Love, has made it impossible for preachers and people to align themselves politically in an atmosphere of hostility. While as convinced Protestants we have to discount papal claims of infallibility and supremacy, we seek to cherish every sincere worshipper of our God as a true brother or sister in Christ; and especially in the Ulster context we want to be known as peacemakers, proclaiming by word and deed the message of reconciliation. Numerically we are small alongside other denominations in these islands. We hope that in compassion and in co-operation we will always show a spirit that is broad and generous.

BIBLIOGRAPHY

Ford, Jack, *In the Steps of John Wesley – The Church of the Nazarene in Britain*, Kansas City, Missouri: Nazarene Publishing House 1968

Leadingham, Everett (ed.), *I Believe – Now Tell me Why*, Kansas City, Missouri: Nazarene Publishing House 1994

Manual of the Church of the Nazarene, 1993–97, Kansas City, Missouri: Nazarene Publishing House

All the above are obtainable from Nazarene Literature Department, Nazarene Theological College, Dene Road, Didsbury, Manchester, M20 2GU, England.

BIOGRAPHICAL NOTE

The REV. DAVID TARRANT was born in Surrey in 1920. He was converted and baptised as a youth, joined the Inland Revenue, then entered wartime service. Called of God to preach the gospel, he entered the Nazarene ministry as the war ended, and pastored churches in Carlisle, Portsmouth, Port Glasgow and Edinburgh until 1972, when he was elected District Superintendent of the Church's British Isles North District (which includes Ulster). He subsequently became chairman of the trustees of Nazarene Theological College. He retired in 1987 and remains active in ministry.

14

The
Free Methodist Church

ANDREW BELSHAW

ORIGINS

Many famous names are associated with the development of Methodism in America from 1738, including John and Charles Wesley, George Whitefield, Barbara Heck and Philip Embury. The two people who played the most significant roles in American Methodism, however, were Dr Thomas Coke and Francis Asbury. There was a great need for ordained clergy in the American Church, and when the Bishop of London would not agree to the ordination of Dr Coke, John Wesley decided to ordain him himself as Superintendent and to have Francis Asbury as his assistant.

In 1784 the Methodist Episcopal Church was established. The Church grew large over the next century, but problems were beginning to arise as two camps of Methodists became apparent. Doctrinally, Sanctification became an issue of conflict, as did membership of Secret Societies. Slavery was disfavoured by Wesleyan Methodists as were rented pews. A worldliness crept into Methodism which violated historical Methodist principles and Scripture. These were the deepening conflicts which finally brought into existence a new Methodist denomination.

The Rev. Benjamin Titus Roberts had studied at university as a lawyer, but later he became a minister and saw the effects which slavery and the rental of pews had on the neglected poor. The Church was favouring the wealthy, so he used his skills to fight such favouritism on the basis of the scriptural principle that the gospel is free. He produced an article entitled 'New School Methodism' which highlighted these differences. After being disciplined by the Methodist Episcopal Church for his article he was moved to Pekin, New York. His ministry there was successful but after a further publication of 'New School Methodism' he was expelled.

Roberts appealed to the General Conference. He wanted to stay to promote evangelism and preach the Wesleyan message, but, along with several other sympathising ministers and laymen who shared his beliefs, he found himself deprived of membership. With converts still coming through Roberts's ministry, a spiritual home was needed. So on 23 August 1860, eighty laymen and fifteen ministers met in Pekin, and established the Free Methodist Church.

For another century, the denomination in America grew substantially. Then thirty years ago Free Methodism came to Britain and Northern Ireland.

DENOMINATIONAL SURVEY

The Free Methodist Church has at present approximately 170 fully active members plus other attenders in Northern Ireland, with churches in Bangor, Dundonald, Glengormley, Belfast, Lisburn and Dungannon.

The early years of Free Methodism in Northern Ireland saw many churches being established, but again through doctrinal differences a number of members felt that standards were not adequate and therefore left to form their own denomination. The number of people involved as members has fluctuated, perhaps as a result of the many changes in leadership and the impact on such a young denomination of a loss of continuity. At present, however, the Free Methodist Church is putting into place structures that will take it into the next millennium with great vision and purpose.

DOCTRINAL POSITION

The Free Methodist Church is based upon historical Wesleyan Methodist principles. It continues to stress the reality of an inner cleansing and power that affirm the doctrine of 'Entire Sanctification', as taught by John Wesley.

Free Methodists are committed to working in the world for the salvation of all men. Their commitment is to Christ and therefore conforms to the will of God, which is made known in the Scriptures.

Free Methodists' beliefs are the standard beliefs of evangelical Arminian protestantism. They believe the gospel is for all, but sense a special obligation to preach the gospel to the poor. There is also a strong belief in the mission of the Church, so there is a keen sense of responsibility for stewardship in the area of finance. Commercial efforts to raise funds to support the cause of Christ are not engaged in.

Free Methodists believe in one God, but in the unity of this Godhead there are three persons: Father, Son and Holy Spirit. God was in Jesus Christ reconciling man to God. He was born of the virgin Mary but conceived by the Holy Spirit. God in human flesh was truly God and truly man. He suffered, was crucified, died and was buried. He became as a blameless sacrifice for our sin. He is our Saviour, the only perfect mediator between God and man. He rose victorious from the dead, ascended into heaven, sits at God's right hand as our exalted Lord. He will return to judge all men. The Holy Spirit, the third person of the Trinity, proceeds from the Father and the Son. He is equal in Deity, Majesty and Power and continues to reveal and glorify Jesus. He is effective in creation and life and is the administrator of the work of Christ enabling and empowering the believer to make real the Lordship of Christ in his life and in the Church.

The Bible, consisting of the Old and New Testaments, is God's inspired written Word, written by men, moved by God through the Holy Spirit, to each generation. It is the Free Methodists' basis of authority to teach the truth about God and mankind and its destiny. It teaches the way of Salvation and the life of faith. If certain teachings and beliefs are not found in the Scriptures, they are not required as an article of belief, neither are they necessary for Salvation.

Man is created by God in His image, to love Him and to love his neighbour.

Salvation is through Christ, who offered the one perfect sacrifice for the sins of the whole world. A new life and right relationship is possible through Jesus Christ.

The Church is created by God. It is the people of God with Christ as the head and the Holy Spirit as its life and power. It is where the Word of God and the Sacraments are administered.

Christ will return and may return at any moment, but we do not know when. The dead of the just and the unjust will rise in bodily form, the good unto eternal life and the evil unto eternal damnation. God has an appointed day in which He will judge the world in the light of the gospel and people's works in this life.

SACRAMENTS

Free Methodists believe that Baptism and the Lord's Supper are the Sacraments of the Church based on the Scriptures.

Baptism is a symbol of the new covenant of grace commanded by Christ. It is to be administered to believers as a declaration of their faith in Jesus Christ as Saviour.

The Lord's Supper is a sacrament of our redemption, remembering Christ's death. The bread resembles the body of Christ and the cup is a partaking of the blood of Christ. There is no change in the bread or the cup. They are not literally the body and blood of Christ, neither is there a literal presence of Christ in the elements. They are emblems of worship eaten in faith by those who are redeemed.

MEMBERSHIP

For a person to become a full member of the Church, there are certain requirements, such as a personal experience in regeneration, seeking to live a holy life and Christian Baptism. Acceptance of the Articles of Religion, Guidance for Christian Living and the Book of Discipline in matters of church government are necessary, as well as a pledge to live in fellowship with the members and a covenanted support of the Church, through a declaration of membership vows. Any member may participate in the sacraments and ordinances of the Church as well as vote and hold office in the Church. Membership is seen as a privilege and a responsibility. The Scriptures teach that members enter into a covenant relationship with Jesus Christ. There should be evidence of a desire to sustain that relationship with God, to preserve the unity of the Body of Christ and of the Free Methodist Church.

CHURCH GOVERNMENT

Each Free Methodist Church has a pastoral charge. The churches in Northern Ireland constitute the United Kingdom–Northern Ireland Conference. Each year the Northern Ireland Conference meets to organise the work of the Free Methodist Church at Annual Conference. A lay delegate represents each church along with the minister and is entitled to vote on issues regarding the ongoing work in Northern Ireland. Each Annual Conference has an overseer known as the Superintendent. The Area Bishop, who is based in America and has charge of many conferences, is the President of the Conference.

Local church government is in the hands of the minister and church board. The minister is the overseer of the local church and is therefore the chairperson at each business session of the official board meeting. Those serving on church boards are Trustees, Lay Delegates, Treasurer, Secretary and leaders of various departments of the church (for example, Sunday School, Women's Ministries, Youth, et cetera). These positions are voted on at each local church Annual General Meeting by members of that church. They serve in the departments to which they are elected until the next local church Annual General Meeting.

MINISTRY

There are four stages to becoming a fully ordained Free Methodist minister. The person sensing the call of God and the Church to ministry is first licensed as a local ministerial candidate. The second step involves acceptance by the Annual Conference as a ministerial candidate. During this two-year period the candidate prepares for the third step, ordination as a Deacon. Usually after a further two years, ordination to Elders' Orders completes the ordination process.

Certain skills and qualities are required and sought by Annual Conference in this period of training: spiritual qualifications, personal characteristics, pastoral care, communication and leadership. At this stage the pastor becomes a member of Conference instead of a local church.

The Superintendent Minister is elected by the pastoral and lay leadership of each local church within the Conference. He vacates the pastoral position of a church to attend to the group of churches and pastors that make up the Conference.

WORSHIP AND LITURGY

The Free Methodist Church believes worship provides an opportunity to give God praise, to gain insight into the will of God and to enable individuals to commit themselves to God. Worship includes congregational singing, reading from the Scriptures, pastoral prayers and preaching. Healing and sharing and less formal structures of worship are encouraged. The formality of the worship service varies from church to church.

BUILDINGS

Each Free Methodist Church is of a simple but presentable nature. The structure of each church is laid out in a formal setting of rows of cushioned pews facing towards the pulpit at the front. Adjacent to the sanctuary of each church are suites of rooms and a minor hall, which are used to facilitate other functions and departments of church life.

CHURCH AND COMMUNITY

It is the aim of each Free Methodist Church to reach its community with care and concern for its many needs, physically, emotionally and, of course, spiritually, and to present to them the life-changing Gospel of Christ. The Free Methodist Church seeks to provide a service and a witness for each sector of its community from youth up to senior citizens. Various clubs, social programmes and meetings function from week to week to cater for each person. Within each community the Free Methodist Church links up with other evangelical denominations in various inter-church efforts such as missions, social welfare programmes and the like. Ministers meet up with the local fraternity to discuss and address the community's differing problems so that together we might be able to make Northern Ireland a better place to live.

BIBLIOGRAPHY

Bastian, Donald, *Belonging: Adventures in Church Membership*, Light and Life Communications 1996

Knox, Lloyd H. (compiler and editor), *Faith and Life of a Free Methodist*, Free Methodist Publishing House 1976

Marston, Leslie R., *From Age to Age: A Living Witness*, Light and Life Press 1960

1995 Book of Discipline: Free Methodist Church, Free Methodist Publishing House 1996

1996 Yearbook: Free Methodist Church, Light and Life Communications 1996

BIOGRAPHICAL NOTE

ANDREW BELSHAW successfully completed his theological studies in 1991, since when he has been engaged in pastoral work, particularly in the Free Methodist Church. In 1994 he was ordained as a minister and is now senior pastor of the Dundonald Free Methodist Church. He is married to Elizabeth, an English teacher, and they have a two and a half year old son, Daniel.

15

The Fellowship of
Independent Methodist Churches

R.H. SCOTT

ORIGINS

The Fellowship of Independent Methodist Churches in Ulster was founded in 1974. Its roots, however, may be traced back to 1964, for it was in that year that a number of Christian laymen within the Methodist Church met to discuss teachings and trends within their denomination which they felt were proving detrimental to the spiritual well-being of its members. In particular they were concerned about the modernistic approach to the Bible, the increasing worldliness of the Church's social activities, contacts between the Methodist clergy and the Roman Catholic Church with mixed gatherings for young people and the involvement in the World Council of Churches.

In order to seek to stem the tide of apostasy an organisation was formed known as the 'Irish Methodist Revival Movement'. Under this banner rallies were held and a magazine entitled *Whither Methodism?* was issued quarterly to sound the alarm. While the founders sought to remain loyal to their denomination they realised after some years that the hierarchy of the Methodist Church was bent on a course of ecumenical involvement and was rather indifferent to their concerns.

There were moments of great heart-searching while wondering what was the best spiritual way to preserve the Methodist heritage and to ensure that their children would be nourished in the doctrines of the Christian faith. The decision was finally taken that separation from the denomination was a necessity and that a fresh source of fellowship be found.

Members of the Revival Movement were not anxious to form a new denomination so contact was made with the 'Free Methodist Church of

North America'. They associated with this Church for a short time but eventually decided along with some ministers to form the 'Fellowship of Independent Methodist Churches'.

DEVELOPMENT

At the time of writing the denomination has sixteen churches in the province. Two of the churches are in Belfast and the remainder are in all six counties of Ulster. In addition to these fully constituted churches there are Independent Methodist Outreach centres where regular Sunday evening services are held. Two of these are in Éire, in Cos. Donegal and Monaghan. A residential Bible College, known as 'Bethel Bible College', has been established for the training of ministers, evangelists and missionaries. The denomination issues a bi-monthly magazine, the *Alert*, and there is a constant evangelistic thrust through missions and house-to-house visitation. Camps for young people are conducted each summer.

DOCTRINAL POSITION

In doctrine the Fellowship is Methodist. Its members believe in the Deity of Christ; the doctrine of the Trinity; that Christ died to provide atonement for all; that man can be saved from sin only through the new birth; the personal visible return of Christ; the ministry of divine healing; future rewards and punishments. Each believer can know cleansing from all inward sin and be filled with the Holy Spirit. All members are expected to enjoy this experience or seek diligently until they obtain it.

CHURCH GOVERNMENT

Recognising the headship of Christ each local church is self-governing and self-supporting. A Leaders' Board is democratically elected each year from the membership and is responsible for the day-to-day running of the church.

A General Council exists in order that the witness of the denomination be co-ordinated in matters of church extension and fellowship. It is composed of the minister and one layman from each church. Responsibilities include supervision of Bible College administration and appointment of staff. It appoints a minister for oversight in a vacant church in agreement with the Leaders' Board. All candidates for the ministry must have the approval of the Council.

MINISTRY

Each church appoints its own minister. To be called he must obtain a 75%

vote of the members attending a members' meeting convened for that purpose. Lay members may be elected as local preachers who will be responsible for services during the minister's absence.

SACRAMENTS

Two sacraments are observed by the denomination: Believers' Baptism and the Lord's Supper. The former is administered to those desiring it and subsequent to their salvation. With regard to the Lord's Supper ministers emphasise that only those who are born again and are walking in obedience to God's revealed will are eligible to participate.

INFANT DEDICATION

We practise infant dedication and reject infant Baptism as there is no scriptural authority for it. We oppose the dogma of baptismal regeneration on the grounds that it rules out personal faith and makes Christianity magical and not spiritual.

WORSHIP

Public worship is free and non-liturgical. Services consist of singing of hymns, prayer, the reading of God's Word from the Authorised Version of the Bible and preaching. Sinners are urged to repent of their sins and personally trust in Christ as Lord and Saviour. Believers are exhorted to grow in grace and the knowledge of the Saviour and to live holy lives.

ATTITUDES TO OTHER DENOMINATIONS

We respect all other denominations who endeavour to hold faithfully the teachings of Holy Scripture as contained in the sixty-six books of the Bible and who believe that these alone constitute the divine rule of Christian faith and practice.

We are opposed to the present false ecumenical movement and to the World Council of Churches and we do not share in any of their activities. We are glad to have fellowship with born-again members of other denominations.

BUILDINGS

Our church buildings tend to be of plain design with suitable accommodation for Sunday School and youth work. The pulpit occupies the central point at the front of the main sanctuary and on the wall behind a text of Scripture is generally inscribed. No images or pictures adorn the walls.

While our denomination may be small, yet we trust in the purpose of

God, we will continue to expand. We feel it has a vital role to play in the evangelisation of our society and the spread of scriptural holiness across our land.

BIOGRAPHICAL NOTE

The REV. R.H. SCOTT, a native of Co. Fermanagh, became a Christian during a Gospel mission conducted by the late Rev. W.P. Nicholson in Enniskillen. He and his wife served as missionaries in Zambia and returned to Ulster in 1973. He then was called to the pastorate within the Fellowship of Independent Methodist Churches, and is at present the pastor of Lisnaskea Independent Methodist Church. He has served the denomination as Secretary of the General Council from 1974 until 1985, lectured on Methodism in Bethel Bible College and is the current editor of the *Alert*.

16

The
Religious Society of Friends (Quakers)

ARTHUR CHAPMAN

ORIGINS

The first Quaker settlement in Ireland was founded in Lurgan in 1654 during the troubled years of Cromwell's Commonwealth. Meetings were soon established in many of the Ulster towns as well as among English settlers in Leinster and Munster. By the end of the seventeenth century there were some five thousand members throughout the country. As Quakers were at that time debarred from entry to the professions, they were mostly small farmers, weavers and shopkeepers in areas where English influence was strong.

In the succeeding centuries Friends in Ulster became concentrated in the Lagan Valley and the area south of Lough Neagh. Today there are fourteen meetings in Northern Ireland with an approximate membership of nine hundred out of a total of sixteen hundred in Ireland. Most meetings have been in existence for over a century, but some small new groups have been established in recent years. Friends in Ulster preserve the original form of worship and organisation, but within the membership many strands of theological outlook, both evangelical and liberal, are represented. The British Isles and North America are considered the homeland of the movement, but as a result of emigration and missionary and relief work Quaker meetings or churches of many different types are now found in most parts of the world. These groups are linked by the Friends World Committee for Consultation, which brings together Quakers from all backgrounds for regular conferences.

The Quaker movement originated as a realisation of the direct and immediate presence of Christ which could be found and experienced by each individual. The founder, George Fox (1642–91), describes how he had been disappointed in his quest for God through his experiences with organised religion. He tells how 'when all my hopes in all men were gone, so that I had nothing outwardly to help me, nor could tell what to do; then, oh! Then, I heard a voice which said: "There is one, even Christ Jesus, that can speak to thy condition"; and when I heard it my heart did leap for joy.' Inspired by this direct revelation of the Light of Christ to the human heart, he travelled widely through the British Isles and beyond, proclaiming that 'Christ has come to teach his people himself'. Many 'Seekers' readily accepted this message and found a vital Christian experience in the form of worship practised by Quakers.

DOCTRINES AND BELIEFS

While retaining the essential doctrines of the Christian faith, Friends have always laid stress on the capacity of each individual to respond to God through a divine Light or Seed present *in every person*. They emphasise the supremacy of direct guidance by the Light of Christ rather than the authority of tradition. The Bible is prized and accepted as divinely inspired, but it is to be understood and interpreted through the illumination of the Holy Spirit. Religious traditions are not to be followed uncritically, but examined in the light of the Spirit. Friends do not find their faith can be satisfactorily distilled into the formal words of a creed but express their belief by a commitment and obedience to God's Light in all issues of everyday life. The distinctive testimonies and practices of Friends derive from this search for the will of God as applied to the issues of contemporary life.

ORGANISATION

In organisation the system adopted by Friends is highly democratic and all members, men and women alike, are expected to play their part in business matters. In accordance with their belief in the direct leadership of Christ there is no hierarchical mode of authority and there are no specially ordained priests or clergy specifically charged with preaching or conducting other religious duties. These responsibilities are undertaken by all members. Elders and overseers are, however, appointed for a specific period of time, the former to ensure the right holding of public worship and the latter to attend to pastoral duties. Decisions are made by the entire group accepting 'the sense of the meeting' rather than by voting to determine the opinion of the majority. For business matters there are three regional meetings (known as Lisburn, Lurgan, and Grange and Richhill Monthly Meetings) and one Quarterly Meeting embracing all the meetings in Northern Ireland.

'Meeting for Worship' is the chief corporate activity of Friends. Unlike the services of most other Churches there is no pre-arranged programme or liturgy. There is no appointed leader to conduct the service or to deliver a prepared sermon. However, as one meets in silence one is aware of the promptings of the Holy Spirit, and ministry is shared by all who feel called to share the message which has been given to them. This may take the form of prayer, reading or exposition from the Bible or sharing of some significant experience. A 'gathered' meeting has a strong sense of God's presence and, while the quality of worship does not depend on human words, it is evident in the continuity of messages which are delivered. Anyone, whether male or female, young or old, member or visitor, is free to take part in ministry if felt led to do so. Meeting lasts about one hour and children, for whom this is a long time, leave for their own special Sunday School after about twenty minutes. In addition to Meeting for Worship other meetings are held to provide teaching in basic Christian issues and distinctive Quaker principles.

Marriage and funeral services, too, are conducted within the framework of a public meeting for worship. In the case of a wedding the bridal pair rise to their feet during a specially appointed meeting and in turn solemnly promise before God and the assembled gathering to be loving and faithful to one another for the remainder of their lives. The marriage certificate is then signed by the bridal pair, the witnesses and the registering officer.

SACRAMENTS

The outward sacraments of the Lord's Supper and Water Baptism are not formally observed, but their inward spiritual significance is stressed. Friends believe that entry into the Church of God demands no rite of baptism whether by immersion or sprinkling; true spiritual baptism is through a change of heart, a rebirth of spiritual values. Communion with Christ in the deepest sense can be achieved in waiting and listening to His voice as He ministers in the silence. Friends hold that these 'means of grace' should not be limited to set occasions, but that in a very real sense the whole of life is sacramental.

BUILDINGS

Buildings used for worship are simple and functional in nature. The word 'church' is not applied in this context, being reserved for the community which makes up the body of Christ. In line with the belief that worship is a spiritual exercise there are no elaborate furnishings of symbolic nature, such as stained-glass windows, memorials, pulpit, communion altar. In older meeting houses a ministers' gallery is found, but in recent constructions the seating pattern is more likely to be rectangular or circular. Burial grounds often adjoin meeting houses and headstones which mark graves are uniform in size and inscription.

SOCIAL AND COMMUNITY INVOLVEMENT

In the middle period of Quaker history, viz. in the eighteenth and nineteenth centuries, Friends tended to be somewhat aloof from the community in which they lived. Their distinctive garb and testimonies and mode of worship encouraged this withdrawal. However, their concern for the welfare of their fellow men and their desire to apply the principles of the Kingdom of Heaven to the world around them led them to involvement in many areas of social reform, such as the anti-slavery movement, prison reform and relief action in the Great Famine of 1845-6. In Ulster the 'model village' of Bessbrook, built to house the workers in the linen mill of John G. Richardson and to provide them with a more congenial environment, is perhaps the best example of how faith was demonstrated in social action. The well-known pacifist principles of Friends are expressed not only in their condemnation of war, but in active measures of reconciliation and resolution of conflict. The Ulster Quaker Peace Committee and the Service Committee have been particularly active since 1970 in projects involving prisoners and in bringing harmony and understanding to divided communities in inner-city areas.

Education has always been of concern to Quakers because of the need to train each individual for potential leadership. Friends' School in Lisburn was founded in 1774, solely for the children of members, but for the past century it has served the entire community as a boarding and day establishment.

Encouraged by similar Quaker programmes in England and the United States, a Quaker Peace Education Project specialising in conflict management was set up in association with the University of Ulster in 1988. Camps for children and young people are held at Moyallen, Co. Down, each summer and are attended by many from a wide variety of backgrounds.

INTER-CHURCH ACTIVITY

The Religious Society of Friends is a member of the Irish Council of Churches and co-operates at a local level in many interdenominational activities. Friends lend support to various inter-church projects and many have an active interest in home and foreign mission work.

BIBLIOGRAPHY

Burke, E., *Transactions of Central Relief Committee of Friends during the Famine in Ireland*, reprinted by Edmund Burke 1995

Christian Experience (extracts from minutes, advices and the writings of individual Friends), 5th edn available from Religious Society of Friends in Ireland, Swanbrook House, Bloomfield Avenue, Donnybrook, Dublin 4

Gorman, George, *Introducing Quakers*, Friends Home Service Committee 1981

Grubb, Isabel, *Quakers in Ireland 1654–1900*, Swarthmore Press 1927

Hubbard, Geoffrey, *Quaker by Convincement*, Quaker Home Service 1985

Sharman, Alison, *You and the Quakers*, Quaker Home Service 1985

Wigham, Maurice, *The Irish Quakers*, Historical Committee of the Religious Society of Friends 1992

BIOGRAPHICAL NOTE

ARTHUR CHAPMAN was Headmaster of Friends' School, Lisburn, from 1970 to 1989. A lifelong member of the Religious Society of Friends, he is currently an overseer in the Portadown Friends' Meeting and was for a time Clerk of the Ireland Yearly Meeting's Committee (the executive body of the Friends in Ireland). He is Chairman of Craigavon Historical Committee and author of a history of Friends in the Lurgan area.

17

The Evangelical Presbyterian Church in Ireland

ROBERT C. BECKETT

ORIGINS

The history of the Evangelical Presbyterian Church (EPC) is deeply rooted in the history of Irish Presbyterianism, which traces its ancestry back to the Scottish Reformation. In 1927 the Evangelical Presbyterian Church emerged as a distinct denomination from the Presbyterian Church of Ireland (PCI).

In the early years of the twentieth century liberal 'Higher Criticism' of the Bible and 'Modernist' theology became firmly established in the Assembly's Presbyterian College in Belfast, which had begun as a thoroughly orthodox establishment in the aftermath of the 1859 revival. This departure from its biblical foundation caused great concern amongst people of evangelical and conservative Reformed thinking and as a result the 'Bible Standards League' came into being to contend for orthodox theology. One of the leading exponents of this liberal theology was Professor J.E. Davey. A group of evangelical ministers and laymen, deeply troubled by the effect of Professor Davey's views, brought charges of heresy against him, alleging that what he was teaching and writing was contrary to the doctrinal standards of the Irish Presbyterian Church and to the Bible. Five specific charges were laid against him:

1. A denial of the doctrine of Imputation (or transference) of our guilt to Christ and his righteousness to us.

2. A denial of the Impeccable (or perfectly sinless) character of Christ.

3. A denial of the Infallibility of the Bible.

4.   The view that in some way God was responsible for man's sin.

5.   A denial that the doctrine of the Trinity was taught in the Bible.

Despite his plea of 'justification' on four of the five heresy charges, evidence drawn from his own published writings and notes taken in his classes, in 1927 both the Belfast Presbytery and the General Assembly found him 'not guilty' on all five charges. The Presbytery proceeded to ban all discussion of the subject and a Commission armed with Assembly powers was formed to silence protest within the Church. As a result two ministers resigned their charges and membership of the Irish Presbyterian Church in July 1927. In October of that year the **Irish Evangelical Church** came into being in response to numerous little groups of Christians alarmed by proceedings who had withdrawn from their Irish Presbyterian Churches. There was never any attempt to organise divisions. People left as they were compelled by their own consciences before God. They were convinced that God's Word required them to separate from PCI as it had officially approved heretical teaching and had opposed truth. They now stood in the traditional position occupied by historic Presbyterianism as distinct from the new liberal position of PCI.

The name of the church was changed in 1964 to the **Evangelical Presbyterian Church**, a title which was a more accurate reflection of the denomination's stance.

RELATIONS WITH OTHER CHURCHES

The EPC, while it fully believes in the necessity of separation from error, deplores schism. Schism rightly understood is not the act of separation itself, but the departure from the truth that makes such an act necessary. The EPC believes in the true unity of all 'Born-Again Christians' and consequently seeks to co-operate with other biblical Christians in witnessing for Christ. Its bookshop, the Evangelical Bookshop, at 15 College Square East, Belfast, has a highly respected influence among the many ministers and members of various denominations who frequent it.

Subsequent events within PCI have fully vindicated the concerns of 1927, with involvement in unbiblical ecumenism, an increased degree of liberal theology in Union Theological College and the ordination of women. The EPC is fully convinced that a separate existence from PCI is required in order to be faithful to God's Word. It does, however, seek to encourage all within PCI who are seriously contending against error and striving to restore purity to it. It longs for a return by PCI to its former biblical position so that the separate existence of the EPC is no longer necessary.

The EPC is a founder member of the British Evangelical Council (see p. 140) and the International Conference of Reformed Churches, bodies that seek to promote biblical church unity amongst those who take seriously the Bible's claims to be the inspired Word of God and the only infallible rule for faith and practice. It has always rejected the unbiblical ecumenism of the World Council of Churches, and has never been a member.

It enjoys a cordial working relationship with the Free Church of Scotland, with whom it co-operates in missionary work in India, Peru and South Africa. It has close links with the Reformed Presbyterian Church in Ireland, the Evangelical Presbyterian Church in England and Wales, the Reformed Churches in the Netherlands (Liberated) and the Orthodox Presbyterian Church in the USA.

CURRENT STATISTICS

The EPC consists of eleven congregations, six in Belfast (at Knock, Stranmillis Road, Lisburn Road, Finaghy, Crosscollyer Street and Somerton Road), two in Co. Antrim (at Ballyclare and Crumlin) and one each at Richhill, Omagh and Dublin. In addition there are two Mission churches at Bangor (Co. Down) and Blackburn (Lancashire).

Communicant membership is based on a personal credible profession of faith in Jesus Christ as Saviour and Lord and members are expected to be actively involved in the life of their local congregation. Total communicant membership at the end of 1995 was 458. Average attendances at morning and evening Sunday worship during 1995 were 662 and 478 respectively with 223 attending the midweek meetings for Prayer and Bible Study. Whilst most other denominations have experienced a significant drop in membership in recent years, the EPC has known growth and expansion. There are currently ten full-time ministers installed in congregations, one minister involved in missionary work in Nigeria and two students undergoing theological training in preparation for the ministry. There is also one member serving God as a pharmacist in Uganda, and others engaged in evangelism among students in the Ukraine and France.

DOCTRINAL POSITION

The Word of God, as set forth in the scriptures of the Old and New Testaments, is the only infallible rule of faith and practice, and is the supreme standard of the EPC. As a Presbyterian Church its doctrinal position (Subordinate Standards) is defined by the *Westminster Confession of Faith* and the *Larger* and *Shorter Catechisms* prepared by the Westminster Assembly. All ministers and other office-bearers must subscribe fully and without reservation to these standards at ordination/installation. A 'formula of subscription', used by many other Presbyterian bodies as a device to weaken the terms of subscription, is not permitted.

The Westminster Confession of Faith is accepted with the following three amendments:

1.   Chapter XXIII – Of the Civil Magistrate
   'This chapter is not recognised in any sense as meaning that the Civil Magistrate has a controlling power over Synods or Councils, with respect to the exercise of their ministerial authority, or power to persecute any for their religion.' (This understanding excludes the state from interference in church affairs.)

2.   Chapter XXIV – Of Marriage and Divorce
   'All the statements of this chapter are accepted *except the last sentence* of paragraph IV which is omitted entirely.' (This sentence excluded remarriage to a close relative *of a former marriage partner*.)

3.   Chapter XXV – Of the Church
   From paragraph VI in this chapter the following words are omitted: '*but is that antichrist, that man of sin, and son of perdition that exalteth himself against Christ, and all that is called God*'.

   The revised paragraph VI reads:

   > There is no other Head of the Church but the Lord Jesus Christ: nor can the Pope of Rome in any sense be head thereof. The claim of any man to be the Vicar of Christ, the Head of the Church, is Unscriptural, without warrant in fact, and is a usurpation, dishonouring to the Lord Jesus Christ.

   (This amendment, while allowing the antichrist to be identified as the Pope, permits other identifications to be made.)

MEMBERSHIP AND CHURCH GOVERNMENT

Membership, church organisation and patterns of worship are based on the 'Regulative Principle'. This principle affirms that God has given instructions in the Bible how he wishes His Church to be governed and how He desires to be worshipped and served. The EPC does not accept that man is free to organise God's Church, or worship God in any way which merely seems attractive to him personally.

Communicant membership is based on a personal confession of faith in Jesus Christ as Saviour and Lord. Children of believing parents are baptised and brought under the umbrella of the Church until such time as they make their own personal profession or proclaim that they are not believers.

Government of each congregation is by a Kirk Session composed of three or more Elders (including the Minister) chosen by the democratic vote of a clear majority of the members. The Minister is regarded as a *Teaching* Elder as distinct from the other *Ruling* Elders. The Minister has primary responsibility for worship services and the administration of the sacraments, and has equal responsibility with each of the other elders in the government of the church. He is chosen by majority vote of the congregation. Deacons, also elected by the congregation, look after the church finances, maintenance of property, care of the needy and other matters which are more indirectly related to the spiritual ministry of the church. Matters involving discipline within the congregation are handled by the Kirk Session. Elders are elected for life. Deacons serve terms of three to five years and are eligible for re-election.

The EPC has one Presbytery composed of ministers and representative elders from each congregation. It meets seven times each year to consider matters relating to the denomination as a whole. There is also an Annual Presentation of Presbytery Reports in which a summary of all the activities of Presbytery and its various committees is presented to the Church. Guest delegates from other denominations are invited to this event and bring greetings. A Moderator is elected annually by Presbytery. He acts as Chairman of Presbytery Meetings and officially represents the EPC during his year in office. The office of Moderator rotates around both Ministers and Ruling Elders. Presbytery and all congregations annually make available audited reports of all finances.

SACRAMENTS AND ORDINANCES

Two sacraments ONLY are recognised as having been given to the Church by Jesus Christ: Baptism and Communion. Administration of both sacraments normally takes place during regular worship services.

Communion, or the Lord's Supper, is observed monthly. The **significance** of eating the bread and drinking the wine follows the explanation given by Christ (John 6:35, 40, 54, 63). It is maintained that the bread and wine do *not* change into the literal body and blood of Christ. The blessing obtained from receiving the sacrament occurs through the SPIRITUAL reception of Christ into the communicant's life. The elements are regarded as visual reminders (1 Corinthians 11:23–6) of the sufferings of Christ for sin, and in themselves have no power to confer forgiveness.

Participation in Communion is limited to those who profess to be 'born again' by the Holy Spirit. The Lord's Supper is regarded as a 'fellowship meal' for the Lord's people rather than a way of gaining entrance into heaven. There is an 'Open Table' in that the onus is put on the individual participant to examine himself regarding his fitness in accordance with 1 Corinthians 11:27–32. The Kirk Session exercises its powers of discipline in barring from Communion those whose way of life is contrary to the standards of holy Christian living.

Baptism is administered to adults who have not previously been baptised on profession of faith, and to the children of believing parents. It is performed by sprinkling or pouring in accordance with the established rite of purification given by God to the Old Testament Church. The method is not regarded as essential to the validity of the sacrament, and the EPC receives into membership those who have been baptised by immersion. Baptism by water is not understood to convey any spiritual grace to the recipient nor to cause the removal of 'original sin' nor bring about 'Baptismal Regeneration'. It is understood as a visual representation of the invisible Baptism by the Holy Spirit through which a sinner is cleansed and renewed in holiness. The application of clean water is a symbolic indication by the appointed officers in God's Church that God has cleansed a sinner from sin. The Baptism of children where at least one of the parents is a professed 'Born-Again Christian' (1 Corinthians 7:14) recognises the promise given by God that his Covenant Relationship with his people will also embrace their children (Genesis 17:7; Acts 2:38–9) and continues the pattern of circumcision in the Old Testament (Colossians 2:11, 12). Its application to young infants is an act of faith by the parents and the Church in God's promises. It is also a recognition that salvation is solely by God's grace and is not dependent on the intellectual attainments of the individual.

Ordination: All Elders (both Teaching and Ruling) are ordained into office by the Presbytery, by the laying on of hands and prayer. Deacons are similarly installed by their local Kirk Session.

WORSHIP AND SPIRITUALITY

True worship is dependent on inner attitudes of heart rather than on outward ritual. While the beauty of many of the prayers in, for example, the Anglican Prayerbook is recognised, the concept that they alone must be used in the public worship of God is rejected. Pulpit prayers in the EPC are extempore and reflect the changing needs of the congregation at the time. In this way worship is always fresh and avoids liturgical repetition, which often bypasses the mind. The **focal point** is always the pulpit and great emphasis is put on the expository preaching of the Bible with application to present-day events. One of the prime aims is to hear God speaking through the Scriptures. Worship is simple, reverent and God-centred with a definite consciousness that one is in the presence of Almighty God. The EPC believes that the completion of the Scriptures brought to an end the revelatory gifts of the Holy Spirit experienced by the Church in New Testament times and that all such gifts are now ceased (1 Corinthians 13:8).

The Book of Psalms (Psalter), the hymn book given by God to the Old Testament Church, has a regular place in the public worship of all EPC congregations. As its revelation of Christ was incomplete, more modern hymns which are doctrinally sound are also sung. In addition to the Psalter, the Trinity Hymnal produced by the Orthodox Presbyterian Church in the USA is used. An organ normally accompanies singing.

The EPC recognises that God has appointed both men and women to distinctively different areas of service in his Church. It rejects the idea that women are in any way inferior to men. It holds strongly that the Bible forbids the entrance of women into the office of either Minister or Ruling Elder (1 Timothy 2:11–15). Women are not allowed to preach, but do function as teachers of the young and of other women.

CHURCH AND COMMUNITY

The Church is recognised as the people rather than the buildings, and facilities are usually multi-purpose to maximise efficiency of use. Many buildings are used for children and youth activities on weekdays. Outreach into the community with a primarily evangelistic emphasis is a feature of all EPC churches. There are Mission Sunday Schools, youth clubs, children's meetings, and mother and toddler groups. Door-to-door evangelism along with open-air preaching occur frequently as the Church seeks to present the gospel of Jesus Christ in a non-sectarian way. For over sixty years the EPC has organised summer camps, and approximately 150 young people from both within and outside the denomination participate each year. The denomination's magazine, the *Evangelical Presbyterian*, is published bi-monthly and has an international circulation far beyond the bounds of the EPC.

While recognising the essential relevance of the truths and principles of the Bible to politics, the EPC has never taken a party political position. It values the importance of Christians functioning as 'salt and light' in every area of society and has no objections to its members being involved in politics on a purely personal level. It believes that Church and government are separate and distinct authorities established by God with different spheres of operation. Both are seen as servants of a Sovereign God, each answerable to him. They should be mutually supportive. Within the EPC there is a primary focus on the everlasting Kingdom of Heaven rather than on the temporary Kingdom of this World.

BIOGRAPHICAL NOTE

The REV. DR ROBERT C. BECKETT is the Clerk of Presbytery of the Evangelical Presbyterian Church. He spent his formative years in the Crumlin EPC congregation, where his parents were members. He studied Agriculture at Queen's University, Belfast, and then engaged in postgraduate studies in the USA, receiving a Ph.D. in animal breeding from Ohio State University. After working for some years as an animal geneticist for the NI Department of Agriculture, he studied theology at the Reformed Presbyterian Church College, Belfast, and was ordained into the ministry of the Evangelical Presbyterian Church. For sixteen years he has worked on the Peace Line of North Belfast and he is currently minister of the joint congregations at Crosscollyer Street and Somerton Road. He combines his disciplines of science and theology by lecturing on topics such as evolution and creation, ecological issues and science and ethics. He is married with four children.

18

The
Moravian Church

JOE COOPER

ORIGINS

The Moravian Church had its beginnings in Moravia and Bohemia, now called the Czech Republic, and its roots in the teaching of *Jan Hus*, a Professor of Philosophy and a priest. His protest against the abuses he saw in the Church led to a charge of heresy and Hus was condemned at the Council of Constance and burned at the stake on 6 July1415. Following his death the country was plunged into the long and bloody Hussite wars. The Moravian Church emerged out of that turmoil when in 1457 a group of peace-loving people came together in an attempt to live out the Sermon on the Mount, calling themselves *Unitas Fratrum*, a Unity of Brethren. This was sixty years before the start of Luther's Reformation.

The small society grew into a large Church: it created an Episcopal ministry, took a charitable outlook towards other Christians, and in 1501 published a hymn book. The Bible was translated into Czech, and influenced the Czech language in much the same way that the King James version did the English. During the Thirty Years War the population of Bohemia and Moravia decreased from three million to nine hundred thousand, and it seemed as though the Church was finished. However, *Bishop John Amos Comenius*, an outstanding educationalist, believed that a Hidden Seed of his beloved Church would survive and one day flourish again. In that faith he consecrated his son-in-law a Bishop so that the succession would not be lost.

THE RENEWED CHURCH

When the Church in Bohemia and Moravia was virtually wiped out in 1628 many members left the country looking for refuge in other lands, but some kept the traditions alive by worshipping in secret and in 1722 a group of their descendants found a haven on the estate of a German noble-man, *Count Nicolaus Ludwig von Zinzendorf*, who became an important figure in the history of the Moravian Church. The refugees were given a tract of land and built a village which they named *Hermhut* – the Lord's Watch.

Looking for opportunities to channel their Christian faith, in 1732 members of the Community started on a worldwide mission project. Their first assignment was St Thomas in the West Indies, followed by Greenland, Lapland, Georgia, Surinam, Africa, the North American Indians, Ceylon, Romania and Constantinople. Between 1732 and 1742 more than seventy from a community of six hundred had answered the call to mission service. Later missions were established in Jamaica and other West Indian islands, Ladakh, Russia, Labrador, Tanzania, Guyana, Hon-duras, Nicaragua and Costa Rica. Some work was started and handed over to national Churches, e.g. the work among the Australian Aborigines was handed to the Presbyterian Church of Australia. Work today continues in many of these places, the largest numbers being in Tanzania, North America and South Africa.

At Hermhut the inhabitants were divided according to age and sex, each group with specific roles to perform. The single men and women had their own community houses, each with its own leader. In the early days this settlement pattern was established wherever the Church went. On the mission field it provided work for people and money to maintain the mission, and in the home countries was a base where men and women were trained for the mission work.

This was an era of experiment: the Christmas Candle (Christingle) Service, Early Easter Morning Burial Ground Service; Lovefeasts; Holy Week Readings; Daily Watchwords (first printed in 1731 containing Scripture texts and hymn verses and Bible readings for each day of the year, and today published in forty-one languages, with over one million copies printed in German alone); Hourly Intercession (Prayer Watch kept by the Church throughout the world). All of these remain part of Moravian Church custom today. It was at this time that the ministry was renewed and the old episcopal orders of the *Unitas* were transferred to the Renewed Church.

THE WORK IN ENGLAND AND IRELAND

Moravians visiting London became members of a religious society meeting in Fetter Lane. The Wesley brothers were members, but disagreements led to John Wesley and his followers leaving, and in 1742 the Fetter Lane Society became the first English congregation. 'Moravian' became the popular name for the Church in the English-speaking world, and in 1749 the British parliament gave formal recognition to the 'Moravian Church'.

John Cennick, a successful evangelist in the west of England, joined the Moravians and was invited to Ireland, arriving on 3 June 1746 in Dublin, where a congregation was soon established. In August he was invited to Ballymena, but it was not until the next visit in June 1748 that a start was made in establishing the work. Whilst many societies were formed, the policy of building settlements continued. The work Cennick started in Gloonen (near Ahoghill, Co. Antrim) was transferred to Gracehill (1759), which became the chief settlement in the north of Ireland and is still the largest congregation. There are now five congregations in Northern Ireland (two in Belfast, Ballinderry, Kilwarlin and Gracehill) and a small fellowship which holds occasional meetings in Dublin. The total connected, adults and children, is six hundred members and approximately two hundred adherents.

BELIEFS AND RELATIONSHIPS WITH OTHER CHURCHES

The key to the ethos of the Moravian Church is found in its official name, *Unitas Fratrum*, a Unity of Brethren. From the beginning an attempt was made to show how Christians could live together in fellowship with each other through fellowship with Christ and a greater emphasis was placed on conduct than on creed. Zinzendorf's theology was 'Christocentric'. He spoke about 'heart religion' and Moravians, still following his lead, say that the Church is a fellowship in which Jesus Christ is Lord of every sphere of life.

Moravians believe that there is nothing which should separate all who truly believe in Jesus Christ. They believe in the authority of Holy Scripture, but refrain from adopting any special theory of inspiration or saying how it should be interpreted. They use an old motto adopted by Comenius:

> *In things essential, Unity;*
> *In things non-essential, Liberty;*
> *In all things, Charity.*

Zinzendorf impressed this message on the Church. He saw around him rival denominations each claiming to possess the only true form of Christianity. In all of them were good Christians who held to the essentials: a saving experience of the Saviour and devotion to him. Their differences were about the non-essentials. The *Unity Synod* (see below) has ruled that each province should co-operate with other Christian Churches in its area, and each is encouraged to apply for membership of National Councils of Churches and the World Council of Churches.

Whilst the policy of the Moravian Church is pro-ecumenical and encourages good community relations, it is made up of individuals and, as with all churches, one cannot guarantee the opinion of every member. Where feasible the Church has joined with other denominations in community issues, but because of the scattered membership of the congregations individuals are encouraged to become involved with work in the area where they live.

WORSHIP

A Prayer Book is used with set liturgies, but there is also freedom to adapt worship to suit the needs of the occasion. The Church has its own hymn book, but many hymns are held in common with other denominations. Advent is marked by the hanging of a thirty-two-point lighted star in the church, an Advent wreath, and a Christingle service (which originated in the Moravian tradition but is now widely used in other denominations). In Holy Week there are services each day with readings from 'Passion Week and Eastertide' (a liturgical harmony of the gospels) interspersed with hymns, and Holy Communion on Maundy Thursday.

SACRAMENTS

Baptism is normally administered to infants and confers membership of the Church. Adult Baptism is offered for any not baptised as infants. A recent Synod decided to permit baptised children to partake of Holy Communion. Confirmation is also practised.

Holy Communion is usually celebrated monthly, following either a Lovefeast (an informal Family Service in which tea and buns are served, Moravian and general church news is imparted and a short homily is given) or a Public Service, and is open to bonafide members of all Churches. The elements are distributed to members by the minister during the singing of hymns, and at the end of the service the communicants give each other the right hand of fellowship during the singing of a 'Covenant verse'. The minister wears a white surplice for the sacraments, but apart from that robes are optional.

MINISTRY AND LEADERSHIP

Ordination as Deacon establishes a man or woman in the Pastoral Office and gives authority to administer the sacraments. It is a 'supervised ministry'. Deacons are *Consecrated* to the Office of Presbyter after several years in the ministry. Bishops are elected by Synod and *Consecrated* to their office, which is purely spiritual. Bishops have responsibility for Ordinations (at the request of the Governing Boards), prayer and acting as 'pastor to the pastors'. Ministers are selected, trained and called to service by the province. All receive the same salary.

BUILDINGS

Church buildings are generally simple. Older ones, like Gracehill, have the pulpit and Communion Table on the long wall. Services are conducted from the Communion Table, the pulpit being used for the sermon only. A distinctive Lamb and Flag crest with the motto *Vicit agnus noster eum sequamur* (Our Lamb has conquered; let us follow Him) is usually prominently displayed. This is the official seal or emblem of the Church.

ORGANISATION

The Unity Synod, held once every seven years, comprises representatives from all countries where the Church has congregations, and is the supreme legislative body in matters of faith and order.

Moravian work worldwide is divided into provinces. The Irish District is part of the British province, which has its headquarters in London. Each province is self-governing with its own Synod made up of lay and ministerial representatives. The Synod elects a Governing Board to administer the affairs of the Church between Synods.

The District Conference, which comprises representatives from a group of congregations (such as Ireland), has little legislative power but is a forum for discussing local work and issues.

The Congregation Council Meeting is the legislative gathering of the communicant members of an individual congregation. It elects an executive committee to attend to day-to-day affairs.

BIBLIOGRAPHY

Daily Watchwords (annual publication also containing a directory), British edn, London: Moravian Bookroom

Fries, Adelaide L., *Customs and Practices of the Moravian Church*, Moravian Church USA 1949

Rican, Rudolph (trans. C.D. Crews), *History of the Unity of the Brethren (The Bohemian Church)* (first published in Czech in 1957), Bethlehem, Pennsylvania: Moravian Church USA 1992

Shawe, C.H., *The Spirit of the Moravian Church*, London: Moravian Bookroom 1993

Taylor, J. & Kenneth G. Hamilton, *History of the Moravian Church (1722–1957)*, Moravian Church USA 1967

Through Five Hundred Years (popular history), Moravian Church USA 1957 (and reprints)

All the above books are usually available from:

Moravian Bookroom, 5 Muswell Hill, London, N10 3TJ, England

The following booklets are available from Gracehill Moravian Church:

A History of Gracehill Moravian Settlement
Extracts from the Journals of John Cennick
Moravians in Ireland
James Montgomery, Moravian Hymnwriter
Three Generations of the La Trobes

BIOGRAPHICAL NOTE

The RT. REV. J.H. COOPER was baptised and confirmed in the Moravian Church at Bath, England. After army service, he did theological training in the Moravian College and at Manchester University. Ordained in 1950, he served several congregations in England and came to Ireland in 1963. Joe Cooper was consecrated a Bishop in 1976 and retired from congregational work in 1990. From 1994 to 1996 he served as President of the Irish Council of Churches.

19

The
Lutheran Church in Ireland

PAUL G. FRITZ

ORIGINS

The Lutheran Church is represented in Northern Ireland by a congregation in Belfast which, together with eight other congregations (Dublin, Castlepollard, Cork, Galway, Killarney, Limerick, Sligo, Wexford), forms the **Lutheran Church in Ireland**. The other name of this church, *Evangelisch-lutherische Kirche in Irland,* indicates its German origins. The Church was initially founded in Dublin by German merchants in 1697, who were able to consecrate their first chapel in 1725 (the German Lutheran Church of the Most Holy Trinity).

Although up to now in Ireland it is a distinct minority of mostly German origin, numbering about a thousand on the entire island, it belongs to the worldwide family of Lutheran Churches, one of the largest branches of Protestantism, and is as such recognised by the Lutheran World Federation. Since Lutherans come from all over the world, members of the Irish Church also include Scandinavians, Americans and even Australians.

DOCTRINE, AUTHORITY AND SACRAMENTS

Lutherans are of course Christians first. They follow Jesus Christ, not Martin Luther (1483–1546). Yet they take the great reformer's life and teachings very seriously, trusting that justification is by faith in Christ alone. The Bible is the Church's final rule and norm. Lutherans hold to the three ancient ecumenical creeds (the Apostles' Creed, the Nicene Creed and the Athanasian Creed) and they subscribe to the Augsburg Confession

(1530), the basic doctrinal statement of all Lutheran churches.

Lutherans recognise two sacraments: Baptism and Eucharist (the Communion). The Eucharist is celebrated every Sunday within the sung service.

CHURCH GOVERNMENT AND MINISTRY

The local administration and supervision of the Lutheran Church in Ireland is in the hands of an elected Church Council, of which the Pastor is the ex officio chairman. He is sent out on a six-year term of duties (renewable) by his bishop through the Evangelisch Kirche in Deutschland (EKD) in Hanover, which also partially finances the running costs.

The Lutheran community in Ireland has only one Pastor, an episcopally ordained theologian, who is assisted by two Lay Readers (one Irish, one German). Based in Dublin, the Pastor is in charge of activities on the entire island. His monthly visits to the Belfast congregation are among his special duties, looking after and caring for some fifty families in Northern Ireland. He is also responsible for the German Mission to Seamen and religious education at St Kilian's German School, Dublin.

INTER-CHURCH RELATIONS

Because the Lutheran Church understands itself to be a reform movement within the Church universal, it is pressing towards greater unity (Lutheran Archbishop Nathan Söderblom was one of the pioneers of the Ecumenical Movement). Yet Lutherans propose an ecumenical concept of church 'unity in reconciled diversity', rather than the organic merger of Churches; this they view as an unhistoric resolution to the problem. The unity of all Christians already exists in Christ himself. The Churches respond to this given unity by co-operating with and recognising each other. Thus the Lutheran Church in Ireland is a member of the Irish Council of Churches, the Irish Inter-Church Meeting, the Dublin Council of Churches (the Pastor being one of the Patrons), and the Irish Council of Christians and Jews.

The Lutheran Church in Ireland is a signatory of the 'Leuenberg Agreement of Reformation Churches in Europe', and is therefore in full communion with the Presbyterian Church in Ireland. Through its administrative body in Germany, the EKD, it also has close ties with Anglicans (the Meissen Agreement) and Methodists. In Ireland, where only the mother parish in Dublin has a church building (St Finian's Church, rented from the Church of Ireland for ninety-nine years), churches of other denominations host Lutheran services outside Dublin. (In Belfast services are held at the Moravian Church on University Road.)

The Lutheran Church gratefully appreciates and enjoys good ecumenical relations with all other Churches. This was evident in 1995 when representatives of all other Christian Churches participated in the commemoration of the fiftieth anniversary of the martyrdom of Dietrich Bonhoeffer, the great Lutheran theologian who was executed by the Nazis for his involvement in the assassination plot against Hitler. Lutherans share with all other Christians the burning desire for peace and justice here and all over the world.

BIBLIOGRAPHY

See references to Martin Luther and Lutheranism in any encyclopedia
Burgess, Joseph A., 'Who Are the Lutherans Today?' in *Christianity, A World Faith*, Lion Handbook 1985
Long, Roy, *The Lutheran Church*, Christian Denominations Series, Religious & Moral Education Press 1984

BIOGRAPHICAL NOTE

The VERY REV. PAUL GERHARD FRITZ became Pastor of the Lutheran Church in Ireland in 1985 with responsibility for the congregations in both the Republic and Northern Ireland. He was born in 1934 in Berlin, where he lived, throughout the momentous events of the Second World War and the Cold War, until 1972. He studied theology, philosophy, literature and music at the Universities of East and West Berlin, Erlangen, Zurich and Basel, numbering among his teachers such great names as Karl Barth and Paul Hindemith. Ordained in 1962, he worked in parishes and secondary schools in East and West Berlin. From 1972 to 1978 he was Director of the Lutheran Institute of Adult Education in Hermannsburg/Hanover, and then became Superintendent (local Bishop) of Göttingen until his appointment to Ireland. In Ireland he was involved in various inter-church organisations including the Executive Committee of the Irish Council of Churches. He retired in 1996.

20

New Churches

BILL ROY AND PAUL REID

In a province and culture where 'the last thing we need is more churches', what possible explanation could there be for the upsurge and growth of the new church movement? Yet churches such as Christian Fellowship Church (Strandtown, Belfast), Coleraine Christian Centre and King's Fellowship (Bangor) have been on the scene for the last fifteen years or so. Without exception they are charismatic in their expression of historic Christianity and most, while still breaking down into house groups mid-week, now have buildings. Numbering around the four to five thousand mark, they are generally self-governing autonomous churches in good relationship with each other. In recent years many have come together to form a 'Network' or a more closely aligned grouping called *LifeLink*. Most of them have common values such as an emphasis on Praise and Worship, Prayer and Bible Teaching, an obvious ministry of the Holy Spirit, every-member participation, the development of open and committed relationships with each other, evangelism, mission overseas, social justice and a real heart for Christian unity and reconciliation.

Fellowships with these common values are found all over the world and include *New Frontiers International* under Terry Virgo's leadership, *Pioneer* under Gerald Coates's direction and the *Icthus Fellowship* in London led by Roger Foster. New Churches in Northern Ireland have close links with these groupings and others across the globe.

ORIGINS

Most have their origins in the Charismatic Renewal of the 1970s. The spiritual gifts found in 1 Corinthians 12, such as speaking in tongues, prophecy, healing, et cetera, formerly mainly experienced in Pentecostal Churches, were now expressed in the mainline denominations. This led to conflict and many of those who had experienced *the baptism in the Holy Spirit* left to form new churches. These came from churches as diverse as Christian Brethren and Roman Catholic, but mainly from a Protestant Evangelical background. Although the Charismatic Renewal deeply touched many Roman Catholics, most of these stayed in the Catholic Church.

While originally a reaction to what some saw as 'dead orthodoxy', the new churches quickly became 'Restoration Churches'. They believed that the Church, instead of decreasing in numbers and declining in influence, should be vibrant, relevant and growing in quality and numbers. This led to many of the young and gifted leaving the established Churches to give expression to what they saw as the New Testament Church. The core beliefs of historic Christianity remained a common factor, with the new churches continuing to have communion and baptism, although for most this was 'believers' baptism' by immersion. One of the key distinguishing marks was flexibility and the disappearance of the distinction between clergy and laity. Clive Calver, former General Secretary of the Evangelical Alliance, said that 'the division among evangelicals at present is between flexible churches and inflexible ones'.

SMALL GROUPS

Many fellowships have their origin in small prayer groups. Indeed some have remained ostensibly just that – a small community group consisting of twelve members continuing to meet in a specific locality with many of its members joining for celebration and worship in a larger gathering primarily on a Sunday. Others, like Christian Fellowship Church for example, have grown into a network with up to two thousand people being involved. However, even in groups of this size there remains a zealous commitment to the dynamics of the cell group or home group – a place where people can appreciate deeper levels of relationship and fellowship, very much in keeping with Acts 2:46. All Christians are likely to agree that the good news of the Kingdom should be brought to every man, woman and child in this province and beyond, and new churches have, in many cases, a stated policy of establishing small groups in as many streets and communities as possible. This is not an alternative to corporate meetings, but rather a natural progression and expression of them, in order to express the love of God at a more local and personal level. Small groups, it could be argued, are the 'lifeblood' of the new churches, they provide a safe arena for members to appropriate ongoing preaching and teaching, develop and mature in the use of spiritual gifts and generally engender a greater sense of belonging.

WORSHIP

The vast majority of new worship songs have come from so-called new churches. Here in Northern Ireland the work of Robin Mark, for example, is appreciated by Christians from many different Christian perspectives and increasingly beyond our shores. The new church movement has facilitated, in a very conscious way, the development of men and women to lead the church in new spheres of worship, for example exuberant praise, dancing, using the whole of your body to worship God and not just your voice, allowing many people to feel that they are able to express more personally and intimately their love and appreciation for God. Taking the Scriptures and setting them to modern music played with contemporary instruments has injected a freshness into the understanding of the psalms and scriptural truths in general.

The euphoric, charismatic displays of liberty and celebration may yet draw scepticism and suspicion from some quarters but the new churches have many men and women of God serving within them who are urging holiness, prayer and wholesome relationships and a proper regard for all of Scripture. They are making Bible reading, prayer, fasting and evangelism acts of discipline, joy and celebration. It is no surprise therefore that they are in demand here in our own province, in the South of Ireland, in Britain and abroad. It is said, of course, that many have their roots in the more traditional streams of the Church in the province. Many would readily acknowledge this and express genuine appreciation for their spiritual heritage.

EVANGELISM, MISSION AND SOCIAL ACTION

Bringing much of their evangelistic enthusiasm with them, the new church members have a broadly holistic approach to ministry. An integral part of mission is treating men and women as equals and seeing that Christ's ministry is to the whole person, i.e. body, soul and spirit. While the salvation of a person's soul is seen as vital, it is never to be divorced from the need of the whole person. While it is true that originally most of the new churches comprised former members of other Churches, this is changing. More and more unchurched people are coming to faith in Christ through the evangelistic efforts of the members. Courses such as the *Alpha Course* have been particularly successful as a means of communicating the gospel in a postmodern age. In *Alpha* people invite their friends to a ten-week course on Christianity and each session is characterised by food, teaching and small discussion groups. People form relationships while learning about Christianity in an informal and relaxed way.

The need of the nations has seen a recent upsurge of missionary interest among new churches. People are going overseas as church planters, with relief agencies, with traditional missionary societies and building links with overseas churches.

EVERY–PERSON MINISTRY

One of a number of obvious similarities between the new churches is the emphasis on *every-person ministry*. There is a commitment within most of the new churches to a move away from one-person ministry, particularly in aspects of church life such as pastoral care, training and discipleship, teaching and prayer. It is also important to note that the commitment of the new churches to an obvious ministry of the Holy Spirit has served to reinforce the conviction that spiritual gifts are for today. The new church movement is committed to the development, teaching and training that is necessary for the edification of the Church, the releasing and empowering of individual believers to match the words of Jesus with the works of Jesus.

RECONCILIATION

As the Charismatic Renewal of the 1970s included Roman Catholics, new churches have been very open to joint worship with any Christian no matter what church they belong to. Their view is that there is only one invisible church to which every genuine believer in Christ belongs, although there are different expressions of that same church locally. This had led to good relationships, joint conferences and worship with such groups as the Lamb of God Community on the Antrim Road, Belfast, and Youth Initiatives of Belfast.

THE WAY AHEAD

Many believe that legitimacy and credibility, indeed the importance of the existence of the new churches, will continue to become more established over the next few years. There is, in these days, a deepening desire for mutual recognition and respect – a growing commitment to unite under the Lordship of Jesus Christ, to be a prophetic voice to this nation, proclaiming anti-sectarian Christianity and a commitment to the unity of all believers regardless of church affiliation. No one stream of the Church has a franchise on the good news of the Kingdom but each has a unique contribution to make in order to see Ireland once again become a 'light to the nations'.

BIOGRAPHICAL NOTES

BILL ROY is pastor of Gateway Church, Carrickfergus. Formerly a deputy headmaster in a large primary school, he has been involved in Christian work for many years. As well as his local church responsibilities he travels extensively and has a particular interest in India. He is committed both locally and nationally to reconciliation and the unity of the body of Christ. He is married to Margaret and they have two sons.

PAUL REID is the Leader of the LifeLink Team, a group of churches in Ireland committed to church planting and resourcing other churches, and is also Senior Pastor of Christian Fellowship Church in Belfast. He travels extensively and has a vision to see the Gospel brought to the nations in his lifetime. Paul is committed to reconciliation in his own country and to the principle of the Unity of all believers, which he sees as essential if the Christian message is going to be effective in reaching the world. He is married to Priscilla and they have four daughters.

21

The
Belfast Chinese Christian Church

WAI KUEN MO

WAI KUEN MO

ORIGINS

The Church's origins date back to Easter 1975, when the Rev. Ronnie McCracken and Mr Nai Bob Cham started some evangelistic work amongst the local Chinese in Belfast. As a result of the work, a small group of believers started to meet together regularly every Sunday at the Queen's University Methodist Chaplaincy at Elmwood Avenue, Belfast. This group of believers became known as the Belfast Chinese Christian Fellowship (BCCF). The BCCF did not really expand until February 1987, when a sudden influx of new Chinese students started to attend the Sunday meetings. The numbers kept on increasing to such an extent that a new place was sought to accommodate the growing congregation. When the congregation of Windsor Baptist Church heard about the BCCF's need for a larger meeting place, they kindly offered the use of their church halls on Sunday afternoons. In June 1988, by the grace of God, and with a large step in faith, the BCCF moved to Windsor Baptist Church.

Around 1994 the church work began to expand to such an extent that there were meetings, either in the church or at various homes, taking place on almost every day of the week. Apart from the need for more space, many in the congregation also realised that the Chinese Church should have a larger church building of its own which it could also truly call 'home'. Again by the grace of God, Ulsterville Presbyterian Church informed the BCCF in 1995 of its intention to sell its side halls at Lorne Street. At a Special General Meeting on 20 October 1996, BCCF members made a decision to proceed with the purchase of the Lorne Street Halls. Another important step taken by the BCCF was the adoption of a new

Constitution and Trust Deed on 3 November 1996 which instituted the first Chinese Church in Northern Ireland with the name of the Belfast Chinese Christian Church (BCCC).

At the time of writing, the legal formalities for the purchase of the Lorne Street Halls have not yet been completed. However, the BCCC has moved out of Windsor Baptist Church, with its blessing, and has been meeting in the Lorne Street Halls since May 1997.

NATIONAL AND INTERNATIONAL LINKS

The BCCC is one of many Chinese Churches and fellowships spread out throughout the UK and Europe. For the past few decades, the Chinese Overseas Christian Mission (COCM), based in London, has been instrumental in helping to establish Christian fellowships and churches in cities and towns where a sizeable Chinese community exists. The BCCC is officially linked to COCM and through it maintains a close relationship with other Chinese Churches and fellowships in the UK. Chinese Churches and fellowships which are linked to COCM, including BCCC, are mostly evangelical and non-denominational. For the past four years, COCM has helped BCCC by sending Pastor Sam Sham and his wife and family to Belfast to engage in missionary and pastoral work for the church.

CHURCH GOVERNMENT AND MINISTRY

Church government at the BCCC is through its Board of Elders, which consists of the pastor of the church and elders elected by members of the BCCC. Once elected, elders are expected to serve a maximum period of three years, after which they must be renominated and re-elected to serve any further periods. The Board of Elders has responsibilities in matters of doctrine, financial policy, pastoral care, organisation of public worship, baptismal services, Holy Communion and the admission and discipline of members. Apart from the Board of Elders, there is an annually elected committee of deacons which has the responsibility of carrying out some of the practical tasks of the Church. Advisers to the BCCC are also appointed annually.

BAPTISM AND COMMUNION

The two recognised ordinances of the BCCC are baptism by full immersion and Holy Communion. Two baptismal services are normally held each year – one in April and the other in December. Baptism is normally performed by the Pastor of the church. Holy Communion is held on the first Sunday of each month and is led by someone from the leadership.

RELATIONS WITH OTHER CHURCHES

With the BCCC being a 'Chinese' Church, most members of the congregation would be of Chinese origin. The ethnic uniqueness and independence of the BCCC has helped it to foster good relationships with other denominations who hold similar doctrinal views. Indeed, some members of the congregation were members of other denominations, such as the Brethren, Baptist and Elim, before they joined the BCCC. Pastors and Ministers of those Churches and other local churches are often invited to speak at the BCCC, and members of BCCC have often been invited to take part in other church services. The BCCC also has contacts, through ex-members and COCM, with other Chinese Churches in the UK, Canada and Hong Kong.

GROWTH

With the BCCC now having a building of its own, the leadership prays that the Church can reach out more effectively to the Chinese in Northern Ireland. But since many local Chinese still see Christianity as a Western religion, the task of preaching the Cross to the Chinese people will continue to be a difficult one. But we do praise God that the work continues to grow and the congregation continues to increase in numbers. We believe that with the Holy Spirit's help, more Chinese in Northern Ireland will come to believe in Christ in years to come.

BIOGRAPHICAL NOTE

WAI KUEN MO was born in Hong Kong but emigrated, with his parents, to Northern Ireland in 1971. He is a full-time systems analyst in the NI Civil Service and is married with three children. Originally a nominal Buddhist, Wai Kuen accepted Christ as his personal Saviour in 1980 and attended the Broadway Gospel Hall until 1987, when he joined the BCCF. Wai Kuen is currently the Chairman, and an elder, of the Belfast Chinese Christian Church.

22

The
Orthodox Churches

GEORGE WOODMAN

The small community of Orthodox Christians in Ireland represents one of the largest Christian groupings worldwide. They belong to the family of churches originating in the part of the Roman Empire round the Eastern Mediterranean, whose common language was Greek.

ORIGINS AND DEVELOPMENT

By the fourth century Christianity had spread throughout the Roman Empire and to certain areas beyond it. In 312 it was adopted by the Emperor Constantine as the official religion. In 330 he proclaimed Byzantium at the meeting point between Europe and Asia on the Bosphorus as the imperial capital, renaming it Constantinople, city of Constantine. A series of Ecumenical Councils, of which the first was at Nicea in 325, defined the limits within which Christian doctrine could develop. These were attended by representatives of the Church throughout the world. In 451 five senior bishoprics, known as patriarchates, were established of which Rome was the senior and Constantinople the second. Gradually Greek East and Latin West grew apart. They no longer understood each other's languages and developed different ways of thinking and of organisation. This led to disagreements and eventually to the Great Schism which developed from the ninth century onwards. The Schism was completed when Latin Christians sacked Constantinople in 1204, although unsuccessful attempts were made to heal it during the next two centuries. During the ninth and tenth centuries missionaries from Constantinople established Christianity in Bulgaria, Serbia and, somewhat later, in Romania. Russia embraced Christianity in its Byzantine form in 988, eventually becoming the largest and, after the conquest of Constantinople by the Turks in 1453, the most powerful Orthodox nation.

ORTHODOX IN THE WORLD TODAY

It is estimated that there are about eighty-five million Orthodox Christians in the world today. In addition to the Greek-speaking world and the countries evangelised from Constantinople where Orthodoxy remains the principal faith, there are communities in Albania, Turkey and throughout the Middle East. Many of these communities have suffered from emigration as a result of political pressures. There are in addition Orthodox churches in Finland and the Baltic, Central Europe, the Far East and East Africa. As a result of emigration, flourishing Orthodox communities have been created in Britain, Western Europe, America and Australasia. There have been many converts to Orthodoxy in the West. In Ireland as a whole there are about five hundred Orthodox.

DOCTRINE

The sources of the Orthodox faith are the Nicene Creed, the Bible and the first seven Ecumenical Councils. Dogma is less codified than in Roman Catholicism or Protestantism. Tradition, the living continuity of the Church, is much stressed. Differences from Western theology tend to be more of emphasis than of belief.

The Trinity is all-important. Orthodox stress the threeness of the Persons working actively. The work of the Holy Spirit receives greater attention than in the West. The Nicene Creed originally described the Holy Spirit as 'proceeding from the Father'. In the sixth century the Western church, in an attempt to combat heresy, added 'and from the Son' (Latin *Filioque*). The East objected strongly. The Creed belonged to the whole Church and one part had no right to alter it. Many Eastern theologians considered that the *Filioque* clause had no theological basis and diminished the equality of the Three Persons.

Deification is a very important concept. Through the Incarnation God became one of His own creatures and drew all creation into the work of salvation. Humankind is made in the divine image and should be drawn into God's actions.

The Mother of God is honoured above all creation as the human agent of the Incarnation, the supreme human co-operator in the Divine Work. She is known as the *Theotokos* (she who gave birth to God). Awareness of tradition and of the Kingdom of Heaven leads to reverence towards the Saints. The whole Church, living and departed, is seen as worshipping and praying together.

Orthodox theology finds expression in **icons**, pictures representing incidents in the life of Christ, the Mother of God and the Saints which are painted according to strict rules of symbolism and arranged in churches in a prescribed order. Worshippers reverence them both in churches and in their homes. Icons bear witness to the Incarnation, to the human and therefore representational form of God and to man's potential to become God. In recent years they have become familiar in the West, rather out of context, as religious pictures.

AUTHORITY AND MINISTRY

Orthodox Christians, while acknowledging the primacy of the See of Rome, could not accept the Papacy as the ruler of the whole Church with absolute power, as it came to be seen in the Western Church in the ninth century. The Patriarch of Constantinople is known as the Ecumenical Patriarch and enjoys a position of special honour. Orthodox Christians are organised into independent local churches, usually of people belonging to a particular national group. The Ecumenical Patriarch's position does not entitle him to intervene in these churches. However, Greek émigré churches are mostly in dioceses under his direct jurisdiction. The parish in Dublin to which most Irish Orthodox belong is in one such diocese. There are divisions among Russian émigré churches as a result of disputes after the Russian Revolution in 1917.

Orthodox Christians have the threefold ministry of bishops, priests and deacons. Parish clergy are normally married and must be married before ordination. Bishops are always monks. Monasticism, both male and female, is an important feature of Orthodox life. Monasteries are independent with no structure of religious orders.

CHURCH BUILDINGS

Churches are normally square in shape with a large central area covered by a dome. There are icons on the walls and at the east end there is a screen made up of them called the iconostasis. In it there are three doors, with the altar behind the central door. There are either no seats at all (in the Russian tradition) or a few seats round the wall (in the Greek tradition). The Orthodox parish church in Dublin, which has been skilfully adapted from a schoolroom, shows most of these features. People normally stand in the centre of the church during services.

WORSHIP AND SACRAMENTS

For Orthodox Christians worship is paramount, the principal means of expressing and understanding the Christian faith.

The main sacraments are Baptism and the Eucharist. Baptism and

Confirmation, known as Chrismation, take place together so that children may communicate from the earliest years. A great variety of other blessings, such as those of corn or fruits or homes, are also used.

All services are sung and the vernacular is used (albeit in both Greek and Slav traditions in an archaic form). The main service is the Eucharist, known as the Divine Liturgy or simply the Liturgy. Services tend to last rather longer than in the Western traditions.

The main feast of the Christian year is Easter, the date of which is calculated in most Orthodox churches by the Julian calendar so that it falls a week or more later than in the West. Next in importance come the Twelve Great Feasts, which include Christmas and Pentecost. Epiphany (which in the East commemorates Jesus' Baptism in the Jordan) and the Transfiguration are celebrated more than in the West. There are many other feasts and also fasts.

PERSONAL DEVOTION

Devout Orthodox pray regularly morning and evening before the icons in their homes. Another common devotion is the Jesus Prayer: *Jesus Christ, Son of God, have mercy on me*. This can be repeated constantly in the midst of daily activity. The Jesus Prayer is now much used by Christians in the West.

Fasting is also important as a means for the whole Church to live a disciplined life. Lent (known as Great Lent) is the major fast but there are many others. During them meat, fish and all animal products are forbidden.

CHURCH AND COMMUNITY

More than most Western Christians, Orthodox have experienced non-Christian and, on occasion, hostile rulers, mainly under the Turks and Communist governments. The strong ethnic identity of the churches has made them a force for national survival, notably after the German invasion of Russia in 1941, but also, it must be said, has led to a tendency towards aggressive nationalism. There have always been Orthodox thinkers who have resisted this. Patriarch Pavle of Serbia provided strong moral leadership in the Yugoslav Civil War, bravely condemning atrocities and seeking reconciliation with other religious leaders. Orthodox churches in Eastern Europe experienced varying degrees of persecution under Communist governments and are now coming to terms with a new era.

Orthodox have always (when the state has allowed them) been strong on practical charity. However, with some exceptions, they have not developed a social theology.

The Orthodox parish in Dublin is at present engaged in valuable pastoral work among refugees and asylum seekers from Eastern Europe.

In recent years the Orthodox awareness of creation has led to a strong participation in environmental concerns.

CATHOLICS OF THE EASTERN RITE

Over the centuries since the Schism, groups of Orthodox have acknowledged the authority of the Pope and formed churches linked to the Roman Church. They have retained their own liturgy and customs (including married clergy) and are known as Greek Catholics or Catholics of the Eastern rite. (An older name, *Uniates*, has hostile overtones.) They have provided a distinctive voice within Catholicism, especially at the Second Vatican Council. The largest and best-known Church is in the Ukraine. There are other communities in Central and Eastern Europe and the Middle East (where they are known as Melkites). There are also flourishing émigré churches. Under Communism governments forcibly united them to Orthodox churches but since its collapse they have re-emerged strongly, leading to serious disputes about the ownership of churches. Different in origin are the Maronites of the Lebanon. This ancient Church, with an Arabic Eastern liturgy, has been united to Rome since at least 1184. Senator George Mitchell, a prominent member of the United States Maronite community, has been involved in Northern Ireland as independent chairman of the political talks.

ORIENTAL ORTHODOX CHURCHES

Some Churches did not accept the Christological definitions of the Fourth Ecumenical Council of Chalcedon in 451. These Oriental Orthodox Churches have existed separately ever since. They were mainly in areas outside the Roman Empire and include the Ethiopian Church, the Coptic Church in Egypt, the Armenians and the ancient churches of South India and Syria. The Assyrians, based in Syria and Turkey, refused to accept the definitions of the Third Ecumenical Council at Ephesus in 431. They were originally known as Nestorians. All these churches have émigré branches. In Ireland there is a Coptic parish centred in Bray, south of Dublin. In recent years relations between Orthodox and Oriental Orthodox have become warmer, the theological difficulties now being seen as arising out of linguistic misunderstandings.

RELATIONS WITH OTHER CHURCHES

Most Orthodox churches belong to the World Council of Churches and, in Europe, to the Council of European Churches. The Irish Orthodox parish has recently joined the Irish Council of Churches. A process of dialogue has begun with the Roman Catholic Church, but serious problems have arisen, largely over the Eastern Rite Catholics. Anglican contacts with the Orthodox have been long and close. The Anglican–Orthodox Dialogue (of which the Anglican co-chairman was for many years Dr McAdoo, former Archbishop of Dublin) produced agreed statements in 1976 and 1984. Dialogues have also been started with Lutherans and other Protestant Churches. Orthodox regard communion as a sign of achieved unity, so that intercommunion is not allowed.

The Fellowship of St Alban and St Sergius is an organisation founded in 1928 to encourage contact between Anglicans, and later other Western Christians, and the Christian East. There has been a branch in Belfast since 1986. Based in the Department of Greek and Latin at Queen's University, it regularly invites Orthodox speakers to Belfast.

ORTHODOX IN NORTHERN IRELAND

Seventy-two people described themselves as Greek Orthodox in the 1991 Northern Ireland Census. Those who are practising belong to the Greek parish in Dublin.

In the 1950s Metropolitan Anthony of Sourozh, the Moscow Patriarchate Archbishop in Britain, visited Northern Ireland several times. He also spoke to the Connor Diocesan Clerical Union (Church of Ireland) on 22 September 1959. Archbishop Isidore of Pelusium, the Melkite Greek Catholic Patriarchal Vicar for Antioch, celebrated the Liturgy at Clonard Monastery on 19 November 1994.

The Orthodox bear witness to the historical core of the Christian faith and provide a direct link to the Early Church. In an Irish context, they furnish a salutary reminder that Christianity is wider than the Western world and broader than the division between Protestant and Catholic.

BIBLIOGRAPHY

Hackel, Sergei, *The Orthodox Church* (rev. edn.), Oxford: St Stephen's Press 1994. Clear and well-illustrated short introduction. Useful for schools.
Hill, Henry (ed.), *Light from the East: A Symposium on the Oriental Orthodox and Assyrian Churches*, Toronto: Anglican Book Centre 1988. Valuable survey on churches briefly touched on above.
Meyendorff, John, *The Orthodox Church: Its Past and its Role in the World Today*, 3rd edn, Crestwood, NY: St Vladimir's Seminary Press 1981. Important historical and doctrinal survey.

The Orthodox Way, London: Mowbray 1979. An examination of various theological problems and Orthodox approaches to them. Includes a useful anthology of Orthodox writings.

Ware, Timothy (Bishop Kallistos of Diokleia), *The Orthodox Church* (rev. edn), Harmondsworth: Penguin 1996. Comprehensive historical and theological survey. Standard work.

BIOGRAPHICAL NOTE

GEORGE WOODMAN is a librarian by profession. A member of the Church of Ireland, he has been involved in its work at university chaplaincy, parish and diocesan level and is at present a member of the General Synod. He has been interested in Orthodoxy for over thirty years and since 1991 has been Secretary of the Belfast branch of the Fellowship of St Alban and St Sergius.

PART 2

Reflections
across the
Traditions

The
Living Tapestry
Introduction to Part 2

NORMAN RICHARDSON

In the title of this book Christianity in Northern Ireland is likened to a tapestry. This is very appropriate, because not only is the tapestry a positive image – creative and colourful – but its very construction provides a helpful parallel with the two parts of the book.

Just like the *warp* on the loom the lengthways or vertical threads of Christian experience in Northern Ireland remain in parallel relationship – some closer than others, but all discrete and singular. These are the Churches, the denominational traditions described in Part 1. Yet they only really fit properly into the overall picture when the *weft* is applied, the horizontal strands which weave the warp into a rich and diverse community of pattern and colour. This is the wide range of issues, structures and 'isms' which bind the whole together into the pattern of contemporary faith; perhaps a way of seeing 'the Church' through the confusion of 'the churches'.

To read about the denominational traditions as stand-alone phenomena, diverse and fascinating as they are, would be to see only a part of the whole, to miss the pattern. If we wish to gain some sense of how these traditions contribute to the broad religious scene in Northern Ireland then we must consider their sources, their relationships – or lack of them – to each other, their alliances, their undercurrents – recognised or otherwise. The writers of the ensuing chapters all have experience beyond the boundaries of their own denominational traditions and are well equipped to read and interpret these cross-denominational strands and to offer a view on the resulting picture, warp and weft combined.

All imagery has its limitations, of course, and this image of *tapestry* falls down in that the resulting picture is constantly changing, in part depending on the viewer's own standpoint, but more importantly because the corporate Christian experience in Northern Ireland, as elsewhere, is a living organism, not a once-and-for-all snapshot in time. Even the very act of reflection and interpretation is a part of that process of change which makes all the difference between the observation of a dead specimen and the experience of something very much alive.

Perhaps, one might say, the tapestry is still, and hopefully will always be, in the process of being woven.

23

Differences and Commonalities

DAVID STEVENS

Through the centuries Christians have expressed their understandings differently – in essential belief, in ways of expressing their faith, in ways of worship and in the form and structures of church life which reflect different understandings of authority in the Church.

Of particular importance have been differences of belief and church order. Some Churches baptise infants; others administer baptism only to those who have made a profession of their faith. Some Churches have bishops whose consecration to office is traced back to the apostles; others do not even set aside people to an ordained ministry. Some Churches call on the Virgin Mary and other saints in their intercessions; others say this contradicts the unique mediating role of Jesus Christ. Some Churches set great store by the affirmation of historic creeds; others believe such formulas restrict the freedom of the individual Christian. Some Churches use a wide variety of hymns in their worship; others insist on using only versifications of the Psalms.

In fact, the situation is even more complicated. Churches which sing only the Psalms have divided over whether or not it is proper to accompany their singing with musical instruments. Differences about baptism among Churches which baptise infants may be as sharp as their differences with Churches which baptise only adults. Some of these differences, which once led to anathemas and excommunications, may seem, in some cases, unimportant today. But at one point in Church history they represented something over which Christians were ready to break fellowship.

Ruptures in a fellowship often create considerable bitterness and conflict. In particular, the rupture in medieval Christendom created by the Reformation meant that Churches which emerged from that period defined themselves over and against each other (especially for Protestant denominations over and against the Roman Catholic Church). Differences were emphasised, rather than the things held in common. It is really only in the twentieth century that this has begun to alter significantly.

Among the Protestant Churches differences, rifts and splits have been a prominent feature since the Reformation. The history of Ulster Protestantism, in particular, reveals a story of inter- and intra-denominational conflict. Particularly since the beginning of the nineteenth century there has been an increasing fragmentation of Ulster Protestantism. With fragmentation went competition for members.

NON-THEOLOGICAL FACTORS

Different understandings of faith have been powerfully moulded and accentuated by human factors in the societies in which they have appeared. Politics, culture, economics, ethnicity, nationalism, powerfully influence religion and are influenced by religion. This is particularly true in Ireland. It may be that the animosities of Christians in Ireland partly had their roots in cultural divisions and differences between the Irish and the English and Scottish. In any event the religious communities in Ireland developed their identities in opposition to each other. The Presbyterian/Anglican antipathy was, in part, overcome in the nineteenth century, but it was subsumed into a heightened pan-Protestant/Catholic difference and antagonism. But the Protestant/Catholic divide was not only a difference in religion; it became a difference between 'national' communities. Thus the majority of Roman Catholics became nationalists and the majority of Protestants became unionists. This remains the case in Northern Ireland. The consequence was that the purely religious differences between the two communities were reinforced. Ecumenism could even be seen by some as a political betrayal. The interaction between religion and politics is a particularly important one, especially in Northern Ireland.

AN EMPIRICAL PERSPECTIVE

A Protestant conservative/liberal split

A Presbyterian Church Board of Social Witness survey[1] shows a split between Presbyterians who believe in the necessity of a 'born-again' experience to be a Christian and those who don't. Bruce & Alderdice[2] found that between one-fifth and one-quarter of all Protestants were people who say that they are born again or had a 'born-again' experience.

Probably as many as one-third of regular churchgoing Protestants would be in this 'born-again' category. Boal, Campbell & Livingstone in their 1983 survey of churchgoing Protestants in the Belfast area[3] found that more than a quarter of regular churchgoers belong to a group identified by their insistence on the all-importance of a conversion experience and on a strictly inerrantist view of the Bible. 'Liberals', who did not accept these two notions, were well over 50% of those surveyed. Boal, Livingstone & Campbell found that the conservative–liberal split cuts across all the Protestant denominations, but cuts across them differently. For instance, 76% of members of the Church of Ireland were 'liberals', 53% of Presbyterians and 55% of Methodists, but only 6% of Baptists and 4% of Brethren.

Thus Ulster Protestantism is characterised not only by denominational cleavages but by a conservative/liberal divide. There are 'conservatives' in all the Protestant Churches and this shows the importance that evangelicalism has played in Ulster Protestant life. Evangelicals will come together in a variety of non-denominational organisations which will express a commonality of evangelical faith and worship. The diversity and individualism of Ulster evangelicalism should also be emphasised and it can be difficult for evangelicals to work together because of theological and personal differences. The role of the Orange Order in bringing Ulster Protestants together across class and denominational lines should also be mentioned, although there are many more Protestants outside the Order than inside it.

Boal, Livingstone & Campbell's research shows that some Protestant Churches are relatively homogeneous theologically (e.g. Brethren, Mission Hall, Evangelical Presbyterian, Baptist) but others are theologically diverse (e.g. Church of Ireland, Presbyterian and Methodist).

The liberal/conservative split relates to a number of religious, moral and social issues; indeed, conservatives tend to give a higher priority to 'religious' issues than to 'social' issues. The split also has political consequences; for instance, Boal, Livingstone & Campbell found that 'conservatives' are much more likely to vote for the Democratic Unionist Party, whereas 'liberals' are more likely to vote for the Official Unionist Party or the Alliance Party.

The split is, however, limited to certain issues. The vast majority of Protestants, irrespective of theological conviction or denominational affiliation, in the Boal, Livingstone & Campbell survey expressed their belief that the Protestant opposition to a united Ireland sprang primarily from a fear about the role the Catholic Church would play under such a constitutional arrangement. This shows again the way religion and politics are linked in the Protestant community.

Catholic divisions

There do not appear to be the same kind of theological divisions within Catholicism.[4] There are divisions within the churchgoing community, particularly between young and old and between those who are more educated and those who are less. Those who are older and less educated are more likely to be more orthodox and to see the Northern Ireland conflict as religious rather than political. There is only a weak association between religious views and voting patterns, i.e. religious views cannot be used as a predictor of what party someone is likely to vote for, unlike in the Protestant community.

Morrow suggests[5] a growing problem for the Church within the Catholic community in the sphere of personal morality issues, e.g. contraception and what to do about family breakdown. Compton & Coward have found[6] that Catholic attitudes towards family planning have been moving towards those held by Protestants, while suggesting that a significant factor in larger Catholic family size in Northern Ireland remains the role of religion. Montgomery & Davies found[7] that Catholic women were more inclined to favour easier divorce than Protestant women. There appears to be an increasing plurality of opinion developing among Catholics which is often at variance with the official standpoint of the Catholic Church.

Attitudes to ecumenism

The 1983 and 1993 surveys of Belfast churchgoing Protestants found that only a minority (35% in 1983 and 39% in 1993) were willing to worship with Catholics.

The 1993 survey found that 54% of Church of Ireland members, 47% of Presbyterians and 44% of Methodists were 'happy to take part in a joint service of worship with Catholics'. In the case of Catholics 78% were happy to worship with members of the Church of Ireland, 48% with Presbyterians and 42% with Methodists.

Only 10% of Protestants in both the 1983 and 1993 surveys of Belfast churchgoers thought that the aim of relations with the Roman Catholic Church should be unity. Forty-eight per cent in 1983 (47% in 1993) expressed a desire for greater co-operation with the Roman Catholic Church in both religious and social matters. The vast majority of the 'liberals' in the 1983 survey expressed a desire for co-operation with the Roman Catholic Church in both religious and social matters, but the 'conservatives' were not interested in extending relationships beyond the social sphere. Indeed, one-third of 'conservatives' wanted no dealings with the Roman Catholic Church whatsoever.

Catholics appear not to fear the Protestant Churches in the same way as Protestants fear the Catholic Church. The 1968 Rose survey found[8] that five-sixths of Catholics said there was nothing they disliked about the Protestant Churches. In the 1993 Belfast churchgoers survey 47% of Catholics thought that the aim of inter-church relations should be unity and another 46% thought that the aim should be greater co-operation on religious and social matters. This is very significantly different to Protestant attitudes as revealed above.

Moral attitudes

The 1989 Social Attitudes survey found[9] that churchgoing Protestants and Roman Catholics in Northern Ireland shared a common conservative position on censorship, abortion, homosexuality and pornography. There are disagreements between Protestants (particularly Presbyterians) and Roman Catholics when it comes to gambling, use of alcohol, capital punishment, attitudes to prisoners and to some extent on abortion (e.g. when it comes to choosing between the mother's or the baby's life, or on the possibility of defects to the foetus). According to Cairns[10] Catholics hold more radical views on questions concerning the distribution of wealth, welfare, law and order and support for political protest. On the issue of law and order in particular, Protestants take a much more conservative position.

WHERE WE ARE TODAY

In the twentieth century there has been a move among 'mainline' churches towards a more positive evaluation of each other's traditions. Vatican II in the Roman Catholic Church and the ecumenical movement have altered attitudes. Many Churches have begun to discover that, despite much diversity in theological expression and difference in church order, there is a lot they have in common in their understanding of the faith. Many promising convergences have emerged in doctrinal matters. Some would talk of a real but imperfect unity which now exists. There has been a decline in bitterness and rivalry between many Churches. Co-operation in a variety of fields has increased. The relations between many Churches and many Christians have been significantly transformed. People meet and worship together in ways that they did not do in the past.

Important theological disagreements continue to hold Churches and Christians apart and cause difficulty in how they relate together, for example over mixed marriage and intercommunion. For some evangelicals the theological disagreements remain such that they continue to find it difficult to accept the Roman Catholic Church as a Christian Church. Some would find it impossible even to accept that individual Roman Catholics could be Christian. The research evidence quoted earlier shows that there is a considerable reserve about ecumenism, particularly among Protestants.

Groups like the *Inter-Church Group on Faith and Politics* and the *Evangelical Contribution on Northern Ireland* (ECONI), and other work within the Churches, has meant that there has been some progress in separating religious commitments from political commitments in Northern Ireland, and thus separating political differences from religious differences. This work has a long way to go, but it has commenced.

IN CONCLUSION

In this century there has been developing a coming together of churches (especially 'mainline' Churches) and Christians. There is an increasing awareness that much is shared, even though important differences remain. At the same time there has been an even greater fragmentation of Protestantism going on in Northern Ireland. In particular there has been a growth in evangelical and fundamentalist Churches at the same time as the 'mainline' Churches have declined in membership. There is, also, the reality of differences within denominations and this may be growing too. Thus overall there is a paradox: a growing awareness of the commonalities of faith among some and the continuing reality of differences – and these differences may be increasing as new religious groupings and movements come on the scene.

NOTES

1. D. Bamford & B. McCullough, *Burning Issues* (Belfast: The Board of Social Witness, Presbyterian Church in Ireland 1990).
2. S. Bruce & F. Alderdice, 'Religious Belief and Behaviour' in P. Stringer & G. Robinson (eds.), *Social Attitudes in Northern Ireland: The Third Report* (Belfast: Blackstaff Press 1993).
3. 1983 Belfast Protestant Churchgoers Survey – some of this research is written up in F. Boal & D.N. Livingstone, 'Protestants in Belfast: A View from the Outside', *Contemporary Review*, 248, no. 1443 (April 1986), pp. 69–175 and F. Boal, J.A. Campbell & D.N. Livingstone, 'The Protestant Mosaic: A Majority of Minorities' in P. Roche & B. Barton (eds.), *The Northern Ireland Question: Myth and Reality* (Aldershot: Avebury 1991).
4. For the 1993 Belfast Churchgoers Survey see F.W. Boal, M. Keane & D.N. Livingstone, *Them and Us? Attitudinal Variation among Churchgoers in Belfast* (Belfast: Queen's University Institute of Irish Studies 1997).
5. D. Morrow, *The Churches and Inter-Community Relationships* (Coleraine: Centre for the Study of Conflict, University of Ulster 1991).

6. P. Compton & J. Coward, *Fertility and Family Planning in Northern Ireland* (Aldershot: Avebury 1989).
7. P. Montgomery & C. Davies, 'A Woman's Place in Northern Ireland', in P. Stringer & G. Robinson (eds.), *Social Attitudes in Northern Ireland: 1990–91 Edition* (Belfast: Blackstaff Press 1991).
8. See R. Rose, *Governing without Consensus: An Irish Perspective* (London: Faber & Faber 1971).
9. R. Jowell, S. Witherspoon & L. Brook (eds.), *British Social Attitudes – The 7th Report* (Aldershot: Gower 1991 [1989 Social Attitudes survey]).
10. E. Cairns, 'Is Northern Ireland a Conservative Society?' in P. Stringer & G. Robinson (eds.), *Social Attitudes in Northern Ireland: 1990–91 Edition* (Belfast: Blackstaff Press 1991).

BIOGRAPHICAL NOTE

DR DAVID STEVENS is General Secretary of the Irish Council of Churches, which brings together the largest of the Protestant Churches in Ireland and some of the smaller. He is a Presbyterian elder, a member of the Corrymeela Community and of the Faith and Politics Group. He was a founder member of the Northern Ireland Community Relations Council.

24

Spirituality
in Contemporary Ireland

JOHNSTON McMASTER

It is hardly surprising, given the diversity of human persons, that spirituality is also diverse. Throughout almost two millennia of Christian history it would be more accurate to speak of spiritualities. The paradoxes contained in the mystery of human lives require diverse approaches and expressions. The ultimate mystery, God, cannot be encapsulated or totally experienced in any one spirituality. The very nature of God requires diversity.

All expressions of holistic spirituality, and there is a rich diversity, have four interconnected and interrelated essentials. These may be defined in brief as:

- a way of seeing and experiencing God
- a way of seeing and experiencing self
- a way of seeing and experiencing others
- a way of seeing and experiencing the world

All belong together and if one essential is left out, neglected or ignored, the expression of spirituality will be deficient. Spirituality is essentially an experiential vision which embraces the totality of relationships. The divine, personal, communal and ecological are all held together in a way of seeing, experiencing and relating. Diverse Christian spiritualities will settle for no less.

The purpose of this chapter is to explore three expressions of spirituality which have come alive for people in contemporary Ireland.

1. CELTIC SPIRITUALITY

The twelfth-century Bernard of Clairvaux claimed that everyone ought to be able to drink from their own well. Celtic spirituality can claim to be the oldest expression of Christian spirituality in Ireland. It was the spirituality that took root in Irish culture and life when the gospel itself reached these shores. In that sense it is indigenous spirituality.

At the same time it is not exclusive to Ireland. Celtic spirituality took root and developed also in Scotland, Wales, Cornwall, the Isle of Man, Brittany and parts of England, particularly the north. Northern Irish Presbyterians, with their Scottish connection, have as much claim to drink from the well as Irish Catholics and the Church of Ireland. Indeed the historical Presbyterian tradition of dissent is much more expressive of the fierce spirit of independence and nonconformism of the early Celtic Church, than the historical experience of other Irish Churches.

Celtic spirituality is our oldest form of spirituality, older than anything that divides Irish Christians and reaching far behind the historical causes of division. Though historical and political events suppressed the Celtic cultural and spiritual tradition, they never totally destroyed it. It became an underground cultural and spiritual stream which, from time to time, pushes its way to the surface. The last quarter of the twentieth century seems to be such a time when Celtic spirituality is being rediscovered, not in any one denominational tradition, but across the inter-church spectrum. The rediscovery is not a nostalgic or romantic recovery of a distant past, but of a spirituality that enables a holistic way of seeing and experiencing in the contemporary world.

Historical roots

Whatever Patrick did and achieved, he was not the first to bring Christianity to Ireland. There is the tradition of Palladius 'sent to the Irish who believe in Christ'. Not only is there general acceptance that Palladius predates Patrick, but the documented reference indicates a Christian community already in Ireland. It is even thought that a Christian community existed in Ireland almost a century before Patrick came. This is not impossible given the movement of captured slaves from Britain, where Christianity was known to be present by AD 200. Ireland also had extensive trading links in the fourth century with Britain and mainland Europe. There is also documentation of a fourth-century migration of Gaulish Christians fleeing persecution to Ireland.

Whatever the origins of Celtic spirituality in Ireland, it did take root and developed with the great Celtic Church, which was essentially a monastic or community model. The Celtic Church became renowned for its biblical scholarship, wide-ranging cultural learning and missionary tradition. This monastic Church was also characterised by a breadth of tolerance, lack of centralised structure and a spirit of independence of thought and expression. Though by no means flawless and without need of reform, the Celtic Church birthed a living, vital, holistic spirituality that renewed the flame of spirituality in Europe. The Celtic contribution to a Europe where the flame of faith had almost gone out is a remarkable one. It is also a contribution which contemporary Irish Christians, living through the birth of a new Europe, too easily overlook or fail to appreciate.

Essential characteristics

(a) SPIRITUAL FREEDOM. Celtic spirituality perceived truth as a multifaceted diamond. There are many ways of holding a diamond up to the light and viewing it. What is revealed is of rich, diverse beauty and splendour. It was this essential way of viewing reality that gave Celtic Christians an intense sense of spiritual freedom to quest, explore and discover the incredibly rich diversity, breadth and depth of God's grace in all sorts of people, places, events, sights and sounds. Spirituality for Celtic Christians was essentially a journey. It was a journey into God, worshipped and adored as Trinity and which never ends.

(b) ARTISTIC AND POETIC. Celtic Christians were also artistic and poetic. The interwoven and interlaced patterns of Celtic artwork provide a visible expression of the mystery of things. The spiralling and interwoven patterns have no beginning or end. Here is a visible symbol of the interweaving of eternity and time as Celtic Christians lived with the deep sense of belonging to two worlds which are but one. God is in all things and all things are in God and the pattern of personal, communal and ecological lives goes on being woven into greater patterns still, shot through at every twist and turn with the divine. In its artistic work, also given rich expression through gospel books such as the Book of Kells, Celtic spirituality engages the visual and sees and experiences God through the imagination and art.

Celtic spirituality is highly poetic. Celtic poems are prayers and Celtic prayers are poems. It is a spirituality which makes use of the word but in a rich poetic way. Language is used metaphorically not literally. The strict literal meaning of a word has little appeal for Celtic spirituality, not because words are unimportant but words and language have too much depth, richness and mystery to have only one meaning or to be taken literally. Conversation with God, the ultimate mystery, is through the poetic. Metaphors abound.

There are many anthologies of Celtic poetry from Ireland and Scotland. Two of the best-known poems for Irish Christians of all traditions are 'Patrick's Breastplate' and 'Be thou my Vision'.

The Breastplate was not written by Patrick, but is a later composition in the well-known Celtic style known as the Lorica. It was probably a morning dressing prayer as one bound to oneself the Trinity for all the meetings, activities, encounters, journeys and relationships of the day. At least three essential characteristics of Celtic spirituality are highlighted.

(c) ROOTED IN THE TRINITY. Celtic spirituality is rooted in the Trinity, which is an expression of mystery and the mystical at the heart of spirituality. The Trinity was also experienced by Celtic Christians in 'friendship and affection'.[1] Friendship and affection, therefore, are at the heart of the mystery. Celtic spirituality has a deep sense of mystery, warmth, intimacy and divine–human friendship.

Celtic spirituality is also intensely practical. The mystical and the practical are held together. The Trinity is essentially perceived as relational. For Celtic spirituality the Trinity is about harmonious relationships; a model of community in which there is diversity in unity and unity in diversity. Rooted in the Trinity, Celtic spirituality is oriented to community and relationships. Significantly some aspects of late-twentieth-century theology are recovering this mystical–practical insight.

(d) LOVE OF NATURE. One stanza from the Breastplate is full of ecological metaphors and insights. The sun, moon, rocks and sea all become windows into the God of all life. Celtic spirituality has a profound love of nature and a deep sense of harmony with nature. It is the Celtic sense of the sacredness of all things and the awareness of the divine presence in all things. It is an environmentally friendly spirituality which produces a sense of partnership, with reverence and respect for nature and creation.

(e) CHRIST-CENTRED AND RELATIONAL. Two stanzas of the Breastplate highlight the Christ-centredness of Celtic spirituality. The entire Christ-story is rehearsed in eight lines. From birth to the end-hope the whole Christ is embraced. This too is a highlighting of the Bible story. For Celtic spirituality Scripture is the norm and the volume of Scripture copying, translation, reflection and scholarship that emerged from the Celtic Church is an indication of the centrality of the Scriptures for worship, faith and practice.

But Celtic spirituality is not primarily a spirituality of the book. It is a spirituality of the person and of relationships. It is not just that the whole Christ is embraced, but that the whole Christ embraces the whole person.

> Christ be with me, Christ within me,
> Christ behind me, Christ before me,
> Christ beside me, Christ to win me,
> Christ to comfort and restore me,
> Christ beneath me, Christ above me,

Christ in quiet, Christ in danger,
Christ in hearts of all that love me,
Christ in mouth of friend and stranger.

Celtic spirituality makes much of the image of the circle with the idea of wholeness and inclusiveness. All of life and relationships are encompassed and encircled by Christ. All relationships are held in the circling of Christ. The encounters with friend and stranger are encounters with Christ. Celtic spirituality is essentially relational and communal. It is about Christ in the whole of life and in the whole of relationships. It is therefore a spirituality with profound personal, social and political implications.

(f) VISION AND WHOLENESS. 'Be thou my Vision' (the familiar versified form is by Eleanor Hull from an earlier and more literal translation by Mary Byrne of an eighth-century Irish form) also embraces the whole of life in relationships and community, including economic life and relationships. It defines the essence of Celtic spirituality as vision. Vision is a way of seeing and perceiving as well as experiencing reality. The ultimate vision is of God, but God who is inclusive of all human and ecological reality. This again requires metaphors and this piece of Celtic poetry is typically full of metaphors drawn from Celtic culture and society. Celtic spirituality has the ability to perceive images and models of God and life within a contemporary cultural and social context.

(g) SUMMARY. The essential, though not exhaustive, characteristics of Celtic spirituality are as follows:

- Rooted in the Trinity
- The Communion of Saints
- Love of Scripture
- The Whole Person
- Down-to-Earth Spirituality
- Hospitality
- Love of Nature
- Austerity and Suffering

Celtic hospitality today is about social, economic and political justice while the Celtic approach to suffering is a creative alternative to passivity, fatalism or determinism; it is a creative solidarity with the suffering of Christ.

That an indigenous well has been rediscovered is evident from the plethora of publications, and it is embodied by places like the Iona Community and the interpretative centres on ancient Celtic Christian sites such as Glendalough, Nendrum and Clonmacnoise. The contemporary appeal is also crossing the age barrier. In three descriptive words, Celtic spirituality is a holistic, relational and embodied spirituality.

2. TRADITIONAL SPIRITUALITIES

As spiritualities develop, traditional experiences continue to nurture many Irish Christians. Even here traditional does not always mean unchanging. The old, which once was new, can and sometimes does find renewed emphasis and meaning in the changing context of people's lives.

Protestant expressions

Protestantism encompasses a broad spectrum and has never been monolithic. In Ireland political exigencies have often created a Protestant unity which has obscured real and sometimes even historically bitter differences. Protestant expressions of spirituality are equally diverse. There is no one Protestant spirituality. Quaker, Church of Ireland, Calvinist and Wesleyan spiritualities are richly different. There are nuances and emphases, often coming out of different historical experiences, which create a rainbow, even a kaleidoscope of spiritualities. The denominational chapters of this book indicate the range of diversity. What follows are a few of the broad brush strokes in traditional Protestant expressions.

(a) THE WORD. *Sola Scriptura* is a central Protestant emphasis. The Word of God in Scripture is the ultimate authority. The Bible is essential for the nourishment of the spiritual life. The various Protestant expressions of spirituality would therefore claim to have scriptural foundation.

Protestant spirituality has made use of Scripture in two ways. There is the formal use of Scripture when the Word of God is read in the worshipping congregation. The Word is also proclaimed within the congregation through preaching, which often dominates traditional Protestant worship, especially Presbyterian and Methodist and many of the smaller denominations. The ministry of the Word is the heart of worship and is the primary channel of spiritual nourishment and means of encounter with God.

The other use of Scripture is more informal and finds expression through the private or individual prayerful study of the Bible. This is essentially a devotionalist approach to Scripture. For some it is also a very literalistic approach to the text. For others the critical and devotionalist approaches are held together and individual Bible study becomes a wrestling with the Word.

Various Bible reading notes and devotional commentaries are used alongside the text and the study often leads to prayer.

(b) THE PRAYER MEETING. The prayer meeting has been and remains a spiritual dimension of Protestant Christian fellowship. This is an informal meeting, additional to the Sunday worship of the congregation. Prayers are vocal, spontaneous or extempore. The form is quite different from the Catholic Prayer Service, a more formal service used on non-sacramental occasions.

The prayer meeting is often held on a weeknight and will include prayers for the congregation, the sick, those facing various difficulties and the mission of the Church. The evangelical revivals of the eighteenth and nineteenth centuries enhanced such prayer. It was the evangelicals who introduced the term 'prayer meeting' in the early nineteenth century.

It is probably true to describe the traditional prayer meeting as a minority activity in most congregations and something which has declined over the years. However, in some situations, fresh impetus has been given to the prayer meeting by the Charismatic Renewal Movement.

In the Calvinist tradition a mature relationship with God is centred in prayer. John Calvin's rules of prayer have been applied to private prayers as well as the prayer meeting and public prayer at worship.

- The mind must rise to a purity worthy of God.
- We are to ask only so far as God permits.
- We are to ask only for things really needed, and with ardent desire, whether for ourselves or not.
- Prayer should be utterly humble, and yet confident.
- The model prayer is the 'Our Father'.

(c) HYMNOLOGY. The greatest use of hymns in spiritual nurture and prayer has been in the Wesleyan tradition. Charles Wesley remains the most prolific hymn writer in the history of English language hymnology. In the eighteenth century he and his brother John realised that one of the key ways to develop and nurture faith was to sing it. At the same time Methodists have always used their hymn books as prayer books. Wesley hymns have had a prime place in Methodist devotion, underlining the reality that the deepest language of prayer is often poetic and metaphoric.

Many modern Methodists find Wesley's poetic theology less appealing, though for significant numbers the hymn book remains a prayer book.

Presbyterians have always cherished the Psalms, singing the Hebrew songs in their metric version. The Psalms were the Hebrew song and prayer book. Their appeal has been universal, expressing as they do the whole range of human emotions in relationship to God. Psalms continue to be a vital part of Presbyterian worship, including the old metric and modern versions.

Fresh impetus has been given to the role of hymnology in spirituality by the outpouring of new hymns and songs characteristic of the last two decades. Twentieth-century song and hymn writers such as Fred Kaan, Sydney Carter and Graham Kendrick have all contributed from their diverse Christian perspectives to the praise of God. Taizé chants and *Wild*

Goose Songs in the modern Celtic tradition from the Iona Community (many of them written by the prolific writers John Bell and Graham Maule) are also increasingly used. Charismatic songs and African music provide expressions of worship for a diverse Christian community.

(d) THE LORD'S DAY. Traditional Protestant spirituality has been influenced not only by the evangelical revivals, but by Puritanism, an influence clearly seen in the traditional Protestant emphasis on the Lord's Day. Sabbath observance remains for not a few a significant dimension of their spirituality. Though not as strictly observed as a century ago or even less, the day of rest given to worship and devotion, and in which play, work and trading have little or no part, is still a traditional Protestant characteristic.

Within the practising Protestant spectrum the level of observance may vary, but the emphasis remains. It is reflected by the representation of the largest Protestant denomination in Northern Ireland, the Presbyterian Church, to the Prime Minister at a meeting in Downing Street in July 1995, expressing opposition to the planned reduction of Sunday trading restrictions.

Catholic expressions

Traditional Catholic spirituality also emphasises the need for a scriptural foundation. Pope Paul VI in *Marialis Cultus* (1974) reminded Catholics that devotion to Mary must be based on Scripture. Medieval monasticism, often rooted in the Rule of Benedict, placed much emphasis on the private meditative reading of the Bible. *Lectio divina*, sacred reading, almost exclusively of Scripture, led to *meditatio*, the turning over in the mind and on the lips of the text read. The content of the traditional Catholic expressions of spirituality highlighted below is essentially biblical.

The Second Vatican Council (1962–5) has been a focal point of renewal for the Catholic Church. New models of Church, mission and liturgy emerged and new insights and impetus have been given to spirituality. There has been renewed emphasis on the liturgy, the Bible and retreats as sources of spiritual nourishment. However, as one Catholic author has observed, 'Since 1965 devotional expressions such as stations of the cross, novenas, holy hours and special practices in honour of the Eucharist, the Heart of Jesus and the Blessed Virgin have sharply declined in many places, not without serious loss, when they have not been replaced by something better.'[2]

These traditional devotional expressions have not disappeared completely. Not a few Irish Catholics continue to find meaning and nurture in their practice. Four traditional expressions are highlighted here.

(a) MARIAN DEVOTION. Much of the devotion is focused on the Marian feasts celebrated in the calendar and liturgy of the Catholic Church. Catholic theology has always very carefully drawn the distinction between worship, ascribed only to God the Trinity, and honour or veneration, due to Mary. From early times Mary was honoured with the title 'Mother of God', which was essentially a Christological statement. The main feasts honouring Mary are as follows (in theological rather than chronological order):

The Immaculate Conception	8 December
The birthday of the Blessed Virgin	8 September
The Annunciation	20 December
The Visitation	2 July
The Purification	2 February
The Assumption of Mary	15 August

The month of May is also dedicated to Mary.

The main focus of these feasts is not primarily Mary, but Christ. They are essentially Christocentric feasts celebrating Mary's unique honour of being the mother of humanity's saviour and redeemer.

Again, Pope Paul VI reminded Catholics that devotion to Mary must be based in Scripture. Pope John Paul II in his homily at Knock during his visit to Ireland in 1979 underlined the Christocentric nature of this traditional devotion by reflecting on and repeating the words of Mary in the story of the wedding feast at Cana (John 2): 'Do whatever he tells you.'

(b) THE ROSARY. The Rosary is a form of prayer which engages the voice, body and mind. Familiar prayers are repeated with meditation on selected mysteries of the faith. In *Marialis Cultus* Pope Paul VI described it as a gospel prayer deriving from and leading to the liturgy.

The Rosary consists of fifteen decades of 'Hail Mary', each decade preceded by an 'Our Father' and concluded by a 'Glory be'. There are fifteen mysteries grouped in series of fives. They are as follows:

The Joyful Mysteries
annunciation
visitation
nativity
presentation in the temple
finding in the temple

The Sorrowful Mysteries
agony in the garden
scourging

crowning with thorns
carrying of the cross
death on the cross

The Glorious Mysteries
resurrection
ascension
coming of the Holy Spirit
assumption of the Virgin Mary
coronation of the Virgin Mary and glory of all the saints

These are essentially meditations with a central Christological emphasis.

(c) THE STATIONS OF THE CROSS. This traditional devotion probably goes back to the early pilgrimages to Jerusalem which followed the 'way of the cross'. By the nineteenth century nearly all Catholic churches had fourteen stations arranged around the internal walls or sometimes in the church grounds. The fourteen stations are selected incidents from the final journey of Christ.

As a devotion the stations can be used privately, silently and informally, or as a public celebration especially during Lent and Passiontide.

More recent historical development has seen the addition of a fifteenth station representing the resurrection. Again the devotion is essentially Christocentric and the meditations are rooted in Scripture. The fifteen stations are as follows:

Jesus is condemned to death.
Jesus takes up his cross.
Jesus falls for the first time.
Jesus meets his blessed mother.
Simon of Cyrene helps Jesus to carry his cross.
Veronica wipes the face of Jesus.
Jesus falls the second time.
The women of Jerusalem mourn for Jesus.
Jesus falls the third time.
Jesus is stripped of his clothes.
Jesus is nailed to the cross.
Jesus dies on the cross.
Jesus is taken down from the cross.
Jesus is placed in the tomb.
Jesus is raised from the dead.

(d) THE EASTER VIGIL. The Easter Vigil is the celebration of the passion, death and resurrection of Christ on the Saturday night and Sunday morning of Easter. It is the recognition by the people of God that they exist only through the saving events of cross and resurrection. Far from being a mere recollection of the past, the celebration looks forward to Christ's coming again in glory to bring the work of redemption and the Kingdom to perfect completion. The celebration, therefore, is a living encounter and a renewed experience of the Lord.

The vigil goes back to the first century when the emphasis was on the Eucharist. By the second century the focus included baptism. The introduction of the lighting of the fire was introduced by the Celtic Church. The vigil is therefore characterised by the use of Word, symbol and sacramental celebration. The word-service rehearses and celebrates God's saving deeds in the Scriptures. The story of redemption is read and heard.

The symbolism of light and fire precedes the word. The church is in darkness and the new fire is lit. From the fire the Paschal candle is lit. 'Christ our light' is celebrated in song and then follows the lighting of the people's candles. The Easter Proclamation leads into the hearing and proclamation of the saving deeds of God in the Scriptures.

After the homily the baptismal water is blessed and candidates, if any, are baptised. Then the people are sprinkled with water and baptismal promises renewed. This leads into the liturgy of the Mass and the celebration of the risen and present Christ.

The entire vigil, therefore, is a celebration of the redeeming work of Christ.

(e) THE EUCHARIST. Central to Catholic spirituality is the Eucharist. The word is of Greek origin, meaning thanksgiving, and is derived from the Last Supper of Jesus with his disciples. Included in the thanksgiving is remembering, confessing and proclaiming what God had done. The Eucharist is at the heart of Catholic worship and essential to it is a high view of the real presence of Christ.

Anglican theology and the theology of the Wesleys also hold a high view of the real presence, though the conceptual frameworks differ.

The centrality and frequency of the Eucharist (daily or weekly) is a strong characteristic of Catholic spirituality. Within the Protestant traditions frequency can range from monthly to twice per year. Infrequency in contrast to Catholic practice does not suggest a low view of the sacrament. All the traditions hold to the high significance and importance of the Eucharist or Lord's Supper, which leads some to frequent participation and others to infrequent practice.

The Liturgical Renewal Movement of the twentieth century has sought the recovery of early Christian practice. This means restoring the Eucharist to its central place in Sunday worship as a corporate, congregational celebration. This aspect of the Liturgical Movement has had limited impact on Irish Protestant Churches, however.

For Catholics, the Eucharist remains at the heart of worship and spirituality.

3. CHARISMATIC SPIRITUALITY

Charismatic renewal has found expression in all of the mainstream Churches in Ireland. It has also been experienced by those who belong to the Religious Society of Friends. Within the House or Fellowship church movement (the 'New Churches' are described elsewhere in this book) the signs of charismatic renewal exist, often it seems, combining Brethren and pentecostal emphases. Charismatic spirituality, therefore, is a significant expression of spirituality among Irish Christians of various traditions. It is a spirituality with a particular emphasis on the Holy Spirit and renewal. It is about thirty years since the renewal experience first reached Ireland and there are now those who speak of the need for a renewal of the renewal.

Historical roots

The earliest roots of the twentieth-century phenomenon can be traced to the USA. Charismatic renewal began as a pentecostal movement. From 1901 various claims have been made for origins, but many now agree that the moment of catalyst was in 1906 in Azusa Street, Los Angeles.

From a sociological perspective it was a strange beginning to the pente-costal phenomenon. Peter Hocken, a scholarly historian of the pentecostal and charismatic movements, highlights the surprising features of the Azusa Street event:

- its interracial character
- the make-up of the crowds who came from far and near
- its fringe character in relation to society
- its fringe character in relation to mainline denominations[3]

Clearly it was something which cut across expectations, barriers and structures in a surprising way. What happened to people in Azusa Street also surprised many. The characteristics of the phenomenon have been described as follows:

- people spoke in unknown tongues
- people prophesied
- people raised their various voices in simultaneous praise
- some were healed
- people spoke of experiencing 'Pentecost'
- people spoke of being baptised in the Holy Spirit[4]

The mainstream churches did not recognise what was happening as the work of the Holy Spirit. But the pentecostal movement was born and the 'first surprise' as Hocken describes it, was, after several years, repeated in the historical Protestant traditions. The second surprise of charismatic renewal in the historical Protestant Churches became clear around 1960. The third surprise was the spread of charismatic renewal to the Roman Catholic Church. The renewal emphases of the Second Vatican Council had focused on liturgy, biblical studies, catechetical reform and lay participation. The restoration of the *charismata pneumatika* of 1 Corinthians 12 was not on the agenda, but by the late 1960s it had become the experience of lay Catholics in the United States.

Hocken sees the pentecostal movement as 'the mother of these surprises', and suggests that 'baptism in the Spirit is the common grace'.[5]

It was in the early 1970s that charismatic renewal came to Ireland. The earliest experiences of renewal were centred on Queen's University in Belfast and University College Dublin. The initial spark came through the Student Christian Movement, a large group in the late 1960s. There were individual meetings between Catholics and Protestants, and a large meeting in Dublin addressed by Revs. Tom Smail and Joe McGeady proved a catalyst, prompting follow-up meetings in the Quaker Hall in Eustace Street, Dublin.

The experience of charismatic renewal in Ireland had crossdenominational participation from the beginning. Prayer groups developed all over Ireland with attendance ranging from twenty to two hundred. Conferences were organised in Dublin and Belfast and a particular high point was reached in 1978 when an International Charismatic Conference was held in the Royal Dublin Society (RDS) arena attended by twenty thousand people.

The RDS conference was exclusively Catholic, which created some tensions given the cross-denominational dimension to the renewal experience in Ireland. Today there are people in every mainstream Irish Church who have experienced charismatic renewal and the Christian Renewal Centre in Rostrevor is well established as a focus on charismatic renewal in the Holy Spirit.

Essential characteristics

At the heart of the Charismatic Renewal Movement is an understanding and experience of the Trinity in the Church and in personal lives. There is also a strong emphasis on the full restoration of the gifts of the Holy Spirit. Together these emphases highlight the deeply experiential nature of the renewal movement. There is a living, immediate sense of the awareness of God. God is not distant but personal.

Personal testimony or witness, an important feature of meetings, often speaks of empowering, an awareness of a personal relationship with God and a deeper sense of joy. The sense of personal relationship is rooted in God's love, and worship or liturgy becomes alive with a sense of the celebratory.

The experiential is central, not that theology is unimportant, but if anything, it is the articulation of the experience. In this sense the Charismatic Renewal Movement is a protest against a cerebral form of Christianity. Church history suggests the emphasis on the cerebral cannot continue indefinitely, but personal, experiential and emotionally satisfying expressions of faith will emerge. The twentieth-century Charismatic Renewal Movement would seem to be such an expression of Christian faith and spirituality. What are the essential characteristics?

(a) DIVERSE STREAMS. In global terms the Charismatic Renewal Movement has diverse expressions. It began as a pentecostal experience, but as the twentieth century progressed the experience impacted others. There are now five diverse streams of renewal

- Pentecostal
- Protestant Charismatic
- Catholic Charismatic
- Messianic Jewish
- Independent Charismatic

The last stream is itself a diverse grouping of independent charismatic assemblies where there are full-time workers but no received pattern of ordained ministry or ministerial training. They are, in a sense, non-denominational and may be described as independent networks.

Messianic Judaism, like the independent charismatic stream, came into being in the 1970s. It has also been described as a distinctively Jewish form of Christianity and in one sense is a protest against an exclusively Gentile church. Messianic Jews accept Jesus as the Messiah but continue to affirm their Jewish heritage and identity. Messianic synagogues celebrating Jewish feasts and confessing Jesus as Messiah are developing outside the historic Churches. Though part of the broad charismatic stream, Messianic Judaism does not really feature in Irish experience.

Globally, then, charismatic renewal expresses itself through diverse forms and structures. There are diverse streams, but Hocken believes that they 'all belong to the one overall outpouring of the Spirit'.[6]

The Rev. Cecil Kerr of the Christian Renewal Centre in Rostrevor draws attention to the following five particular emphases of the charismatic experience.[7]

(b) AN EXPERIENCE OF THE TRINITY. In experiential terms God as Father becomes a living reality. The awareness of God in charismatic renewal is immediate and personal. There is a real spirit of sonship or being a child of God.

This also includes a deeply personal relationship with Christ and an experience of the reality of Jesus as personal saviour.

The third person of the Trinity, the Holy Spirit, is experienced as personal empowerment and there is the reality of the gifts of the Spirit.

(c) UNITY. The unity of God's people is a high priority in charismatic renewal. This emphasis on unity has not been worked out in any theological or ecclesial sense, but again is an experiential unity.

The experience of unity begins with baptism in the Spirit and is one of the gifts of the Spirit. This experience of unity as a gift is given concrete expression through bringing together Protestant and Catholic Christians. The experience has also created communities such as the Renewal Centre in Rostrevor and the Lamb of God Community in Belfast. Charismatic renewal and the experience of unity is believed to be the most significant grass-roots ecumenism in Ireland since the early Celtic Church. A major challenge, Hocken believes, for all those who have experienced Spirit-baptised unity, is how to relate it to doctrinal, pastoral and governmental unity in the Church.[8]

(d) THE IMPORTANCE OF SCRIPTURE. In charismatic prayer meetings Scripture is central. It is not just a textbook but is read and studied as a daily guide. The Spirit illuminates Scripture and through the Word God speaks. Bible reflection is part of the sharing experience of the prayer meeting. The reading of a Bible passage out loud and slowly is in the context of prayer in and to the Spirit with opportunity for people to share from their prayerful reflection.

(e) OUTREACH AND EVANGELISM. Within the charismatic renewal experience there is a strong link between the gift of the Spirit and evangelism or evangelisation. The biblical model is the Pentecost story from the Acts of the Apostles when the disciples, empowered by the Spirit, began to preach the good news. Baptism in the Spirit gives impetus to share a living faith.

Testimony is an important part of the charismatic prayer meeting when people relate and share their personal experiences. Pat Collins believes that an important task for charismatic renewal is to re-evangelise society and he sees the prayer meeting as a key place for regular reflection and discussion on:

- the nature of evangelisation
- the many compelling motives there are for spreading the Good News

- the practical means whereby this could be done in a personal and communal way[9]

(f) BAPTISM IN THE SPIRIT. This emphasis is central to the charismatic experience. It is also the common factor in each of the otherwise diverse streams. Hocken describes it as foundational grace and highlights the relevant Scripture data and the contemporary experience.[10]

In relation to twentieth-century origins, the experience was central to the Azusa Street Pentecostal phenomenon and was believed to be the grace of Pentecost. The Spirit-baptism terminology, despite early criticisms, has been retained in charismatic experience.

It is baptism in the Spirit which gives an immediacy of relationship to the Persons of the Trinity and is seen as the restoration of the Christianity of the New Testament. Spiritual gifts are given to empower ministries and to build up the Body of Christ. The gifts are the characteristic signs of the divine sovereign intervention of baptising with the Holy Spirit.[11]

The Scripture basis for the *charismata pneumatika* is found in 1 Corinthians 12:8–10, with Romans 12:6–8 also cited. They are, as the Pauline words suggest, gifts of grace or charisms. In 1 Corinthians 12 there are nine such gifts: wisdom, knowledge, faith, healing, miracles, prophecy, discernment of spirits, tongues and interpretation of tongues.

While the experience is common there are nuances of understanding within the Christian denominations. Catholics tend to see baptism in the Spirit as a release of the Holy Spirit related to the sacraments of baptism and confirmation. Many Protestants would take the Pentecostal approach of being born again and then baptism in the Holy Spirit. The Anglican approach would relate the baptism in the Spirit to the sacrament of baptism in terms of the later experience as an entering into one's inheritance. Whatever the nuances and however related to a denominational tradition, the experience is common and central.

The experience at the heart of charismatic spirituality is given expression through the prayer meeting, which incorporates spontaneous prayer and praise as well as biblical reflection. In those Christian traditions with a sacramental emphasis, there has been for those baptised in the spirit an experience of sacramental renewal. Life in the Spirit seminars provide teaching on the basic truths of salvation, enable an immediacy of awareness of God's unconditional love and assure participants that the gift of power is transformative.

Charismatic spirituality is a spirituality of empowerment, restoration and reconciliation. As such it contributes to the spiritual and relational life of Irish Churches and the search for reconciliation in the community.

At the end of the twentieth century there is a search for meaningful spirituality. This is often in contrast to disillusionment with institutional or organised religion. The new millennium may well see a reclaiming of spirituality in fresh and varied ways.

NOTES

1. Esther de Waal, *The Celtic Vision* (London: DLT 1988), p. 10.
2. Edward Malatesta, 'Current Spirituality: Roman Catholicism' in Cheslyn Jones, Geoffrey Wainwright & Edward Yarnold, SJ. *The Study of Spirituality* (London: SPCK 1986), p. 525.
3. Peter Hocken, *The Glory and the Shame* (Guildford: Eagle 1994), p. 17.
4. Ibid. p. 17.
5. Ibid. p. 22.
6. Ibid. p. 194.
7. Cecil Kerr, Interview with Johnston McMaster (Rostrevor, May 1995).
8. Hocken, *The Glory and the Shame*, p. 84.
9. Pat Collins, *Maturing in the Spirit* (Dublin: Columba Press 1994), p. 66.
10. Hocken, *The Glory and the Shame*, pp. 37f.
11. Ibid. p. 49.

BIOGRAPHICAL NOTE

JOHNSTON MCMASTER is a native of Portavogie in the Ards Peninsula, Co. Down. As a Methodist minister he has worked on Methodist Circuits in west Cork, Wicklow and north Belfast. Following eight years as General Secretary of the Irish Methodist Youth Department, he worked with Youth Link:NI, the inter-church youth service agency with responsibility for developing cross-community work. In 1997 he joined the staff of the Irish School of Ecumenics as Lecturer in Ecumenical Theology and Co-ordinator of the Northern Ireland Adult Education Programme. He is also co-convenor of the Inter-Church Relations Committee of the Methodist Church in Ireland.

25

Evangelicalism
and Fundamentalism

ALWYN THOMSON

INTRODUCTION

Evangelicals, it seems, are more than a match for Heinz – fifty-seven varieties, probably many more! While evangelicalism in Northern Ireland may not reflect the same degree of diversity found elsewhere, there is a lot more to evangelicalism in this community than many people think.

The Presbyterians preserve an evangelicalism with a reformed emphasis, while Reformed or Evangelical Presbyterians preserve it in their own distinctive ways. The Anglican and Wesleyan evangelical traditions are reflected in the Church of Ireland and the Methodist Church respectively. Elim Pentecostal churches are reminders of this century's first wave of pentecostalism, while many of the independent churches – some big, some small – reflect its more recent manifestations.

Then there are Brethren Assemblies – closed and open, City Mission halls, the Salvation Army, Congregationalists, Baptists, Free Presbyterians and more besides.

As well as the churches there are the many *parachurch* groups – distributing evangelistic tracts, producing Christian literature, supporting missions, advocating Christian values in society, working for those in the developing world, working with young people – all having their own distinctive evangelical ethos.

Yet while these are all evangelical, or have an evangelical dimension, some would have little or no contact with others – often as a matter of deliberate policy.

Hence, those who write or speak about evangelicalism – whether or not they identify with the movement – need to bear in mind the varieties of evangelicalism to be found in Northern Ireland. Evangelicalism is not a narrow and rigid movement. It is more like an extended family. However, as with all families there are ties that bind and there are conflicts and disagreements that divide.

The diversity to be found among evangelicals is often a consequence and reflection of those conflicts and disagreements. Sadly, the disagreements can lead to quite open and aggressive hostility. So, if evangelicalism is a family, it is, if not a dysfunctional family, a fractured family.[1]

This chapter is in three parts. The first section attempts to describe the nature of evangelicalism. The second deals with the particular form of evangelicalism known as fundamentalism. The third part locates evangelicalism within the wider Christian tradition in Northern Ireland, focusing on evangelicalism and Roman Catholicism, evangelicalism and ecumenism, and evangelicalism and ecclesiology.

EVANGELICALISM

The past decades have witnessed a steady growth of this movement, both in the major denominations and in new churches. More recently, evangelicals have risen from relative obscurity to a position of some prominence. In July 1990 George Carey, an avowed evangelical, was chosen to be Archbishop of Canterbury. The Evangelical Alliance, an umbrella body representing many different groups, is often asked to comment on matters of political or social concern.

Even the media have recognised this phenomenon, with religious documentaries focusing on the identity and role of evangelicalism. Whether discussing religious education in schools, child abuse or aspects of social legislation, evangelical views are reported in the press – though sometimes with a certain bemusement.

Clearly, evangelicals have a higher profile now than for many years. Yet there is still a great deal of confusion and misunderstanding about them.

In Northern Ireland, of course, evangelicals have always had a high profile. Significant numbers of people, especially in the Protestant community, identify themselves in this way. Mission halls and little churches turn up among the hedgerows and fields in the country. In the cities and towns evangelical churches of all denominations and none stand side by side. Yet despite this, many in Northern Ireland still have little understanding of the nature of evangelicalism.

So, who are the evangelicals?

To answer this question, one common misunderstanding needs to be cleared up – that is, the idea that evangelicalism is a coherent group with a single creed or unifying structure. However, no one who has studied evangelicalism or knows it intuitively from the inside could make this mistake.

Any attempt to understand the nature of evangelicalism has to recognise both the coherence that enables very diverse groups of people to be so identified and the flexibility that enables evangelicalism to accommodate these very diverse groups.

Moreover, this diversity does not merely reflect denominational differences. The trends within evangelicalism are transdenominational, while all kinds of evangelicals can be found in non-denominational groups.

Thus, for example, evangelicals within a Presbyterian church may feel a stronger sense of community with their fellow evangelicals in the local Methodist church than they do with those in their own denomination who do not share their evangelical convictions. This evangelical transdenominationalism is also clearly seen in the parachurch groups, who draw their workers and supporters from a wide range of denominational groups.

A shared evangelical identity is more important than a shared denominational identity. Defining the richly patterned phenomenon that is evangelicalism is no easy task. Writers on evangelicalism have used a number of metaphors to explain its nature. For some, it is a mosaic; for others, a kaleidoscope; recently, it has been compared to a Rubik's cube.[2]

Others have offered concise summaries of what holds evangelicalism together. Evangelicals are Bible people and gospel people, says John Stott.[3] George Marsden offers a fuller definition. Evangelicals are:

> Christians who typically emphasise (1) the Reformation doctrine of the final authority of Scripture; (2) the real, historical character of God's saving work recorded in Scripture; (3) eternal salvation only through personal trust in Christ; (4) the importance of evangelism and missions; and (5) the importance of a spiritually transformed life.[4]

David Bebbington argues that evangelicalism is marked by four key characteristics – biblicism, crucicentrism, conversionism and activism.[5]

Yet, while different writers offer differing definitions of evangelicalism, there are a number of discernible common themes:[6]

The supreme authority of Scripture

Evangelicals believe that the Bible is the Word of God – breathed into existence by the Holy Spirit. It is truthful and authoritative.

Scripture is interpreted and proclaimed by the Christian community –

the church of Jesus Christ – through the Holy Spirit, but the community itself stands under the authority of Scripture.

As a consequence, Christian people, if they are to respond to the Word of God, must be willing to scrutinise all areas of life and to test them against God's truth.

The majesty of Jesus Christ, both as incarnate God, and as saviour through his work on the cross

Evangelicals affirm the traditional faith of the Church that God came to us in human form in the person of Jesus – true God and true man.

Evangelicals emphasise strongly the significance of Jesus' death on the cross. Jesus died as an atonement for our sin. Through his death and resurrection a fallen and condemned humanity can be reconciled to God.

Evangelicals put particular emphasis on the need for a personal and individual response to the work of Jesus. The call to be 'saved' or 'born again', common in evangelical circles, reflects the sense of the seriousness of humanity's rebellion against God, and the consequences of rejecting God's salvation in Christ.

The lordship of the Holy Spirit in creating and sustaining Christian life

Evangelicals stress the sovereignty of God in creating new life, in making men and women Christians. Salvation is, in its entirety, the work of the Holy Spirit. The Spirit not only gives new life but sustains that life and brings about spiritual growth.

In recent decades the growth of the charismatic movement – while sometimes controversial – has given new emphasis to the role of the Spirit in the Christian life and in the Church. This movement is widespread within, but not limited to, evangelicalism.

The need for a personal response of faith

'At the heart of evangelical spirituality lies the concept of a personally appropriated faith.'[7]

While evangelicalism has often focused upon a dramatic conversion experience, it is widely recognised that this need not be the experience of everyone. 'It is present convertedness rather than the memory or experience of past conversion which is of fundamental importance.'[8]

The necessity of evangelism

Evangelicals believe that all human beings are separated from God by their sin. Yet God, in his love and mercy, has made it possible for men and women to be forgiven and to be reconciled to him.

God's desire is that the good news of Jesus Christ should be made known to all men and women and the task of achieving this is given to his people.

Consequently, evangelicals have often been at the forefront of evangelism, both in their own communities and overseas.

In recent decades evangelicals have rediscovered the importance of Christ's command that his followers be salt and light in society. As a consequence many evangelicals now recognise the necessity for true Christian witness to address all aspects of human need – both spiritual and social.

The importance of the Christian community for Christian life and growth.

It is often assumed by some that evangelicals lack a doctrine of the Church. The evangelical emphasis on personal salvation leads people to conclude that the Church plays little part in their thinking.

However, while evangelicalism does indeed lack a specific doctrine of church order, it is not lacking in the conception of the Church as the body of Christ. In the practice of church life – of Christian people meeting together to worship God and proclaim his truth – it is evangelical churches that tend to be full.

As noted earlier, evangelicalism, as a consequence of its understanding of Christian community, is a genuinely transdenominational movement. Indeed, while there is a separatist tradition within some evangelical groupings, evangelicals on the whole tend to be better at crossing denominational divisions than most since they tend to identify themselves primarily as evangelicals rather than as members of particular denominations.

These fundamental convictions serve both to unite evangelicals around a common identity and to distinguish them from other groups.

However, evangelicalism need not be understood solely as involving adherence to a set of shared doctrinal beliefs. Marsden argues that it can be interpreted, not so much as a 'category', but as 'a dynamic movement, with common heritages, common tendencies, an identity, and an organic character.'[9]

This more dynamic approach does justice to the diversity to be found among different groups of evangelicals. It also allows room for that other defining feature of evangelicalism – constant infighting.

EVANGELICALISM AND FUNDAMENTALISM

To understand the relationship between evangelicalism and fundamentalism there are two misconceptions that need to be addressed. First, the misconception that evangelicalism and fundamentalism are discrete movements, and, second, the misconception that evangelicalism and fundamentalism are one and the same.

'Fundamentalism', however defined, is an integral part of evangelicalism. Perhaps the simplest approach is to think of evangelicalism as a spectrum. Fundamentalism is an integral part of that spectrum. Moreover, what many often fail to realise is that fundamentalism itself is best thought of as a spectrum. Among fundamentalists there is often a great deal of diversity.

Sadly, both fundamentalism and evangelicalism have consistently been misunderstood, because of either prejudice or laziness. Evangelicals of all kinds are lumped together as fundamentalists and their beliefs described in a flawed and misleading way.[10]

So what is fundamentalism? This question can be answered only by taking a brief look at the roots of fundamentalism and the place of this movement within the wider history of evangelicalism – not least in order to challenge the false views of fundamentalism all too common today.

The historical framework for understanding the origins and nature of fundamentalism is a North American one. While this may not seem to be directly relevant to Northern Ireland, a knowledge of this framework is a prerequisite for any true understanding of what fundamentalism is and, therefore, for any true understanding of what evangelicalism is.

Howard Marshall, a respected evangelical New Testament scholar, sums up the prevalent view of fundamentalism thus:

> The popular picture of fundamentalists is of people (1) who adhere to the literal interpretation and the supreme authority of some ancient religious book, and who hold fast to it even when to everybody else it seems totally anachronistic; (2) who are aggressive in urging other people to accept their beliefs; (3) and who are fiercely intolerant of anybody who does not share their views.[11]

In this popular picture, fundamentalists are those practitioners of religion from whom respectable people shy away, identifying them as fanatics and extremists. Fundamentalists are those Muslims who call for the death of Salman Rushdie. Fundamentalists are those Jews who massacre Palestinians at prayer. Fundamentalists are the televangelists of the United States, exploiting the weak and defrauding the state. Fundamentalists are the preachers and marchers of Northern Ireland who proclaim 'Not an Inch' and who despise Catholicism. They are considered to be politically reactionary, narrow-minded, intolerant, anti-intellectual, aggressive, uncompromising and sometimes violent.

To its critics fundamentalism is seen as a monolithic movement. The most extreme examples are used as the basis for the description of the nature of the movement. These examples are then woven together into a comprehensive picture of 'fundamentalism'. Having been so described, fundamentalism is then dismissed as an embarrassing relic of another age not worthy of serious consideration by sensible people.

This superficial and pejorative use of the term is increasingly common. Critics of religion hold 'fundamentalism' up as an example of everything that is bad about religious belief. Those whose religion is of a liberal persuasion label as fundamentalists those whose beliefs are conservative. Even some evangelicals have begun to use the term in this sense. Embarrassed by their shared theological and historical roots, they define fundamentalism in a way that allows them as 'evangelicals' to distance themselves from 'fundamentalists'.

The irony is that in creating this caricature of fundamentalism the people responsible are doing exactly the thing they criticise 'fundamentalists' for doing – condemning those they neither know nor understand. Fundamentalism so perceived exists more in the minds of its critics than in reality.

The most obvious weakness of this approach is the refusal to take fundamentalism seriously as a theological and historical phenomenon. Yet unless fundamentalism is so understood any discussion of it is at best uncontrolled and at worst prejudiced.

Defining fundamentalism

A key event in the history of fundamentalism was the publication of a series of booklets, *The Fundamentals – A Testimony to the Truth*, between 1910 and 1915. These essays summarised many of the concerns that had been growing in the previous decades.

> Their topics laid down the gauntlet for a confrontation with the theology of the Modernists with attacks on higher criticism, evolution, socialism, and modern cults. They affirmed the sinful nature of humanity, the need for regeneration, biblical infallibility, the deity of Christ, the Virgin birth, and the importance of morality.[12]

While fundamentalist leaders debated on a broad front, one key issue dominated their agenda – the influence of 'higher criticism' of the Bible.[13]

Fundamentalism and the Bible

The key area of theological concern for fundamentalists was – and remains

– the question of the place of the Bible in Christianity. The new critical approaches were premised on the assumption that the Bible was a human book – a record of religious experience, whose expression was shaped by the cultural and religious patterns of the world in which the writers lived. This belief struck at the very heart of evangelical faith.

In contrast, fundamentalists, like other evangelicals, believed that the Bible should be accepted as inspired by God and authoritative as God's self-revelation.

Confronted with this new approach to Scripture, some – notably B.B. Warfield – tried to maintain an evangelical and professional scholarship. However, although such scholars displayed a willingness to adopt and adapt the methodologies of contemporary biblical criticism while rejecting its assumptions, many fundamentalists opposed even this. The very methods were considered to be an assault on the Bible, and those evangelicals who made use of these methods were considered to have compromised in the vital areas of revelation and authority.

Down through the decades, fundamentalist convictions about the Bible have shown themselves in two key areas of concern: the question of the interpretation of Genesis 1–3 – that is, the question of creation and evolution – and the debate over the nature of inerrancy. Both of these issues are well to the fore in contemporary debate within American evangelicalism.

These two areas also highlight two of the distinguishing marks of fundamentalism. The first shows the extent to which the issue of biblical authority is linked with matters of biblical interpretation. An affirmation of the authority of Scripture is not sufficient. It must be backed up with a commitment to certain key interpretations.

The second area shows the degree of suspicion with which some fundamentalists regard some evangelicals, even when there is a common recognition of biblical authority.

Discussing this phenomenon, Mark Noll wrote:

> Evangelical Bible scholars live in Christian communities where fidelity to Scripture is both a badge of honour and an excuse for recrimination. This wider world is one in which dogmatic 'separatists' lambaste the inconsistencies of other self-confessed 'fundamentalists', who in turn deny the wishy-washiness of 'conservative evangelicals', who in their turn snipe at the innovations of 'progressive evangelicals', who look down their noses at all of the benighted brethren to their right.[14]

However, to say this is not to say that fundamentalism is anti-intellectual. Fundamentalists are opposed only to a certain way of 'doing' biblical and theological studies. For them, biblical study starts with belief in the authority of God's revelation in Scripture. To that extent they are no more at odds with the mainstream of academic biblical scholarship than most evangelicals.

The distinctive aspect of fundamentalism is the strength of opposition to, and separation from, this mainstream. Fundamentalism has long been known for its opposition to modern presuppositions about the way the Bible should be studied. Perhaps this gives us a clue to understanding the fundamentalist attitude. For fundamentalists are not so much anti-intellectual as anti-modern. Again, evangelicalism generally is anti-modern to some extent, but fundamentalism is characterised by the degree of hostility and the sense of defensiveness.

The effects of this can be seen in the gradual disengagement from the mainstream of biblical scholarship that accompanied the growth of the fundamentalist movement. Moreover, this disengagement not only affected the field of scholarship but had wider implications for the role of evangelicals in society.

By the 1920s, as a result of these and other developments, evangelical Protestantism had acquired a reputation for being backward-looking and anti-intellectual – a reputation which, to a significant degree, survives to this day.

Fundamentalism, as a consequence of its withdrawal from society, had nowhere to go. While fundamentalists forged their own academic and social institutions, it became increasingly clear that they had no future outside the subculture they had created for themselves. However, it also became clear to many that this level of withdrawal could only be considered a denial of evangelical faith.

It was the recognition of this that led to the rise of the 'new evangelicalism' in the years immediately after the Second World War.

Advocates of the new evangelicalism maintained their commitment to the theological heart of the evangelical faith but rejected the disparagement of scholarship and the withdrawal from society which characterised fundamentalism. Thus, while related to fundamentalism, the new evangelicalism was distinct from it. Gradually, its ideas and values spread within American evangelicalism, largely through the influence of the National Association of Evangelicals, an umbrella body for American evangelicals founded in 1942, and Fuller Theological Seminary, founded in 1947. They were reinforced and further disseminated through the magazine *Christianity Today*, founded in 1956 and aimed at a general audience, and through the ministry of Billy Graham.

However, influential as the new evangelicalism became, it did not spell the end for fundamentalism. Instead, the two tendencies within the evangelical movement developed alongside one another, and with the passing of time the lines of demarcation shifted, blurred and fractured. The result was the creation of the evangelical spectrum that now exists, not only in North America, but wherever evangelicalism is found.

Clearly, then, relationships within the broad church that is evangelicalism are a great deal more complicated than many imagine. But how do evangelicals view relationships with those from other traditions?

EVANGELICALISM AND CHRISTIAN TRADITION IN NORTHERN IRELAND

Before looking briefly at evangelical attitudes to Roman Catholicism and ecumenism it is worth noting again the evangelical view of the Church, since this will help in understanding the broader evangelical perspective.

Evangelicalism and ecclesiology

Evangelicals are not particularly concerned with the details of church order, though among evangelicals many will argue strongly for the validity of their own particular way of doing things. However, the evangelical emphasis is always primarily on the Church as the body of Christ – a community of people who believe in Jesus.

Membership of this community comes through a response in faith to the gospel. Through baptism, communion, prayer, worship, teaching and proclamation, those people God has called into his Church grow in their faith and make the gospel known.

Evangelicals do not believe that any church has the power or authority to make any person a member of the Church of Jesus Christ. To put it somewhat crudely, evangelicals are people who believe that, in relation to the Church in its biblical sense, we are out until we opt in and not vice versa.

This view of the Church affects how evangelicals understand wider questions of their relationship with other traditions. At the heart of any relationship must be the question of truth. On the one hand there must be a shared commitment to the truth, who is Jesus Christ – a commitment understood in the evangelical sense noted above. On the other hand there must be a commitment to the truth in a theological sense. Evangelicals do not see the different traditions as simply different ways of being Christian. Instead, all traditions – including their own – must be tested by the authoritative revelation given by God in Scripture.

Thus, evangelicals would not wish to identify with any tradition that in its beliefs or practices obscures or undermines the gospel message.

This evangelical understanding of the Church, together with the other distinctives of evangelical theology outlined above, shape attitudes towards both Roman Catholicism and the ecumenical movement.

Evangelicalism and Catholicism

Evangelicalism is often seen as being strongly separatist and exclusivist. It is often perceived as having a negative and hostile spirit, particularly in relation to Roman Catholicism. However, while this is true of some evangelicals, it is wrong to ascribe these attitudes to them all.

As a movement within conservative Protestantism, it is inevitable that the relationship between evangelicalism and Roman Catholicism has been marked at times by fear, suspicion and hostility, although it should be recognised that these negative attitudes have not been all one way. This relationship is currently the subject of intense debate in the English-speaking world and in Latin America. A number of factors have driven the debate – the changes in Roman Catholicism since Vatican II; the growth of the renewal movement within Roman Catholicism, which has led to the phenomenon of individual Catholics who openly describe themselves as evangelical; the growing self-confidence and maturity among evangelicals; and a recognition that both evangelicals and Roman Catholics face a world which does not discriminate in its hostility towards Christianity.

In Northern Ireland this debate is also inevitably influenced by the religious dimension to our wider political problems. Though it is impossible to summarise the debate, it is possible to make two basic points from an evangelical perspective.

Firstly, there is a difference in belief between Roman Catholicism and evangelicalism. When all misunderstandings are clarified, these core differences remain. It is pointless, not to say dishonest, to pretend otherwise. There are many areas of official Roman Catholic teaching that evangelicals cannot accept without denying their own evangelical beliefs – beliefs which they see as lying at the heart of God's revelation and what it means to be a Christian.

Secondly, because of the nature of evangelical belief about the Church, the issue of relationships between the Churches – understood as ecclesiastical bodies, denominations – is much less important for many evangelicals. However, many recognise that increasing numbers of individuals within the Roman Catholic Church have a faith that has much in common with evangelicalism. The challenge for evangelicals is to recognise and respond positively to this development.[15]

Evangelicalism and ecumenism

Evangelicalism is normally perceived as being hostile to traditional ecumenism. And generally speaking most evangelicals are. However, in many cases this is the consequence not of intolerance or bigotry, but of legitimate concerns about the extent to which the ecumenical movement has obscured elements of the gospel which evangelicals see as vital to the integrity of the Christian message.

They are concerned that the movement tolerates those whose theological beliefs are at odds with Scripture, setting out no clear standard of orthodoxy. They are also concerned that the goal of the movement is a structural or formal unity, a unity that is not based on true belief or true faith in Christ.

Evangelicals are concerned by these things because of their understanding of what the Bible has to say about the human condition and humanity's fate without God, and because of their understanding of the absolute necessity of personal faith in Christ if men and women are to know God's salvation.

It is worth noting in passing that it is not only evangelicals who have expressed concerns about the nature and direction of the ecumenical movement; the Orthodox Churches of the East share these same concerns.[16]

CONCLUSION

The diversity of evangelicalism makes it difficult to offer a conclusion that would satisfy everyone professing to be evangelical. Given this, I conclude with a number of personal reflections.

All evangelicals believe that the whole of life should be lived in obedience to God as he makes himself known through Scripture. No evangelical believes that we do so perfectly. Thus self-examination is always a necessary part of evangelical spirituality. In the context of Northern Ireland, this evangelical self-examination has perhaps been lacking.

Evangelicals need to ask if they have been obedient, or if they have instead allowed themselves to be conformed to the pattern of this world (Romans 12:2), which is often expressed in the political traditions of this community.

Evangelicals also believe in the power of God to change people. After self-examination can come a new commitment to obedience and a new confidence in God to transform us.

Faith in God's transforming power is exciting because the evangelical community undoubtedly has great potential to be a force for good in our country. Evangelicals are in a position to respond distinctively and constructively. They can respond distinctively because their convictions are shaped by biblical values and by Christian discipleship. They can respond constructively because their hope and trust is in God.

BIBLIOGRAPHY

McGrath, Alister, *Evangelicalism and the Future of Christianity*, London: Hodder & Stoughton 1994

Marsden, George (ed.), *Evangelicalism and Modern America*, Grand Rapids: Eerdmans 1984

Noll, Mark, *Between Faith and Criticism: Evangelicals, Scholarship and the Bible*, Leicester: IVP 1991

Tidball, Derek, *Who Are the Evangelicals?*, London: Marshall Pickering 1994

NOTES

1. Some of the material in this chapter is adapted from the ECONI booklet *The Fractured Family* by Alwyn Thomson. This booklet looks at the nature of evangelicalism and fundamentalism with particular reference to the identity and work of ECONI (Evangelical Contribution on Northern Ireland).

2. Cullen Murphy described evangelicalism as a '12-ring show', while Timothy Smith lists fourteen varieties of evangelicalism. See George Marsden, 'The Evangelical Denomination' in George Marsden (ed.), *Evangelicalism and Modern America*. Derek Tidball lists six approaches to the church, six to the world and five to spirituality found among evangelicals which can be combined in a host of different ways. (*Who Are the Evangelicals?*, pp. 19–24).

3. John Stott, *What is an Evangelical?* (London: CPAS 1977).

4. George Marsden, 'The Evangelical Denomination' in Marsden, *Evangelicalism and Modern America*, p. x.

5. David Bebbington, *Evangelicalism in Modern Britain: A History from the 1730s to the 1980s* (London: Routledge 1989), pp. 2–19.

6. See Alister McGrath, *Evangelicalism and the Future of Christianity*, pp. 51–80; Kenneth Kantzer & Carl Henry (eds.), *Evangelical Affirmations* (Grand Rapids: Eerdmans 1990), pp. 27–38.

7. McGrath, *Evangelicalism and the Future of Christianity*, p. 67.

8. McGrath, *Evangelicalism and the Future of Christianity*, p. 70.

9. George Marsden, 'The Evangelical Denomination' in Marsden, *Evangelicalism and Modern America*, p. x

10. James Barr's work *Fundamentalism* (London: SCM 1977) is only the most obvious example of this approach.

11. I.H. Marshall, 'Are Evangelicals Fundamentalists?' in *Vox Evangelica*, XXII (1992), p. 10

12. Bill J. Leonard, 'The Origin and Character of Fundamentalism' in *Review and Expositor*, LXXIX.1 (1982), p. 12.

13. See Mark Noll, *Between Faith and Criticism*.

14. Mark Noll, 'Evangelicals and the Study of the Bible' in Marsden, *Evangelicalism and Modern America*, p. 109.

15. A fuller discussion of evangelical attitudes to Roman Catholicism can be found in the ECONI booklet *Beyond Fear, Suspicion and Hostility* by Alwyn Thomson.

16. A forthcoming ECONI booklet, *A Bridge Too Far?*, will offer an evangelical perspective on the ecumenical movement.

BIOGRAPHICAL NOTE

ALWYN THOMSON was born and raised in Belfast. After studying Theology and Philosophy of Religion he joined Evangelical Contribution on Northern Ireland (ECONI) as Research Officer. He has written or edited a number of ECONI publications, including *The Fractured Family: Fundamentalists, Evangelicals and ECONI; Faith in Ulster*; and, most recently, *The Politics of Holiness*. He is married to Viki and they are members of Windsor Baptist Church.

26

Ecumenism

IAN M. ELLIS

The word 'ecumenism' itself has often been misunderstood in Northern Ireland. There may be various reasons for this, but surely a major one lies in the way in which those who have opposed ecumenism have organised their campaign; the genuine fear of loss of identity, and the 'fear' of the other community, have undoubtedly been exploited. Many people have thought that ecumenism is about the Protestant Churches reuniting with the Roman Catholic Church, and they often have been led to believe that there is a secret, hidden agenda with political implications. In fact, ecumenism is about the unity of the whole Church and involves all the Churches working together towards visible unity 'in truth and holiness'. It is not about surrender but about the search for agreement in faith and order and for unity in the Churches' life. It is no more about Protestants becoming Roman Catholics than about Roman Catholics becoming Protestants. It is about being Christians together. The editors of the *Dictionary of the Ecumenical Movement* have written as follows:

> At its best, the ecumenical movement has been a search for unity in the truth as it is found in Jesus (Ephesians 4:21), and into which the Holy Spirit leads (John 16:13). It has not been a matter, on the one hand, of creating a super-orthodoxy uniformly formulated or, on the other, of doctrinal compromise or indifferentism. Rather, the churches have together searched the scriptures, the venerable Tradition of the church, and the belief and practice of the contemporary communities with the aim of reaching a 'common expression of the apostolic faith today'.[1]

In a community in which not merely political but national allegiance has been relatively clearly divided along the parallel lines of religious adherence, it is perhaps understandable that there should have been suspicion of anything that crossed community barriers. The deep-seated religious, even denominational, consciousness in Northern Ireland has led to suspicion of anything that might have hinted at compromise of cherished beliefs and customs. However, at a popular level, even in the midst of a peace process, there are still often great difficulties in crossing the religious divide, although it has to be said that in recent times advances in that direction have certainly become increasingly evident.

THE DEVELOPMENT OF ECUMENISM

Ecumenism is both a movement in the thinking and attitude of Christian people and one that involves the Churches as institutions in their official relationships. The modern ecumenical movement, which is generally recognised to have its origins in the 1910 Edinburgh Missionary Conference, has been very much a mixture of these two strands – personal and public. There is, however, a third dimension: the ecumenical movement has also been a global movement and for that reason it is impossible to consider ecumenism in Northern Ireland without relating it both to Ireland as a whole (for almost all the Churches in Ireland are all-Ireland institutions) and to the wider world scene. These three geo-ecclesiastical aspects of ecumenism in Northern Ireland – the Northern Ireland setting, the all-Ireland dimension and the global context – are all inextricably linked.

The Edinburgh Missionary Conference of 1910, in which there was Irish participation, marked the beginning of the modern ecumenical movement because it brought into focus the experience of missionary endeavour and saw clearly that in the mission field there was no room for denominational competition. The missionary cause could be advanced throughout the world only by the missionary bodies and the Churches actively co-operating. The Roman Catholic Church at this stage did not wish to be associated with any ecumenical moves; it still held the position that it and it alone was the Church. Changes in this outlook came only with the Second Vatican Council (announced by Pope John XXIII in 1959, and opened in October 1962), which actually committed the Roman Catholic Church to ecumenical involvement. This change in approach did not come out of the blue, however. There had been a process of more liberal thinking expressed by various Roman Catholic scholarly writers; it was in this 'new theology', emanating principally from France, that lay the foundations for the Second Vatican Council's fundamental change of direction as far as ecumenism was concerned; Vatican II's *Decree on Ecumenism* and *Constitution on the Church* are the chief, relevant documents.

Pope John XXIII had called the Council the Church's *aggiornamento*, the opening up of the Church to what was happening in the wider world. It was the end of the Roman Catholic Church's self-sufficient isolationism. From a Protestant perspective, however, the Council did not go far enough; it did not bring its logical train of thought to a proper conclusion, for the ecclesiology, if not the ecclesiastical politics, of Vatican II remained to a large extent that of 'the true Church' and 'the separated brethren'. It would not be an ecumenism of equals, in Roman Catholic eyes, but at least there was ecumenism. The Vatican Council had developed a theory of 'degrees of ecclesialness', using itself as the ultimate, and true, model. The further a Church got away from that model, the less a 'Church' it was. However, a new era in ecumenism had begun with the recognition by the Roman Catholic Church of the authentic Christian life and witness of other Churches.

ECUMENISM IN THE HISTORICAL NORTHERN IRELAND CONTEXT

At the beginning of this century the whole of the island of Ireland was part of the United Kingdom, but no matter how constitutionally integrated Ireland was into the national life of the United Kingdom, a movement was gaining ground for Irish national independence. The striving for national independence and the Home Rule debate had their repercussions in church relations, moreover, for when it came to independence for the twenty-six counties and the consequent partition of Ireland, it was impossible to disentangle the basically pro-British mentality of the Protestant Churches and pro-nationalist mentality of the Roman Catholic Church. With the passage of time, Protestants in the Republic have come to identify much more specifically with the Irish state, but at the time of the Home Rule debate and partition Protestants in the South had not, generally speaking but with clear exceptions, identified with the nationalist cause. That of course is still the case within Northern Ireland today.

When the Protestant Churches founded the Belfast-based *Irish Council of Churches* in 1923 it was an important step in terms of inter-Protestant relations. Protestantism in Northern Ireland is often viewed as a single tradition, but that is far from the case. In the early years of this century there were still bitter feelings between Presbyterians and Anglicans stemming from memories of the period of Church of Ireland establishment. The ease of contemporary Church of Ireland–Presbyterian relations should not be permitted to blur the historical reality at the beginning of the century when the legacy of the relatively recent past still caused acrimony.

When the Irish Council of Churches was formed, there was a desire on the part of the Protestant Churches to come closer to one another. This was in part a result of the developing, worldwide ecumenical movement, but it was also partly due to the political need for Protestants to come together in an Ireland that, for them, was in many ways coming apart. Indeed, F.S.L. Lyons has referred to the revival of Orangeism with the rise of the Home Rule movement, illustrating Protestants' desire for greater solidarity.[2]

Then again, Protestants of all denominations were outraged at the Roman Catholic Church's *Ne Temere* (literally: *not rashly*) decree, which was introduced into Ireland in 1908, requiring the presence of a Roman Catholic priest at any marriage involving a Roman Catholic; J.A.F. Gregg, later Church of Ireland primate, summed up Protestant feelings when he wrote that this law was really designed to ensure the Roman Catholic upbringing of any children of an inter-church marriage, for no Roman Catholic priest would 'dare to be present' unless such an agreement had been made.[3]

Many people in Northern Ireland today are of the opinion that the repressive *Ne Temere* is still in force in the Roman Catholic Church, but it has in fact been superseded by more liberal regulations. The effect of *Ne Temere*, however, has been long-lasting; it is ingrained in the Protestant consciousness in particular because of the steep decline of the Protestant population in the Republic – although *Ne Temere* was by no means the only factor that led to this decline.

The experience of a dramatic fall in numbers in the Protestant Churches in the Republic is relevant to the outlook of Northern Ireland Protestants because it gave grounds for real fears about their ultimate survival in an Ireland in which the overall majority would be nationalist and Roman Catholic. The decline also has often been cited as an example of alleged Roman Catholic hostility to Protestants and therefore of ecumenical 'sham'. Those who wish to perpetuate division do not wish to recognise that *Ne Temere* has been replaced within the councils of the Roman Catholic Church. That is not to say that all is well in the still sensitive area of Protestant–Roman Catholic marriages, but conditions have undoubtedly improved immensely since the days of the infamous *Ne Temere*.

THE IRISH COUNCIL OF CHURCHES (ICC)

The ICC was, and is, a body with the aim of promoting and enabling inter-church co-operation. However, the scope of its work has expanded considerably since the Council's formation in the 1920s. During and after the Second World War years, it was very much taken up with the cause of refugee relief; the Roman Catholic Church was not a member and, as far as the war was concerned, was totally opposed to any form of conscription in Northern Ireland – in contrast to Protestant opinion, which, as generally unionist in orientation, wanted Northern Ireland to be treated on the same basis as the rest of the United Kingdom. The difference in outlook could not have been sharper and the situation was impossible; conscription was not introduced in Northern Ireland. After the Second World War, the Irish Council of Churches continued its work on social concerns and promoted co-operation among the Protestant Churches. In the early stages of the Northern Ireland Troubles that began in 1968–9, the ICC Executive Committee often made statements on the current situation on behalf of its member Churches, but the emergence of regular church leaders' meetings (of the four largest Churches) tended to take over that particular role.

The Irish Council of Churches was not, and has not been, involved in direct discussions about actual church unity. That has not been part of its remit from the Churches. Instead, the Protestant Churches in the course of this century have approached the issue of church union on a bilateral or tripartite basis. The Church of Ireland, the Presbyterian Church and the Methodist Church considered proposals from the *Tripartite Consultation* for organic union in 1973, but these came to nothing. A chief stumbling block was the issue of the ordained ministry. Tripartite discussions came to an end in 1988, but the Church of Ireland and the Methodist Church continued, and still are continuing, to discuss possibilities for union (at the same time, coincidentally, as the Lambeth Conference of Anglican Bishops and the World Methodist Council have formed an Anglican–Methodist International Commission).

BALLYMASCANLON

Ecumenism in Northern Ireland became a topic of current controversy especially when the first 'Ballymascanlon Talks' were held in 1973, so called because they were convened at the Ballymascanlon Hotel, Dundalk. These were leadership-level discussions between the member Churches of the Irish Council of Churches and the Roman Catholic Church. The background to these talks lay, ultimately, in the already established ecumenical commitment of the Protestant Churches and in the new commitment of the Roman Catholic Church following the various related decisions of the Second Vatican Council.

Vatican II, as we have noted, committed the Roman Catholic Church across the world to involvement in the ecumenical movement. Each national Hierarchy was left to work out the implications of the principles of Vatican II for the situation in each country. Already before the first Ballymascanlon meeting, the Roman Catholic Hierarchy in Ireland had in 1970 entered into an official ecumenical body known as the Joint Group on Social Problems. The Joint Group, made up of representatives of the

Protestant and Roman Catholic Churches, in turn formed working parties to produce reports on various social problems. Although this was at the early stages of the Troubles in Northern Ireland, the Joint Group was not permitted by the Churches to engage with what was evidently the most major of social problems, namely violence. The reasoning was that to have taken on this topic would have brought the Churches, at a very early stage in their official, co-operating relations, into a direct discussion of specifically political and national issues. In 1976, however, following special permission from the Churches, a report entitled *Violence in Ireland* was produced by the Joint Group and was a most forward-looking document. In subsequent years its conclusions were often quoted in church circles.

Perhaps it was at least partly the relative success of the working of the Joint Group that encouraged the Irish Council of Churches and the Roman Catholic Hierarchy to agree to a full joint meeting of church leaders. There was, naturally, a high degree of media interest in this unprecedented and in many ways fascinating event. The Ballymascanlon Talks, specifically at the request of Cardinal Conway, included theological dialogue. This was a very wise insistence because it made it quite clear that the talks were about religious matters and were not, as the media liked to portray them, a kind of forum for peace negotiations. This was a serious, ecumenical initiative, no doubt partly encouraged by the need for the Churches to confer in the midst of the developing turmoil of Northern Ireland and to witness to peaceful ways, but essentially was inspired by the ecumenical spirit of the age.

ECUMENISM AND PEACE

What has been said about Ballymascanlon is not, of course, to say that the Churches and church people have not been involved in specifically peace moves. The contrary is the case. There have been specific church campaigns and initiatives for peace and reconciliation throughout the years of the Troubles. The Irish Council of Churches collaborated in a most creative way with the Roman Catholic Hierarchy's *Irish Commission for Justice and Peace* in the promotion of peace education in schools. In recent times, there has been the behind-the-scenes involvement of the Church of Ireland Primate, Archbishop Eames, in promoting reconciliation, in laying the ground for peace and in trying to break the political logjam, a role for which he was honoured by the Queen in 1995 with a life peerage. Then again, there was the role played by the Presbyterian minister the Rev. Roy Magee in liaising with hardcore loyalism as the 1994 ceasefire was being framed. Cardinal Daly has spoken and written extensively about peace,[4] and Monsignor Denis Faul has been a consistently outspoken critic of all forms of injustice. There have been countless efforts by church people – some of them private efforts, some denominational, some ecumenical – to bring about a peaceful resolution of the problems of Northern Ireland.

One of the best known of these took place on 10 December 1974 when there was a most controversial incident involving a secret meeting between leading Protestant ecumenists and the IRA at Smyth's Hotel, Feakle, Co. Clare, which did in fact lead to a temporary ceasefire. The scene at the conclusion of those daring discussions has been vividly and atmospherically recorded by the ecumenical pioneers Eric Gallagher and Stanley Worrall, in what must be one of the most memorable passages from any book emerging from Northern Ireland during the years of the Troubles:

> The room was a single sitting-room above a mainly one-storey hotel; the stairs came up directly into the room. The eight of us sat in silence as a good deal of uneasy shuffling was heard at the foot of the stairs. The first thing to appear above the floor line was the muzzle of a sub-machine gun, followed a moment later by the tense face of the policeman holding it. When he saw no guns covering him he advanced more confidently, and soon the room was full of policemen. The officer in charge demanded our names. 'Arthur Butler, Bishop of Connor.' 'Harry Morton, General Secretary of the British Council of Churches.' 'Jack Weir, Clerk of the Presbyterian General Assembly.' 'Eric Gallagher, former President of the Methodist Church in Ireland.' 'Arthur MacArthur, of the British Council of Churches.' 'Ralph Baxter, Secretary of the Irish Council of Churches.' 'Bill Arlow, his assistant.' 'Stanley Worrall, retired headmaster of Methodist College.'
>
> Blank bewilderment and disbelief! Downstairs they had found Rory O'Brady, President of Provisional Sinn Féin, reading by the fire. He was not on the wanted list and is reputed to have said, 'You will find the men you are looking for upstairs.' But in fact the men they wanted had fled some hours before.[5]

The Ballymascanlon Talks convened irregularly. The pace was indicative of caution in a politically volatile situation and in ecclesiastically uncharted waters. In due course, however, the talks were formalised and became what is now known as the *Irish Inter-Church Meeting*, convening in full session every eighteen months and with the executive Inter-Church

Committee and two Departments – Social Issues and Theological Questions – meeting much more regularly. The recent report, *Sectarianism*[6] was produced by a working party of the Department of Social Issues; an extensive chapter in the report, entitled 'Ways Forward and Recommendations', provides a challenging agenda for the Churches. Similarly, the 1997 publication of the Department of Theological Questions, *Freedom, Justice and Responsibility in Ireland Today*, is full of challenges for the Churches in the current situation.[7]

ECUMENISM: CHALLENGE AND PROGRESS

In broad terms, the people of Northern Ireland saw the need for such inter-church contact when their society at times seemed to be inexorably plunging from one depth to another of violence and despair. There were objectors, but the vociferousness of the objectors sometimes suggested that they had more support than was in fact the case. All the main Protestant Churches and the Roman Catholic Church were involved in ecumenical contact without exception and in public. Fundamentalists would from time to time condemn 'ecumenical churchmen', but their complaint did not prevent inter-church co-operation. Nevertheless, conservative theological elements undoubtedly contributed to the Presbyterian Church's withdrawal from the World Council of Churches in 1980 and, ten years later, to its refusal to join the new Council of Churches for Britain and Ireland.

The experience of the Churches over the past thirty years of violence in Northern Ireland has also been an ecumenical learning experience; Christians have grown to know and love one another more. Archbishop Eames, in his 'Ecumenical Vision' lecture for the Irish School of Ecumenics in 1995, spoke these words, which convey an unmistakable optimism and hope for the future:

> In the past few years or so there has developed a much more united Christian voice from the Churches which has learned to speak as much of injustice in the experience of others as it has addressed perceived or real injustice for 'our own people'. The Christian vision of the just, reconciled and peaceful society has now become the authentic voice of the Irish Churches. There is a new integrity in our public utterances. If twenty-five years of suffering has in fact been our Calvary experience – we may just be beginning to sense our Easter message.[8]

The criticism has often been voiced that ecumenism in Northern Ireland is remote from parish life. Meetings of church leaders and distant ecumenical boards and committees, it is held, are irrelevant to the situation of ordinary church members. There may be an element of truth in this, but there is another point of view. The fact is that without what is called 'top-down' ecumenism it is doubtful that there would have been much ecumenism at all in Northern Ireland. The 'top-down' ecumenism has in fact provided ecumenical leadership and has created an environment in which some local ecumenical initiatives – including not a few local ecumenical, clerical groups – have been inspired and perhaps even made possible. Without the leadership of the Churches having taken the initiative, the Churches would in all probability have remained in a more polarised world. Many church people involved in ecumenical dialogue even at senior level have been able to take part only because they have had sufficient courage of their convictions, and real courage was needed in such a mould-breaking role. With more and more people working and praying for a true and lasting peace, there are definite signs that despite continuing sectarianism, ecumenical leadership is beginning to bear fruit in Northern Ireland in a growing number of local ecumenical initiatives that simply could not have taken place even five years ago.

NORTHERN IRELAND'S ECUMENICAL FUTURE

The official ecumenical structures that are in place today reflect the historical conditions of the times of their formation. The Irish Council of Churches broadly reflects the situation in the pre-Vatican II years when the Roman Catholic Church would not participate; the Irish Inter-Church Meeting (formerly the Ballymascanlon Talks) reflects the position after Vatican II, with full Roman Catholic involvement. The merging of these two bodies would appear to be the natural progression, and there are currently specific proposals for this before the Churches. There is undoubtedly considerable duplication of effort as things stand and many of those involved in ecumenical work are becoming increasingly frustrated by the cumbersome nature of the process. As an initial step towards rationalisation, one of the Irish Council of Churches' Boards, that of Community Affairs, has recently been stood down and its work transferred in totality to the Inter-Church Meeting's Department of Social Issues. Because of the increasingly ecumenical nature of the times, and with the emergence of the much more fully ecumenical Council of Churches for Britain and Ireland, ecumenical business requires as inclusive participation as possible.

A merging of the ICC and the Inter-Church Meeting would be a very hopeful sign of the times for Christianity in Northern Ireland, for it would signal a deeper mutual commitment among the Churches and across the divide. That deepening of mutual commitment is taking place and sooner or later it must find expression in a single, renewed ecumenical body.

Ecumenism, of course, is not to be understood only as a movement in church relations. It is that, but it is also much more. It is about justice, peace and ecology and about relations between the races and different world religions. It is about the unity of creation in its every aspect. It is, essentially, a spiritual movement.

The desire for the unity of Christians is a desire that springs from fidelity to Christ and his commands. In one sense, there always has been an 'ecumenical movement' in the Church, because as long as there has been a Church there have been divisions and dissensions. This recurring problem in church life is already seen within the New Testament Church itself. In Northern Ireland, as elsewhere, the modern ecumenical movement is underpinned by the continuing movement of prayer for unity – in the annual Week of Prayer and in the regular prayers of the faithful day by day and week by week.

The spiritual dimension to ecumenism is its powerhouse; as long as Christians pray for reconciliation in faith and life, as they do so often in Northern Ireland where ecumenism has been at the cutting edge, the ecumenical movement will progress and bear fruit. There is fruit-bearing and there will be more fruit-bearing, even if it requires patience and perseverance, and even if the fruit is not entirely what is expected. The pilgrimage is one of discovery, not of manufacture. Despite what more pessimistic commentators might say, the people of Northern Ireland are discovering one another across barriers that have been dividing us for generations. Similarly, the majority of Christians in Northern Ireland are in fact discovering one another, and in discovering one another we are also discovering new and truly joyful dimensions to our common discipleship of Jesus Christ. Ecumenism in Northern Ireland has very often been surrounded by controversy, but at the same time it has never been without many committed advocates. One might venture to suggest that the future life of the Churches will be increasingly influenced by ecumenical perspectives. Despite contrary indicators, such as problems during the annual 'marching season' (which are more political than religious in nature), we do appear to be entering an era of possibilities when, even in Northern Ireland, ecumenism will more and more become an accepted, if not a required, pattern of specifically church life. Difficult though it may be at times to see, such surely is our Christian future, sooner or later.

The reasons for what has been experienced as ecumenism's lack of widespread enthusiasm in Northern Ireland undoubtedly lie in the tangled nature of the web of political, constitutional, cultural and religious allegiances. However, as this tangled web is gradually untangled through increased dialogue across the spectrum of religious and political life, the reasonableness and indeed the imperative of ecumenism will become more obvious. The ecumenical movement will continue to progress not because of any ecclesiastical power politics but because the Churches all know that they must seek to obey the sovereign will of Christ, who prayed 'that they all may be one' (John 17:21).

NOTES

1. *Dictionary of the Ecumenical Movement* (Geneva: World Council of Churches/ London: Council of Churches for Britain and Ireland 1991), p. xii.
2. F.S.L. Lyons, *Ireland Since the Famine* (Weidenfeld & Nicolson 1971), p. 13.
3. J.A.F. Gregg, *The 'Ne Temere' Decree* (APCK 1943), pp. 9f.
4. See Cahal B. Daly, *The Price of Peace* (Blackstaff Press 1991).
5. E. Gallagher & S. Worrall, *Christians in Ulster* (Oxford University Press 1982), p. 1.
6. *Sectarianism: A Discussion Document* (Department of Social Issues of the Irish Inter-Church Meeting 1993).
7. *Freedom, Justice and Responsibility in Ireland Today* (Department of Theological Questions of the Irish Inter-Church Meeting 1997).
8. Quoted from manuscript copy.

BIOGRAPHICAL NOTE

DR IAN ELLIS was ordained in St Patrick's Church of Ireland Cathedral, Armagh, in 1977, and has served in parishes in Co. Armagh and Co. Down. He has been Rector of Newcastle since 1993. From 1980 until 1998 he was Honorary Secretary of the Church of Ireland General Synod's Committee for Christian Unity and he is widely experienced in national and international church relations. He was a founding member of the Council of Churches for Britain and Ireland in 1990 and has been closely involved in the Anglican Consultative Council's Ecumenical Advisory Group. In 1998 he was elected vice-president of the Irish Council of Churches.

27

Christian
Reconciliation Movements

JOHN MORROW

Reconciliation is a term which gives rise to a good deal of suspicion, both from those seeking radical social change, who often feel that it is an attempt to blur the issues or cover over the cracks, and from conservative church circles, where it may acquire the connotation of 'selling the pass' or compromising over principles. But any thoughtful examination of the New Testament shows that a concept of reconciliation which emerges as an interpretation of the significance of the life, death and resurrection of Jesus Christ can hardly be based on a denial of truth. Christian Reconciliation Movements are anxious not only to give the concept a central place, but also to recover its full dimensions as a challenge to those who would turn principle into prejudice or a struggle for justice into tribal enmity. Reconciliation means change and transformation so that former conflicts can find resolution in new relationships and new frameworks. But it also means forgiveness, the healing of past wounds and the letting go of past hurts if we are to find the way to that new future.

Any selection of Christian Reconciliation Movements is bound to be somewhat arbitrary, partly because there are so many peace and reconciliation groups in Northern Ireland which have some degree of Christian influence – for example, *Women Together* or the *Community of the Peace People* – but which are not explicitly Christian Reconciliation Movements. At the other end of the spectrum there are groups which have been set up officially by the Churches or which have grown out of the ecumenical movement in recent years. In this chapter the intention is to concentrate on the more unofficial or spontaneous movements or groups which have emerged over the past thirty years or so. It is hoped to indicate some of the factors which have brought them into existence and any special focus which they give to their life and work.

FELLOWSHIP OF RECONCILIATION (FoR)

The oldest Christian Reconciliation Movement in Europe is probably the *International Fellowship of Reconciliation* (IFOR), which emerged at the beginning of the 1914–18 war, when an English Quaker and a German Lutheran declared 'We are one in Christ and so can never be at war.' Out of this grew an international movement based on 'faith in and allegiance to the God of Love'. The aims were to bring about peaceful relations between divided communities, with an emphasis on disarmament, mediation and active non-violent ways of resolving conflict and removing injustice. Since 1949 there has been a branch of FoR in Northern Ireland so it was natural that it would become involved in the work of reconciliation here, especially from 1969 onwards. In addition to encouraging efforts to understand the sources of the Northern Ireland conflict, it has engaged in many practical community projects for children and young people and in the promotion of a non-violent training project. Although FoR is inter-denominational, until recently it has probably found its main support from Quakers and other Protestant denominations.

PAX CHRISTI

From within the Roman Catholic Communion a similar movement emerged towards the end of the Second World War called *Pax Christi* (the peace of Christ). This was founded in France to foster reconciliation between French and German people. Bishop Theas, a prisoner of war who was known for his teaching on the Gospel command to forgive enemies, was a significant figure in the early years. The movement, based on prayer, study and action for the peace of Christ, spread to many countries and a branch was founded in Ireland in 1967 and in Belfast in 1982.

Specific aims of Pax Christi include:

- propagation of Christian teaching on peace and justice and its application to our society; exposing the futility of violence and the efficacy of non-violence;
- provision of a meeting point for Christians who wish to be committed to peacemaking;
- education and training of peace leaders;
- collaboration with all other bodies with similar aims to create peace and justice in the world.

In Ireland Pax Christi has been active in peace education; promoting dialogue; retreats; vigils and prayers; acting as observers in potentially violent situations, et cetera. Members have sometimes led public vigils after violent events as a witness to their conviction that violence is not the way forward. In one particular situation after the killing of many policemen in Newry a silent candlelit walk and vigil organised by Pax Christi members expressed the revulsion of many people in a deeply moving and dignified way. Gestures like this have helped to save Northern Ireland from total polarisation at times.

THE CORRYMEELA COMMUNITY

Probably the first fully indigenous Christian Reconciliation Movement to emerge in Northern Ireland in recent years was the Corrymeela Community, which was founded in 1965 under the leadership of Ray Davey (Presbyterian Chaplain and Dean of Residence at Queen's University, Belfast, and a former prisoner of war in Italy and Germany, 1942–5). The founding group, which included a majority of students or former students, was influenced by many different 'streams'. These included the ecumenical movement, Vatican II, new Christian communities like *Iona* in Scotland, *Taizé* in France, and *Agape* in northern Italy. It was also aware of post-Second World War movements in Europe seeking to relate Christian witness more sharply to the concrete issues in wider society and to affirm the Christian lay vocation in the Church and in the world.

Although strongly Presbyterian in its origins, it was interdenominational from the start and full Roman Catholic involvement was quickly achieved. Also, although holding to an explicitly Christian basis, the Community welcomes people of all faiths or none to participate in most of its programmes and seeks to nurture a spirit of acceptance and mutual respect. It operates as a dispersed network of people who seek to work out their vision in family, work, church or local community, often meeting in small local support groups. The key visible focus of the Community is a major residential centre for meeting and reconciliation near Ballycastle, Co. Antrim, from which it takes its name. There is also a resource centre in Belfast for administration and for fieldworkers to plan and follow up cross-community projects with youth, schools, families and churches, many of which take place at the Ballycastle centre. More recently a small centre has been established on the slopes of nearby Knocklayd for more intimate meeting, reflection and prayer.

Some of Corrymeela's aims and objectives are:

- to be a sign and symbol that Protestants and Catholics can share in a common witness and ministry of reconciliation
- to provide opportunities for dialogue and learning to dispel ignorance, prejudice and fear and to promote mutual respect, trust and co-operation

- to address contemporary issues of faith and ethics and to develop new expressions of Christian community life and worship

Volunteer involvement, including a very significant international dimension, has been very important in the life and work of Corrymeela. The Community was founded before the outbreak of violence, and was not simply a response to violence, but a movement seeking renewal and reconciliation in Church and society. It has sometimes been described as *a question mark* to the Churches in Ireland or a search for a new kind of witness in a divided society.

Over the years many new initiatives have emerged out of the Community and become independent movements – for example, the *Northern Ireland Mixed Marriage Association* (NIMMA); the *Cross Group* (a support group for families bereaved in the Troubles); the *Corrymeela Singers*; the *Inter-Church Group on Faith and Politics* (jointly sponsored by Corrymeela, Glencree and the Irish School of Ecumenics); *Understanding Conflict and Finding Ways Out* (a training and learning project linked with the University of Ulster). [A fuller account of the Inter-Church Group on Faith and Politics is given in Chapter 29, 'Churches and Politics'.]

PROTESTANT AND CATHOLIC ENCOUNTER (PACE)

One of the first Christian Reconciliation Movements to emerge after the outbreak of violence in 1969 was PACE. It was initiated by a group of clergy and laity from the main Christian traditions in Northern Ireland, many of whom were very involved in other aspects of reconciliation work and processes of inter-church understanding.

The objectives of PACE are:

- to promote harmony and goodwill between religious and political communities in Northern Ireland
- to demonstrate that although people may be separated by differences of conviction, there are many ways in which they can freely unite in order to work for the common good
- to work with all who desire the establishment of a social order based on justice and charity, in order to eliminate factors which produce harmful divisions in society

One of the great strengths of PACE was that it developed a model which was transportable into any local community, and active groups grew up in Ballymoney, Bangor, east Belfast, Ormeau, Dunmurry, Holywood, Lisburn, Newcastle, Portadown and other areas. The regular publication of the *PACE Journal* contributed much to promote reflection and action on many of the issues facing our society.

After an initial period of enthusiasm the membership remained rather static for a period of years and inevitably became older. More recently the dynamic efforts of the PACE field officer, David McKittrick, led to the development of Encounter Group work, Youth Drama projects, conferences on key issues, interdenominational services and to the involvement of a whole range of new people. A decision by the Northern Ireland Community Relations Council in 1997 to cease funding for PACE, however, has created difficulties for the movement's future.

CORNERSTONE COMMUNITY

The special symbolism which gave focus to this Christian Reconciliation Movement was the call to be a witness for reconciliation on the 'peace line' in inner-city west Belfast. The Springfield Road forms the dividing line between the Shankill and the Falls Roads. In 1982 this was not only a flashpoint for conflicts between local groups or between the police and army and paramilitaries, but an area where there were stretches of abandoned housing forming a kind of no man's land.

The group had its origin in a prayer group based at nearby Clonard Monastery, where Protestants and Catholics had been meeting together for a number of years. They aimed to bring together people who either lived or had a work base in the lower Falls or Shankill areas. Members established a community house at 443–5 Springfield Road where a residential core group live together. They seek to be 'a servant of God's reconciling grace in the Shankill and the Falls', believing that the people of both traditions belong to one another in the family of God. In this spirit they try to enable those around them to discover the bonds which unite and to learn respect for differences.

The men and women who make up the membership of the community and staff include the Leader, a family and community worker and a youth worker. Due to their composition they have close links with many grassroots activities and people and a kind of natural outreach into the district. In addition to community meetings the house is widely used for prayer, ecumenical Bible study, support of victims or distressed people, hospitality, peace education, et cetera. A unique form of joint ministry to the bereaved was carried out when sectarian violence was rife in the district for several years. In addition to their continuing links with Clonard Monastery, they have established a close connection with the local Methodist church and with the more recently formed Currach Community (see below). All of this has led to a greater involvement in local community development in a project called 'ForthSpring' (based on the names of housing estates within the area) and to a ministry which seeks to empower people to share in the renewal of the area as they attempt to set the period of violence behind them.

CURRACH COMMUNITY

The Currach Community was founded by Sr Noreen Christian OP (a member of the Cornerstone Community) as a small residential community of Protestants and Catholics based in a house on the interface of the Shankill and Falls Roads. Currach seeks to be a witness to reconciliation and to enable local communities to share experiences and empower them to work together for the common good. It is a partner in the ForthSpring project and has become a catalyst for many small initiatives.

COLUMBANUS COMMUNITY OF RECONCILIATION

Fr Michael Hurley SJ, founder of the Irish School of Ecumenics, led a further initiative in north Belfast in 1983. The aim was that by living and sharing together as an interdenominational community they would be a model and an example of what a more united Church, a more just society and a peaceful world might look like. This community has a more explicitly ecumenical focus than most of the others and from the beginning has involved representatives of the main Churches as active patrons and sponsors. The reason for this was to avoid the danger of Churches regarding new communities as optional extras while still avoiding facing up to the challenge to overcome their divisions and rediscover their unity in Christ.

The small group of Community members live together in the Community house on the Antrim Road, sharing in daily worship and going out to work with or support local projects. This house, like many of the others associated with groups described here, has become a resource to many activities, some of which are organised by the members. Others, such as local courses in Ecumenics, are organised from outside the Community. The Community also employs a Schools' Worker who seeks to promote and support the work of Education for Mutual Understanding in the city's schools. (At one stage a youth worker was also employed.) Particularly valuable is the additional residential accommodation, which provides an important ministry of hospitality. Retreats and quiet days have been much valued by many exhausted bridge-builders in Ireland over recent years.

One difficulty which they have faced, however, has been in the recruitment of Northern Ireland Protestants into Community membership. This may be partly because the concept of the Community as a kind of religious order is difficult for those outside the Roman Catholic tradition.

CHARISMATIC RENEWAL AND HEALING MOVEMENTS

In the early 1970s a worldwide movement often described as Charismatic Renewal began to make an impact in Ireland, touching both Roman Catholic and Protestant traditions. There was a strong emphasis on prayer and openness to the gifts of the Holy Spirit as a healing, renewing and reconciling power. In 1974 the Rev. Cecil Kerr (at that time Church of Ireland Chaplain at Queen's University) and his wife, Myrtle, felt led to set up the **Christian Renewal Centre** at Rostrevor, Co. Down. Over many years now this Centre has brought together people from all traditions who have been separated by fear, suspicion and ignorance and has helped them to rediscover that they are brothers and sisters in Christ. It has given a special emphasis to the need for the removal of deep blockages caused by past hurts, wounds and resentments as a vital part of the work of healing and reconciliation. Although its work is mainly within and between the Churches, it has had a significant ministry with some fomer paramilitary activists from both loyalist and republican backgrounds. A small core residential community is based at the Centre, and in addition to many programmes based there it has a wide outreach and many contacts throughout the province.

Among the other groups which have a close link with the Christian Renewal Centre is the **Lamb of God Community**, which was founded (in 1977) and led by Larry Kelly. Its base is Shalom House, Cliftonville Road, a sensitive cultural interface area of north Belfast. It seeks to promote inter-church renewal, cross-community dialogue and social outreach to youth, the elderly and victims of violence. **Columba House** in Derry, founded in 1980 by Fr Neal Carlin, has taken a special initiative in the promotion of symbolic liturgical occasions where acts of mutual repentance have been shared by representatives from different traditions in Ireland and Britain. It has also given considerable support to ex-prisoners and to others who have been badly damaged by the events of the Troubles. Both of these groups have made an impact in their local areas, where they run houses which are a resource to the community, offering prayer, counselling and other forms of support. A more recent project which shares much with this tradition, called **Restoration Ministries**, has been founded by a Presbyterian minister, the Rev. Ruth Patterson, and is especially focused on the need for support and healing for those who carry a heavy burden in caring for others. Personal counselling, programmes for the deepening of spiritual life and opportunities for more intimate inter-church sharing form part of a developing outreach. Restoration Ministries has been considerably inspired and influenced by the visits and spiritual writings of Jean Vanier, the French-Canadian founder of *L'Arche Communities*.

Not everyone is comfortable with the presuppositions of the Charismatic Renewal Movement and some would feel that it can be unduly emotional or even manipulative at times. However, no one can doubt the important changes which have taken place in the lives of many people and the commitment to reconciliation which has resulted from the work of these centres. It has also had an impact on many of the other groups mentioned and on all of the Churches.

CHRISTIAN RECONCILIATION MOVEMENTS IN EDUCATION

Whilst it is the case that many Christian Reconciliation Movements have an educational component, some groups in particular have emerged to give this their main priority.

The **Irish School of Ecumenics** (ISE) was the first of these and was founded by Fr Michael Hurley SJ in 1970. Although the main centre of the School is in Dublin, it has always served the whole island and the international community as well. In recent years its work in Northern Ireland has been expanded, especially in the area of adult education and in a major research project entitled *Moving Beyond Sectarianism*.

The central inspiration of the School comes from the worldwide Ecumenical Movement for Christian Unity, Renewal and Common Witness. The relevance of this movement to our divided society has been obvious from the start to all except those who wish to deny the significance of the religious dimension of the Troubles. Fr Hurley was deeply conscious of the need for the Churches to break free from their sectarian history. The widespread ignorance, stereotypes and distrust of each other's tradition and the lack of awareness in Ireland of the worldwide development of dialogue, co-operation and theological convergence, was seen to be a major obstacle to the work of reconciliation in Ireland.

The need to prepare leaders such as clergy, teachers, church members and community workers for this challenge was felt to require serious research, good academic study and practical application. Since 1970 over nine hundred students have been taught by the ISE and many of them are now in positions of leadership in church and community in Ireland and throughout the world. Research projects have been carried out on mixed marriages, human rights, the healing of memories and sectarianism. Postgraduate degrees and diplomas in Ecumenics and Peace Studies are based in Dublin, but shorter certificate courses and other local courses, open to all, have been set up in Northern Ireland in a growing number of centres, including Belfast, Derry, Armagh, Newry and Enniskillen.

The School has been handicapped by lack of resources to expand its work in recent times. The Churches have had a somewhat ambivalent relation to the ISE, supportive at times but also, perhaps, seeing some of its work as a threat to their identity in the long term, which makes it difficult for them to give their wholehearted support.

The ISE is now in the process of adapting its courses to grass-roots communities and making them generally more accessible. Much of its work fits closely with the Northern Ireland schools' curriculum theme of Education for Mutual Understanding and is of special value to teachers. The urgent need to retrieve the rich resources of the Gospel message of reconciliation (which all traditions share) and to recall the Churches to a fresh vision is the continuing task of the School. Finally, its work in the area of inter-faith relations is becoming increasingly important, even in Northern Ireland, as we seek to build a society in which all minorities are understood and respected.

Another educational focus which emerged in the early 1970s was that of *Integrated Education*. **All Children Together** (ACT) was very much a Christian Reconciliation Movement set up by Protestant and Roman Catholic parents who wished to have their children educated in shared Christian schools. Their vision was for schools which would be acceptable to those from all religious and cultural traditions, and they had hoped that the Churches would provide religious education and pastoral care.

In the early years a great deal of work and self-sacrifice went into the raising of public consciousness and the establishment of the first 'planned integrated schools' such as Lagan College, at a time when government support was very limited. They also campaigned for changes in legislation in order to enable the creation of new shared schools for those parents who desired it. (Legislation was, in fact, gradually introduced, culminating in significant new provisions for support and funding of integrated schools in the Education Reform Order of 1989.)

Not all of those working to develop integrated schools have done so from a Christian perspective. As the integrated education movement has grown, however, ACT has continued to place special emphasis on the shared religious dimensions of the curriculum, and much of its thinking is evident in the approach of the Northern Ireland Council for Integrated Education (NICIE), of which ACT is now a component member. (The NICIE Statement of Principles echoes this in saying that the integrated schools movement must 'ensure that each integrated school community welcomes, respects and cherishes the children of parents having other or no religious convictions while remaining loyal to its own essentially Christian character'.)

Members of ACT in particular have been very disappointed by the lack of support for integrated education from the Roman Catholic Hierarchy and by the rather tepid support from the Protestant Churches. However, many individual clergy are among their strongest supporters. Apart from fears of a diversion of funding from existing schools (expressed at times in both Protestant and Catholic educational circles), the main criticisms made by the Catholic Hierarchy have been that they fear such schools will end up as a lowest common denominator and not sustain the particular ethos which they feel is necessary for Catholic education. ACT would claim that its philosophy is to encourage the full expression of all traditions, cultural and religious, and not in any way to water them down. Above all it hopes to create an atmosphere in which real trust, friendship and mutual understanding can be achieved and all can benefit from full access to the diversity present and also recognise much that is held in common.

With the development of many autonomous integrated schools from the late 1980s onwards the role of ACT has been changing. It continues to promote widespread debate and discussion on many aspects of integrated education and support for groups of parents who wish to pursue this vision. The experience of those who have taken part in this form of education has so far been very positive but it is clear that it cannot serve the majority of children at present while there is widespread social segregation. Nevertheless, as a pioneering part of the integrated schools movement, ACT has been significant in enabling many parents and pupils to build strong and lasting relationships across the religious and cultural divide.

A different kind of contribution to Christian reconciliation in education has been made by the **Churches' Peace Education Programme**, which since its establishment in 1978 has involved close co-operation between the *Irish Council of Churches* (Protestant) and the *Irish Commission for Justice and Peace* (an Irish Catholic Episcopal Commission). Valuable materials, for schools and for adult Christian education programmes, have been prepared on themes such as inter-church studies, conflict management and cultural diversity, and a Resource Centre has been established for clergy, teachers and others. Since the early 1980s the staff of the programme have been closely involved in the establishment and development of Education for Mutual Understanding and other educational community relations programmes.

The Northern Ireland branch of the **Christian Education Movement** (CEM) has also given a high priority to the work of reconciliation through its programmes of area and residential conferences, mainly for sixth-formers. These occasions bring together pupils from all traditions for shared study and dialogue. CEM staff have also produced a number of *Church Trails* which enable children in a particular area to visit a range of the local churches in order to explore aspects of the different Christian traditions.

EVANGELICAL CONTRIBUTION ON NORTHERN IRELAND (ECONI)

For some time in the early 1980s a group of evangelical Christians from all the main Protestant denominations were reflecting on the implications of the Gospel of Christ for their witness in a divided society. They felt that there had been a serious neglect of the social dimension of the Gospel within their tradition and a failure to embrace the call to a full ministry of reconciliation and peacemaking. They believed that for some evangelicals a suspicion of ecumenism was being used as a cover for opting out of many dimensions of ministry and for failing to address the idolatrous over-identification of Protestantism with unionism. Thus ECONI was founded in 1987 to challenge this significant constituency within all the main Reformed Churches. The new energy and courage of this movement has led to the production of books and pamphlets, the organising of occasions for dialogue, conferences, workshops and roadshows.

Particular emphasis has been given to the theme of Christian citizenship, involving the whole spectrum of political parties in an open reflection on the relationship between faith and politics. The *Belfast City YMCA*, itself increasingly involved in cross-community activities, has given special support to this movement and ECONI's offices are based there. It has also received encouragement and inspiration from a group of *Mennonites* from the United States – one of the historic peace churches which has been working in Ireland over a period of years. (It is worth noting that several other developments owe much to the Mennonites, in particular *Mediation Network*, which came to public attention for its work in mediating on the disputes around marches and parades in the mid-1990s.) Although not a Christian Reconciliation Movement as such, ECONI has been significant in the evangelical constituency in stimulating active concern about reconciliation in Northern Ireland. (A fuller account of ECONI is given in Chapter 29, 'Churches and Politics'.)

WOMEN'S WORLD DAY OF PRAYER

Another group which is not a reconciliation movement as such but which has enabled valuable inter-church relationships to develop effectively if quietly over many years is the Women's World Day of Prayer. This movement was set up in the United States as long ago as 1887 on the initiative of an American Presbyterian, Mary Ellen James, and is carried out today by women in 170 different countries from all regions of the world. Each year women gather on the first Friday of March, often along with many men, to pray, using a common theme developed each year by a different group of women and translated into many languages. The theme of the prayers normally relates to world issues, justice, human rights, peace and reconciliation, with the motto of 'Informed Prayer and Prayerful Action'. A national committee for England, Wales and Northern Ireland includes representatives from a surprisingly wide range of Protestant denominations as well as the Roman Catholic Church, and at the time of writing the national president is from Northern Ireland. Local groups around Northern Ireland gather each year for the special service. In 1982 the order of service was prepared by women from Ireland and the logo which they designed for that year (a Celtic cross made up from four stylised kneeling figures) was later adopted as the logo for the whole movement.

CONCLUSIONS

In any selection of this kind it is always difficult to decide what should be included and how to deal with those groups which overlap different categories. For example, it would be easy to regard the Society of Friends (Quakers) as a Christian Reconciliation Movement as well as a particular denomination. Friends have shown themselves to be active not only as a Society but in co-operation with just about every group mentioned above.

As the various processes of peacemaking in Northern Ireland develop, all of these groups will find that their focus will have to change to some extent. Some may even feel that they should cease to exist if their agenda is embraced by the Churches at large. However, it seems unlikely that they will be redundant in the short term and the work of reconciliation is likely to require many special contributions for some time to come, whatever political settlements may be agreed. They will, however, need a constant self-critical spirit if they are to learn from past experiences and remain relevant to the tasks of tomorrow.

The emergence of Christian Reconciliation Movements is partly the result of a deep sense of frustration, felt by some church members from different traditions, about the failure of the Churches to take seriously the implications of the Christian message for the work of reconciliation in Church and society. Those who founded them felt a call to be signs of reconciliation within their society; to create opportunities for dialogue and meeting; to be channels for common witness and service; to be vehicles for new initiatives in peacemaking. Many of them have continued to work for change in the Churches, though so far with limited success. It could be argued that without them our society would have become much more polarised than it is, even to the extent of full-scale civil war. However, the task of working for peace and reconciliation in the future will require fresh vision and should have no place for nostalgia.

BIOGRAPHICAL NOTE

The REV. DR JOHN MORROW comes from a farming background and studied agriculture at Queen's University before going on to prepare for ordination in the Presbyterian Church of Ireland. As a student in Scotland he became a member of the Iona Community, and he was later a founder member of the Corrymeela Community. After early ministry in the Belfast area he moved into student chaplaincy work in Glasgow, Dublin and Belfast before being appointed as Leader of Corrymeela in 1979 following the retirement of Ray Davey. In 1993 he was appointed Northern Ireland Lecturer with the Irish School of Ecumenics, from which he retired in 1997. John Morrow is married with four children and several grandchildren.

Contact addresses for many of the organisations described in this chapter are given in the Appendix.

28

Women
in the Churches

Catholic and Protestant Perspectives

BERNADETTE TOAL AND LIZ HEWITT

One of the major sociological phenomena of the second half of the twentieth century has been the way in which the role, status and expectations of
women have changed significantly. This is evidenced in employment
patterns, in family life, in equality legislation and in many other areas of
human experience and activity. Churches around the world have increasingly played their part in these developments, despite many counter-
pressures, and the Irish Churches are no exception.

It is sometimes rather naively perceived that the points at issue are
'women's concerns' and 'women's issues', but this would be to neglect
the fact that many men have shared these concerns with women and,
equally, that women have been just as divided on the issues as men.
Although the concerns and emphases vary between denominations and
theological positions, the basic issues are about acceptance, equality and
participation. Many Christians, male and female alike, would thereby
wish to argue that these are not just 'women's issues' but rather issues for
the whole Church.

In this chapter two Christian women from Northern Ireland, one
Catholic and one Protestant, offer their personal perspectives on the
changing role of women and the ways in which the Churches are respond-
ing. A joint conclusion looks forward to future developments.

A Roman Catholic Perspective

BERNADETTE TOAL

When the question of the role of women in the Roman Catholic Church arises, the focus of the debate is often on the fact that women cannot be part of the ordained ministry and are thereby excluded from the official, decision-making, leadership roles in the Church. The story is told of the little girl who was asked the question: 'How many sacraments does the Church have?' She replied truthfully: 'The Church has seven sacraments for men and six for women!' Her reply was correct because women are excluded from the sacrament of Holy Orders.

This is undoubtedly a very serious issue for the Church, especially now when we expect men and women to be given equal treatment in society, but we must not overlook the fact that women do play an important role in church life in all Roman Catholic parishes in Northern Ireland. Their contribution to parish life is such that without them the parish would not be able to function. Women are an integral and important part of parish teams, involved in organising church activities such as liturgy committees, who meet to organise liturgical worship, or baptism teams, who visit those who are to have a baby baptised to help them better appreciate the importance of this sacrament for themselves and their child. Women read the Word of God (the sacred Scriptures) during Mass and on other liturgical occasions. They are commissioned by the church to distribute holy communion as Eucharistic Ministers during Mass and often they bring communion from the Eucharistic table to those who are sick and confined to home. Along with men, or in women-only groups, they gather for *Triduums* (three days) of prayer to celebrate certain feast days and they are involved in organising *Novenas* (nine days of prayer) and *Confraternities* (groups who gather together for prayer). Religious sisters and laywomen lead prayer groups and retreats and act as spiritual directors to those who come to them for help (both clerical and lay) in leading a more prayerful life. In fact, at parish level and in the prayer life of the church, women are very visible and at any church service there are usually far more women present in the congregation than men.

As well as taking part in the sacramental life of the Church they are usually the ones who do a lot of the less glamorous jobs like cleaning the church building every week or making tea after functions held in the church hall, and it often falls to them to decorate the altar and keep the altar linen in pristine order. (Interestingly enough, however, in my experience counting the money taken up in the collection baskets is usually done by a team of men.) All of these things women do with generosity and love because of their commitment to Christ and the Church and their desire to be of service.

However, there has been rapid change in Western culture over the past twenty years or so and a new consciousness has come about concerning the existence of systematic injustice against women in the home, in the workplace, in education, in politics and also in the Christian community. There have been changes in the roles which men and women play in our society. Male-dominated occupations have been opened up to women so that they might exercise their talents and ability in all areas of human endeavour. Legislation has been passed to ensure that in secular society there is no discrimination in laws and codes of conduct which relate to the treatment of women. An example of this would be the type of question which is allowed to be asked at interview when a woman is the candidate. In the past, women were often asked about their domestic arrangement with regard to their children while men were never asked such a question. There have been changes too in the language we use, so that terms and phrases are specifically inclusive of women and do not presume to refer to them indirectly while using male pronouns like 'him' or 'his' or words like 'mankind' instead of 'humankind'.

These changes have been reflected in the official teaching of the Church. As Pope Paul VI said, during the International Women's Year in 1975, 'a most pressing need at the moment is advancing the cause of women at every level in both society and the Church'.

Pope John Paul II in his Apostolic Exhortation *Vocation and Mission of Lay Faithful in the Church and in the World* (1987) stated that 'confronted with the discrimination, the marginalisation, to which women are subjected just because they are women, there is an urgent need to promote women's personal dignity and their equality with men'.

Statements from the Church which accept the reality of discrimination towards women and urge that it should be combated raise fundamental difficulties for the Catholic Church because there is a discrepancy between what the Church preaches and what she practises. Christianity is primarily a religion about living a way of life in imitation of Jesus. That means it is not a religion which focuses just on knowing the truth or proclaiming the truth but ultimately on *doing* and *living* the truth in love. At present there is a serious credibility gap between the theory and practice of the Catholic Church in regard to women. The visionary statements of the Church concerning equality, justice and participation have not always been followed by much structural change or institutional conversion.

There is a large body of material tracing the view of the inferiority of women held by early church fathers. Today the Church does not think that women are 'defective and misbegotten males', as St Thomas Aquinas thought, but she still operates out of a dual nature anthropology which sees certain roles or attributes as being essentially 'male' or 'female'. This attitude claims that there are two distinct and different ways of being human, namely a male and female way. Qualities such as independence, activity, rationality and strength are regarded as masculine while so-called feminine qualities are relationality, passivity, intuitiveness and gentleness. In this dual approach to what it means to be a human person the Church reflects the general attitude of society, which regards men who are gentle and non-aggressive as wimps while women who are assertive and confident are often labelled 'butch' and regarded as not being feminine. This understanding of what it means to be a man or a woman is seen as part of the divine plan and the social and psychological attributes of each sex are deemed God-given and therefore unchangeable. But Christian theologians are questioning these assumptions and debating these issues in an attempt to create a Church where men and women can both have the fullness of life that Jesus promised when he said, 'I have come that you may have life and have it to the full' (John 10:10).

Traditional theology is being scrutinised and reformulated in order that it should reflect and include the life experience of women. To illustrate the point and give an example let us look at the idea of suffering as it has been traditionally presented. As Christians we were told that to follow Christ meant taking up one's cross daily. For many women, however, this gospel message which should have been interpreted as being faithful to the truth in spite of difficulties was interpreted in a way which kept them in situations where they suffered emotional and sometimes physical violence in the belief that this was their Christian duty; this was the cross which they had to shoulder. The true gospel message about their worth as human beings who are loved by a God who wants all of us to live happy and fulfilled lives was sacrificed to an image of a sadistic God who wants suffering. As some feminist theologians have pointed out, women who were excluded by the Church from presiding at the Eucharistic table 'in the person of Christ' because they had female bodies and not male ones, had no difficulty in emulating the suffering of the crucified Christ in their bodies and were not helped by a theology which glorified suffering without asking, 'Is this really what God wants?' Women have asked why the Hierarchy devotes so much time to issues such as contraception, divorce and abortion and so little time to the violence which women experience in the home and in society generally.

In a recent development a Forum for Catholic Women (FCW) has been established in order to meet the felt need for an organisation equivalent to the (Anglican) Mothers' Union or the Presbyterian and Methodist Women's Associations. An initiative was taken by Dr Cecelia Clegg and colleagues and the FCW was inaugurated in Maghera in November 1997. The organisation seeks

> to vision and develop a model of being church ... that will become an inspiration and alternative experience of authority; to facilitate the formation and education of women so that they understand and claim the theological basis of inclusion in the life of church ... ; to initiate creative dialogue with the 'powers that be'.

Although many women experience great pain and a sense of exclusion at the way they are treated by the Roman Catholic Church, by their actions (and their speaking out about how they feel) they have proved their love for the Church. They want to be fully involved in her development not because they are interested in control or power but because they feel that the Church herself is impoverished by not making full use of the contribution which women have to make. Their insights and talents both in practical matters and in theological debate will be invaluable if the Church is to be relevant to the lives of her people in the future.

A Protestant Perspective
LIZ HEWITT

A report presented to the Methodist Conference in 1997 stated:

> The attitude of the Church, and of individual Christians, towards women should be modelled on Christ's behaviour and attitude ... Through his words and actions he demonstrated towards [women] a caring attitude: he made time to speak, and listen, to the women with whom he came in contact. He offered these women a dignity and a role which they did not receive in the culture and under the Rabbinical teaching of their society ... Against [the] background of rapid change in our contemporary society, the Church needs to reflect upon the teaching and example of Christ and to rediscover Paul's vision of a liberated society in which 'there is neither Jew nor Greek, there is neither bond nor free, there is neither male nor female; for you are all one in Christ Jesus' (Galatians 3:28).

The same report goes on to discuss the issues relating to the role of women in the Church under the headings of *Attitude, Language,*

Enablement, Representation, and *Ordination,* and these headings indeed provide some indication of the agenda for the wider discussion of the role of women in the Irish Protestant Churches in general.

Protestant Churches are diverse and varied, within as well as between denominations, and this is no less so in relation to attitudes towards, and the actual practice of, women's roles. Some denominations – especially those which do not have a strong sacramental theology such as the Salvation Army and the Religious Society of Friends (Quakers) – have always been significantly open to the ministry of women (a fact undoubtedly related to the lack of a need in such traditions to place emphasis on the role of the male priest). Among the larger denominations Methodism has had a tradition of involving laywomen as Local Preachers going back as far as Wesley's times. Certain other denominations – particularly those with a strong conservative evangelical or even fundamentalist theology – completely rule out such a role for women on biblical grounds (citing passages such as 1 Corinthians 14:34–6 – see below). In some other cases internal division is evident. Thus in the Presbyterian Church in Ireland, while women have been admitted for ordination as ruling elders (i.e. laypeople) for many decades and as teaching elders (i.e. ministers) since the early 1970s, a significant number of congregations have been unwilling to 'call' women to minister in either capacity and there have even been some moves to impede the advancement of women in ordained ministry. When the Church of Ireland voted to accept women into the ordained priesthood in 1990 a number of senior clergy made public their opposition and a small group actually left the denomination to form the independent *Church of Ireland: Traditional Rite.*

These variations in attitude and practice are not confined to Irish experience. Sometimes, however, when the practices of the wider world Church are taken into account, it may appear that there is a relatively more conservative attitude among Protestant Christians in Ireland towards the role of women. In Britain, for instance, Presbyterian denominations (such as the Church of Scotland and United Reformed Church) have been very affirmative of women's ministry in a wide range of ways. On the other hand it must be acknowledged that the fierce continuing arguments and threats of schism over women's ordination in the Church of England have never been mirrored in its Irish Anglican partner, the Church of Ireland (in which there is no significant 'High Church' or Anglo-Catholic wing).

For many of those who are opposed to permitting a fuller role for women in the Church the underlying difficulty relates to their understanding of authority in the Church. In almost all denominations positions of theological and administrative authority have traditionally been held by men, who have exercised control over the interpretation of the sources of authority, the Bible and the Church. A theology defined and shaped by men will naturally emphasise the male role, the inevitable corollary of which is that women's roles have at best been hidden.

When women are engaged in roles of authority in the Churches, many church members may even find that the female approach to authority is slightly threatening and unsettling. Men are often familiar and comfortable with a pyramid model of authority, which has traditionally been how denominations and local congregations have been run in the great majority of cases. For many women, however, a collegiate model, in which collaboration, participation and inclusion are the key concepts, is much more appropriate.

Some women are themselves responsible for perpetuating the traditions of male-dominated leadership in the Churches. It is not uncommon in many congregations to find women accepting men's perceptions of their role. Men are perceived as competent in committees or financial matters, while women may be seen as fully confident in the preparation of food for church functions but may well apologise for themselves if they are taking a lead in other areas of church activity. This may relate to a broader problem relating to a traditional understanding of ministry whereby the (male) minister's primary job is seen as that of teaching and preaching, which, once again, raises issues of authority. The deep-seated feeling that 'men should be in charge' has presented real difficulties for women taking up duties as members of the clergy. The request made to one Irish female minister that she should find 'a real minister' to take a funeral service was not an isolated case.

The male image in relation to authority is still dominant in Ireland, especially at the level of official denominational structures and events. At Church Conferences, Assemblies, Synods, et cetera, the platform party is usually all-male. Even in inter-church and ecumenical structures men continue to be in a significant majority. At the congregational level, however, women's representation is improving and in some congregational committees there are certainly more women than men (mirroring the situation in the pews each week). It is clear that this is now being taken more seriously at the level of denominational decision making, as for instance in the Methodist Church in Ireland, which, while rejecting a quota system for its official committees, has nevertheless set in place a formal monitoring process to ensure a balance in terms of gender, age and lay/clergy participation.

There is much in Scripture to encourage a very positive approach to the role of women in the Church. The possibility of female leadership is by no means absent from the Old Testament, despite the tendency to offer a stereotypical interpretation of characters such as Miriam, Sarah, Esther,

Deborah, Naomi and Ruth. In the New Testament the Gospels indicate how Jesus was prepared to discuss theology with women, and Paul commends certain women, such as Phoebe, Dorcas and Lydia, for their leadership qualities. Yet certain texts are often quoted by those who object to a leadership role for women as though there is nothing more to be said on the matter: 'Wives submit to your husbands . . . for a husband has authority over his wife just as Christ has authority over the Church' (Ephesians 5:22–3); 'The women should keep quiet in the meetings. They are not allowed to speak . . . they must not be in charge' (1 Corinthians 14:34). Such texts from the developing experience of the Early Church must surely be balanced against those which seem much more open to a leadership role for women, such as 1 Corinthians 11:5, which suggests that it was quite common for women to 'pray or proclaim God's message in public worship' (and in relation to which Paul was concerned about appropriate customs of dress and appearance rather than whether they should or should not take part in these ways). We need to keep in mind the predominantly male context and culture in which much of the Bible was written and in which it has been read and interpreted over the centuries. The ways in which Christians read, interpret and teach the Bible today are most important and there is a growing awareness among Christians of the need to recover the ability to perceive female perspectives on and in Scripture.

Exclusive language is yet another way of 'hiding' women. In order to help develop a mood of acceptance and equal participation many Christians have increasingly made themselves aware of the use of language in liturgy as in everyday conversation. The encouragement of inclusive gender-free language has not yet been fully evidenced in the published orders of service of the denominations which use set liturgical forms, but there is considerably more awareness of the importance of doing so. For instance, a hymn book supplement published by the Church of Ireland in 1990 accepted this principle, and it is now not uncommon to hear clergy informally 'editing' phrases in set liturgies such as 'all men' to 'all people', or simply 'all'. Many newer editions and revisions of English language Bible translations have also taken on board the use of inclusive language. While some have feared that this indicates an unhealthy tokenism or a trendy desire to be politically correct, an increasing number of Christians would recognise that the purpose of modifying linguistic uses to more inclusive forms is to help create a more inclusive ethos in the Church.

While the three larger Irish Protestant denominations (as well as some of the smaller ones) now admit women to the ordained ministry, progress has been slow. The number of female candidates for ordination has been relatively small and in some traditions there are still discouraging factors such as the difficulty of finding a congregation willing to accept a woman or the male 'colleagues' who refuse to take part in ordination services (as, for instance, is officially permitted in the Presbyterian Church by means of a conscience clause). For those women who are currently engaged in parish or congregational ministry there seems to be limited opportunity to serve in more senior positions. In the Church of Ireland, for instance, no women, at the time of writing, have been appointed to senior positions such as Dean or Bishop. It may take some considerable time for women to work their way through the system in this regard, but the situation does seem likely to change. Part of the problem may be that while the Churches debated significantly the issues relating to the admission of women to ordination, they did not take the time to reflect on the ongoing roles of women in ministry or on the consequences of such admission.

There have undoubtedly been positive developments in relation to the role of women in the Protestant Churches in recent years. A greater local acceptance of women in leadership roles in many congregations would seem to stem from a growing awareness of male/female diversity of gifts. There is an increasing recognition of the presence of women in ordained ministry, and, as the number of female clergy grows (albeit somewhat slowly), women entering the ministry now have the opportunity of discovering female role models. Similar developments in the world Church have encouraged the growth of more inclusive male–female partnerships in ministry here in Ireland.

At the same time there is still a need for improvement in certain areas. The role of women in ministry is part of a wider question of the nature of ministry in general, and relates closely to issues of training and enablement for participation and partnership with laypeople. There must be continuing discussion of the theological issues relating to authority and inclusivity, but at a more practical level opportunities need to be created for women to be able to participate more equally with men in the structures of the Church.

CONCLUSIONS

Despite the reservations and objections which are held by some Christians from both the major strands of Christian tradition in Northern Ireland, it is the belief of the authors of this chapter that there is significant and perhaps growing agreement among many Protestants and Catholics on the importance of broadening the opportunities for women to participate in all aspects of ministry in our Churches.

It was in this spirit that a group was set up in 1997 entitled *Women In Faith* 'to acknowledge and celebrate the work that women in the Churches in NI have done and are doing [and] to challenge women of faith to examine ... initiatives that they might jointly undertake to help build a more harmonious society in NI'. Originating in an initiative of Lady Jean Mayhew in 1996, the group is led by local women from various Christian traditions.

In order to strengthen all these developments we believe that certain key areas of the lives and thinking of our Churches will require special attention.

(a) We look forward to seeing a much greater importance attached to the involvement of both men and women in all aspects of lay ministry in our Churches. Some churches (denominationally and/or locally) already take this very seriously; others less so.

(b) We believe that there is a need for ongoing consideration of the theological objections to the participation of women in certain aspects of the life of the Churches and a deepening consciousness of the contrary arguments.

(c) We believe that a more sensitive awareness of the importance of inclusive *language* in the liturgy and teaching of our Churches would contribute substantially to the creation of an inclusive *ethos* throughout the life and work of a parish or congregation.

(d) In our view a mature development along these inclusive lines would inevitably strengthen the existing changes which are taking place to ensure the fuller participation of women in the structures of church government.

(e) The involvement of women in ordained ministry in some traditions seems more remote, but can be encouraged through the work and example of, for instance, clergy fellowships in which existing women clergy take a full and creative role.

(f) Above all there must be a recognition that the Church as a whole will be enriched by a greater sense of *partnership* between men and women in all aspects of fellowship, worship, church government and mission.

BIBLIOGRAPHY

Ariarajah, Wesley, *Did I Betray the Gospel? The Letters of Paul and the Place of Women*, World Council of Churches 1996

Byrne, Lavinia, *The Hidden Tradition*, SPCK 1991

Carr, Anne E., *Transforming Grace – Christian Tradition and Women's Experience*, Harper 1990

Furlong, Monica (ed.), *Feminine in the Church*, SPCK 1984

Johnson, Elizabeth A., *She Who Is – The Mystery of God in Feminist Theological Discourse*, Crossroad 1992

Keay, Kathy (ed.), *Men, Women and God: Evangelicals and Feminism*, Marshall, Morgan & Scott 1987

Murphy, Claire Colette, SHCJ, *An Introduction to Christian Feminism*, Dominican Publications 1994

Thurston, Anne, *Because of her Testimony*, Gill & Macmillan 1995

Wren, Brian, *What Language Shall I Borrow?*, SCM Press 1989

BIOGRAPHICAL NOTES

BERNADETTE TOAL is a postgraduate theology student at the Milltown Institute of Theology and Philosophy in Dublin. Born in Belfast, she grew up in the Ardoyne area. She lived in England for several years and is now living in Dublin. Bernadette has always been actively involved with the Church at a pastoral level. She serves on the South Dublin Women's Deanery Forum, on the Diocesan Prayer Initiative Committee and on her local Augustinian Parish Forum. In 1995 she was the Irish lay representative at the Augustinian General Chapter in Rome.

The REV. LIZ HEWITT OBE is currently Superintendent Minister of Ballynahinch Methodist Circuit. She began her career as a primary school teacher and was then appointed as Children's Secretary in the Methodist Youth Department. She candidated for the Methodist Ministry in 1979 and was ordained in 1983. Liz has a keen interest in developing links between the churches in the local area. She is also a member of the Methodist Inter-Church Relations Committee, the Irish Inter-Church Committee and the Council of Churches for Britain and Ireland.

29

Churches
and Politics

JOHNSTON McMASTER

Consider, for example, Jesus' 'very spiritual' sounding prayer: 'I thank thee, Father, Lord of heaven and earth, that thou hast hidden these things from the wise and understanding and revealed them to babes' (Matthew 11:25). He was referring here to a concrete historical experience. The powerful of his day were rejecting his invitation and plotting to murder him. Soldiers were being sent after him. And he saw that those who were listening were the poor, who had no significance in the life of the people. It was they who were given the gift to understand and were following him. So it is a spiritual expression – 'I thank you that this Kingdom is passing through the poor' – but it is also a prayer that cannot be understood apart from a real political confrontation.[1]

This insight is a reminder that the prayer of Jesus had a historical and political context. Jesus did not live nor even pray in a vacuum. The same is true of most prayers in the Bible. They have a historical dimension and are of a political nature. Seldom is attention paid to this context, which often results in an over-spiritualised biblical text with little to say to our social and political lives.

In almost two thousand years of church history, the Christian community has never been politically neutral. Sometimes political structures have been explicitly supported. At other times a critical and even subversive voice has been heard. At yet other times a deafening silence has left the status quo unchallenged. Whichever response, Churches are always political and political neutrality is an illusion.

> Whether by action or abstention, Christians are always
> immersed in the world of human co-responsibility which
> we call politics. Prayer and concern for the *polis*, concern for
> human beings, are always together.[2]

Historically this has always been the case and Irish Churches are no exception. Churches and politics have always been and remain inseparable.

1. IRISH CHURCHES AND POLITICAL ORIGINS

Irish churches took root in political soil. Each of the four larger Churches
was shaped by historical dynamics and political forces. Origins are found
not only in God, but also in political contexts. It is important to recognise
these political origins when dealing with Irish denominational histories.
Denominational memories, like biblical texts, can be over-spiritualised.

(a) The Roman Catholic Church

Both the Catholic Church and the Church of Ireland have claimed historical continuity with the early Celtic Church. Until early this century
the claims were more polemical than historical. Whatever the historical
basis or lack of it, the latter half of this century has greatly reduced the
polemic. A more critical view of history has highlighted discontinuity
with the Celtic Church.

The history of the Celtic Church may be said to span the fifth to the
twelfth centuries. Though the Church had a loyalty to the Pope, it was
also characterised by a spirit of independence which frequently gave the
central Roman authorities cause for concern. The ninth-century Viking
invasion put pressure on the Celtic Church to conform to the centralised
Roman system. Viking bishops gave their allegiance to Canterbury and
through Canterbury to Rome.

The Anglo-Norman invasion of the twelfth century added to the pressure. By the mid-century the monastic structure of the Celtic Church was
giving way to the diocesan model.

The Anglo-Norman factor was complicated. A deposed Irish King
brought the Normans to Ireland, but a major factor also was the role of
the Pope. In 1155, Pope Adrian IV donated Ireland to the English King
Henry II. This 'donation' was later confirmed by Pope Alexander III. The
Celts of Ireland were considered barbarians in need of civilisation and the
Church so decadent that it needed radical reform. This really meant conformity to the Roman system.

The twelfth century saw the beginning of twin processes as Anglicisa-
tion and Romanisation imposed English laws and language and Roman

structures and liturgies on Celtic culture and religion. By the time of the Tudor conquest the processes were almost complete. Gaelic resistance, though, continued in Ulster until the Flight of the Earls in 1607.

The Celtic Church as such came to an end in the twelfth century and the much more centralised Roman model began to dominate. In a very real sense the Catholic Church replaced the Celtic Church, certainly in structure and form, and historical dynamics and political forces were prominent in a very significant development in Irish church history.

(b) The Church of Ireland

By the fifteenth century the Irish Church was Catholic in conformity to Rome. The Tudor political conquest brought the Protestant Reformation to Ireland, as part of legislation for royal supremacy in Ireland.

It was at the Irish Reformation Parliament of 1536–7 that Henry VIII asserted royal authority over against papal authority and centred all power in Church and state in himself. Henry VIII's Act of Supremacy was passed in 1534 'which decreed that Henry and his heirs and successors were to be the only supreme heads of the Church and of the whole of Ireland, Hibernia ecclesia'.[3] Power was transformed from papal curia to royal administration. What emerged was a Church of Ireland within the Anglican communion. A dissolution campaign was begun against religious houses and monasteries. The Church was on its way to establishment.

In 1559 the Acts of Supremacy and Uniformity were passed by Elizabeth I. Elizabeth was declared supreme governor of the Church of Ireland and the Act of Uniformity decreed that liturgical practice in Ireland should be in keeping with the norms of the 1552 Book of Common Prayer.

The Church of Ireland was now established and all appointments within the Queen's service had to acknowledge the authority of the monarch in spiritual and temporal affairs. So Protestantism came as a political imposition and the established Church of Ireland or national Church represented only 10% of the total population.

(c) The Presbyterian Church in Ireland

Presbyterianism came to Ireland from the outside. It arrived in the northeast of Ireland or in Ulster from Scotland. The Scottish settlers, who were part of the early-seventeenth-century plantation of Ulster, brought with them their stern Calvinism, which introduced another form of the Reformation to Ireland.

Six of the nine Ulster counties were officially planted, with Antrim and Down planted through the entrepreneurship of Hugh Montgomery and James Hamilton.

The 1609 plantation was not so complete as intended with the result that planters and Gaels found themselves living in closer proximity than envisaged. Patterns of suspicion, hostility, mistrust and sectarian hatred were constitutionally established and have remained to the present.

The worst fears and insecurities of the planters were realised with the Catholic rising of 1641. In April 1642 General Robert Monro arrived in Ulster with an army of ten thousand soldiers. The Scots Covenanting army was largely successful in defeating most of the rising activity. Many of the officers were Presbyterian elders and in the summer of 1642, with Monro, they formed the first Irish presbytery in Carrickfergus. Presbyterianism was taking form and shape and it is to 1642 that the Presbyterian Church in Ireland looks for its founding event.

Presbyterian roots, therefore, were put down in Ulster soil through the events of Plantation and Rising in the first half of the seventeenth century. Political events played a significant part and the politics of the planters was undergirded by theology.

(d) The Methodist Church in Ireland

Irish Methodism traces its roots to 1747 and the first visit of John Wesley to Dublin. He was to visit Ireland some twenty-one times before his death in 1791. It is to Wesley that Irish Methodists look for their origins.

Methodism took root in Georgian Ireland, which was the golden age of the Protestant Ascendancy. It was the century without wars, unlike the seventeenth century in Ireland, but it was also the Ireland of Penal Laws.

The Penal Laws excluded Catholics from public life and any form of Catholic education was made illegal. It was also illegal for Catholics to buy land, obtain a mortgage, rent land or even inherit it. Queen Anne's Test Act of 1704 was of particular significance and was passed 'to prevent the further growth of popery'. The Act imposed a sacramental test on all office-holders under the Crown. Eucharistic participation in the established Church of Ireland was a condition of holding office under the Crown. This, in effect, excluded Catholics and Protestant Dissenters. Any process of repealing the Penal Laws did not really begin until 1772. Catholic Emancipation came in 1829.

John Wesley commented on the role of the Volunteers, a defence force first formed in Belfast in 1778, that 'if they answer no other end, they at least keep the Papists in order'.[4] Wesley, was, in fact, in favour of keeping the remaining Penal Laws. 'I would not have the Roman Catholics persecuted at all. I would only have them hindered from doing hurt.'[5]

Though Methodism in Ireland was not the result of political imposition, it was generally pro-Ascendancy. With consistency Irish

Methodists opposed during the nineteenth century Catholic Emancipation, National Education, the Repeal of the Union Campaign, the
Maynooth Grant and even the Disestablishment of the Church of Ireland.
Early Methodism was not politically neutral and its anti-Catholic and
sectarian spirit was based on 'a settled religious conviction that the Roman
Catholic religion was the primary cause of all the other Irish problems.
Thus, political remedies whose effect was to undermine the Protestant
foundations of Church and state could only perpetuate the very evils they
were designed to remove.'[6]

The major evangelistic initiative of the Irish Methodist Conference in
1799 was as much motivated by sectarian politics as it was by a sense of
divine calling.

2. POLITICAL CHURCHES — A CASE STUDY

Between 1886 and 1912 three attempts were made to give Ireland Home
Rule. Gladstone, the British Prime Minister, was defeated in his attempts
of 1886 and 1893. The 1912 Bill was shelved because of the outbreak of the
Great War, 1914–18. The 'resolution' in 1920/21 was to partition Ireland.
During the first three Bills, Irish Churches played a political role.

(a) The Catholic Church

Prior to the 1880s the Catholic Church 'had found the United Kingdom a
reasonable context in which to advance the best interests of its people, and
even regarded the British empire as a wider world rife for the spread of the
Catholic faith'.[7] By the beginning of the Home Rule era there was a dis-
like for British rule, though in no way would the Catholic Church support
the use of force to replace it. Catholic clergy attended county conventions
to select election candidates for Parnell's Irish Parliamentary Party. Each of
the thirty-two conventions held in connection with the 1885 election was
attended by an average of fifty priests.[8]

In 1886, as the first Home Rule Bill emerged, four Irish Catholic Arch-
bishops met in Dublin to prepare for a forthcoming national synod. They
came out in favour of Home Rule, stating that it alone 'can satisfy the
wants and needs of the Irish people'. George Boyce has described this
stance as 'the high water mark of clerical influence in the party'.[9] Their
statement not only identified the Catholic Church with the nationalist
cause, it also identified Catholicism with Irishness.

By 1890 Home Rule politics were dominated by Parnell's relationship
with Kitty O'Shea. Cardinal Logue did not have much time for Parnell
and publicly declared that 'a man having the destinies of a people in his
hands and bartering it away for the company of an old woman is certainly

not a person to beget confidence'.[10] All the Northern bishops signed the Hierarchy's address against Parnell. Meanwhile the Catholic Church was concerned about the effect of Home Rule on its role in education and in 1893 Logue wrote to Rome expressing the view that the 1893 Bill was 'not satisfactory to Catholic interests'. He believed that 'the bill will not pass and the bishops should avoid the odium of defeating it'.[11]

The reunified Irish Parliamentary Party under John Redmond was blessed by the future Cardinal, Bishop O'Donnell. He, in fact, acted as treasurer of the Parliamentary Party Fund. In 1905 the entire Hierarchy encouraged Catholics to support the Fund. Bishop McHugh, consecrated Bishop of Derry in 1907, put pressure on the Irish Parliamentary Party 'for a more aggressive campaign on Home Rule'.[12]

However, events such as the papal decree Ne Temere of 1908 convinced unionists that Home Rule would result in Catholic domination. Ne Temere confirmed the teaching of the Council of Trent that marriages must be celebrated before a Catholic priest and that children must be brought up as Catholics. Though universally applied, the decree, in the Irish context, confirmed the unionist fear of Home Rule leading to Rome Rule. The political role of the Catholic Church in the Home Rule campaign became increasingly overshadowed by the equation. By the time of the third Bill in 1912 unionists were prepared to use force and violence to defeat it and had a provisional government in the wings. On 6 December 1912 Cardinal Logue wrote to Bishop O'Donnell of Raphoe that 'as far as the Church's interests were concerned it might be best to continue to live under an Imperial than a Home Rule parliament'.[13] Catholic leaders feared that a compromise with unionists in the North would lead to dominance and oppression of Catholics, and that the Orangemen would interfere with Catholic education.

(b) The Protestant Churches

Each of the three larger Protestant Churches was strongly opposed to Home Rule. Protestant prosperity, rights and religion were bound up with the Union, and any attempt to dissolve the Union and give Ireland its own legislature, even a domestic one, was perceived as a grave risk to Protestant identity, prosperity, freedom and religion.

Evangelicalism was particularly strong in Irish Protestant denominations during the nineteenth century. It was also anti-Catholic, and the Home Rule era not only saw the development of unionism, it also gave Protestant Churches a sense of unity which obscured real differences between them.

A Methodist editorial in 1886 identified the Crown rights of England with the Crown rights of Christ: 'The interests threatened in Ireland touch the very heart of the Kingdom of God. Home Rule for Ireland means not only war against the Crown rights of England, but war against the Crown rights of Christ.'[14]

Early in 1886 a manifesto of the Presbyterian Church pledged total opposition to the demands of the Catholic Hierarchy for educational representation and control, which Presbyterians viewed as tantamount to political and religious ascendancy. The Pastoral of the Church of Ireland Bishop of Down, Connor and Dromore saw Home Rule as increasing wicked agitation and other evils including the dismemberment of the Empire and the persecution of the Anglican Church.[15] Anti-Home Rule resolutions were carried by Presbyterian Presbyteries, Diocesan Synods of the Church of Ireland, Methodist District Committees and a petition from the Moravian Church in Ireland.

In the 1890s Irish Methodist clergy were heavily involved on party political platforms in Britain and Ireland. This led to bitterness between ministers and members of the Irish and British Conferences, but the Irish Conference never commented on its clerical politicians.

Early in 1893 the Ulster Convention League held a large Unionist demonstration in the Ulster Hall, Belfast. Church of Ireland, Presbyterian and Methodist clergy spoke in support of the determined opposition to Home Rule.

A special General Synod and a General Assembly were called. The General Synod met on 14 March 1893 and the Government Committee of the Presbyterian Church requested the Moderator to call a meeting of the General Assembly on the basis that 'our civil and religious liberties are menaced'.

Within two weeks the Assembly met in May Street Church, Belfast, and a series of resolutions were moved expressing determination to resist every attempt to destroy the Legislative Union. The Primate at the General Synod meeting in Dublin expressed the view that the Bill should be called 'a Bill to suppress the Protestant faith'. It would harm almost every aspect of life and would set up a Roman Catholic ascendancy. The Archbishop of Dublin thought that the Irish grievances to which Home Rule was a response were an intolerable sham. The Bishop of Derry believed that the protest voice against Home Rule was that of the Episcopalians, Orangemen, the voice of about 550,000 Presbyterians and other forms of Protestantism.[16]

Resolutions against Home Rule were passed by the Quakers, Congregationalists, Evangelical Alliance and the YMCA.

The third Home Rule Bill was introduced in 1912 and this time unionist and Protestant Churches responses were more organised than

before. The crisis produced the Ulster Covenant, a politico-religious document, based on an earlier Scottish Solemn League and Covenant. The
Covenant was drafted by a leading Presbyterian elder, Thomas Sinclair,
and submitted to the Protestant Churches for approval.

Prior to Covenant Day the Methodist Church held a Convention on 14
March in the Ulster Hall. The Presbyterians had held a similar Convention
in February. Special trains ran from all over Ulster and Methodists
attended from every Irish Methodist Circuit. Strong speeches were made
against Home Rule and Methodist Home Rulers were verbally dismissed.
The Ulster Unionist Council, the Loyal Orange Institution and the
Unionist Clubs of Ireland made arrangements for Ulster Day on Saturday,
28 September 1912. Solemn religious services were held at 11.00 a.m.,
followed by the signing of the Covenant.

The Protestant Churches had blessed and approved the Covenant text
with its pledge to 'using all means which may be found necessary to defeat
the present conspiracy'. The sentence implied violence and military dril-
ling and negotiations for arms were already under way.

At the religious service in the Ulster Hall, James Craig asked that there
be no applause because it was a religious service.

> The packed congregation sang 'O God our help in ages past'
> and after prayers and lessons had been read, the former
> Presbyterian Moderator, Dr William McKean, rose to
> deliver his sermon, taking as his text 1 Timothy 6:20: 'Keep
> that which is committed to thy trust.'[17]

Later in Belfast City Hall the Covenant was signed, first by Sir Edward
Carson. Among the first seven signatories were the Church of Ireland
Bishop of Down, the Presbyterian Moderator and the President of the
Methodist Church in Ireland. The Bishop had earlier spoken in St Anne's
Cathedral of 'patriotic devotion' and the Moderator told his congregation
in the Assembly Hall that Home Rule beyond doubt would create a
Roman Catholic ascendancy. In Ballynafeigh Methodist Church a former
Methodist President, the Rev. Wesley Guard, saw the issue as 'a momen-
tous crisis in the history, not only of Ireland, but the United Kingdom'.
The God who had delivered their ancestors would do so again.

3. CONTEMPORARY RESPONSES

Irish Churches have never been politically neutral, but politically
involved, often in a partisan and sectarian way. However, as a peace process is developed Churches must develop new ways of exercising a prophetic ministry which will need to be critical and political. This will

require the development of political theology which will mean the relating of faith values and insights to political realities. What the Churches
have often expressed in the past has been politicised theology which has
tended to be a 'God on our side' theology, which is a civil religion. Political theology will be critical of all political ideologies and will envision
inclusive community and inclusive structures. It may not provide a political blueprint for Northern Ireland or Ireland, but it will provide a moral
framework on which just and peaceful community structures and relationships can be built. The Churches in the political arena can facilitate the
release of social and political imagination without which social and political policies will be sterile and ineffective. There are some hopeful signs of a
new model of religion and politics.

(a) An Inter-Church Group on Faith and Politics

This Group has been born out of the post-1969 events. 'It represents by far
the most hopeful dialogue since the Troubles broke out.'[18]
  The initiative followed the 1983 Greenhills Ecumenical Conference
which called for a Christian Centre for Political Development to analyse
the relationship of Churches to politics in Ireland. The scheme proved too
ambitious, but the steering committee evolved into the present Group.
  Since 1985 a number of significant documents have been produced.

- *Breaking Down the Enmity* (1985)
- *Understanding the Signs of the Times* (1986)
- *Towards an Island that Works* (1987)
- *Towards Peace and Stability: A Critical Assessment of the Anglo-Irish Agreement* (1988)
- *Remembering our Past: 1690 and 1916* (1991)
- *Burying our Dead: Political Funerals in Northern Ireland* (1992)
- *The Things that Make for Peace* (1995)
- *Liberty to the Captives* (1995)
- *Forgive us our Trespasses . . . ?* (1996)
- *Doing unto Others* (1997)

(The earlier documents [1985–92] are now included in one publication,
Breaking Down the Enmity.)
  Though it was not initiated by the Group, some members were
involved in drafting *A Declaration of Faith and Commitment* (1986). The
Declaration, published almost three months after a Unionist Day of
Action in 1986 related to the Anglo-Irish Agreement, asserted that Catho-
lics and Protestants in Northern Ireland were called to put their allegiance
to Christ above all else. This was a recall to the priority of the lordship of

Christ over political commitment.

The underlying philosophy of all these documents is the serious attempt to apply Christian principles to the political sphere. In the conclusion to *Towards an Island that Works* it is stated that 'there is a need for Christians to show that they are willing to make sacrifices for the sake of reconciliation and justice'.[19]

The Group's critical assessment of the Anglo-Irish Agreement asks the Catholic Church to take more seriously the deep-seated distrust among Protestants of Catholic ecclesiastical power. It also asks the Protestant Churches to examine honestly their anti-Catholic bias and to show some understanding of the sense of grievance and injustice of many Catholics. In mapping out approaches to the Northern Ireland problem ten realities and criteria are set out. These include the reality that neither community in Northern Ireland can be coerced or dominated and therefore each should be given parity of esteem and treatment. Later the politics of reconciliation is described as the only realistic and responsible politics in Northern Ireland.[20]

The documents produced between 1995 and 1997 highlighted the new opportunities and context following the paramilitary ceasefires of 1994. They deal with the sensitive issues of forgiveness, dialogue, parity of esteem and sovereignty, and go on to explore the key issues of weaponry, policing and security, and prisoners.

In a section in *The Things that Make for Peace* dealing with the Churches there is the call for the Churches to acknowledge their part in the conflict and to recognise how as institutions they have contributed to community division and sectarianism. There is need too for long-term healing of relationships within and between the two islands. God is affirmed as 'the God of hope, who, again and again, can break into our lives and communities, can disturb our complacency, undermine our unjust structures and help transform our views of one another'.[21]

Two important affirmations sum up the objectives of this Group:

> Christian faith does not, however, suggest that there is or should be a uniformity of political positions for Christians.
> A proper Christian concern is going to have at its heart the development of new and just relationships between communities.[22]

The core objective is to see how Christian faith is to inform politics in Northern Ireland.

(b) Evangelical Contribution on Northern Ireland (ECONI)

ECONI brings together a diverse group of evangelicals in Northern Ireland. The organisation, founded in 1987, is by no means inclusive of all evangelicals, but nevertheless involves a significant group.

Given the evangelical emphasis on Scripture as the Word of God, ECONI seeks to identify biblical principles pertinent to a Christian response to the conflictual situation. It describes itself as 'a single issue movement. The issue in question is the role of evangelical Christians in our divided community – a single issue, but perhaps the most important one facing us as Christian people in Northern Ireland.'[23] The goal is defined as testing all ideologies by Scripture and ordering life by its teaching.

ECONI does not believe that this has always happened. Indeed one view is highlighted which it believes is in direct opposition to its position. The view is a kind of religious nationalism, summed up in the phrase 'For God and Ulster'.[24]

ECONI believes that it is wrong to claim that any one country is uniquely special to God, and that there is no biblical basis for claiming that any one nation has a privileged position before God. It believes Scripture is clear:

> The people of God are not to be identified with any religious community, not even the Protestant people of Ulster; the people of God are not to be identified with any national group; the land of Northern Ireland is not uniquely special to God. The people of God are those who have faith in Jesus Christ. The people of God transcend the identity of religious communities and denominations. No nation can claim God's special favour.[25]

In keeping with the strong biblical emphasis, ECONI has published an Action Pack series exploring such key words as reconciliation, peace, citizenship, justice and righteousness.

Another significant publication is *Beyond Fear, Suspicion and Hostility*. This booklet explores evangelical–Roman Catholic relationships and while it does not directly address the resolution of different national and political identities, it does take seriously the traditional and often bitter division between evangelicals and Catholics. It challenges the merging of an extreme religious and extreme political view, i.e. the Protestant, often evangelical view, that Irish nationalism and the Irish state are simply instruments of Rome, and that the constitutional or terrorist attack on Northern Ireland is an attack on Protestantism and the true gospel.[26]

ECONI, like the Inter-Church Group on Faith and Politics, is a response to the Troubles. It represents evangelicals attempting to break out of un-biblical, anti-Catholic, traditional evangelical rhetoric and asserts the role of evangelical Christians from a biblical perspective within a divided com-munity. Such a role cannot be politically neutral and as ECONI seeks to make a faith response to citizenship and living together in community, it is beginning to develop a political theology.

(c) The Irish Inter-Church Meeting

In 1987 Archbishop Robin Eames and the late Cardinal Tomás Ó Fiaich suggested that the Churches needed to examine more closely the lethal toxin of sectarianism. A working party was set up and in 1993 it presented its report.[27]

The document is a significant piece of work by the institutional Churches rather than a group of individual church members. It is also sig-nificant in that it not only addressed theological issues in sectarianism, and division and reconciliation, it also tackled structural issues in Northern Ireland and issues relating to the Republic of Ireland. There was recogni-tion that organisations and institutions can sustain and perpetuate sectar-ianism, both directly and indirectly.

The final chapter on 'Ways Forward and Recommendations' returned to the structural issues. Again there was recognition that 'sectarianism gains its peculiar virulence because it involves not only religion, but religion combined with a tangle of other factors – for example, culture, politics, economics and national identity'.[28] So, the Northern Ireland problem contains the central constitutional problem, social and economic inequal-ities, cultural differences, security and human rights problems and religious difference. The chapter went on to address the issues under twelve differ-ent headings.

A specific action recommended to the Churches was to refuse to use politics or the state to sustain religious identity. A further recommendation was to hear and acknowledge the fears and hurts of the other tradition. The adverse role of Churches in politics was acknowledged with the call for Churches to 'seek as far as possible to remove, or at least mitigate, some of the adverse social consequences of theological or doctrinal differences [e.g. over mixed marriages or attitudes to the Roman Catholic Church]'.[29]

On the more explicit political recommendations there was the call for a Bill of Rights for Northern Ireland to give explicit recognition in the con-stitutional and legal system to respect for basic human rights and freedoms. Discrimination on grounds of religion was declared abhorrent and equal-ity of opportunity everyone's entitlement.

Published with the document was *Roots of Sectarianism in Ireland*, which was an overview of the historical development of Irish sectarianism. The timescale for reflection ranges from the twelfth century to 1921. It shows the interaction between historical events, political forces and religious identity. It contains a quotation from political scientist Frank Wright that 'nationalisms are not merely "like" religions – they are religions'.[30] It is this inseparable identity of religious nationalism and nationalist religion, belonging to both traditional nationalism and unionism, that calls not only for an awareness of sectarian roots, but also for a theological critique of all politicised religion. Perhaps the work of the Irish Inter-Church Meeting will move the Churches towards not only a new model of political theology, but a new model of engagement between Church and politics.

(d) Other Church Responses

Communities such as Corrymeela, Cornerstone and the Redemptorists at Clonard have, over the years, helped Churches relate faith to the hard questions of Northern Irish politics. Their engagement has been not merely theoretic but concrete and practical. Some of these reconciliation groups are dealt with in Chapter 27 by John Morrow.

Youth Link:NI is an initiative of the four larger Churches in Northern Ireland and has developed a particular approach to training and empowering youth workers and young adults for cross-community work. The methodology takes seriously the core issues at the heart of community division: religion, history, cultural traditions and politics.

Brian Lennon, a Catholic, has written *After the Ceasefires: Catholics and the Future of Northern Ireland*. Timothy Kinahan, from the Church of Ireland, followed with a companion volume, *Where Do We Go from Here?: Protestants and the Future of Northern Ireland*. Each has sought to challenge his community to face hard political and community issues in the light of biblical perspectives.

Lennon reflects on two main scriptural themes:

- the call that the Christian God makes to all people to enter into relationships with each other (reconciliation)
- the conflict there is in Christ's life as he opposed those who oppressed the poor (justice)

Kinahan argues from the basis of Scripture that political models (i.e. republicanism, nationalism, unionism) should take second place to the biblical imperative for reconciliation between all the peoples on the island of Ireland. He also challenges many of the certainties that have dominated Northern Irish Protestantism for a long time.

The Inter-Church Relations Committee of the Methodist Church in Ireland has published a series of Bible Studies, *Biblical Perspectives on the Peace Process*. The studies seek to engage an approach to Scripture which takes seriously its social and political context interacting with the contemporary social and political context. One study explores a Christian understanding of political power.

The Presbyterian Church and Government Committee has published *Presbyterian Principles and Political Witness Today in Northern Ireland*. It explores biblical and theological principles and ethical guidelines, applying them to a range of pertinent political issues.

Both Cardinal Daly and Archbishop Eames have published books analysing the community problem and applying Christian insights. Cardinal Daly writes of the political cost of peace, the destructiveness of republican violence in relation to justice, the sectarian factor in loyalism and the search for peace through social justice. Prison and security policies are addressed as is the ecumenical imperative for reconciliation. Archbishop Eames explores the far-reaching effects of sectarianism and interprets the Protestant and unionist psyche. He asserts that everyone has responsibility for a new political future and calls for a new vision that will touch every aspect of community living. The former Presbyterian Moderator John Dunlop has written on Presbyterians and the conflict in Ireland. He explores the identity of modern Irish Presbyterianism, argues against the siege mentality and maintains that the paramount need of the present is for a wider social justice and freedom for all – regardless of denomination.[31]

The Department of Theological Questions of the Irish Inter-Church Meeting has published a reflective report on the ingredients of true peace which examines the biblical and theological aspects of commitment to the values of freedom, justice and responsibility. The economic, political and religious challenges facing Irish society, north and south, are explored, as is the role of the Churches in the areas of ongoing conflict and emerging pluralism. The question is raised as to the feasibility of a public, ecclesiastical confession of sorrow and guilt with respect to the Churches' involvement in the Northern Ireland situation.[32]

The journey continues in Northern Ireland to develop a political theology which recognises that politics and faith cannot be separated, but inescapably belong together. Its role will be critical, especially of civil religion, and it will awaken the political awareness of Christian theology and spirituality. It will give an understanding of faith and church that is public, critical and prophetic.

This critical approach is necessary for the integrity and credibility of Irish Churches. Historically, the Churches have given expression and legitimacy to sectarian politics. A new future calls for repentance. The past needs to be named and owned. But repentance also means turning around to travel in a new direction. Political neutrality is not an option for Irish Churches. From central structures to the local parishes and congregations on the ground, the politics of peace, reconciliation and community reconstruction are major Christian concerns and responsibilities. The faith and the Church are public, critical and prophetic, or they are nothing in the Ireland of the twenty-first century.

NOTES

1. Emilio Castro, *When We Pray Together* (Geneva: Risk Book Series 1989), p. 80.
2. Ibid. p. 81.
3. Colm Lennon, *Sixteenth-Century Ireland: The Incomplete Conquest* (Dublin: Gill & Macmillan 1994), p. 134.
4. Journal, quoted in Jonathan Bardon, *A History of Ulster* (Belfast: Blackstaff Press 1992), p. 217.
5. Ibid. p. 217.
6. David Hempton, *'For God and Ulster': Evangelical Protestantism and the Home Rule Crisis of 1886* (Belfast: Queen's University Papers n.d.), p. 235.
7. George Boyce, *Nineteenth-Century Ireland: The Search for Stability* (Dublin: Gill & Macmillan 1990), p. 174.
8. George Boyce, *Nationalism in Ireland* (London: Routledge 1991, 2nd edn.), p. 218.
9. Ibid. p. 219.
10. Oliver P. Rafferty, *Catholicism in Ulster 1603–1983* (Dublin, Gill & Macmillan 1994), p. 168.
11. Ibid. p. 169.
12. Ibid. p. 188.
13. Ibid. p. 190.
14. *The Irish Christian Advocate*, 8 January 1886.
15. Ibid. 15 January 1886
16. Ibid. 17 March 1893
17. Bardon, *History of Ulster*, p. 437.
18. An Inter-Church Group on Faith and Politics, *Breaking Down the Enmity: Faith and Politics in the Northern Ireland Conflict* (Belfast 1993), p. 5.
19. Ibid. p. 107.
20. Ibid. pp. 136–9.
21. An Inter-Church Group on Faith and Politics, *The Things that Make for Peace* (Belfast 1995), p. 5.
22. An Inter-Church Group on Faith and Politics, *Breaking Down the Enmity*, p. 22.
23. Alwyn Thomson, *The Fractured Family* (Belfast: ECONI 1995), p. 20.
24. Ibid. p. 23. (See also the ECONI publication *Faith in Ulster* [1996], which brings together fifty personal responses to the question 'What does *For God and Ulster* mean to you?'.)
25. Ibid. p. 27.
26. Alwyn Thomson, *Beyond Fear, Suspicion and Hostility* (Belfast: ECONI 1995), p. 7.

27. Irish Inter-Church Meeting, *Sectarianism: A Discussion Document* (Belfast 1993).
28. Ibid. p. 99.
29. Ibid. p. 101.
30. Joseph Liechty, *Roots of Sectarianism in Ireland* (Belfast 1993), p. 42. (The Wright quotation is from Alan D. Falconer (ed.), *Reconciling Memories* (Blackrock, Co. Dublin 1988), p. 75.)
31. Cahal B. Daly, *The Price of Peace* (Belfast: Blackstaff Press 1991); Cahal B. Daly, *Peace, Now Is the Time* (Dublin: Veritas Publications 1993); Robin Eames, *Chains to be Broken* (Belfast: Blackstaff Press 1995); John Dunlop, *A Precarious Belonging: Presbyterians and the Conflict in Ireland* (Belfast: Blackstaff Press 1995).
32. Department of Theological Questions of the Irish Inter-Church Meeting, *Freedom, Justice and Responsibility in Ireland Today* (Dublin 1997).

BIOGRAPHICAL NOTE

JOHNSTON McMASTER is a native of Portavogie in the Ards Peninsula, Co. Down. As a Methodist minister he has worked on Methodist Circuits in west Cork, Wicklow and north Belfast. Following eight years as General Secretary of the Irish Methodist Youth Department, he worked with Youth Link:NI, the inter-church youth service agency with responsibility for developing cross-community work. In 1997 he joined the staff of the Irish School of Ecumenics as Lecturer in Ecumenical Theology and Co-ordinator of the Northern Ireland Adult Education Programme. He is also co-convener of the Inter-Church Relations Committee of the Methodist Church in Ireland.

30

Religion,
Sectarianism and Community Relations

JOSEPH LIECHTY

INTRODUCTION

The language of sectarianism – sectarian murder, sectarian employment policies, sectarian attitudes, sectarian politics, sectarian division, sectarian marches – is frequently heard in Northern Ireland. However, on closer examination the concept of sectarianism seems to live separate public and private lives: it is frequently used in journalism and academic circles to describe aspects of public life in Northern Ireland, and yet sectarianism is so emotive and potentially explosive a topic, and so frequently thought of as a term of judgemental abuse, that it is little discussed in private conversations. Sectarianism truly is a difficult topic, and nothing is likely to change that. However, some careful thought about where sectarianism comes from and how it works can allow us to talk fruitfully if not easily about sectarianism, and about how it can be overcome. This essay will give a definition, look at historical roots, develop some ideas about how sectarianism works, and suggest some signs of hope.

DEFINING SECTARIANISM

While many dictionaries offer a definition of sectarianism, none does justice to the nuanced, many-layered character of Irish usage. Fortunately, since the start of the Troubles a few groups and individuals in Northern Ireland have developed definitions more appropriate to this context. From these and from our own experience and reflections, Cecelia Clegg and I, co-workers on the *Moving Beyond Sectarianism* project, have put together a working definition to guide our research:

> *Sectarianism is a complex of attitudes, beliefs, actions, and structures –*
> *at personal, communal and institutional levels – which involve*
> *religion as a significant component, which arise as subversions of*
> *natural and positive human needs for belonging, identity and the free*
> *expression of difference, and which consequently influence or cause*
> *destructive conflict by:*
>
> *– negatively reinforcing the boundaries between myself or my*
> *   community and others*
> *– belittling or demonising others*
> *– overlooking others, or*
> *– justifying or enabling the domination of others.*

With this definition in mind, let us take a look at the historical roots of sectarianism, which will prepare us to consider in more detail facets of sectarianism implicit in this definition.

HISTORICAL ROOTS OF SECTARIANISM

The historical roots of sectarianism in Ireland can be traced back to the Reformation era of the 1500s and 1600s. In this period the state-established Church of Ireland, the Catholic Church and eventually the Presbyterian Church were each closely linked with a particular political option, and these were locked in a bitter struggle for ascendancy or even survival. In this age the Churches shared a combination of three doctrines which fostered sectarian attitudes and actions:

> one true church, outside of which is no salvation;
> error has no right;
> and providence.

One true church is largely self-explanatory – our church is the only true church, and if you are outside it, your chances of salvation are much diminished, at best. *Error has no right* is less well known. This doctrine was developed by St Augustine in the fourth and fifth centuries to justify the use of state coercion to suppress his heretical opponents: because they are radically in error, they have no right to express or hold their beliefs. Ever since, the doctrine has been put to similar use as the principle behind every use of coercion, especially state coercion, for religious purposes. Error has no right is the doctrine behind penal laws, inquisitions, forced conversions and similar episodes in Christian history. The doctrine of *providence* is the simple, basic teaching that God is at work in the world, and beyond that, the belief that a faithful Christian observer of the world can discern God's will and purpose by reading the signs of the times in human events and the natural world.

Specifically, the origin of sectarianism lies in two combinations of these three doctrines. The first combination is *one true church* with *error has no right*. One true church is a truth claim, and like every truth claim it automatically carries with it the danger of arrogance and imposition. But these are only dangers, not necessary outcomes – everything depends on how the truth claim is made, and if made consciously and humbly, it does not have to impose on others. However, if you believe that error has no right, then the chances are your truth claim will be made disastrously, because if your church is the one true church *and* error has no right, then it is your duty to see that error is suppressed by whatever means necessary. From this viewpoint tolerance is no virtue – tolerance is a deadly vice. In terms of our definition of sectarianism, note that this combination of doctrines operates by demonising enemies and justifying their domination. 'Liberty of conscience . . . is the worst thing in the world,' grumbled Pope Clement VIII around the year 1598. At that time Pope Clement's viewpoint was by no means peculiarly Catholic; it was widely shared by pious, zealous leaders, whether Protestants or Catholics, in Church and state. The whole idea of religious toleration was only slowly coming to be accepted, and at first acceptance was mostly a matter of pragmatic, weary bowing to ugly, pluralist reality – no matter how we try, we cannot seem to beat our enemies, so we will have to find a way to live with them. It took hundreds of years for the idea of toleration to be widely embraced as a positive principle.

The other doctrinal combination behind sectarianism begins with *one true church* and *providence*. Again, providence simply teaches that God is at work in the world, which is not necessarily a problematic doctrine. However, if providence is interpreted in light of one true church, it is very easily reduced to 'God is on our side'. Then, if we bring in *error has no right* again, God is on our side is likely to mean, 'God wants us to suppress others'. The disastrous consequences are obvious, as can be observed from episodes in Irish history and elsewhere. Note that in terms of sectarianism, this combination of doctrines leads once again to demonising and dominating.

Several key points about sectarianism follow from these doctrines and combinations. First, these doctrines are much more than intellectual propositions about Christian faith. For the 1500s and 1600s, we might do better to think of these not as mere doctrines but as elements of worldview – these were categories in which people thought, a mental framework, standard assumptions about how the world worked. As such, these doctrines deeply shaped Christian identity.

Second, these doctrines were shared by the three main Churches in Ireland, first Catholic and Church of Ireland and later Presbyterian. They are not doctrines that emerge from small fringe groups. Thus sectarianism is rooted in the Irish mainstream, not in the margins.

Third, these doctrines were not obscure teachings from musty, neglected confessions of faith, they were actively affirmed. They come from the centre of mainstream Christian teaching, not from the fringe.

Fourth, taken together these conclusions about the roots of sectarianism mean that each of the three main Churches was historically either an established church or an establishment in waiting. Given the disproportionate share of power the Church of Ireland held in its traditional role as the Established Church until 1870, it was all but inevitable that the Church of Ireland would be responsible for a disproportionate share of actions with sectarian implications. This hard fact should not be dodged, but at the same time let us be clear that this is a question of power, not of principle – there is little reason to think Catholics or Presbyterians would have behaved any better as an establishment, because they were animated by the same principles. The Jesuit scholar Fergus O'Donoghue pithily summarises the attitude of *all* governments, whether Catholic or Protestant, in the post-Reformation era: 'When practicable, persecute.'[1]

THE NATURE OF SECTARIANISM

With this quick sketch of historical roots in hand, let us turn to consider the nature of sectarianism as it works today.

(1) First a general point: *sectarianism is the Irish version of a universal problem.* For example, in our definition substitute 'racism' for 'sectarianism' and 'race' for 'religion' and we have a workable definition of racism. In other conflict settings, this definition might work for ethnocentrism or nationalism – dividing, demonising, overlooking and dominating are everywhere the mechanisms by which such conflicts operate – and indeed probably every society involves some version of such dynamics. To understand sectarianism we will need always to keep one eye on universal aspects of the problem and the other on the local and particular.

(2) *Sectarianism is a complex of attitudes, beliefs, actions and structures – at personal, communal and institutional levels.* Some interpreters of sectarianism have erred in viewing sectarianism as primarily a matter of personal attitudes, others have seen sectarianism as a primarily social or political issue. This definition attempts to hold both ends of the continuum together.

(3) To identify something as sectarian, it must *involve religion as a significant component.* This religious component may be upfront and obvious or it may be well in the background. Religion may, for example, figure somewhere in the historical background to what may now seem a

narrowly political problem, or religion may be present in the form of
a denominational outcome to an essentially political process. But
religion must be present in some way, or the label of 'sectarian' would
make little sense, and it would probably be more accurate to use other
terms, like bigotry or discrimination, instead of sectarianism. It may
be useful to think of sectarianism as a continuum, one end more
political, the other more religious, but involving some element of
religion at all points.

In Northern Ireland today, religion contributes most significantly
to sectarianism by acting as a key element in reinforcing the
boundaries between rival groups. Elements of division include, first
of all, *church life and religious practice*, which are almost by definition
segregated. Note that this radical division in church life is not
accidental, it is the way the Churches have wanted it. Until the 1960s
it was a mortal sin for a Catholic to worship in a Protestant church;
some Protestant Churches have had a reciprocal doctrine, and in any
case most Protestants seem to have operated in a reciprocal spirit. And
this is not a case of authoritarian church hierarchies foisting divisive
doctrines on the tolerant laity. A Catholic priest, for example, recalls
his childhood in rural Co. Mayo where there were no Protestants.
Visiting cousins in the town of Louisburgh and itching with
curiosity, he tried to persuade them to go with him into a Church of
Ireland church to see what it was like. They warned him, however,
that even to set foot in a Protestant church would be a mortal sin. In
fact merely going into a Protestant church was not a problem, it was
worshipping with Protestants that was a mortal sin, but folk
consciousness had taken the theological prohibition and extended it,
turning it into something approaching a superstition.

Marriage and family life is a second element of division, almost totally
segregated on a religious basis and for deliberate religious reasons.
Education is also segregated on a religious basis, and again because the
Churches have actively sought it for explicitly religious reasons, or
they have happily acquiesced in it. *Housing* too is increasingly
segregated on a religious basis. This is primarily the accidental effect of
almost three decades of violence, but no less important because it is an
accident. So here we have religious practice, marriage and family,
education and housing: the most fundamental elements of
socialisation, and all of them are polarised along religious, sectarian
lines. These are essential structures that socialise people into much that
is very, very good, helping to instil strong values and build strong
families and communities. And yet these religiously divided
structures also socialise people into conflict and into sectarianism.

(4) Elements of sectarianism *arise as subversions of natural and positive human needs for belonging, identity and the free expression of difference.* Social boundaries between groups, for example, are not only good, they are absolutely necessary for cohesion, for socialisation, for a sense of belonging, for personal and communal identity. People who talk as if boundaries were themselves the problem, and we could somehow do without them, are radically mistaken. And yet once sectarian attitudes, beliefs, actions and structures are in place, it is social boundaries which become the chief engine for perpetuating sectarianism, because we subvert the positive role of boundaries and use them to exclude others and foster stereotypes. Therefore we cannot solve our problems by dissolving boundaries, but only by learning new and constructive ways of dealing with boundaries – the ones around ourselves and the ones we approach around others.

As with belonging and identity, so with *the free expression of difference.* Difference so easily leads to conflict that we sometimes act as if difference, in and of itself, is the problem, and unity or reconciliation must mean dissolving difference. But no such thing is possible or desirable. Difference is fundamental to being human, and however problematic difference may be when dealt with in certain ways, we can only solve the problems by learning better ways of dealing with difference, not by suppressing or denying difference.

(5) To be identified as sectarian, an attitude, belief, action or structure must *influence or cause destructive conflict.* In other words, when making judgements about sectarianism, it is important to consider consequences.

Confronted with the idea that something in which they are involved may be sectarian, people turn immediately to their intentions. The autumn 1995 referendum on divorce in the Republic of Ireland provided some striking examples. That autumn, as part of a day-long workshop on sectarianism, we pointed out the possible sectarian implications of voting against allowing divorce. The immediate response of some of the anti-divorce activists was revealing: 'We have no sectarian intent, we simply believe that allowing divorce will be destructive of the social good.' That is entirely respectable logic, and it is important that intentions are not sectarian – but it is not the whole story. Given the historical divisions in Ireland, a 'no' vote in the overwhelmingly Catholic Republic of Ireland was likely to confirm Northern Protestant stereotypes of the Catholic-dominated South, thereby deepening sectarian division, confirming fear of potential sectarian domination, and, if not actually causing conflict, at least making its resolution more difficult. In other words, a 'no' vote could have sectarian consequences or implications quite apart from the intentions of those who voted 'no'. Perhaps people could morally justify voting 'no' despite sectarian implications, on the grounds of the lesser of two evils, but it was at least important for them to recognise that despite their good intentions, their actions might have sectarian consequences.

A second example. In the autumn of 1994 Patrick Mayhew, then Secretary of State for Northern Ireland, made public remarks regretting the Orange Order's insistence on marching despite occasions of accompanying violence. The Order's response? We have no intention of causing violence. That is good and important, but it is not the whole story – if sectarian mayhem is the outcome of our actions, we must take this into account, whatever about the purity of our intentions.

Another reason for emphasising consequences is pastoral: how do we approach the problem of sectarianism? Intentions are very, very difficult to address. We all have a great capacity for self-deception, in fact almost certainly greater than we can ever know by ourselves. The same less than pure intentions we fail to see in ourselves, however, we can identify quite clearly in others; but if we accuse someone of having sectarian intentions, a sectarian heart, we are quite likely to have our charges received quite defensively and thrown right back at us. After all, how many people understand themselves to be sectarian? I still have not met anyone. The things we identify in others as sectarianism, they understand instead as defending the truth, standing up for a tradition, protecting community bonds, and so on. That is how we understand what we are doing, and it takes a very high level of personal awareness to understand a thought, a feeling, an impulse as sectarian. We experience these things personally as anger, fear, self-protection, solidarity; that they might also be sectarian is an interpretation we put on them – or more likely that others put on them for us.

Most often awareness of our own sectarian intentions will come only after we have confronted sectarian consequences. Alcoholism is a useful analogy. Denial is a fundamental element of alcoholism: 'I may drink too much occasionally, but I do not have a real problem; I can handle the amount I drink; my drinking does not hurt me or anyone else.' People do not finally come to terms with alcoholism until they are presented with undeniable evidence of the consequences of their actions – a personal breakdown, family breakdown, business breakdown, or whatever. Sectarianism works in a similar way. When we finally confront the sectarian consequences of our actions, only then do we take an honest look inside, and we may discover there problems that we just could not have seen in any other way. When we acknowledge the sectarian consequences of our actions, we may come to see that our intentions were not so pure as we once thought.

Being a member of an inter-church working party on sectarianism from 1991 to 1993 was most instructive in this regard. As a group of people involved in various forms of anti-sectarian work, we faced a continual temptation to regard ourselves as having transcended all these problems, so that we could somehow stand outside the problem and tell those still caught in the sectarianism trap how to get out of it. But I was continually impressed with how rarely Working Party members fell for this temptation. The Working Party often had the feeling of being a recovery group, a group of recovering sectarians. Members did not distance themselves from sectarianism. They recognised that they had been shaped by it, and in our work together, gut responses to certain issues, certain phrases, certain memories, certain experiences, suggested that sectarianism was not something from which we could ever fully separate ourselves. The way members worked at coming to terms with sectarianism was a profound model of dealing with both consequences and intentions, the outward and the inward, and seemed to carry this conclusion: healing from sectarianism is possible, but total distancing from the problem is not. To switch analogies, healing from sectarianism may be less like recovering from a broken leg, in which we are healed once and for all and then return to our usual ways, and more like recovering from heart disease, in which we can expect to lead full and normal lives, but only if we continually attend to living in a new way – if we neglect this and fall into old habits, back the disease comes again.

(6) Finally, sectarianism operates by *dividing (negatively reinforcing boundaries), demonising, overlooking and dominating*. Examples of dividing, demonising, and dominating have been scattered through this text, but none thus far of overlooking, which is one of the more subtle ways sectarianism works. The clearest examples might be the way many Irish Catholics sometimes use the phrase 'the Irish people' and Northern Protestants 'the Ulster people'. Both phrases are superficially inclusive, but they can be used in such a way that they are radically exclusive, overlooking as if they were not there the viewpoints and wishes of the vast majority of Irish Protestants or Northern Catholics, as the case may be.

SIGNS OF HOPE

If sectarianism sometimes seems to be endlessly adaptable and persistent, there are reasons for hope, in fact many more reasons than can be explored here. Taking the long view on just one fundamental issue, however, it is striking that the combination of doctrines from which sectarianism emerged, especially *one true church* and *error has no right*, has been fundamentally altered. During this century the main Churches have recognised each other's basic Christian integrity, if not always full equality, as never before, and they have rejected the idea that error has no right. Of course changing church teachings does not mean that viewpoints formed over centuries will necessarily go away quickly. But it does mean that sectarianism cannot claim doctrinal backing and respectability as it might once have done, and it also means that the many central elements of Christian teaching utterly opposed to sectarianism have an unprecedented opportunity to come into action. Whether or not Christians and their Churches will grasp this opportunity is one of the greatest challenges they face, and one key to peace in Ireland.

NOTES

1. Fergus O'Donoghue, 'The Use of St Augustine's Thought: A Response to Professor Williams', *Milltown Studies*, no. 19/20 (Spring and Autumn 1987), p. 85.

BIOGRAPHICAL NOTE

JOSEPH LIECHTY, a member of the Mennonite Church from Goshen, Indiana, moved to Ireland in 1980. Since completing his Ph.D. in Irish History at the National University of Ireland, Maynooth in 1987, he has worked on issues related to sectarianism, past and present. He is currently employed by the Irish School of Ecumenics as Director of the Moving Beyond Sectarianism project. In the absence of any Mennonite congregations in Dublin, he and his family are happily worshipping at Lucan Presbyterian Church

Appendix

Addresses of
Churches and Other Organisations

CHURCH HEADQUARTERS

NB: A number of the smaller denominations do not have headquarters in Northern Ireland or the Republic of Ireland. Alternative contact addresses elsewhere are given where possible.

Catholic Church in Ireland

Press and Information Office, 169 Booterstown Avenue, Blackrock, Co. Dublin
   tel: 003531-288 5043   fax: 003531-283 4161

Presbyterian Church in Ireland

Church House, Fisherwick Place, Belfast BT1 6DW
   tel: 01232-322284   fax: 01232-236609

Church of Ireland

Church of Ireland House, 61–7 Donegall Street, Belfast BT1 2QH
   tel: 01232-232909   fax: 01232-323554
(NB: The main denominational headquarters is in Dublin:
Church of Ireland House, Church Avenue, Rathmines, Dublin 6
   tel: 003531-497 8422   fax: 003531-497 8821)

Methodist Church in Ireland

1 Fountainville Avenue, Belfast BT9 6AN
   tel: 01232-324554   fax: 01232-239467

Baptist Union of Ireland

117 Lisburn Road, Belfast BT9 7AF
   tel: 01232-663108   fax: 01232-663616

Christian Brethren

The Christian Brethren is not a denomination as such and therefore has no headquarters. Information may be available via the Crescent Church, University Road, Belfast BT7 1NH, or from any local Gospel Hall or other Brethren meeting place.

Free Presbyterian Church of Ulster

Church House, 356 Ravenhill Road, Belfast BT6 8GL
tel: 01232-457106

Congregational Union of Ireland

c/o Secretary of the Congregational Union,
1 Bradford Heights, Carrickfergus, Co. Antrim BT38 9EB
tel: 01960-368292

Elim Pentecostal Church

20 King's Road, Belfast BT5 6JJ
tel: 01232-657744   fax: 01232-471623

Assemblies of God (Pentecostal)

c/o UK Headquarters: 16 Bridgeford Road, West Bridgeford,
Nottingham, England NG1 5GH
tel: 0115-981 1188   fax: 0115-981 3377

Apostolic Church (Pentecostal)

PO Box 389, 24–7 St Helen's Road, Swansea SA1 1ZH
tel: 01729-473992   fax: 01792-474087

Non-Subscribing Presbyterian Church of Ireland

c/o Clerk of General Synod: 102 Carrickfergus Road,
Larne, Co. Antrim BT40 3JX
tel: 01504-272600

Reformed Presbyterian Church of Ireland

Cameron House, 98 Lisburn Road, Belfast BT9 6AG
tel: 01232-660689

Salvation Army

NI Headquarters, 12 Station Mews, Sydenham, Belfast BT4 1TL
tel: 01232-675000   fax: 01232-675011

Church of the Nazarene

c/o UK Headquarters: 29 Packway, Westhoughton,
Bolton, Lancashire, England BL5 2RY
tel: 01942-815036   fax: 01942-810613

Free Methodist Church

c/o UK Headquarters: 290a Blackpool Road, Fulwood, Preston,
Lancashire PR2 3AE
tel & fax: 01772-787991

Fellowship of Independent Methodist Churches

c/o Secretary to the Fellowship: 68 Causeway End Road,
Lisburn, Co. Antrim BT28 2ED

Religious Society of Friends (Quakers)

Swanbrook House, Bloomfield Avenue, Morehampton Road, Dublin 4
tel & fax: 003531-668 3684

Evangelical Presbyterian Church

15 College Square East, Belfast BT1 6DD
tel: 01232-320529   fax: 01232-438330

Moravian Church

Gracehill Moravian Church, 25 Church Road, Gracehill, Ballymena,
Co. Antrim BT42 2NL
tel: 01266-653141
(or via UK Headquarters: 5 Muswell Hill, London N10 3TH
tel: 0181-883 3409   fax: 0181-442 0012)

Lutheran Church in Ireland

Lutherhaus, 24 Adelaide Road, Dublin 2
tel: 003531-676 6548

New Churches

This is a loosely associated group of fellowships, not a denomination as such.
Some information may be available from the Christian Fellowship Church,
171–7 Holywood Road, Belfast BT4 2DG.

Belfast Chinese Christian Church

Lorne Street, Belfast BT9 7DU

Orthodox Churches

Information may be available from the Belfast branch of the Fellowship of
St Alban and St Sergius, c/o the Department of Greek and Latin, Queen's
University, Belfast BT7 1NN. *Alternatively contact* The Greek Orthodox
Archdiocese of Thyateira and Great Britain, Thyateira House, 5 Craven Hill,
London W2 3EN.

OTHER ORGANISATIONS

All Children Together

13 University Street, Belfast BT7 1FY
tel: 01232-327335

Christian Education Movement

c/o 30 Bangor Road, Groomsport, Bangor, Co. Down BT19 6JF
tel: 01247-464259

Christian Renewal Centre
    44 Shore Road, Rostrevor, Co. Down BT34 3ET
        tel: 016937-38492

Churches' Peace Education Programme
    48 Elmwood Avenue, Belfast BT9 6AZ
        tel: 01232-662992

Clonard/Fitzroy Fellowship
    c/o 53 Bawnmore Road, Belfast BT9 6LB
        tel: 01232-662503

Columba House of Prayer
    11 Queen Street, Derry BT48 7EG
        tel: 01504-262407

Columbanus Community of Reconciliation
    683 Antrim Road, Belfast BT15 4EG
        tel: 01232-778009

Cornerstone Community
    445 Springfield Road, Belfast BT12 7DL
        tel: 01232-321649   fax: 01232-327323

Corrymeela Community
    Corrymeela House, 8 Upper Crescent, Belfast BT7 1NT
        tel: 01232-325008   fax: 01232-315385
        e-mail: belfast@corrymeela.org.uk

Currach Community
    2 Workman Avenue, Belfast BT13 3FB
        tel: 01232-312658

ECONI (Evangelical Contribution on Northern Ireland)
    12 Wellington Place, Belfast BT1 6GE
        tel: 01232-325258   fax: 01232-434156
        e-mail: admin@econi.dnet.co.uk

Fellowship of Reconciliation
    c/o 224 Lisburn Road, Belfast BT9 6GE

Inter-Church Group on Faith and Politics
    c/o 8 Upper Crescent, Belfast BT7 1NT
        tel: 01232-325008   fax: 01232-328606

Irish Council of Churches
    48 Elmwood Avenue, Belfast BT9 6AZ
        tel: 01232-663145

Irish Inter-Church Meeting
48 Elmwood Avenue, Belfast BT9 6AZ
tel: 01232-663145

Irish School of Ecumenics (NI)
48 Elmwood Avenue, Belfast BT9 6AZ
tel: 01232-382750

Lamb of God Community
Shalom House, 12 Cliftonville Road, Belfast BT14 6JX

Mediation Network NI
128a Great Victoria Street, Belfast BT2 7BG
tel: 01232-438614   fax: 01232-314430
e-mail: info@mediation-network.org.uk

Pax Christi
52 Lower Rathmines Road, Dublin 6
tel & fax: 003531-496 5293

Protestant and Catholic Encounter (PACE)
174 Ormeau Road, Belfast BT7 1SQ
tel: 01232-232864

Women in Faith
c/o Columbanus Community of Reconciliation,
683 Antrim Road, Belfast BT15 4EG
tel: 01232 778009

Youth Link: NI
143a University Street, Belfast BT7 1HP
tel: 01232-323217   fax: 01232-323247

FOR INFORMATION ON OTHER GROUPS SEE
Inter-Church Directory
Dealing with Difference
Churches Working Together
– all published by the Community Relations Council,
6 Murray Street, Belfast BT1 6DN

Also:
Who's Who in EMU and Cultural Heritage?
– published by the FOCUS Group, c/o EMU-Promoting School Project, Magee
College, Northland Road, Londonderry BT48 7LQ

DENOMINATIONAL AND OTHER CHRISTIAN BOOKSHOPS

Diocesan Resources Centre Bookshop (Roman Catholic)
14 Donegall Lane, Belfast BT1 2LZ

Familybooks (Presbyterian)
Spires Centre, Fisherwick Place, Belfast BT1 6DW

APCK (Church of Ireland)
61–7 Donegall Street, Belfast BT1 2QH

Methodist Bookroom
Aldersgate House, 13 University Road, Belfast BT7 1NA

Beulah Bookshop (Free Presbyterian)
67 Central Promenade, Newcastle, Co. Down BT33 0HH

Christian Bookshop (Elim Pentecostal)
58 Bridge Street, Portadown, Co. Armagh BT63 5AE

Covenanter Bookshop (Reformed Presbyterian Church)
98 Lisburn Road, Belfast BT9 6AG

Evangelical Bookshop (Evangelical Presbyterian Church)
15 College Square East, Belfast BT1 6DD

Faith Mission Bookshop (Interdenominational/Evangelical)
5 Queen Street, Belfast BT1 6EA

Scripture Union Resource Centre (Interdenominational/Evangelical)
157 Albertbridge Road, Belfast BT5 4PS

Index